Bartholomew
CONCISE
WORLD ATLAS

Ian Bell -

Bartholomew
CONCISE
WORLD ATLAS

John Bartholomew & Son Ltd
Edinburgh

Printed in Scotland

Published by John Bartholomew & Son Ltd
Duncan Street
Edinburgh
EH9 1TA

First Edition MCMLXXXIV

ISBN 0 7028 0702 8

B028

CONTENTS

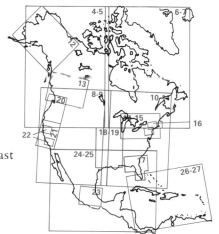

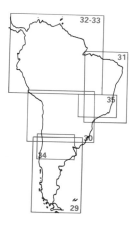

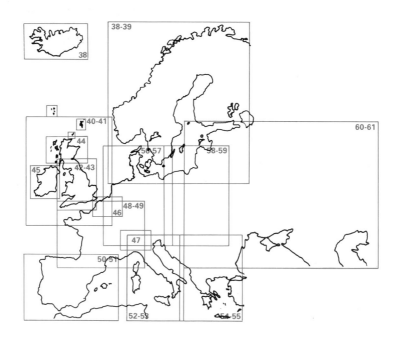

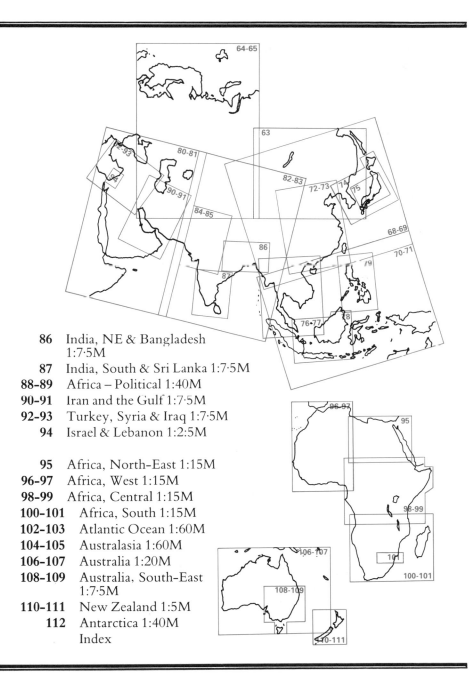

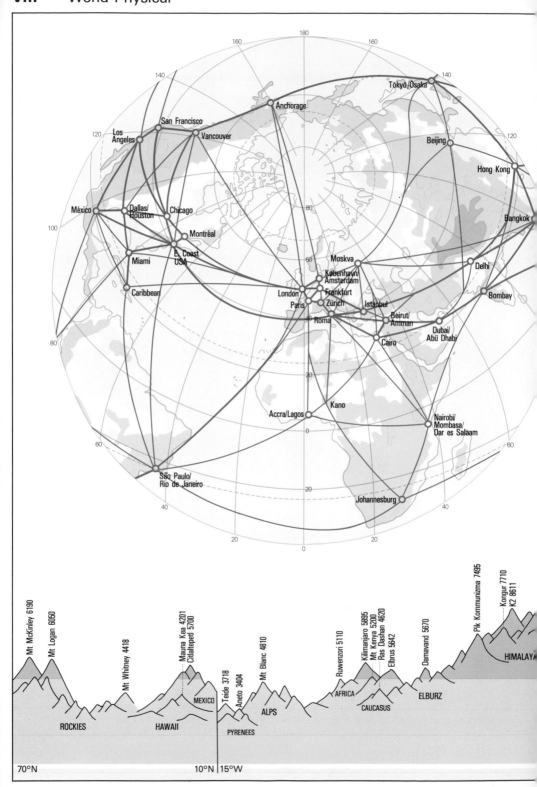

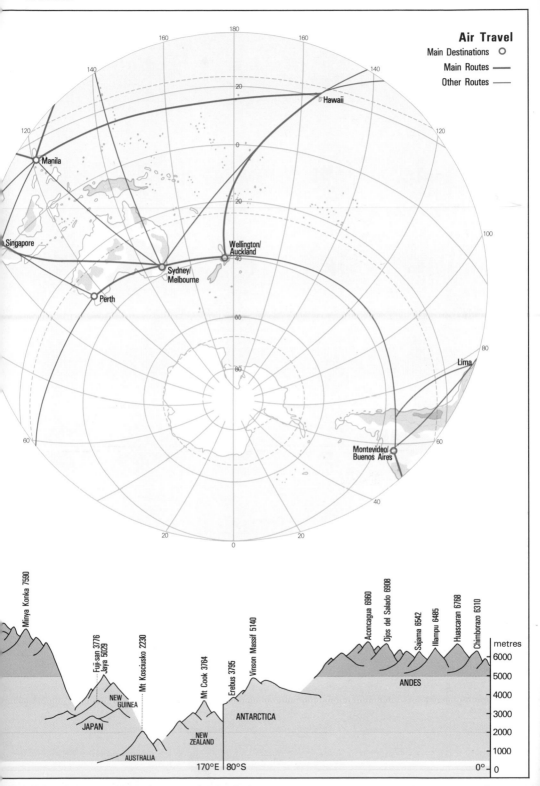

Air Travel
Main Destinations ○
Main Routes ——
Other Routes —

Hawaii

Manila

Singapore

Wellington/
Auckland

Sydney/
Melbourne

Perth

Lima

Montevideo/
Buenos Aires

Minya Konka 7590

Fuji-san 3776
Jaya 5029

Mt Kosciusko 2230

Mt Cook 3764

Erebus 3795

Vinson Massif 5140

Aconcagua 6960

Ojos del Salado 6908

Sajama 6542

Illampu 6485

Huascaran 6768

Chimborazo 6310

NEW
GUINEA

JAPAN

AUSTRALIA

NEW
ZEALAND

ANTARCTICA

ANDES

metres
6000
5000
4000
3000
2000
1000
0

170°E   80°S   0°

Greenland
(Den.)

Alaska
(USA)

ICELAN

Reykjavik

IRELAND

U.
Lon

C A N A D A

Vancouver
Seattle
Portland

Winnipeg

Montréal
Ottawa
Toronto

PORTUGAL
Lisboa

SP

Chicago

New York
Philadelphia
Washington

Açores
(Port.)

M

San Francisco

UNITED STATES
OF AMERICA

Atlanta

Rabat
Casablanca

MOROCC

Los Angeles

Dallas

New
Orleans

ATLANTIC

Canary Is
(Sp.)

A

Houston

Miami

Western
Sahara

Hawaii
(USA)

Guadalajara

México

Havana

THE
BAHAMAS

MAURITANIA
Nouakchott

M

CUBA
JAMAICA

DOM. REP.

CAPE VERDE IS

SENEGAL
THE GAMBIA
GUINEA-BISSAU

Bama

PACIFIC

GUATEMALA
EL SALVADOR

BELIZE
HONDURAS
NICARAGUA

HAITI

GUINEA

SIERRA LEONE

COSTA RICA
PANAMA

Caracas

VENEZUELA

TRINIDAD & TOBAGO
GUYANA
SURINAM
FR. GUIANA

LIBERIA

Bogotá

COLOMBIA

IVORY COAST

G

Equator

Galapagos Is.
(Ec.)

Quito

ECUADOR

OCEAN

Lima

PERU

B R A Z I L

Recife

OCEAN

La Paz

BOLIVIA

Brasília

Salvador

OCEAN

Rio de Janeiro

PARAGUAY

Asunción

São Paulo

Santiago

CHILE

Buenos
Aires

ARGENTINA

URUGUAY
Montevideo

• Denotes capital cities

Falkland Is
(UK)

S. Georgia
(UK)

Major Cities by Continent

Oceania	Pop. '000
Sydney *Australia*	2874
Melbourne *Australia*	2578
Brisbane *Australia*	943
Adelaide *Australia*	883
Perth *Australia*	809
Auckland *New Zealand*	766

Asia	'000
Tōkyō *Japan*	11 696
Shanghai *China*	10 820
Calcutta *India*	9166
Beijing *China*	8626
Bombay *India*	8203
Sŏul *South Korea*	6879
Manila *Philippines*	5901
Jakarta *Indonesia*	5849
Delhi *India*	5277
Bangkok *Thailand*	5154
Tehrān *Iran*	4496
Tianjin *China*	4280
Madras *India*	4277
Karachi *Pakistan*	4000
Shenyang *China*	3600
Dhākā *Bangladesh*	3459
Saigon *Vietnam*	3420
Baghdād *Iraq*	3206
T'ai-pei *Taiwan*	3050
Bangalore *India*	2914
İstanbul *Turkey*	2773

Europe	'000
London *UK*	12 075
Paris *France*	8613
Moskva *USSR*	8099
Leningrad *USSR*	4638
Madrid *Spain*	3188
Berlin *E Ger.-W Ger.*	3056
Roma *Italy*	2830
Birmingham *UK*	2748
Manchester *UK*	2687
Kiyev *USSR*	2144
Athínai *Greece*	2101
Budapest *Hungary*	2064
Bucureşti *Romania*	1934
Tashkent *USSR*	1779
Barcelona *Spain*	1755

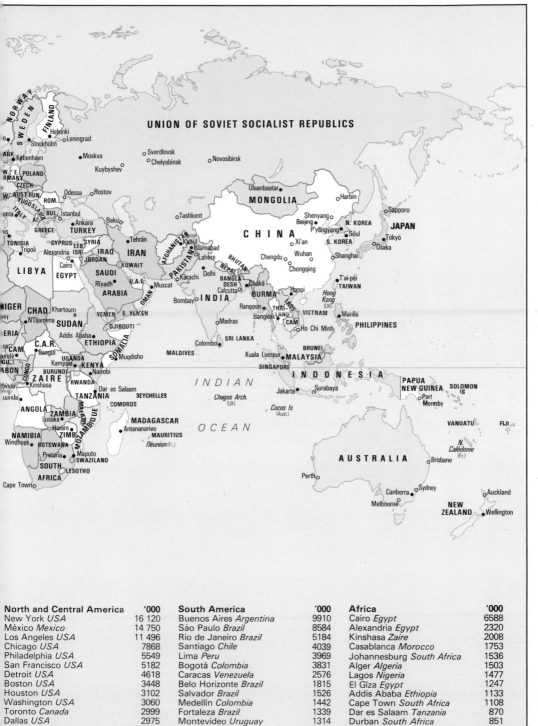

North and Central America	'000	South America	'000	Africa	'000
New York *USA*	16 120	Buenos Aires *Argentina*	9910	Cairo *Egypt*	6588
México *Mexico*	14 750	São Paulo *Brazil*	8584	Alexandria *Egypt*	2320
Los Angeles *USA*	11 496	Rio de Janeiro *Brazil*	5184	Kinshasa *Zaire*	2008
Chicago *USA*	7868	Santiago *Chile*	4039	Casablanca *Morocco*	1753
Philadelphia *USA*	5549	Lima *Peru*	3969	Johannesburg *South Africa*	1536
San Francisco *USA*	5182	Bogotá *Colombia*	3831	Alger *Algeria*	1503
Detroit *USA*	4618	Caracas *Venezuela*	2576	Lagos *Nigeria*	1477
Boston *USA*	3448	Belo Horizonte *Brazil*	1815	El Gîza *Egypt*	1247
Houston *USA*	3102	Salvador *Brazil*	1526	Addis Ababa *Ethiopia*	1133
Washington *USA*	3060	Medellín *Colombia*	1442	Cape Town *South Africa*	1108
Toronto *Canada*	2999	Fortaleza *Brazil*	1339	Dar es Salaam *Tanzania*	870
Dallas *USA*	2975	Montevideo *Uruguay*	1314	Durban *South Africa*	851
Cleveland *USA*	2834	Recife *Brazil*	1241	Abidjan *Ivory Coast*	850
Montréal *Canada*	2828	Brasília *Brazil*	1203	Ibadan *Nigeria*	847
Miami *USA*	2640	Pôrto Alegre *Brazil*	1159	Nairobi *Kenya*	835

| 22 -10 | 23 -11 | 24 | 1 +11 | 2 +10 | 3 +9 | 4 +8 | 5 +7 | 6 +6 | 7 +5 | 8 +4 | 9 +3 | 10 +2 | 11 +1 |

DATE LINE

Monday
Sunday

Anchorage

Vancouver

Winnipeg

Ottawa

8.30

Lond

Denver

Washington

Los Angeles

New Orleans

Miami

México

Ra

Dakar

Panamá   Caracas

8.30

Abid

Equator

2.30

Lima

3.30

La Paz

São Paulo

Zone Times are the Standard Times
kept on land and sea compared with
12 hours (noon) Greenwich Mean Time.
Daylight Saving Time (normally one
hour in advance of local Standard
Time), which is observed by certain
countries for part of the year,
is not shown on the map.

Buenos
Aires

| 180° | 165° | 150° | 135° | 120° | 105° | 90° | 75° | 60° | 45° | 30° | 15° |

Journey Times

Sail (via Cape)
164 days

Steam (via Cape)
43 days

Steam (via Suez)
30 days

Supertanker
(via Cape)
28 days

Singapore ◄——

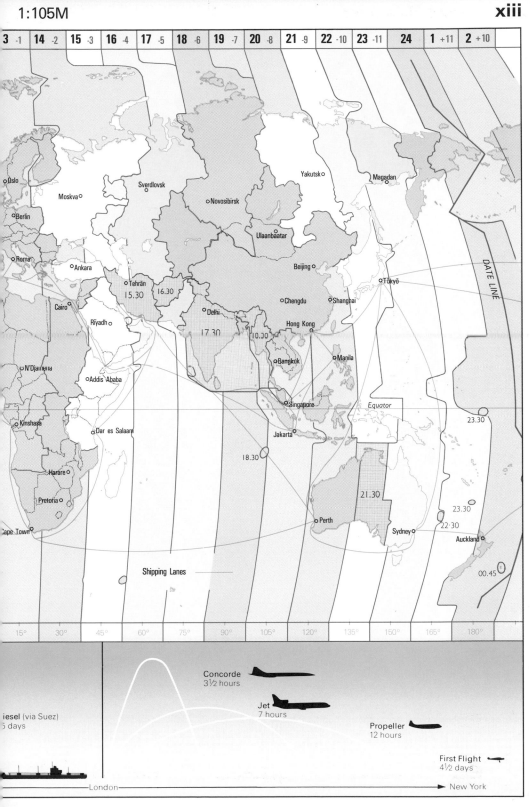

| 3 | -1 | 14 | -2 | 15 | -3 | 16 | -4 | 17 | -5 | 18 | -6 | 19 | -7 | 20 | -8 | 21 | -9 | 22 | -10 | 23 | -11 | 24 | 1 | +11 | 2 | +10 |

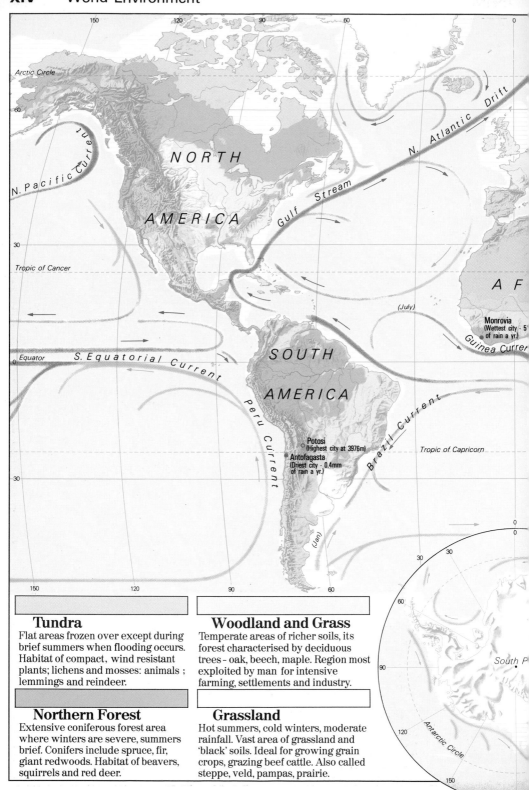

Arctic Circle

60

N. Pacific Current

150   120   90   60   0

NORTH

AMERICA

N. Atlantic Drift

Gulf Stream

30

Tropic of Cancer

(July)

Monrovia
(Wettest city - 5'
of rain a yr.)

A F

Equator

S. Equatorial Current

Guinea Current

0

SOUTH

AMERICA

Peru Current

Brazil Current

Potosi
(Highest city at 3976m)

Antofagasta
(Driest city - 0.4mm
of rain a yr.)

Tropic of Capricorn

30

(Jan)

150   120   90   60

0
0

30   30

60

90   South P

120

Antarctic Circle

150

180

Tundra

Flat areas frozen over except during
brief summers when flooding occurs.
Habitat of compact, wind resistant
plants; lichens and mosses: animals ;
lemmings and reindeer.

Woodland and Grass

Temperate areas of richer soils, its
forest characterised by deciduous
trees - oak, beech, maple. Region most
exploited by man for intensive
farming, settlements and industry.

Northern Forest

Extensive coniferous forest area
where winters are severe, summers
brief. Conifers include spruce, fir,
giant redwoods. Habitat of beavers,
squirrels and red deer.

Grassland

Hot summers, cold winters, moderate
rainfall. Vast area of grassland and
'black' soils. Ideal for growing grain
crops, grazing beef cattle. Also called
steppe, veld, pampas, prairie.

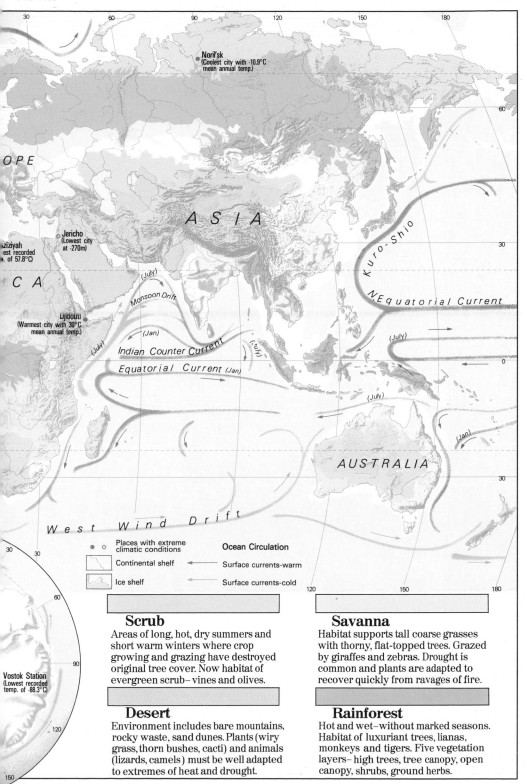

Noril'sk
(Coolest city with -10.9°C
mean annual temp.)

60

O P E

A S I A

Jericho
(Lowest city
at -270m)

30

zīzīyah
est recorded
. of 57.8°C)

C A

(July)

Monsoon Drift

Kuro-Shio

N. Equatorial Current

Djibouti
(Warmest city with 30°C
mean annual temp.)

(Jan)

(July)

(July)

(July)

(July)

0

Indian Counter Current

Equatorial Current (Jan)

(July)

(Jan)

30

AUSTRALIA

30

West Wind Drift

30

30

Places with extreme
climatic conditions

Ocean Circulation

Continental shelf

Surface currents-warm

Ice shelf

Surface currents-cold

120

150

180

60

Vostok Station
(Lowest recorded
temp. of -88.3°C)

90

120

150

Scrub
Areas of long, hot, dry summers and
short warm winters where crop
growing and grazing have destroyed
original tree cover. Now habitat of
evergreen scrub–vines and olives.

Savanna
Habitat supports tall coarse grasses
with thorny, flat-topped trees. Grazed
by giraffes and zebras. Drought is
common and plants are adapted to
recover quickly from ravages of fire.

Desert
Environment includes bare mountains,
rocky waste, sand dunes. Plants (wiry
grass, thorn bushes, cacti) and animals
(lizards, camels) must be well adapted
to extremes of heat and drought.

Rainforest
Hot and wet–without marked seasons.
Habitat of luxuriant trees, lianas,
monkeys and tigers. Five vegetation
layers–high trees, tree canopy, open
canopy, shrubs, ground herbs.

BOUNDARIES

▬▬▬▬▬	International
▬▬ ▬▬ ▬▬ ▬▬	International under Dispute
▪ ▪ ▪ ▪ ▪ ▪ ▪	Cease Fire Line
▬▬▬▬▬	Autonomous or State/Administrative
▬ ▬ ▬ ▬	Maritime (National)
— — — —	International Date Line

COMMUNICATIONS

══════ ════	Motorway/Under Construction
▬▬▬▬▬	Major/Other Road
▬ ▬ ▬ ▬ ▬	Under Construction
▪ ▪ ▪ ▪ ▪ ▪	Track
⟶▬▬⟵	Road Tunnel
▬ ▬ ▬ ▬	Car Ferry
▬▬▬▬▬	Main/Other Railway
▬ ▬ ▬ ▬	Under Construction
▪ ▪ ▪ ▪ ▪	Rail Ferry
⟶▬⟵	Rail Tunnel
┴─┴─┴─┴	Canal
⊕ ✈	International/Other Airport

LANDSCAPE FEATURES

	Glacier, Ice Cap
	Marsh, Swamp
	Sand Desert, Dunes
	Freshwater
	Saltwater
	Seasonal
	Salt Pan

OTHER FEATURES

	River/Seasonal
≍	Pass, Gorge
	Dam, Barrage
	Waterfall, Rapid
	Aqueduct
	Reef
.217 ▲4231	Spot Height, Depth/Summit, Peak
⌣	Well
∆ ▲	Oil/Gas Field
Gas / Oil	Oil/Natural Gas Pipeline
⟨ Gemsbok Nat. Pk ⟩	National Park
∴UR	Historic Site

LETTERING STYLES

CANADA	Independent Nation
FLORIDA	State, Province or Autonomous Region
Gibraltar (U.K.)	Sovereignty of Dependent Territory
Lothian	Administrative Area
LANGUEDOC	Historic Region
Loire **Vosges**	Physical Feature or Physical Region

TOWNS AND CITIES

Square symbols denote capital cities — *Population*

▣	●	**New York**	over 5 000 000
■	●	**Montréal**	over 1 000 000
□	○	Ottawa	over 500 000
▪	•	**Québec**	over 100 000
▫	○	St John's	over 50 000
▫	○	Yorkton	over 10 000
▫	○	Jasper	under 10 000

Built-up-area

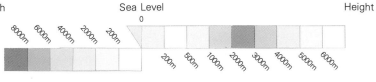

Depth	Sea Level	Height
8000m 6000m 4000m 2000m 200m	0	200m 500m 1000m 2000m 3000m 4000m 5000m 6000m

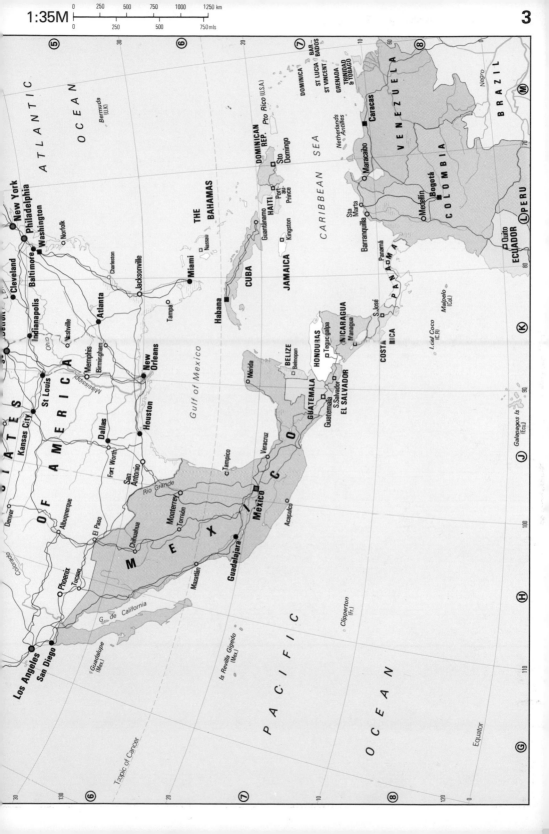

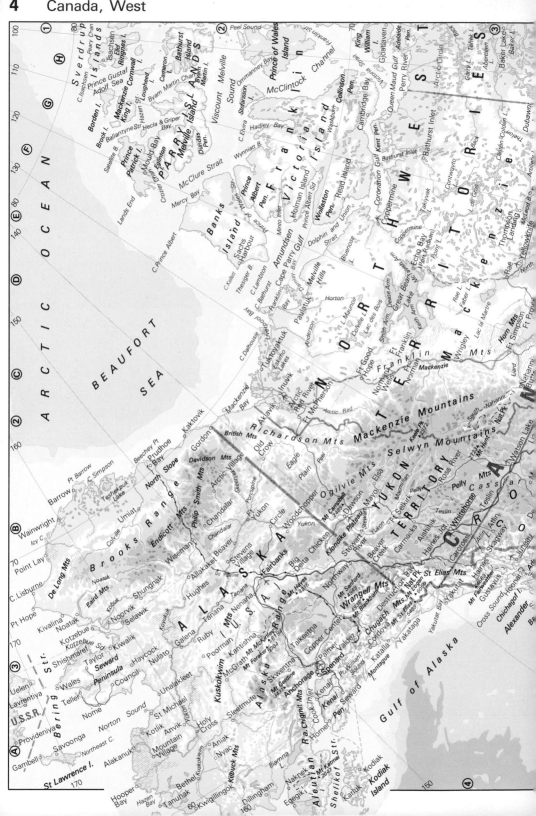

GREENLAND

DENMARK STRAIT

ICELAND

Reykjavík

DAVIS STRAIT

BAFFIN BAY

Baffin Island

HUDSON STRAIT

Labrador Sea

Arctic Circle

Kong Frederik VI Kyst

Kong Christian IX Land

Kronprins Frederik Bjerge

Knud Rasmussens Land

Scoresby Sd.

Mylius Land

Nathorsts Land

Angmagssalik

Kap Farvel

Nanortalik

Julianehåb

Frederikshåb

Godthåb

Sukkertoppen

Holsteinsborg

Søndre Strømfjord

Egedesminde

Christianshåb

Jakobshavn

Godhavn

Disko

Umanak

Upernavik

Thule

QUEEN ELIZABETH ISLANDS

Sverdrup Islands

Axel Heiberg Island

Amund Ringnes I.

Ellef Ringnes I.

Bathurst Island

Cornwallis I.

Devon Island

PARRY ISLANDS

Ellesmere Island

Baffin Island

Lancaster Sound

Melville Peninsula

Boothia Peninsula

Prince of Wales Island

Somerset Island

Prince Regent Inlet

Cumberland Sound

Frobisher Bay

Foxe Basin

Foxe Channel

Foxe Peninsula

Southampton I.

Hudson Strait

Keewatin

Prince Charles I.

Air Force I.

Salisbury I.

Nottingham I.

Coats Island

Resolution I.

Cape Dorset

Wager Bay

Chesterfield Inlet

Baker Lake

Repulse Bay

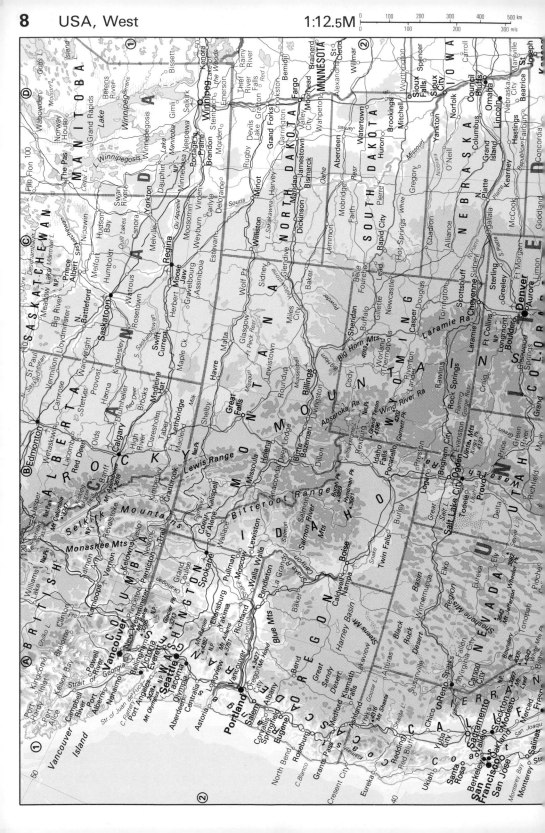

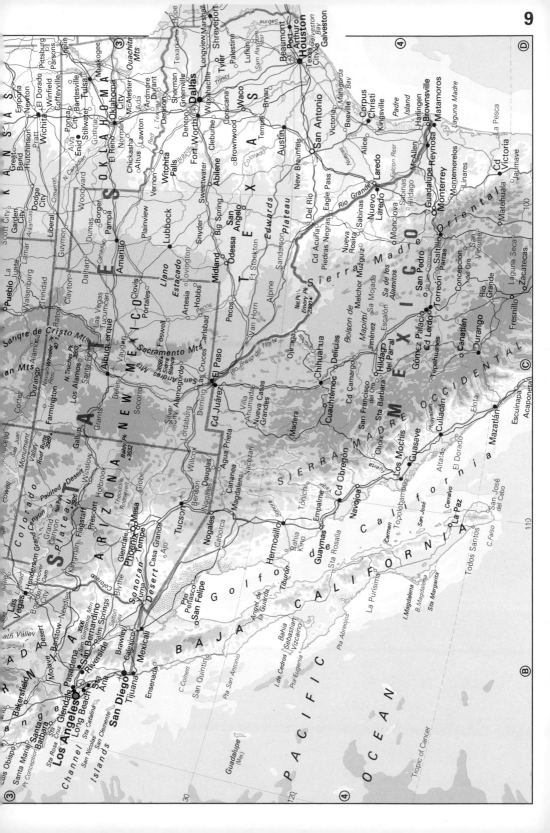

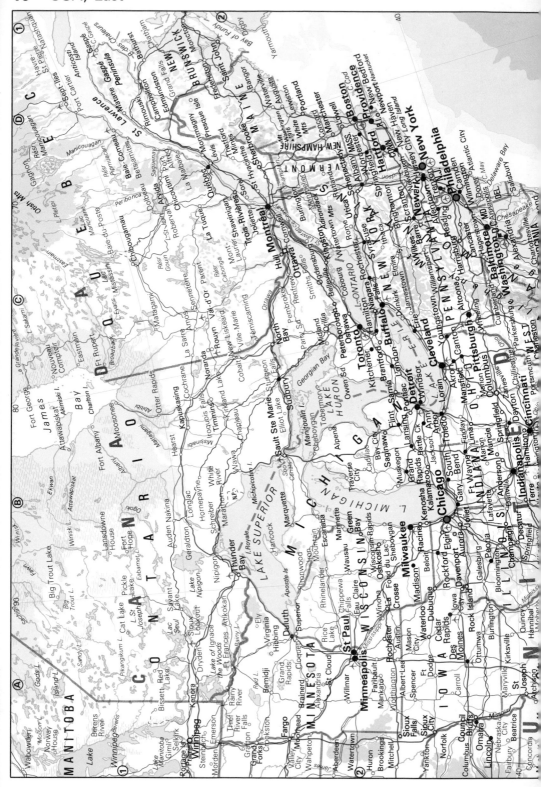

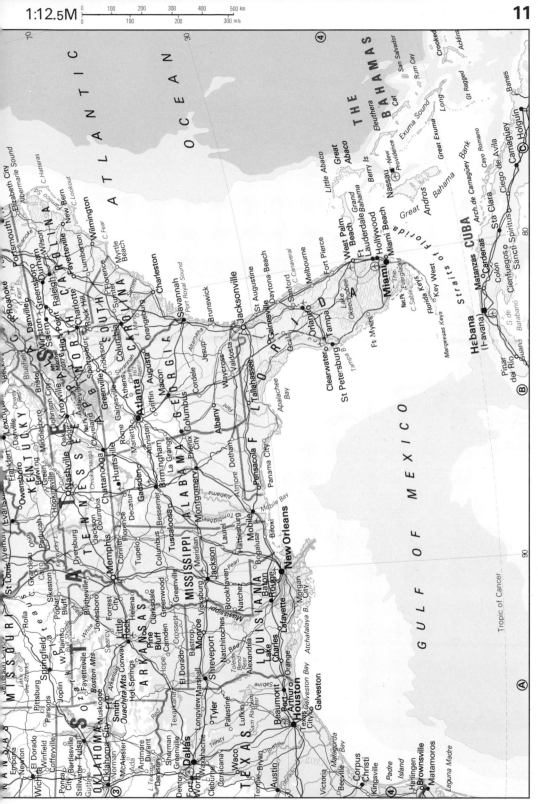

100 200 300 400 500 km
100 200 300 mls

ATLANTIC OCEAN

THE BAHAMAS

San Salvador

Crooked
Acklins
Rum Cay
Long
Cat
Eleuthera
Great Exuma
Exuma Sound
Berry Is
New Providence
Nassau
Little Abaco
Great Abaco
Grand Bahama
Andros
Bahama
Great
Gt Ragged
Banes
Camagüey
Holguin
Cayo de Avila
Arch. de Camagüey Bank
Cayo Romano
Sta Clara
Ciego de Avila
Sancti Spiritus
Cienfuegos
Colón
Cardenas
Matanzas
CUBA
Habana
(Havana)
Pinar del Rio
Guane
G. de Batabano

Elizabeth City
Albemarle Sound
Portsmouth
C. Hatteras
C. Lookout
New Bern
Wilmington
C. Fear
Myrtle Beach
Florence
Charleston
Port Royal Sound
Savannah
Brunswick
Jacksonville
St Augustine
Daytona Beach
C. Canaveral
Melbourne
Ft Pierce
West Palm Beach
Ft Lauderdale
Hollywood
Miami Beach
Miami
Key West
Florida Keys
Marquesas Keys
C. Sable
Nat.Pk.
The Everglades
Lake Okeechobee
Sanford
Orlando
Tampa
St Petersburg
Clearwater
Ft Myers
Ocala
Gainesville

NORTH CAROLINA
Roanoke
Portsmouth
Virginia
Danville
Winston-Salem
Greensboro
Durham
Raleigh
High Point
Fayetteville
Lumberton
Roanoke R.
Neuse R.
SOUTH CAROLINA
Rock Hill
Charlotte
Spartanburg
Greenville
Asheville
Columbia
Sumter
Orangeburg
Santee R.
Savannah R.
GEORGIA
Athens
Augusta
Macon
Columbus
Griffin
Atlanta
Marietta
Rome
Gainesville
Cartersville
Cleveland
Anderson
Dalton
Chickamauga
Chattanooga
Knoxville
Cleveland
Oak Ridge
Johnson City
Kingsport
Bristol
Bluefield
Bluefield

KENTUCKY
Frankfort
Lexington
Danville
Middlesboro
Hazard
Owensboro
Bowling Green
Hopkinsville
Paducah

St Louis
Cape Girardeau
Sikeston
Poplar Bluff
Rolla
Lebanon
Springfield
Joplin
Pittsburg
Parsons
MISSOURI

Evansville
Ohio R.

TENNESSEE
Nashville
Columbia
Dyersburg
Memphis
Jackson
Corinth

Mt Mitchell
2037

ALABAMA
Birmingham
Bessemer
Tuscaloosa
Gadsden
Anniston
Montgomery
Phenix City
Troy
Dothan
Enterprise
Selma
Decatur
Florence
Huntsville
Alabama R.
Tombigbee R.

MISSISSIPPI
Columbus
Tupelo
Greenwood
Greenville
Clarksdale
Meridian
Jackson
Hattiesburg
Laurel
Natchez
Vicksburg
Brookhaven
Pearl R.

GEORGIA
Albany
Cordele
Waycross
Valdosta
Tallahassee
Thomasville
Bainbridge
Flint R.

FLORIDA
Panama City
Pensacola
Apalachee Bay
Apalachicola

Pascagoula
Biloxi
Mobile
Mobile Bay
Bogalusa
New Orleans

ARKANSAS
Little Rock
Pine Bluff
Hot Springs
Conway
Searcy
Jonesboro
Forrest City
Helena
Blytheville
West Memphis
Camden
El Dorado
Crossett
Hope
Texarkana
White R.
Arkansas R.
Bull Shoals L.
Boston Mts
Ouachita Mts
Fayetteville
Fort Smith
Fort Smith

OKLAHOMA
Tulsa
Oklahoma City
Muskogee
McAlester
Ada
Ardmore
Durant
Norman
Stillwater

KANSAS
Wichita
Winfield
Arkansas City
Coffeyville
Newton
El Dorado
Emporia

LOUISIANA
Shreveport
Monroe
Bastrop
Ruston
Alexandria
Lake Charles
Lafayette
Baton Rouge
Natchitoches
Toledo Bend Res.
Red R.
Morgan City
Atchafalaya B.
Sabine R.

TEXAS
Dallas
Fort Worth
Waco
Austin
Houston
Galveston
Beaumont
Port Arthur
Orange
Texas City
Galveston Bay
Lufkin
Palestine
Tyler
Longview
Marshall
Denton
McKinney
Sherman
Denison
Temple
Bryan
Cleburne
Corsicana
Victoria
Corpus Christi
Beeville
Kingsville
Brownsville
Harlingen
Matamoros
Padre Island
Laguna Madre
Matagorda Bay
San Raphael
Brazos R.
Trinity R.
Colorado R.

GULF OF MEXICO

Straits of Florida

Tropic of Cancer

70

80

90

① ② ③ ④

Ⓐ Ⓑ Ⓒ

1:10M

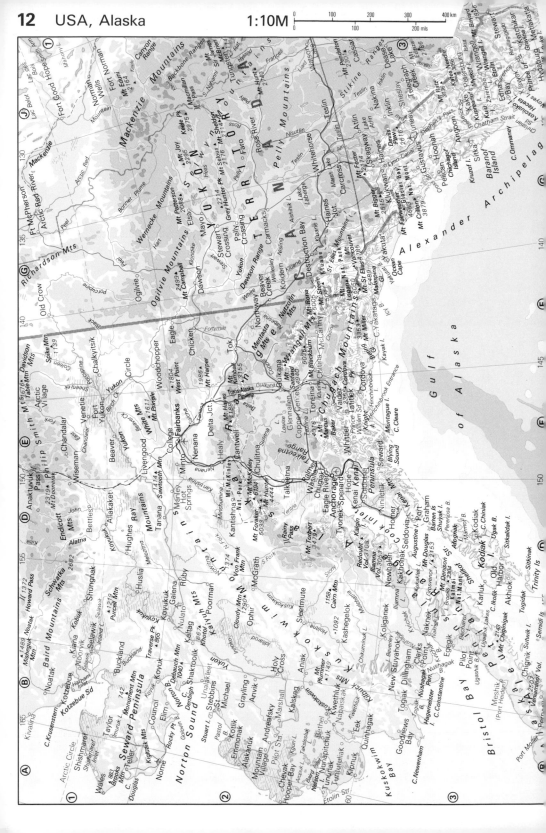

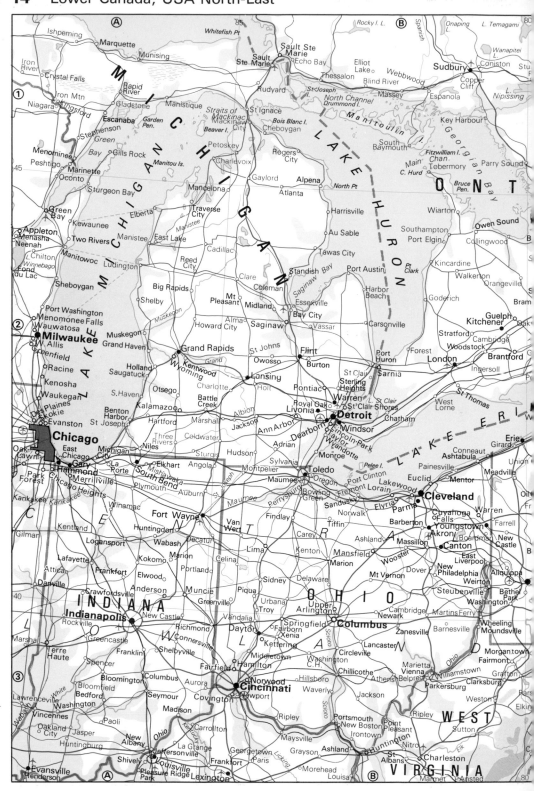

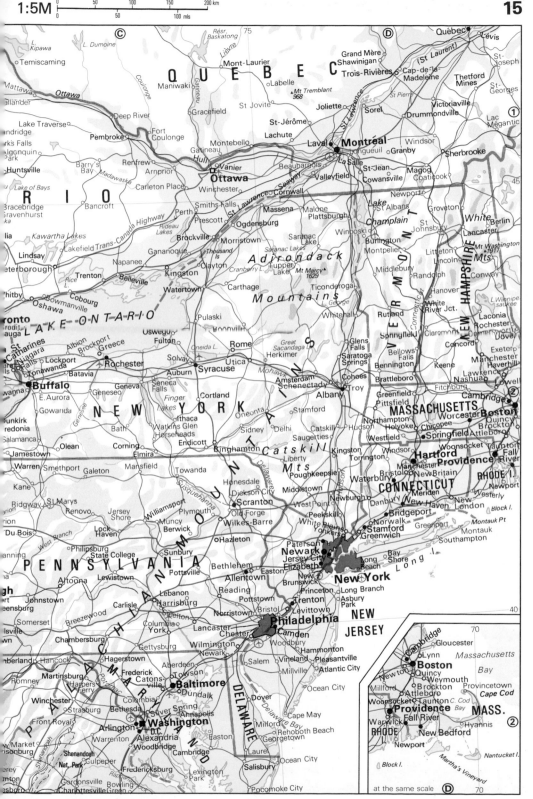

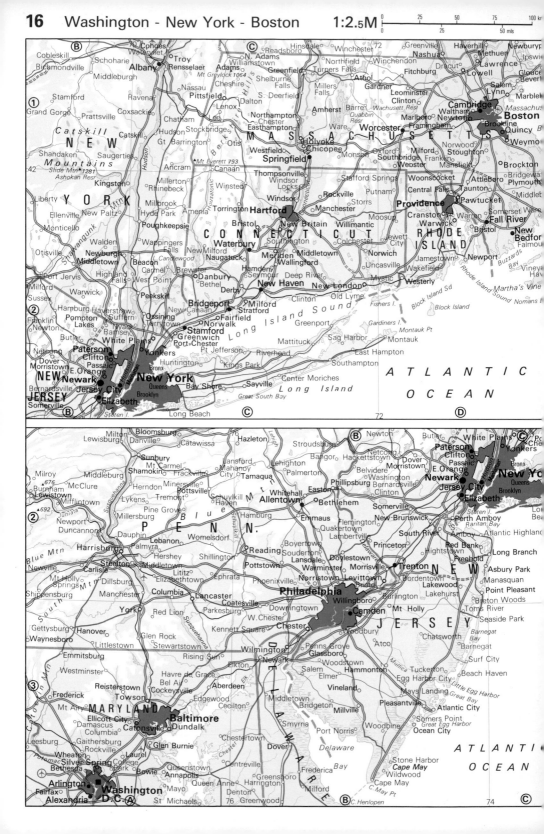

1:5M

50 100 150 200 km
50 100 mls

ATLANTIC OCEAN

GULF OF MEXICO

NORTH CAROLINA
Burgaw, Onslow, Wilmington, Carolina Beach, Cape Fear, Lumberton, Whiteville, Conway, Myrtle Beach, Marion, Georgetown, Cape Romain, Charleston, Cheraw, Darlington, Florence, Lake City, Goose Creek, St Stephens, Walterboro

SOUTH CAROLINA
Chester, Lancaster, Kershaw, Camden, Sumter, Columbia, Cayce, Orangeburg, Bamberg, Allendale, Varnville, Estill, Ridgeland, Beaufort, Port Royal, St Helena Sound, Newberry, Laurens, Anderson, Abbeville, Greenwood, Saluda, Aiken, Augusta, Batesburg, Calhoun Falls, Clark Hill Res., Whitmire, Westminster, Lake City

GEORGIA
Athens, Washington, Thomson, Waynesboro, Statesboro, Swainsboro, Dublin, Vidalia, Lyons, Ludowici, Darien, Brunswick, St Simons I., Windsor Forest, Savannah, Pembroke, Wrightsville, Louisville, Milledgeville, Eatonton, Covington, Atlanta, Decatur, Forest Park, College Park, E. Point, Smyrna, Marietta, Roswell, Buford, Dahlonega, Mt Oglethorpe, Calhoun, Rome, Bremen, Carrollton, Newnan, Griffin, Barnesville, Thomaston, La Grange, Columbus, Phenix City, Opelika, Auburn, Warner Robins, Macon, Perry, Fort Valley, Americus, Cordele, Dawson, Cuthbert, Eufaula, Blakely, Camilla, Bainbridge, Thomasville, Moultrie, Tifton, Ashburn, Fitzgerald, Douglas, Baxley, McRae, Eastman, Hazlehurst, Jesup, Kingsland, Folkston, Waycross, Homerville, Valdosta, Quitman, Jasper, Greenville, Live Oak

ALABAMA
Montgomery, Prattville, Fort Deposit, Greenville, Troy, Ozark, Enterprise, Daleville, Dothan, Union Springs, Tuskegee, Alexander City, Sylacauga, Talladega, Anniston, Gadsden, Attalla, Cullman, Center Point, Mountain Brook, Birmingham, Homewood, Alabaster, Clanton, Scottsboro, Guntersville

FLORIDA
Jacksonville, Jacksonville Beach, Orange Park, Baldwin, Lake City, Fernandina Beach, St Augustine, Bunnel, Ormond Beach, Daytona Beach, New Smyrna Beach, Titusville, Sanford, Winter Park, Orlando, Kissimmee, L. Apopka, Leesburg, Wildwood, Ocala, Gainesville, High Springs, Williston, Crestland, Lake Butler, Macclenny, Perry, Tallahassee, Crawfordville, Carrabelle, Apalachicola, Port St Joe, C. San Blas, St George I., Apalachicola Bay, Panama City, Lynn Haven, De Funiak Springs, Marianna, Chipley, Crestview, Valparaiso, Fort Walton Beach, Andalusia, Florala, St Andrew Bay, St Andrew Sound, Waccasassa Bay, Suwannee, Cedar Key, Brooksville, Hudson, Dade City, Plant City, Lakeland, Tampa, Ruskin, Wauchula, Arcadia, St Petersburg, Pinellas Park, Palmetto, Bradenton, Sarasota, Clearwater, Largo, Dunedin, Winter Garden, Winter Haven, Lake Wales, Avon Park, Sebring, La Belle, Fort Myers, Bonita Springs, Naples, Marco, C. Romano, Ten Thousand Islands, Punta Gorda, Port Charlotte, Charlotte Harbor, Pine I., Caloosahatchee, Peace R., Istokpoga, Okeechobee, Lake Okeechobee, Pahokee, Belle Glade, South Bay, Clewiston, Cape Sable, Ponce de Leon Bay, Big Cypress Swamp, The Everglades, Homestead, National Park, Cutler Ridge, South Miami, Miami, Coral Gables, Miami Beach, N. Miami, N. Miami Beach, Hialeah, Carol City, Plantation, Ft Lauderdale, Hollywood, Pompano Beach, Deerfield Beach, Boca Raton, Delray Beach, Boynton Beach, Lake Worth, W. Palm Beach, Palm Beach, Riviera Beach, Stuart, Jupiter, Fort Pierce, Vero Beach, Gifford, Palm Bay, Melbourne, Cocoa, Rockledge, Cape Canaveral, Merritt Island, Titusville, Key Largo, Islamorada, Marathon, Big Pine Key, Boca Chica Key, Key West, Marquesas Keys, Florida Keys, Florida Bay, Biscayne Bay, St Johns R., L. George, L. Kissimmee

at the same scale

ATLANTIC OCEAN
Long Bay, Cape Fear

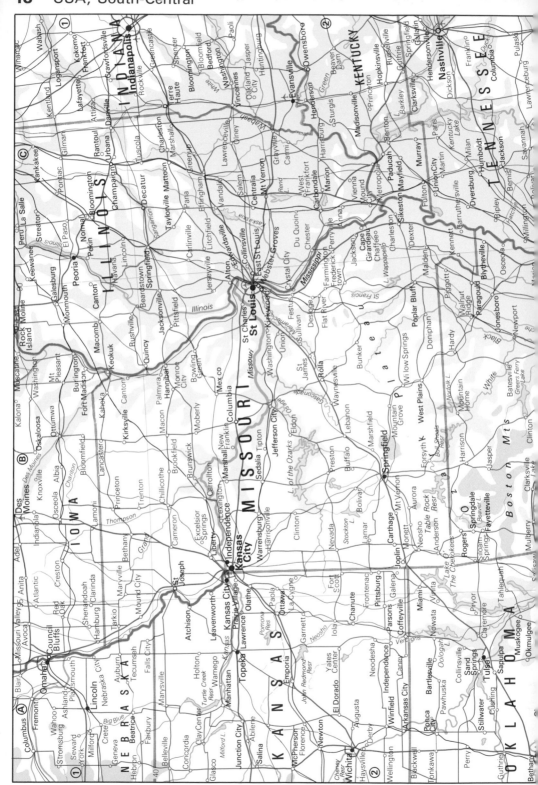

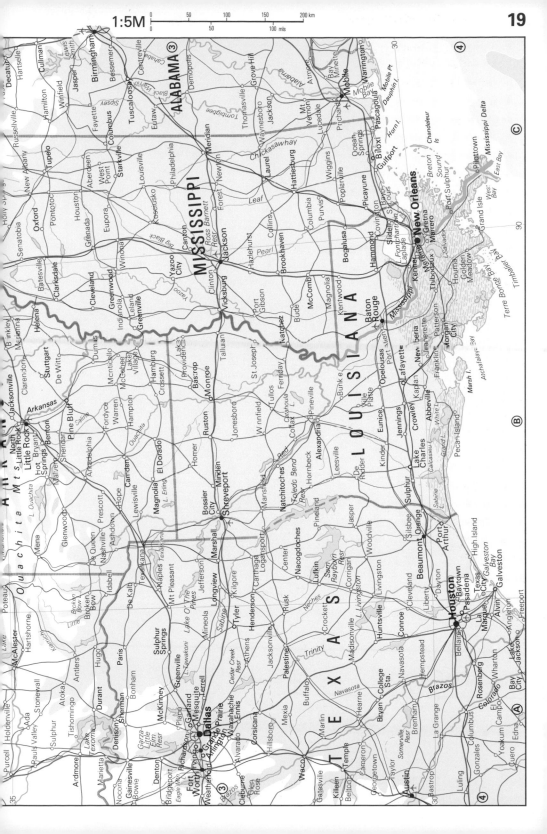

1:5M

0 50 100 150 200 km
0 50 100 mls

ALABAMA ③

MISSISSIPPI

LOUISIANA

TEXAS

A R K A N S A S

Ouachita Mts

④

Birmingham
Bessemer
Centreville
Grove Hill
Mobile
Pascagoula
Biloxi
Gulfport
Mississippi Delta
New Orleans
Gretna
Marrero

Decatur
Hartselle
Cullman
Jasper
Tuscaloosa
Demopolis
Thomasville
Jackson
Mt. Vernon
Prichard
Ocean Springs
Chandeleur Is
Breton Sound
Pilottown

Hamilton
Winfield
Fayette
Columbus
Waynesboro
Lucedale
Pilot

Russellville
New Albany
Tupelo
Aberdeen
West Point
Starkville
Louisville
Philadelphia
Meridian
Newton
Chickasawhay
Laurel
Hattiesburg
Wiggins
Poplarville
Picayune
Slidell
Covington
Hammond
Baton Rouge
Kenner
Laplace
Houma
Golden Meadow

Holly Springs
Oxford
Pontotoc
Houston
Grenada
Eupora
Kosciusko
Canton
Forest
Collins
Columbia
Purvis
Bogalusa
Ponchatoula

Senatobia
Batesville
Clarksdale
Cleveland
Greenwood
Winona
Yazoo City
Jackson
Clinton
Hazlehurst
Brookhaven
Magnolia
McComb
Kentwood

Helena
Indianola
Leland
Greenville
Vicksburg
Port Gibson
Bude
Natchez

Stuttgart
De Witt
Monticello
McGehee
Lake Village
Tallulah
St. Joseph
Ferriday
Bunkie
Opelousas
Lafayette
New Iberia
Jeanerette
Franklin
Morgan City
Patterson

Clarendon
Dumas
Hamburg
Crossett
Bastrop
Monroe
Tullos
Winnfield
Catahoula L.
Pineville
Alexandria
Kinder
Eunice
Crowley
Kaplan
Abbeville

Little Rock
North Little Rock
Hot Springs
Benton
Sheridan
Warren
Hampton
Ruston
Jonesboro
Colfax
Ville Platte
Jennings
Lake Charles
Sulphur

Pine Bluff
Malvern
Arkadelphia
Fordyce
Homer
Rayne
De Ridder
Leesville
Kinder

Hot Bryant Springs
Camden
El Dorado
Minden
Bossier City
Shreveport
Natchitoches
Toledo Bend Resr
Jasper
Woodville
Silsbee
Beaumont
Orange
Port Arthur
High Island

Glenwood
Magnolia
Prescott
Lewisville
Mansfield
Logansport
Pineland

Mena
Nashville
Hope
Ashdown
L. Erling
Marshall
Center
Nacogdoches
Lufkin
Corrigan
Livingston
Cleveland
Dayton

De Queen
Idabel
Texarkana
Naples
Mt Pleasant
Jefferson
Longview
Kilgore
Carthage
Rusk
Crockett
Huntsville
Conroe
Houston
Pasadena
Bellaire

Broken Bow
DeKalb
Paris
Mineola
Tyler
Henderson
Jacksonville
Athens
Palestine
Madisonville
Navasota
Hempstead
La Marque
Texas City
Galveston

McAlester
Hartshorne
Antlers
Hugo
Sulphur Springs
Greenville
Terrell
Mesquite
Garland
Plano
Richardson
Dallas
Waxahachie
Ennis
Corsicana
Mexia
Buffalo
Hearne
Bryan
College Sta.
Brenham
Bellville
Rosenberg
Wharton
Bay City
Lake Jackson
Angleton
Alvin
Freeport

Ada
Tishomingo
Durant
Denison
Sherman
McKinney
Frisco
Fort Worth
Arlington
Grand Prairie
Cleburne
Hillsboro
Marlin
Martin
Navasota
La Grange
Columbus
Gonzales
Edna
Ganado
Yoakum

Purcell
Holdenville
Pauls Valley
Ardmore
Marietta
Gainesville
Bowie
Nocona
Denton
Bridgeport
Weatherford
Granbury
Glen Rose
Gatesville
Killeen
Temple
Belton
Georgetown
Taylor
Bastrop
Austin
Luling
Gonzales

③

④

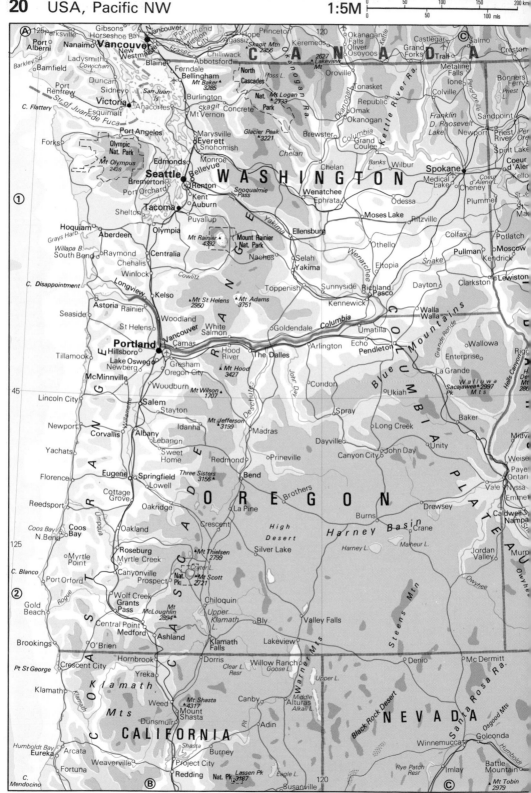

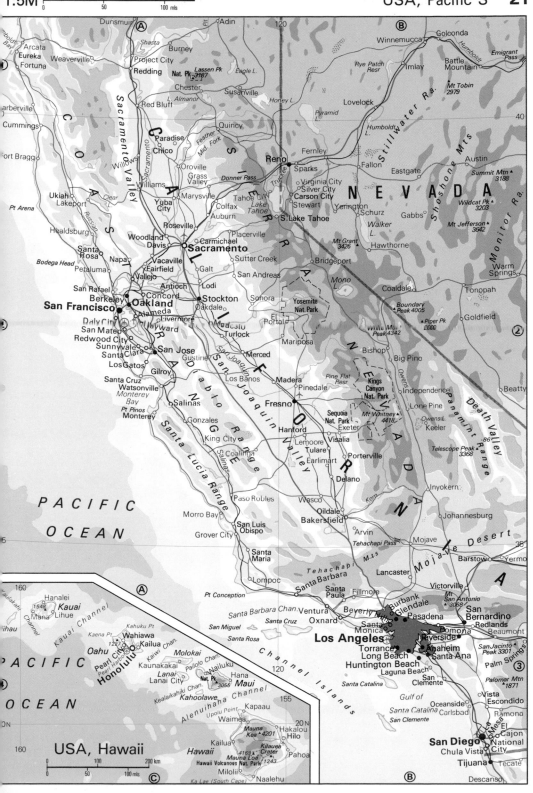

1:5M

0 50 100 150 200 km
0 50 100 mils

PACIFIC OCEAN

NEVADA

Stillwater Ra.
Shoshone Mts
Monitor Ra.
Panamint Range
Death Valley
Mojave Desert

C O A S T   R A N G E S

Sacramento Valley

S I E R R A   N E V A D A

San Joaquin Valley

Santa Lucia Range

Diablo Range

C A L I F O R N I A

Los Angeles

San Francisco
Oakland

Sacramento

Fresno

Bakersfield

San Diego

Dunsmuir
Adin
Winnemucca
Golconda
Arcata
Eureka
Fortuna
Weaverville
Project City
Redding
Nat. Pk.
Lassen Pk.
3187
Eagle L.
Susanville
Rye Patch
Resr
Imlay
Battle
Mountain
Emigrant
Pass
Mt Tobin
2979
Barberville
Cummings
Fort Bragg
Ukiah
Lakeport
Pt Arena
Healdsburg
Santa
Rosa
Napa
Bodega Head
Petaluma
San Rafael
Berkeley
Daly City
San Mateo
Redwood City
Sunnyvale
Santa Clara
Los Gatos
Santa Cruz
Watsonville
Monterey
Bay
Pt Pinos
Monterey
Gonzales
King City
Coalinga
Paso Robles
Morro Bay
San Luis
Obispo
Grover City
Santa
Maria
Lompoc
Pt Conception
Shasta
Burney
Chester
Almanor
Red Bluff
Paradise
Chico
Oroville
Grass
Valley
Williams
Yuba
City
Marysville
Colfax
Auburn
Placerville
Woodland
Davis
Carmichael
Vacaville
Fairfield
Vallejo
Antioch
Concord
Alameda
Hayward
San Jose
Gilroy
Salinas
Salinas
Gustine
Los Banos
Modesto
Turlock
Merced
Madera
Pinedale
Hanford
Lemoore
Tulare
Visalia
Porterville
Earlimart
Delano
Wasco
Oildale
Arvin
Quincy
Honey L.
Lovelock
Pyramid
Humboldt
L.
Reno
Sparks
Fernley
Donner Pass
Feather
Mid Fork
Truckee
Tahoe City
Lake
Tahoe
S. Lake Tahoe
Virginia City
Silver City
Carson City
Stewart
Yerington
Schurz
Gabbs
Walker
L.
Hawthorne
Mt Grant
3426
Bridgeport
Mono
L.
Sutter Creek
Galt
Lodi
Stockton
Oakdale
Sonora
El
Portal
Mariposa
Yosemite
Nat. Park
Boundary
Peak 4005
Piper Pk
10000
Goldfield
Coaldale
Tonopah
Warm
Springs
White Mtn
Peak 4342
Bishop
Big Pino
Pine Flat
Resr
Kings
Canyon
Nat. Park
Independence
Lone Pine
Owens L.
Keeler
Telescope Peak
3368
Sequoia
Nat. Park
Mt Whitney
4418
Exeter
Beatty
Inyokern
Johannesburg
Mojave
Barstow
Yermo
Tehachapi Pass
Tehachapi
Mts
Lancaster
Victorville
Mt
San Antonio
3068
San
Bernardino
Redlands
Beaumont
Pomona
Riverside
Anaheim
Santa Ana
San Jacinto
Peak 3301
Palm
Springs
Palomar Mtn
1871
Vista
Escondido
Oceanside
Carlsbad
Ramona
Chula Vista
Tijuana
Tecate
Descanso
San Diego
El
Cajon
National
City
Mesa
Santa
Barbara
Santa
Paula
Fillmore
Ventura
Oxnard
Beverly Hills
Burbank
Glendale
Pasadena
Santa
Monica
Torrance
Long Beach
Huntington Beach
Laguna Beach
San
Clemente
Santa Catalina
San Clemente
Gulf of
Santa Catalina
Channel Islands
Santa Catalina
Santa Cruz
Santa Rosa
San Miguel
Santa Barbara Chan.
Eastgate
Austin
Summit Mtn
3188
Wildcat Pk
3203
Mt Jefferson
3642
Fallon
Russian R.
Clear
Lakeport
Sacramento
San Andreas
Willow
Lassen

40

120
120
155
20 N
35
36
160
160

USA, Hawaii

PACIFIC
OCEAN

Kauai
Hanalei
1548
Mana
Lihue
Kauai Channel
Kahuku Pt
Kaena Pt
Oahu
Wahiawa
Kailua
Pearl City
Pearl Harbor
Honolulu
Kauai
Channel
Niihau
Kaulakahi Channel
Molokai
Kaunakakai
Lanai
Lanai City
Kahoolawe
Maui
Nat. Pk.
3055
Hana
Kapaau
Upolu Point
Waimea
Mauna
Kea 4201
Hakalou
Hilo
Kailua
4169
Mauna Loa
Hawaii Volcanoes
Nat. Park
Kilauea
Crater
1243
Pahoa
Mililoli
Naalehu
Ka Lae (South Cape)
Kaiwi Chan.
Pailolo Chan.
Nailuku
Alenuihaha Channel
Kealaikahiki Chan.
Hawaii

0 100 200 km
0 50 100 mils

A
B
C
1
2

1:2.5M

0 25 50 75 100 km
0 25 50 mils

San Francisco & Los Angeles map

Lytton, Calistoga, L.Berryessa, Woodland, Folsom, Placerville, Folsom, Camino, Diamond Springs, Markleeville, Topaz, W.Walke
Healdsburg, St Helena, Winters, Davis, Carmichael, **Sacramento**, Highland Pk 3333, Coleville
Forestville, Yountville, Dixon, Elk Grove, Plymouth, Mokelumne, Bear Valley, Dardanelle, Devils Gate 2301, Bridgepc
Santa Rosa, Napa, Vacaville, Galt, Sutter Ck, West Pt, Jackson, Arnold, Sonora Pass 2933, Bridgeport, Resr
Sebastopol, Sonoma, Fairfield, Elmira, Comanche Resr, Mokelumne Hill, San Andreas, Pinecrest, Excelsior Mtn 3790
Petaluma, Napa, Lodi, Clements, Angels Camp, Murphys, S.Fk, Groveland, Hetch Hetchy Resr, Tioga Pass, Mt Dana 3978
Novato, Vallejo, Pittsburg, Isleton, Antioch, Bellota, Melones Resr, Sonora, Mather, Tuolumne Mdws, Lee Vini, Mono Lake
San Rafael, S.Pablo B., Concord, Oakley, Brentwood, Stockton, Farmington Resr, L.Eleanor, Groveland, National, Mt Lyell 3997, Mt Ritter 4010
Mill Valley, Richmond, Berkeley, Mt Diablo 1173, Byron, Tracy, Manteca, Riverbank, Don Pedro Resr, Oakdale, Coulterville, El Portal, Park, Devil Postpi N.M.
Golden Gate, Oakland, San Leandro, Livermore, Pleasanton, Ripon, Ceres, Modesto, McClure L., Wawona, Mariposa, Fish Camp, Mammoth Pool Resr
Daly City, Alameda, Hayward, Fremont, Vernalis, Patterson, Turlock L., Snelling, Yosemite L., Mariposa, Bass Lake, Kaiser Pk 3146, Lakeshore
S.San Francisco, San Mateo, Redwood City, Mountain View, Sunnyvale, Newman, Merced, Planada, Raymond, Mariposa Resr, Huntington L., Shaver L.
San Gregorio, Palo Alto, Santa Clara, San Jose, Coyote, Gustine, Los Banos, Chowchilla, Berenda, Fresno, Millerton, Friant Dam, Humphreys, Pine Flat Resr
Pescadero, Boulder Creek, Los Gatos, Morgan Hill, Volta, S.Luis Resr, Dos Palos, Madera, Firebaugh, Herndon, Friant, Pinedale, Clovis, Patterson Mtn 2489
Davenport, Soquel, Gilroy, Laveaga Pk 1154, S.Luis Resr, Mendota, Kerman, Clovis, Piedra, Minkler, Badger
Santa Cruz, Watsonville, Hollister, Tres Pinos, Herndon, **Fresno**, Sanger, Reedley
Monterey Bay, Castroville, San Juan Bautista, Alisal, Helm, Selma, Kingsburg, Dinuba
Pacific Grove, Salinas, Seaside, Monterey, Gonzales, Pinnacles N.M., Kings

San Luis Valley, San Joaquin Valley, Diablo Range, Gabilan Rge, Santa Cruz Mts, COAST RANGES, SIERRA NEVADA, Yosemite National Park

Carmel, Carmel Valley

Sta Ynez, Los Alamos, Los Olivos, San Rafael Mts, Big Pine Mtn 2081, Gorman, Piru Ck, Lake Hughes, California Aqueduct, Rosamond L., Helendale
Lompoc, Buellton, Solvang, L.Cachuma, Lancaster, Mirage L., Pt Arguello, Santa Ynez Mts, Ojai, Fillmore, Castaic, Palmdale, Adelanto, Victorville
Pt Conception, Gaviota, Goleta, Carpinteria, Santa Paula, Moorpark, Acton, Littlerock, Hesperia
San Miguel, Santa Barbara, Santa Clara R., Newhall, San Gabriel Mts, Wrightwood 3068, San Bernardino
Santa Barbara Channel, Ventura, Oxnard, Camarillo, San Fernando, Mt Wilson 1740, Pasadena, Mt San Antonio, Upland, Colton, Highlan
Santa Rosa, Santa Cruz, Anacapa Is, Port Hueneme, **Los Angeles**, Burbank, Glendale, Hollywood, Monrovia, Pomona, Ontario, Redlands
Santa Cruz Chan., Santa Monica, Beverly Hills, Inglewood, Whittier, Riverside
Channel Islands, Santa Monica Bay, Torrance, Redondo Beach, Lakewood, Fullerton, Anaheim, Orange, Corona, Perris
Santa Barbara, Long Beach, Garden Grove, Santa Ana, Costa Mesa, Santiago Pk 1736, Sta Ana Mts
Huntington Beach, Newport Beach, Laguna Beach, S.Onofre, Elsinore L., Fall brook
San Nicolas, Santa Catalina, Avalon, San Pedro Channel, San Clemente, Oceanside, Vista
Gulf of Santa Catalina, Outer Santa Barbara Channel, Carlsbad, Encinitas, Santa Margarita
Santa Barbara, San Clemente, Del Mar, La Jolla, **San Diego**

PACIFIC OCEAN

1:5M

| 0 | 50 | 100 | 150 | 200 km |

| 0 | 50 | 100 mls |

GULF OF MEXICO

Major cities and places:

Cd Madero · Tampico · Altamira · Panuco · Ebano · Cd del Maiz · Cd Valles · Tamazunchale · Tamuin · Cerritos · San Luis Potosi · Zaragoza · Sta Maria del Rio · Rio Verde · San Bartolo · Cardenas · Aguascalientes · AGS. · Loreto · Encarnacion · Lagos de Moreno · San Felipe · Dolores Hidalgo · San Miguel de A. · Guanajuato · León · Silao · San Francisco del Rincon · Irapuato · Salamanca · Celaya · Querétaro · San Juan del Rio · Guadalajara · Tlaquepaque · Tepatitlán · Chapala · La Barca · Zamora · Jacona · Zacapu · Morelia · Patzcuaro · Uruapan · Colima · Tecoman · Manzanillo · Lázaro Cárdenas · Acapulco · Pto Marquez · Chilpancingo · Iguala · Taxco · Cuernavaca · Toluca · Méxic(o) · Xochimilco · Tlalpan · Contreras · Texcoco · Pachuca · Tula · Tulancingo · Puebla · Tlaxcala · Cholula · Atlixco · Izúcar de Matamoros · Orizaba · Cd Mendoza · Córdoba · Jalapa · Veracruz · Cardel · Huatusco · Coscomatepec · Poza Rica · Papantla · Tuxpan · Naranjos · Tamiahua · Tehuacán · Oaxaca · Tlacolula · Mitla · Etla · Nochixtlán · Huajuapan de León · Acatlán · Tehuantepec · Salina Cruz · Catemaco · S.Andrés Tuxtla · Alvarado · Tuxtepec

Regions/States: NAYARIT · JALISCO · GUANAJUATO · QUERÉTARO · HIDALGO · MICHOACÁN · MORELOS · GUERRERO · OAXACA · Sa. Madre del Sur · Sa. Madre Oriental · Sa. de Juárez · Sa. de Miahuatlán

Features: Vol Citlaltepetl 5700 · Pop(ocatepetl) 5450 · Ixtaccihuatl 5286 · Nev de Toluca 4558 · La Malinche 4282 · Nev de Colima 4330 · Co Tancitaro 3845 · Rio Grande de Santiago · Rio Balsas · Lago de Chapala · Presa del Infiernillo · Lago de Tamiahua · I de Lobos

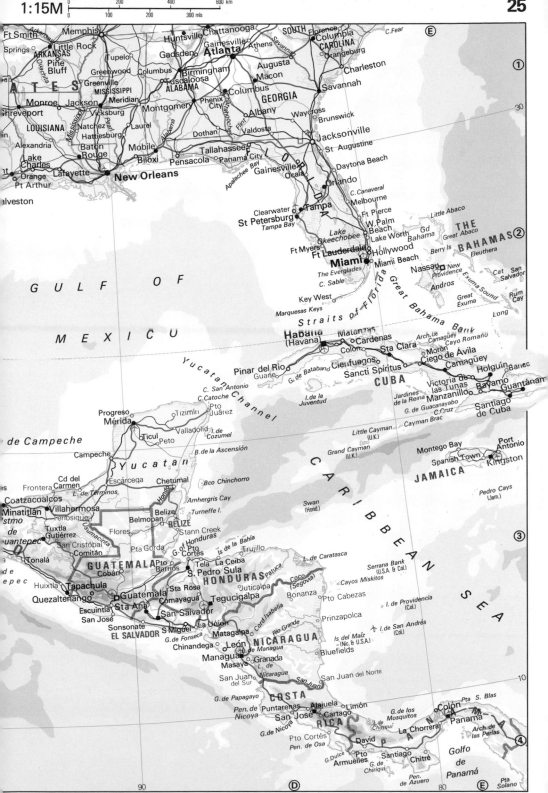

1:15M

0 200 400 600 km
0 100 200 300 mls

UNITED STATES

Ft Smith
Memphis
Springs
Little Rock
Huntsville
Chattanooga
Gadsden
Florence
Columbia
SOUTH
C.Fear
ARKANSAS
Pine Bluff
Greenwood
Tupelo
Gainesville
Athens
Atlanta
Augusta
CAROLINA
Orangeburg
MISSISSIPPI
Greenville
Columbus
Birmingham
Tuscaloosa
Macon
Charleston
Monroe
Jackson
Meridian
ALABAMA
Montgomery
Phenix City
Columbus
GEORGIA
Savannah
LOUISIANA
Vicksburg
Laurel
Albany
Waycross
Shreveport
Natchez
Pearl
Dothan
Valdosta
Brunswick
Hattiesburg
Alexandria
Baton Rouge
Mobile
Tallahassee
Jacksonville
St Augustine
Lake Charles
Lafayette
Biloxi
Pensacola
Panama City
FLORIDA
Daytona Beach
Orange
Pt Arthur
New Orleans
Apalachee Bay
Gainesville
Ocala
Orlando
C.Canaveral
alveston

GULF

OF

St Petersburg
Clearwater
Tampa
Tampa Bay
Lake Okeechobee
Ft Myers
Ft Lauderdale
Hollywood
Miami
Miami Beach
The Everglades
C. Sable
Melbourne
Ft Pierce
W.Palm Beach
Lake Worth
Bahama
Gd Bahama
Little Abaco
Great Abaco
THE
BAHAMAS
Berry Is
Eleuthera
Nassau
New Providence
Andros
Cat I.
San Salvador
Exuma Sound
Rum Cay

MEXICO

Key West
Marquesas Keys
Great Exuma
Long I.

Straits of Florida

Great Bahama Bank

Habana (Havana)
Matanzas
Cardenas
Colon
Sta Clara
Arch. de Camagüey
Cayo Romano
Pinar del Rio
Guane
G. de Batabanó
Cienfuegos
Sancti Spiritus
Morón
Ciego de Ávila
CUBA
Camagüey
Holguín
Banes
C. San Antonio
C.Catoche
Pto Juárez
I. de la Juventud
Jardines de la Reina
Victoria de las Tunas
Bayamo
Manzanillo
G. de Guacanayabo
C.Cruz
Santiago de Cuba
Guantánamo

de Campeche

Yucatan Channel

Progreso
Mérida
Tizimín
Ticul
Peto
Valladolid
I. de Cozumel
B. de la Ascensión
Little Cayman (U.K.)
Grand Cayman (U.K.)
Cayman Brac
Montego Bay
Spanish Town
Port Antonio
Kingston
JAMAICA
Pedro Cays (Jam.)

Campeche

Yucatan

Cd del Carmen
Frontera
Escárcega
Chetumal
Bco Chinchorro
Coatzacoalcos
Minatitlán
Istmo de uantepec
Villahermosa
Tenosique
L. de Términos
Flores
Belize
Belmopan
BELIZE
Amhergris Cay
Turneffe I.
Swan Is (Hond.)
Stann Creek
Pta Gorda
Tuxtla Gutiérrez
San Cristóbal
Comitán
Usumacinta
CARIBBEAN
Serrana Bank (U.S.A. & Col.)
Tonalá
G. of Honduras
Pto Cortés
Is de la Bahía
Trujillo
L. de Caratasca
epec
GUATEMALA
Pto Barrios
La Ceiba
Tela
S. Pedro Sula
HONDURAS
Patuca
Cayos Miskitos
SEA
Huixtla
Cobán
Sta Rosa
Coco (Segovia)
Tapachula
Quezaltenango
Escuintla
Sta Ana
Guatemala
Comayagua
Tegucigalpa
Juticalpa
Bonanza
Pto Cabezas
I. de Providencia (Col.)
San José
Sonsonate
San Salvador
Chinandega
S Miguel
La Unión
Matagalpa
Cord Isabelia
Rio Grande
Prinzapolca
EL SALVADOR
G. de Fonseca
León
Chinandega
NICARAGUA
Is del Maíz (Nic. & U.S.A.)
I. de San Andrés (Col.)
Managua
L. de Managua
Bluefields
Masaya
Granada
L. de Nicaragua
San Juan del Sur
San Juan
San Juan del Norte
G. de Papagayo
COSTA
Pen. de Nicoya
Puntarenas
Alajuela
San José
Cartago
Limón
G. de los Mosquitos
Colón
Pta S. Blas
PANAMA
Panama
G. de Nicoya
RICA
L. de Chiriquí
La Chorrera
Arch. de las Perlas
Pto Cortés
Pen. de Osa
David
Santiago
Chitré
Golfo de Panamá
G. Dulce
Pto Armuelles
G. de Chiriquí
Pen. de Azuero
Pta Solano

1:10M

100   200   300   400 km

100   200 mls

JAMAICA

Montego Bay · Falmouth · Wakefield · St Ann's Bay · Galina Pt · Ocho Rios · The Cockpit Country · Dry Harbour Mts · Moneague · Annotto Bay · Cambridge · Mt Denham 986 · Chapelton · Pt Antonio · Blue Mtn Pk 2256 · Blue Mts · 18

Mandeville · May Pen · Spanish Town · Kingston · lack River · Salt River · Port Royal · Morant Pt

Southfield · Long Bay · Portland Bight · Portland Pt · Morant Bay

1:2.5 M

TRINIDAD L

Chupara Pt · Matelot · Galera Pt · 61
Pt of Spain · Northern Range · Mt Aripo 940 · Tunapuna · San Juan · Arima · Matura Bay
Chaguanas · Upper Manzanilla · Cocos Bay
San Fernando · Rio Claro · Princes Town · Pt Radix · St Joseph
Point Fortin · Débé · Guayaguayare · Ortoire
Fullarton · Siparia · Moruga · Galeota Pt
Gulf of Paria

1:2.5 M · 10

GRENADA M
Bedford Pt · Sauteurs · Mt St Catherine 840 · Grenville · St George's · Pt Salines · Prickly Pt · 12 · 61°45' · 1:2.5 M

ST VINCENT N
Soufrière 1234 · Porter Pt · Georgetown · 13°15' · Barrouallie · Kingstown · Johnston Pt · 61°15' · 1:2.5 M

ST LUCIA P
Gros Islet · Cap Pt · Castries · Dennery · 14 · Soufrière · Mt Gimie 950 · Vieux Fort · C.Moule à Chique · 61 · 1:2.5 M

DOMINICA Q
C. Melville · Marigot · Portsmouth · Morne Diablotin 1447 · 15°30' · Roseau · Rosalie · Grand Bay · 61°30' · 1:2.5 M

BARBADOS R
North Pt · Speightstown · 13°15' · Holetown · Mt Hillaby 340 · Blackman's · Bridgetown · Ragged Pt · South Pt · 59°30' · 1:2.5 M · 3

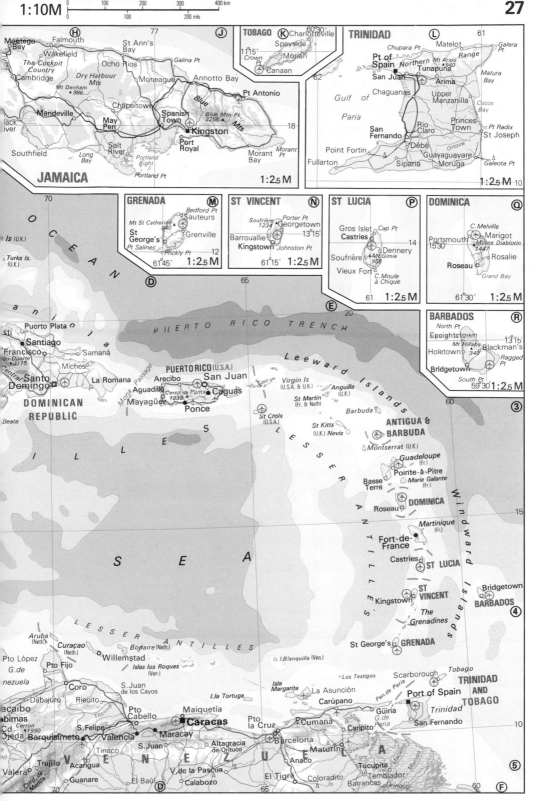

O C E A N

Is (U.K.)

Turks Is. (U.K.)

70

65

20 · E

PUERTO RICO TRENCH

Leeward Islands

sti · Puerto Plata · Samaná
Francisco · co.Duarte 3175 · Miches
Santiago · La Romana · Mona Passage
Santo Domingo · San Juan · Arecibo · Virgin Is (U.S.A. & U.K.) · Anguilla (U.K.)
DOMINICAN REPUBLIC · PUERTO RICO (U.S.A.) · San Juan · St Martin (Fr. & Neth)
Aguadilla · Caguas · Cerro de Punta 1338 · St Croix (U.S.A.) · Barbuda
Mayagüez · Ponce · St Kitts (U.K.) Nevis · ANTIGUA & BARBUDA
Beata · Montserrat (U.K.)

A N T I L L E S

G R E A T E R

L E S S E R

Guadeloupe (Fr.) · Pointe-à-Pitre · Marie Galante (Fr.)
Basse Terre · DOMINICA · 15
Roseau

Martinique (Fr.) · Fort-de-France
Castries · ST LUCIA

C A R I B B E A N

S E A

St George's · Kingstown · ST VINCENT · The Grenadines · GRENADA
Bridgetown · BARBADOS · 4

Windward Islands

L E S S E R   A N T I L L E S

Aruba (Neth.) · Curaçao (Neth.) · Bonaire (Neth.) · Willemstad · Islas los Roques (Ven.) · I.B!anquilla (Ven.)
Pto López · G.de · nezuela · Pto Fijo · Los Testigos · Scarborough · Tobago
Coro · S. Juan de los Cayos · I.la Tortuga · Isla Margarita · La Asunción · Carúpano · Pen.de Paria · Port of Spain · TRINIDAD AND TOBAGO
acaibo · Dabajuro · Riecito · Maiquetía · Pto la Cruz · Cumaná · Güiria · Trinidad · San Fernando
bimas · S.Felipe · Pto Cabello · Caracas · Maracay · Barcelona · Caripito · 10
Cd · Cerron 1990 · Maracay · S.Juan · Altagracia de Orituco · Maturín · Tucupita
Ojeda · Barquisimeto · Valencia · Tinaco · Anaco · Guanipa
Valera · Trujillo · Acarigua · El Baúl · V.de la Pascua · El Tigre · Temblador · Tigre · Orinoco · Barrancas
Guanare · Cord.de Mérida · Guanare · Calabozo · Coloradito · 5
60 · F

V E N E Z U E L A

1:40M

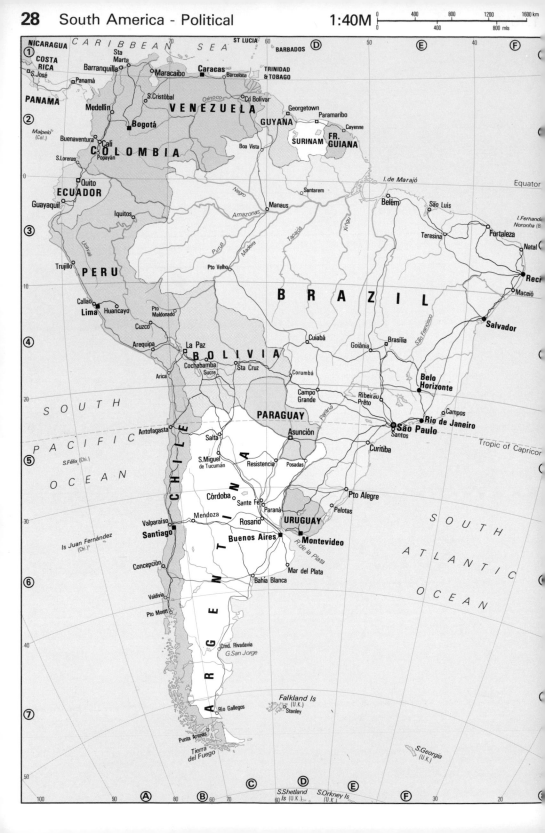

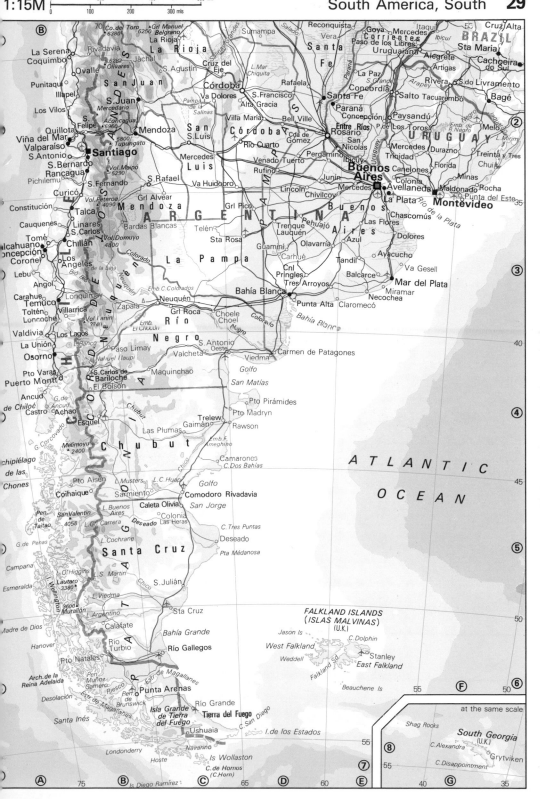

1:15M

200 400 600 km
100 200 300 mls

La Serena
Coquimbo
Rivadavia
6380 6250 Belgrano
Sumampa
Reconquista
Goya Mercedes Itaqui
Vera Paso de los Libres
Uruguaiana Ibicuí
Cruz Alta 55
BRAZIL
Sta Maria

Punitaqui
Illapel
Ovalle
6282
Olivares
Jáchal
S. Agustin
Santa Fe
La Paz
S. Grande
Arapey
Alegrete
Artigas
Rivera S.do Livramento
Cachoeira
do Sul

Los Vilos
S. Juan
Mercedario
Córdoba
Va Dolores
S. Francisco
Alta Gracia
Rafaela
Concordia
Salto Tacuarembó
Bagé

Quillota
Aconcagua 6960
Mendoza
San
Villa María
Bell Ville
Concepción
Paraná
Paysandú
Emb.de
R.Negro
Melo
L. Mirim

Viña del Mar
Valparaíso
S.Antonio
S. Felipe
6800
Tupungato
S. Luis
Córdoba
Cda de
Gómez
Entre Ríos
Rosario
San
P.de los Toros
Durazno
Treinta y Tres
Chuí
URUGUAY

S. Bernardo
Rancagua
Pichilemu
Santiago
Vol.Maipo 5290
S. Rafael
Río Cuarto
Venado Tuerto
Pergamino
Ibicuy
Nicolás
Mercedes
Trinidad
Florida
Minas
2

Curicó
Vol.Petероа 4090
Mendoza
Va Huidobro
Rufino
Junín
Buenos Aires
Avellaneda
La Plata
Colonia
Canelones
Maldonado
Punta del Este
Rocha
35

Constitución
Talca
Grl Alvear
Lincoln
Chivilcoy
Mercedes
Montevideo

Cauquenes
Linares
S.Carlos
Bardas Blancas
Grl Pico
Pehuajó
Las Flores
Chascomús

Tomé
Chillán
Vol.Domuyo 4800
Telén
Sta Rosa
Trenque
Lauquén
Guaminí
Olavarría
Azul
Dolores

Concepción
Coronel
Los Ángeles
Colorado
La Pampa
Carhué
Tandil
Ayacucho
Va Gesell

Lebu
Angol
Carahue
Temuco
Loncoche
Villarrica
Longuimay
Zapala
Grl Roca
Choele Choel
Bahía Blanca
Cnl Pringles
Tres Arroyos
Balcarce
Necochea
Mar del Plata
Miramar
3

Toltén
Vol.Lanin
Neuquén
Río
Colorado
Punta Alta
Claromecó

Valdivia
La Unión
Osorno
Negro
S. Antonio
Oeste
Viedma
Bahía Blanca
40

Pto Varas
Puerto Montt
S.Carlos de
Bariloche
El Bolsón
Paso Limay
Nahuel Huapi
Valcheta
Carmen de Patagones

Ancud
G.de
Ancud
Castro
Achao
Esquel
Maquinchao
Golfo
San Matías
Pto Pirámides

de Chiloé
Chubut
Pto Madryn
Trelew
Gaimán
Rawson
4

G. Corcovado
Melimoyu 2400
Las Plumas
Emb.F.
Ameghino

chipiélago
de las
Chonos
Pto Aisén
Musters
L.C.Huapi
Golfo
San Jorge
Camarones
C. Dos Bahías
ATLANTIC
45

Coihaique
Sarmiento
Caleta Olivia
Comodoro Rivadavia
OCEAN

Pen.
de
Taitao
San Valentin
4058
L. Buenos
Aires
L. Gn Carrera
Deseado
Colonia
Las Heras
C. Tres Puntas

G.de Penas
L. Cochrane
Santa Cruz
Deseado
Pta Médanosa
5

Campana
L.S. Martin
FALKLAND ISLANDS
(ISLAS MALVINAS)
(U.K.)

Esmeralda
L. Viedma
S. Julián
Jason Is
West Falkland
C.Dolphin
50

Madre de Dios
Hanover
Lautaro 3380
L. Argentino
3600
Murallón
Sta Cruz
Calafate
Bahía Grande
Río
Turbio
Río Gallegos
Weddell
Falkland Sd.
East Falkland
Stanley

Arch.de la
Reina Adelaida
Desolación
Santa Inés
Pto Natales
Pen.
Muñoz
Riesco
Pen.
de
Brunswick
Punta Arenas
Beauchene Is
55
F
50
6

Río Grande
Isla Grande
de Tierra
del Fuego
Tierra del Fuego
C. San Diego
at the same scale

Londonderry
Hoste
Ushuaia
Navarino
I. de los Estados
Shag Rocks
South Georgia
(U.K.)
C. Alexandra
8

Is Wollaston
C.de Hornos
(C.Horn)
Grytviken
C.Disappointment

A 75 **B** Is Diego Ramírez **C** 65 **D** 60 **E** **7** 55 40 **G** 35

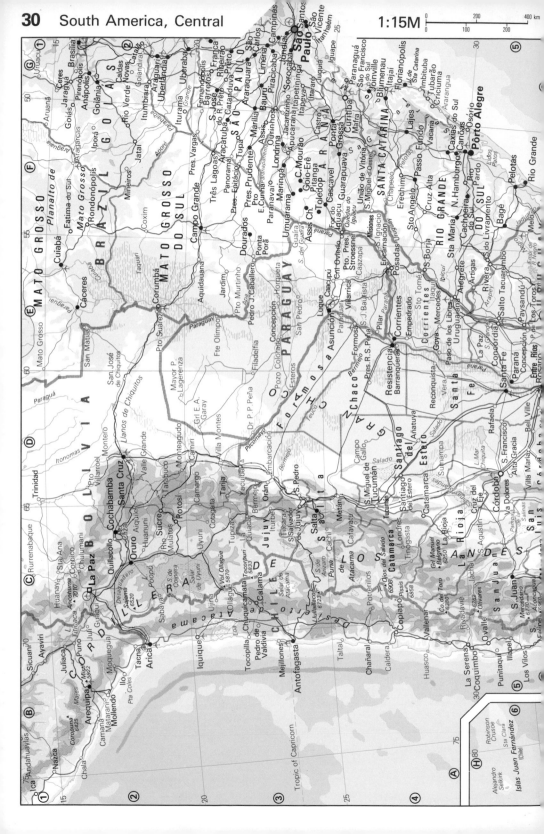

1:15M

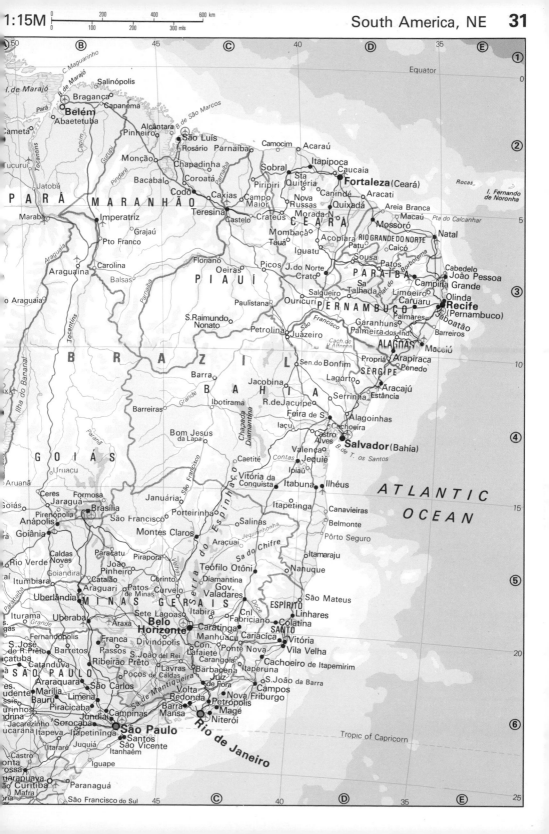

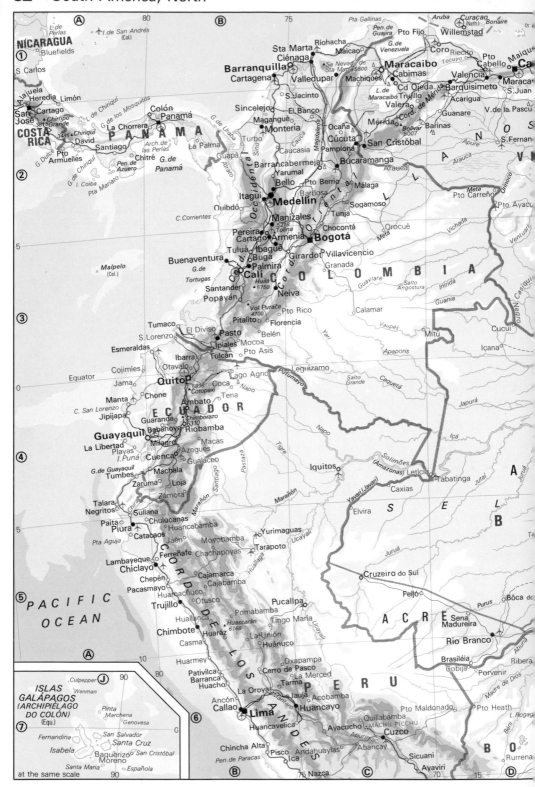

PACIFIC OCEAN

COSTA RICA

NICARAGUA

PANAMA

COLOMBIA

ECUADOR

PERU

VENEZUELA

LLANOS

SELVA

ACRE

BO...

ISLAS GALÁPAGOS (ARCHIPIÉLAGO DO COLÓN) (Equ.)

at the same scale

1:15M

200 400 600 km

100 200 300 mls

GRENADA

St George's

I. de Margarita

La Asunción

Carúpano Pen. de Paria Tobago

Cumaná Güiria Port of

Caripito G. de Spain

Paria Trinidad San Fernando

Maturín

Tucupita

Barrancas

Cd Bolívar Orinoco Cd Guayana

Cd Piar Upata

Emb. de

La Paragua Guri

El Dorado

Salto

del Angel La Gran

Sta Elena Sabana Roraima

2190

Sa Pacaraima

Bonfim

Boa Vista

R O R A I M A

Caracaraí

Negro

Branco

Tefé

Manaus

Manacapuru Careiro Itacoatiara

A M A Z O N A S

Coari

Purus

B R A S I L

Lábrea Madeira

Humaitá

Prainha

Aripuaná

Pôrto Velho

R O N D Ô N I A Serra dos Parecis

Guaporé

Vilhena

Trinidad Mato Grosso

ATLANTIC

OCEAN

Mabaruma

Charity

Suddie Leguan I.

V. en Hoop Georgetown Nieuw Amsterdam

Bartica New Amsterdam

Linden Paramaribo Marienburg

Nieuw Totness

Nickerie Albina Sinnamary

Apoera Witagron I. du Diable (Devil's I.)

Kaieteur Blommesteinmeer Kourou

Fall Cayenne

G U Y A N A S U R I N A M FRENCH Cabo Orange

Julianatop GUIANA

1280 Oiapoque

Serra Tumucumaque Amapá Ilha de Maracá

A M A P A

Sa do Navio

Jari Macapá C. Maguarinho

Pto Santana B. de Marajó

I. de Marajó Salinópolis

Oriximiná Bragança

Obidos Amazonas Capanema

Monte Pará Belém

Santarém Alegre Cametá Abaetetuba

Altamira Tucuruí

Aveiro Jatobá

Itaituba Tapajós

Pimenta P A R Á Marabá Imperatriz

Jacareacanga Pto

Iriri Franco

S. Félix Araguaína Carolina

Xingu Araguaia

Serra do Cachimbo C. do Araguaia

Teles Pires Cachimbo

Tocantins

Juruena São Félix

Arinos Ilha do Bananal

Sa dos Caiabis Sa Formosa

M A T O G R O S S O G O I Á S

Pto Artur

Mato Grosso Aruanã Uruaçu

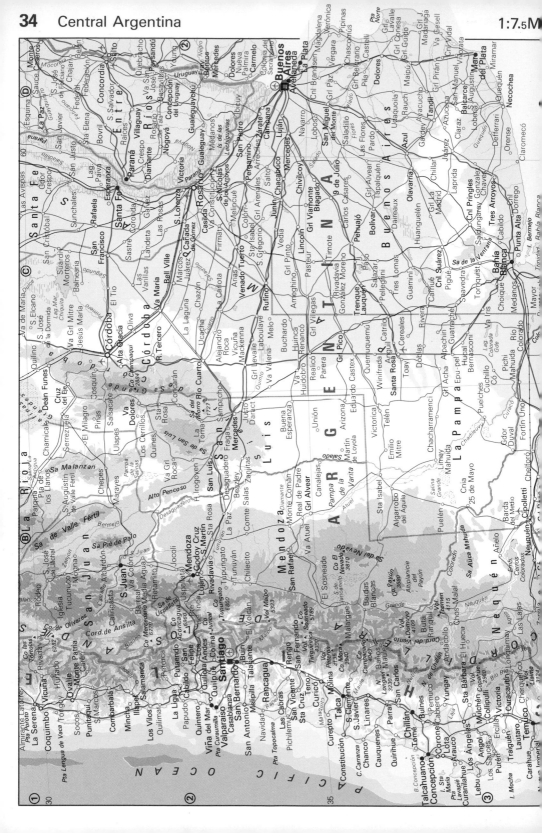

1:7.5M

0 100 200 300 km
0 50 100 150 mls

Tropic of Capricorn

B R A Z I L

ESPIRITO SANTO

MINAS GERAIS

M A T O G R O S S O

DISTRITO FEDERAL

São Paulo

Belo Horizonte

Rio de Janeiro

Niterói

Vitória

Brasília

Goiânia

Anápolis

A T L A N T I C   O C E A N

S A O   P A U L O

P A R A N A

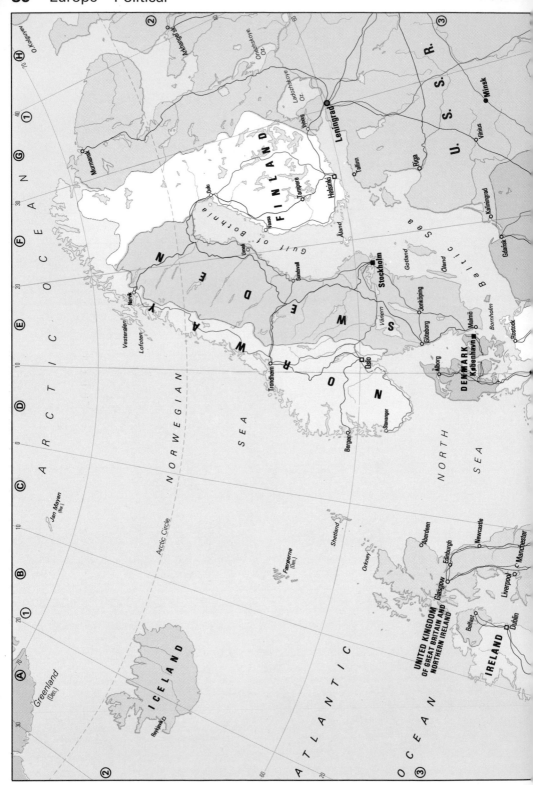

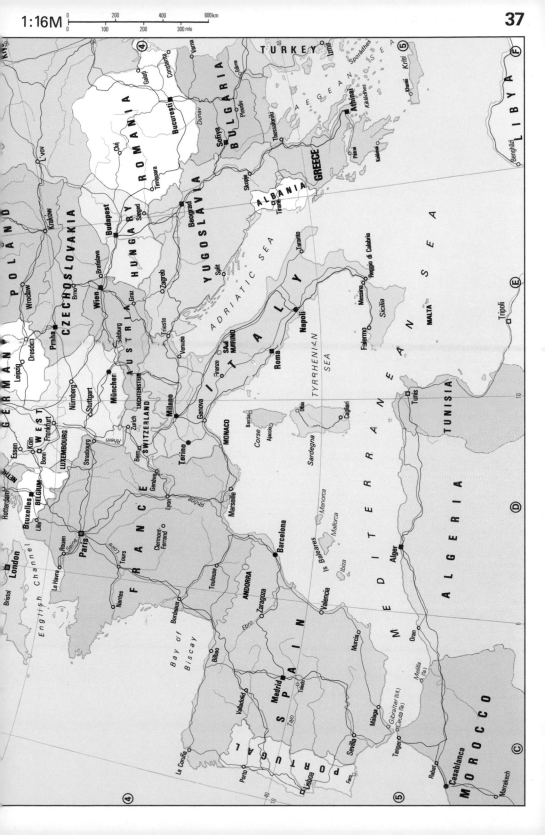

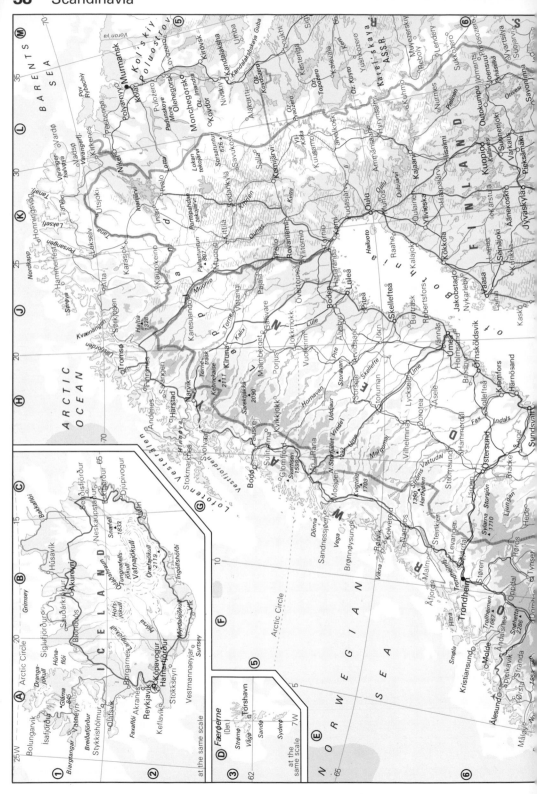

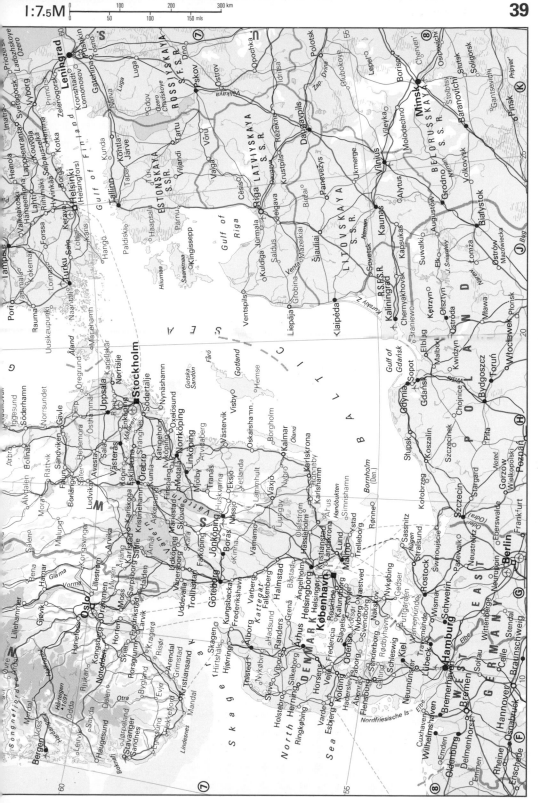

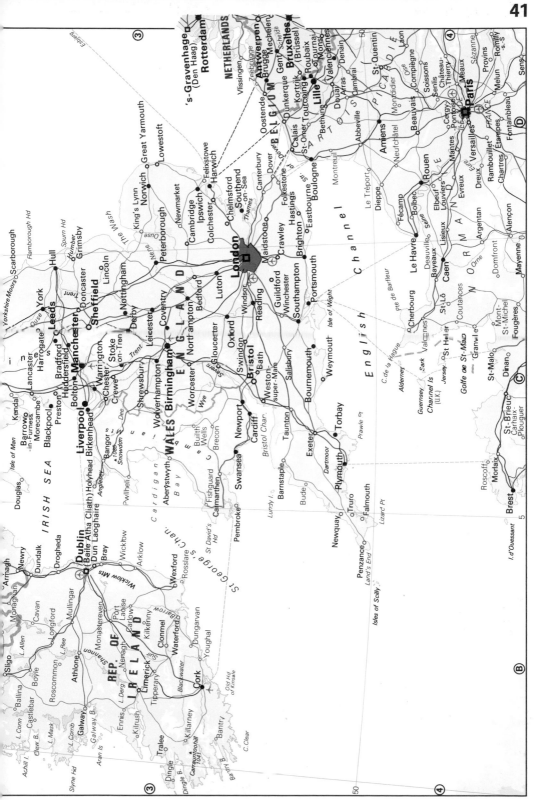

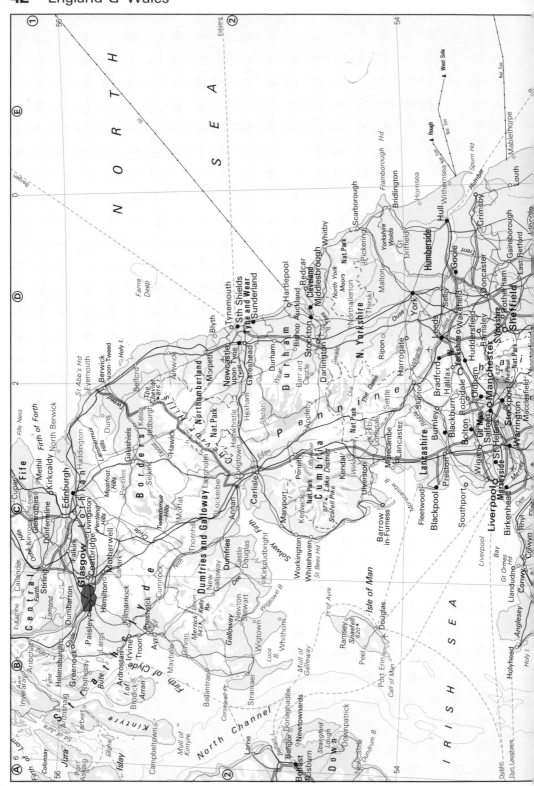

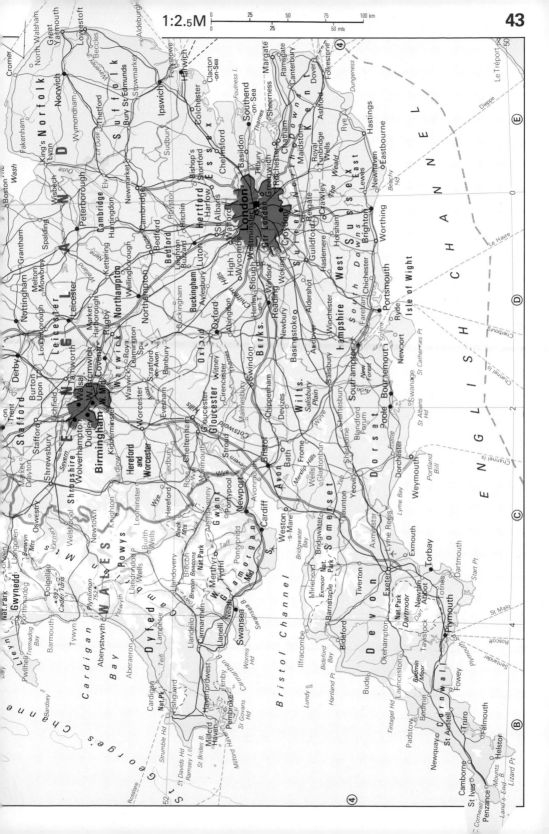

1:2.5M

1:2.5M

0 25 50 75 100 km
0 25 50 mls

Shetland

Herma Ness · Unst · Fetlar · Yell · Whalsay · Isbister · St Magnus Bay · Hillswick · The Faither · Papa Stour · Brae · Voe · Bressay · Ness · Lerwick · Scalloway · Foula · Fitful Hd · Grutness · Sumburgh Hd · Fair Isle · 60 · 58

Aberdeen

Orkney

Papa Westray · N. Ronaldsay · Sanday · Stronsay · Shapinsay · Westray · Eday · Rousay · Kirkwall · Birsay · Mainland · Scapa Flow · Burray · S. Ronaldsay · Stromness · Dunnet Hd · Duncansby Hd · Hoy · Pentland Firth

N O R T H   S E A

Long Forties

Buchan Deep

Kinnaird's Hd · Fraserburgh · Peterhead · Buchan Ness · Girdle Ness · **Aberdeen** · Inverurie · Stonehaven

Ythan · Banff · Huntly · Deveron · Montrose · Arbroath · Brechin · Forfar · N Esk · S Esk · Bervie · Banchory · Dee · Dundee · Tay · Fife Ness · North Berwick · St Andrews · Firth of Forth · Cupar · Kirkcaldy · Methil · Leven · Haddington · Edinburgh

Grampian

Lossiemouth · Elgin · Keith · Dufftown · Spey · Ballater · Braemar · 1155 · Ben Macdui · Lochnagar · Cairngorms 1310

Forres · Nairn · Aviemore · Grantown-on-Spey · Pitlochry · Blair Atholl · Aberfeldy · **Tayside** · Perth · Crieff · Blairgowrie · Glenrothes · Dunfermline · Kinross · Dollar · Stirling · Falkirk · Livingston · Coatbridge

Wick · Lybster · Helmsdale · Brora · Dunnet Hd · John O'Groats · Thurso · Pentland Firth · Burray · S. Ronaldsay · Hoy

Ben Hope 927 · Tongue · Ben Kilbreck 961 · Ben More Assynt 998 · Ben Wyvis 1045 · Ben Dearg 1081 · Lairg · Dornoch · Tain · Dingwall · Beauly · Inverness · Dornoch Firth · Tarbat Ness · Cromarty · Black Isle · Moray Firth · Findhorn · Monadhliath Mts · Kingussie

Highland · **S c o t l a n d** · **G r a m p i a n   M o u n t a i n s**

Loch Ness · Glen Garry · Fort Augustus · Ben Attow 1031 · Kyle of Lochalsh · Glen Affric · Fort William · Ben Nevis 1344 · Ballachulish · Glencoe · Ben Lawers 1214 · Killin · Crianlarich · Callander · Loch Rannoch · L Ericht · L Tay · L Earn · **Central** · Dumbarton · Glasgow · Paisley · Greenock · Helensburgh · Arrochar

Ullapool · Lochinver · Enard Bay · Eddrachillis Bay · Handa · Scourie · C. Wrath · Durness · L. Eriboll · Kinlochbervie · Stoer · L. Broom · L. Maree · Gairloch · L. Torridon · Loch Ewe · Greenstone Pt · Rubha Reidh · Applecross · Raasay · Sd of Raasay · Portree · L. Snizort · L. Bracadale · **Isle of Skye** · Cuillin Hills · Broadford · Bradford · Kyleakin · Glenelg · L. Hourn · L. Nevis · Mallaig · Arisaig · L. Morar · L. Shiel · L. Sunart · Morvern · Loch Linnhe · Oban · Firth of Lorn · L. Awe · Inveraray · L. Fyne · Lochgilphead · Ardrishaig · Tarbert · Loch Long · Port Askaig · Jura · Sd of Jura

Western Isles · Butt of Lewis · Stornoway · Broad Bay · Loch Roag · **Lewis** · North Minch · Tarbert · **Harris** · Sd of Harris · L. Seaforth · E. Loch Tarbert · Scarp · Taransay · Pabbay · Scalpay · Little Minch · Lochmaddy · **North Uist** · Monach Is · Benbecula · **South Uist** · Eriskay · Barra · Lochboisdale · Castlebay · Barra Hd · Flannan Is

Rum · Eigg · Muck · Canna · Ardnamurchan Pt · Coll · Tiree · **Mull** · Tobermory · Ulva · Staffa · Iona · Sd of Mull · Colonsay

Beatrice

Oil

56 · 58 · 60

at the same scale

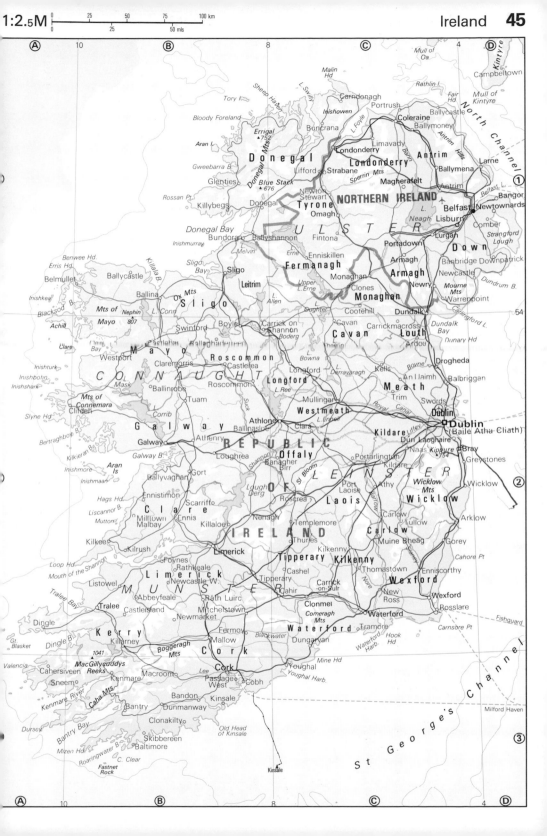

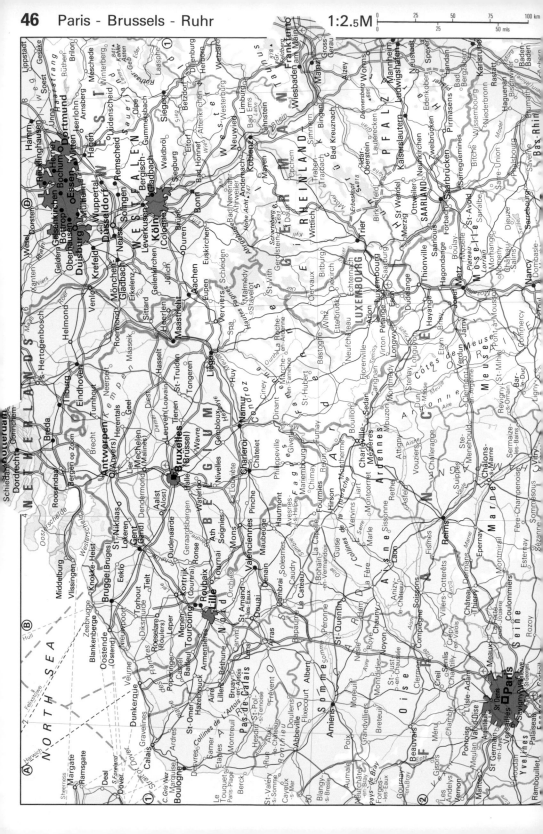

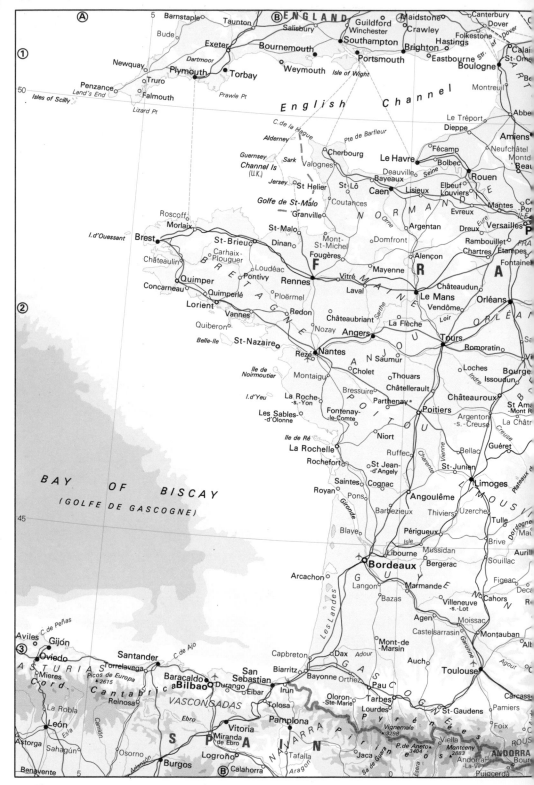

1:5M

0 50 100 150 200 km
0 50 100 mls

issingen
Zeebrugge
Eindhoven
Antwerpen (Anvers)
Düsseldorf
WESTFALEN
Mönchen-gladbach
Köln
Siegen
Erfurt
Eisenach
Jena
Gera
Zwickau
E.GER.
Brugge
Gent
Mechelen
Maastricht
Aachen
Bonn
Bad-Godesberg
Marburg
Bad Hersfeld
Fulda
Werra
Thüringer Wald
Plauen
Hof
Cheb
Brüssel (Bruxelles)
Leuven
Hasselt
St-Truiden
Liège
Euskirchen
Andernach
Koblenz
Limburg
Giessen
Alsfeld
Fulda
HESSEN
WEST
Schweinfurt
Coburg
Bayreuth
Weiden
Roubaix
Tournai
Mons
Namur
Marche
Bitburg
Frankfurt
Wiesbaden
Mainz
Offenbach
Aschaffenburg
Würzburg
Bamberg
Valenciennes
Charleroi
Ardennes
Bastogne
LUXEMBOURG
Trier
Bad-Kreuznach
Bingen
Darmstadt
Worms
Mannheim
Ansbach
Kitzingen
Erlangen
Amberg
Denain
Maubeuge
Fourmies
Sedan
Arlon
Longwy
Luxembourg
SAARLAND
Kaiserslautern
Saarbrücken
Pirmasens
Ludwigshafen
Speyer
Heidelberg
GERMANY
Crailsheim
Nürnberg
Fürth
Rarsberg
St-Quentin
Charleville-Mézières
Laon
Thionville
Saarlouis
Karlsruhe
Heilbronn
BADEN-
Donauwörth
Regensburg
Ingolstadt
Oise
Compiègne
Aisne
Reims
Verdun
Metz
Sarreguemines
Pforzheim
Rastatt
Stuttgart
Ludwigsburg
Esslingen
Heidenheim
Alb
Landshut
teau-erry
Epernay
Chalons-s.-M.
Sarrebourg
Nancy
Strasbourg
Offenburg
Baden-Baden
Tübingen
Reutlingen
Ulm
Augsburg
München
Dachau
eaux
Sézanne
Provins
Troyes
Bar-s-A.
Chaumont
Épinal
St Dié
Colmar
Freiburg
WÜRTTEMBERG
Tuttlingen
Biberach
Landsberg
Starnberg
Rosenheim
Joigny
Châtillon
Langres
Vesoul
Mulhouse
Lörrach
Schaffhausen
Konstanz
Ravensburg
Friedrichshafen
Lindau
Memmingen
Kempten
Bad Tölz
Kufstein
Garmisch-P.
AUSTRIA
Avallon
Vitry-l.-F.
Tour
Romilly-s-S
Bar-s-A
Dijon
Besançon
Belfort
Montbéliard
Basel
Zürich
Olten
Winterthur
St Gallen
Dornbirn
Feldkirch
Innsbruck
Provins
Chalon-s.-S.
Dôle
Biel
Neuchâtel
Bern
Zug
Luzern
Chur
Arosa
LIECHTENSTEIN
Vaduz
Bludenz
Landeck
Wildspitze 3774
Merano
Brunico
Autun
Beaune
Doubs
Pontarlier
Fribourg
Thun
Interlaken
St Gotthard
SWITZERLAND
Schwyz
Rhein
St Moritz
Ortles 3899
Bolzano
Marmolada 3342
Le Creusot
Montceau-l.-M.
Lons-l.-S.
Lausanne
Vevey
Montreux
Brig
Jungfrau 4158
Simplon 2005
Bellinzona
L.di Como
Sondrio
Edolo
Trento
Rovereto
Bassano
FRANCHE COMTÉ
Mâcon
Bourg
Bellegarde
Genève
L. Léman
Martigny
Matterhorn 4477
Col du Gd St Bernard
Domodossola
L. Maggiore
Lugano
Lecco
Lövere
Bergamo
L.di Garda
Vicenza
Digoin
Lapalisse
SAVOIE
Annecy
Aix-l.-B.
Mt Blanc 4807
Aosta
Biella
Varese
Como
Bustp Arsizio
Monza
Brescia
Verona
Rovigo
Vichy
Roanne
Villefranche
Albertville
Gran Paradiso
Ivrea
Novara
Milano (Milan)
Lodi
Cremona
Mantova
Thiers
Tarare
Lyon
Villeurbanne
Chambéry
Vercelli
Pavia
Piacenza
Parma
Carpi
Ferrara
St-Chamond
Vienne
Voiron
Col du Mt Cenis 2803
Susa
Casale Monf.
Alessandria
Reggio n.-E.
Modena
Bologna
St-Étienne
Annonay
Bourg
Grenoble
Massif du Pelvoux
Briançon
Torino (Turin)
Asti
Novi Ligure
Ovada
Piacenza
Mt Cimone 2165
Lempdes
Le Puy
Romans-s.-I.
Valence
Col du Mt Cenis
Corps
Gap
Mte Viso 3841
Alba
Mondovi
Appno Ligure
Taro
Reggio
Genova (Genoa)
Massif Central
Mt Mézenc 1754
Aubenas
Montélimar
Nyons
Sisteron
Mt Pelat 3053
Cuneo
Savona
Rapallo
La Spezia
Carrara
Massa
Pistoia
Prato
Mende
Alès
Bagnols-s.-Cèze
Orange
Carpentras
Cavaillon
Digne
C.de Tende 1870
Mte Cinto 2710
La Spezia
Viareggio
Lucca
Firenze (Florence)
Mt Aigoual 1565
Avignon
Castellane
Draguignan
Grasse
Nice
Monte Carlo
MONACO
LIGURIAN
Pisa
Pontedera
Nîmes
Arles
Salon-d.-P.
PROVENCE
Cannes
St Raphaël
Côte d'Azur
Sea
Livorno
Cecina
Siena
Montpellier
Sète
Martigues
Aix-en-Provence
Aubagne
Marseille
St Tropez
Toulon
Hyères
Iles d'Hyères
Cap Corse
G. de St Florent
Bastia
Elba
Pianosa
Piombino
Portoferraio
Grosseto
Narbonne
Golfe du Lion
C. de Creus
Perpignan
CORSE (CORSICA)
Mt Cinto 2710
Ponte Lecca
Calvi
Ajaccio
C. Rosso
Corte
Montecristo
Giglio
Orbetello
Cateraggio
Follonica

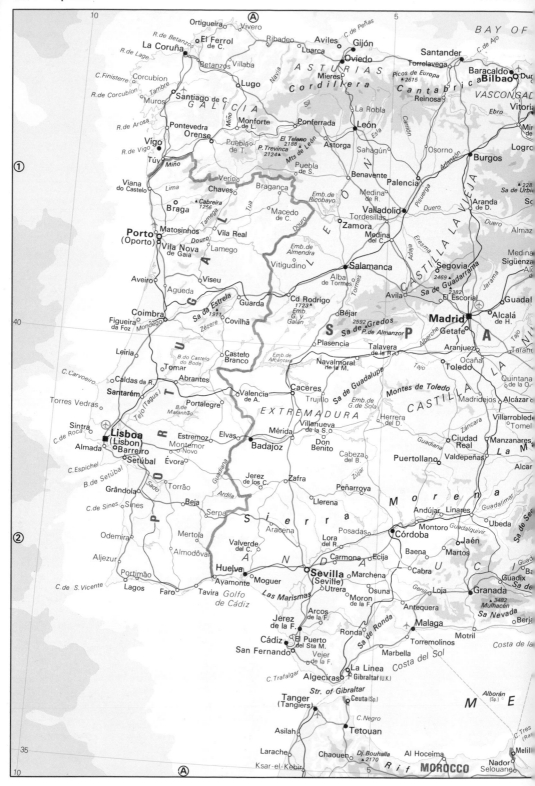

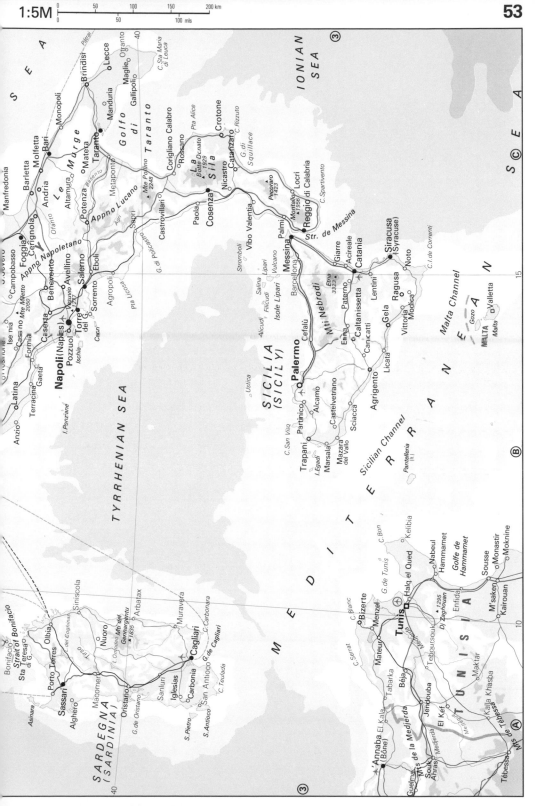

0
50
100
150
200 km

0
50
100 mls

S E A

Patras
Brindisi
Lecce
Monopoli
Otranto
Maglie
Gallipoli
C. Sta Maria di Leuca
I O N I A N   S E A
③
Manfredonia
Barletta
Molfetta
Bari
Andria
Le Murge
Matera
Manduria
Taranto
Golfo di Taranto
Campobasso
Foggia
Cerignola
Altamura
Potenza
Appno Lucano
Metaponto
Corigliano Calabro
Pta Alice
Crotone
C. Rizzuto
Isernia
Benevento
Avellino
Vesuvio 1277
Salerno
Eboli
Sorrento
Agropoli
Appno Napoletano
Basento
Ofanto
Agri
G. di Policastro
Sapri
Castrovillari
Rossano
La Sila
Monte Pollino 2248
Botte Donato 1929
Nicastro
Catanzaro
G. di Squillace
C. Rizzuto
Cassino
Mte Miletto 2050
Napoli (Naples)
Pozzuoli
Torre del G.
Ischia
Caserta
Cilento
Pta Licosa
Paola
Cosenza
Pecoraro 1423
Vibo Valentia
Montalto 1956
Locri
Reggio di Calabria
C. Spartivento
Palmi
Str. de Messina
Giarre
Acireale
Catania
Messina
Str. de Messina
C.I. de Correnti
Ise nía
Formia
Gaeta
I. Ponzane
Stromboli
Isole Lipari
Lipari
Salina
Filicudi
Alicudi
Vulcano
Barcellona
Mti Nebrodi
Etna 3323
Paternò
Lentini
Siracusa (Syracuse)
Noto
Latina
Anzio
Terracina
Ustica
Cefalù
Caltanissetta
Can catti
Enna
Gela
Vittoria
Modica
Ragusa
Catania
Malta Channel
Gozo
Valletta
MALTA
Malta
M E D I T E R R A N E A N
Palermo
S I C I L I A (S I C I L Y)
Partinico
Alcamo
Castelvetrano
Sciacca
Licata
Agrigento
Sicilian Channel
C. San Vito
Trapani
I. Egadi
Marsala
Mazara del Vallo
Pantelleria (It.)
T Y R R H E N I A N   S E A
Kelibia
Nabeul
Hammamet
Golfe de Hammamet
Sousse
Monastir
Moknine
C. Bon
G. de Tunis
Halq el Oued
Tunis
Bizerte
Menzel
Enfida
M'saken
Kairouan
C. Blanc
C. Serrat
Mateur
Medjerda
Téboursouk
Dj Zaghouan 1295
Maktar
Sardegna (Sardinia)
Bonifacio
Strait of Bonifacio
Sta Teresa di G.
Olbia
Siniscola
Porto Torres
Sassari
Alghero
Asinara
Nuoro
Mt del Gennargentu 1835
Arbatax
Muravera
C. Carbonara
Oristano
G. di Oristano
Sanluri
Iglesias
Carbonia
Cagliari
G. de Cagliari
S. Pietro
S. Antioco
C. Teulada
L. Omodeo
Tirso
Annaba (Bône)
El Kala
Guelma
Souk Ahras
Mts de la Medjerda
Medjerda
El Kef
Jendouba
Béja
Tabarka
Kalla Khasba
Tébessa
Mts Tébessa
Maktar
T U N I S I A
③
Ⓐ
Ⓑ
Ⓒ
40
15
10

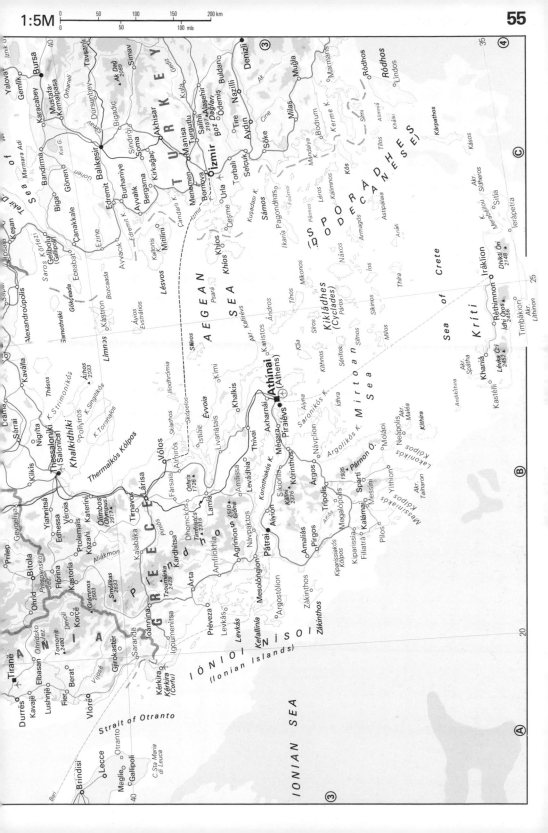

1:5M

0 50 100 150 200 km
0 50 100 mls

TURKEY

Iznik
Yalova
Bursa
Gemlik
Karacabey
Mustafa-Kemalpaşa
Ohhaneli
Dursunbey
Simav
Ak dağ 2089
Tavşanlı
Denizli ③

Sea of Marmara
Tekir Dağı
Bandirma
Gönen
Biga
Çanakkale
Balikeşir
Sindirği
Soma
Kirkağaç
Akhisar
Manisa
Turgutlu
Salihli
Alaşehir
Ödemiş
Buldan
Nazilli
Aydın

Kuş G.
Gediz
Kula
Boz Dağları 2157

Edremit
Burhaniye
Ayvalik
Bergama
Menemen
Bornova
İzmir
Urla
Çeşme
Torbali
Selçuk
Söke
Tire
Ak
Çine
Muğla

Saros Körfezi
Gelibolu (Gallipoli)
Eceabat
Ezine
Ayvacik
Mitilini
Kallonis
Çandarli K.
Edremit K.
İzmir K.
Kuşadasi K.
Mandalya

Alexandroúpolis
Keşan
İpsala
Gökçeada
Bozcaada
Lésvos
Psará
Khíos
Khíos
Sámos
Ikaría
Pagondhas
Foúrnoi
Léros
Kálimnos
Kós
Bodrum
Kerme K.
Sími
Alimniá
Khálki

RODHOS
Ródhos
Líndos
Kárpathos
Kásos

Drama
Kavála
Thásos
Serrai
Nigríta
Kilkís
Thessaloníki (Salonica)
Khalkidhikí
Políyiros

SPORÁDHES
DODEKÁNISOS

Ayios Evstrátios
Límnos
Áyios
Kástron
Samothráki
Skíros
Skópelos
Skíathos
Évvoia

Astipálaia
Anáfi
Amorgós
Náxos
Íos
Páros
Síros
Tínos
Ándros
Míkonos
Dhílos
Sérifos
Kíthnos
Sífnos
Mílos
Sikinos
Thíra
Folégandhros

AEGEAN SEA

Sea of Crete

Kríti
Iráklion
Réthimnon
Dhíkti Óri 2148
Ídhi Óros 2456
Khaniá
Lévka Óri 2452
Akr. Sídheros
Sitía
Ierápetra
Timbákion
Akr. Líthinon
Kastélli
Akr. Spátha
Megháliou

SPORÁDHES (Sporades)
KIKLÁDHES (Cyclades)

K. Strimonikós
Strimón
K. Toronéos
K. Singitikós
Áthos 2033

Kateríni
Thermaïkós Kólpos
Vólos
Othris 1726
Skíathos
Istiáîa
Límni
Khalkis
Kími
Livanátais
Iliodhrómia

Flórina
Kastoría
Kozáni
Yiánnitsá
Véroia
Ptolemaïs
Kalabáka
Tírnavos
Lárisa
Farsala
Dhomokós
Lamía
Almirós
Thívai
Amfissa
Levádhia
Timfristós 2315
Timfrestós 2510

Kilkís
Nigríta
Bitola
Prespansko Jez.
Grámmos 2503
Smólikas 2633
Olimbos Olympus 2917
Smríikas

Edhessa
Tzoúmerka 2429
Píndos
Kardhítsa
Agrínion
Návpaktos
Aíyion
Pátrai
Kórinthos
Sikióna
Korinthiakós K.
Mégara
Axarnaí
Akharnaí
Athínai (Athens)
Piraiévs

 Athens
Saronikós K.
Aíyina
Ídhra
Ándros
Kaíistos
Akr. Kafirévs
Akr.

Kérkira Kérkira (Corfu)
Préveza
Ioánnina
Árta
Amfilokhía
Mesolóngion
Agrínion
Návpaktos

Ohrid
Ohridsko Jez.
Tomorrit 2480
Grirokastër
Berat
Sarandë
Igoumenitsa
Parga

Devoll
Pínios
Akhélöos
Trikkala
Dhomokós

GREECE
GREECE

Kílini
Pírgos
Olimpía
Megalópolis
Amaliás
Trípolis
Argos
Návplion
Sparti 1925
Kalamai
Messíni
Kíparissía
Filiatrá
Pílos
Yíthion
Akr. Maléa
Neápolis
Molái
Parnon Ó. 1935
Ménalon 2376
Zákinthos
Zákinthos
Kiparissiakós Kólpos

Argolikós K.
Lakonikós Kólpos
Messiniakós Kólpos
Akr. Taínaron
Kíthira
Mirtoan Sea
Antikíthira

Préveza
Levkás
Levkás
Kefallinía
Zákinthos
Argostólion

IÓNIOI
NÍSOI
(Ionian Islands)

Tiranë
Durrës
Kavajë
Elbasan
Lushnjë
Fier
Vlorë
Berat
Vijosë

IONIAN SEA

Strait of Otranto

Brindisi
Lecce
Meglie
Gallipoli
Otranto
C. Sta Maria di Leuca
Bari

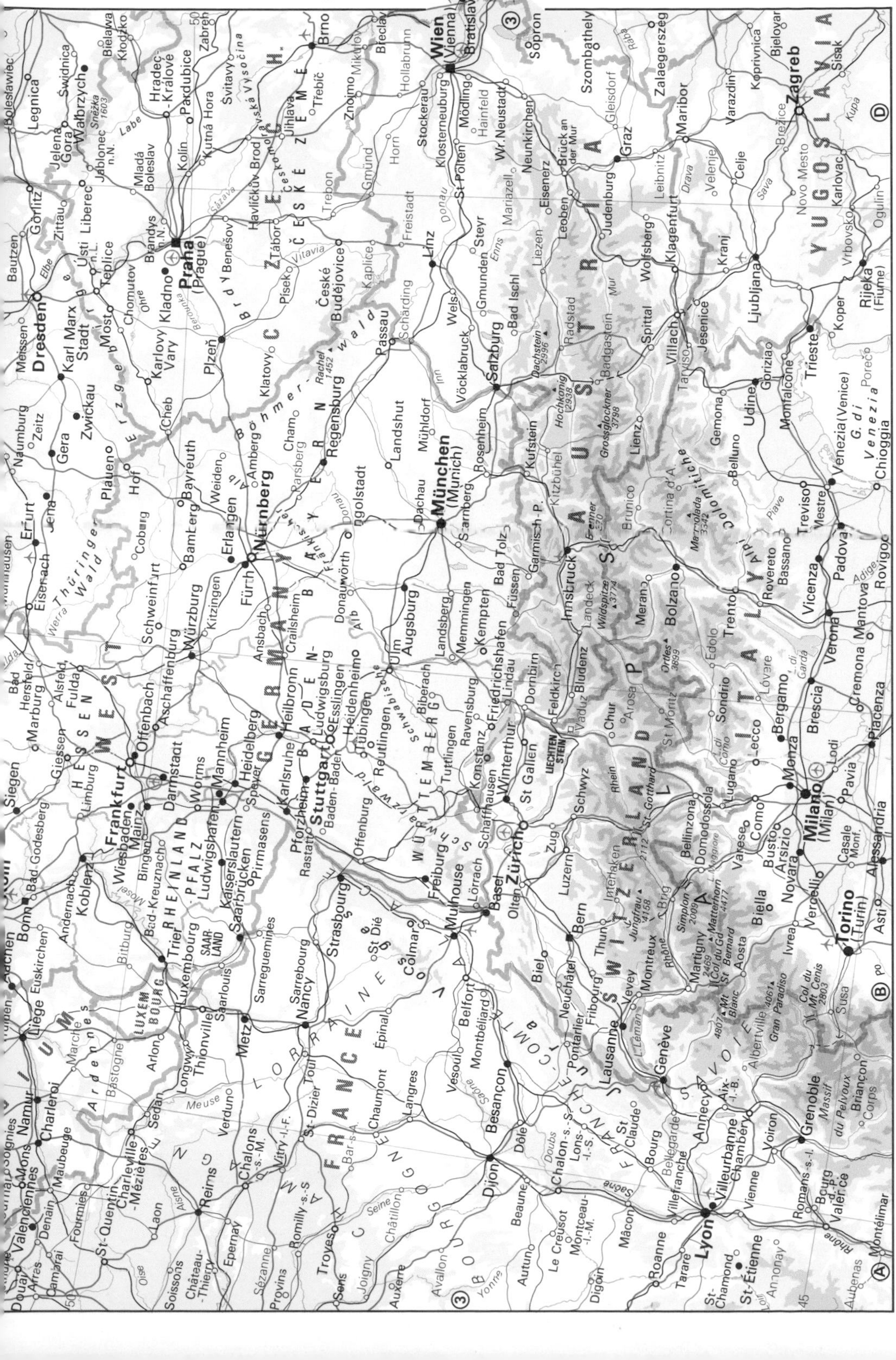

0 50 100 150 200 km
0 50 100 mls

G E R M A N Y

Č E S K É Z E M Ě

A U S T R I A

S W I T Z E R L A N D

I T A L Y

Y U G O S L A V I A

F R A N C E

Dresden · Praha (Prague) · Brno · Wien (Vienna) · Bratislava · Sopron · Szombathely · Zalaegerszeg · Zagreb

München (Munich) · Salzburg · Linz · Graz · Maribor · Ljubljana · Trieste · Rijeka (Fiume)

Nürnberg · Regensburg · Passau · Innsbruck · Bolzano · Trento · Verona · Venezia (Venice) · Padova · Vicenza

Frankfurt · Mainz · Wiesbaden · Mannheim · Heidelberg · Karlsruhe · Stuttgart · Ulm · Augsburg

Strasbourg · Freiburg · Basel · Zürich · Bern · Luzern · St Gallen · Bregenz

Milano (Milan) · Como · Lecco · Bergamo · Brescia · Cremona · Piacenza · Pavia · Torino (Turin) · Novara · Alessandria

Mulhouse · Belfort · Besançon · Dijon · Lausanne · Genève · Lyon · Grenoble · Chambéry · Annecy

Reims · Nancy · Metz · Luxembourg · Trier · Koblenz · Bonn · Liège · Namur · Charleroi

Erfurt · Jena · Gera · Zwickau · Plauen · Hof · Bayreuth · Würzburg · Fürth

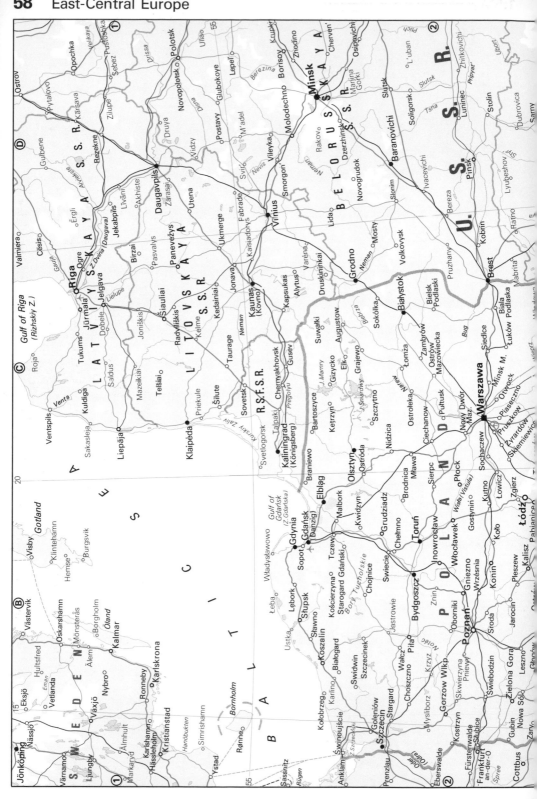

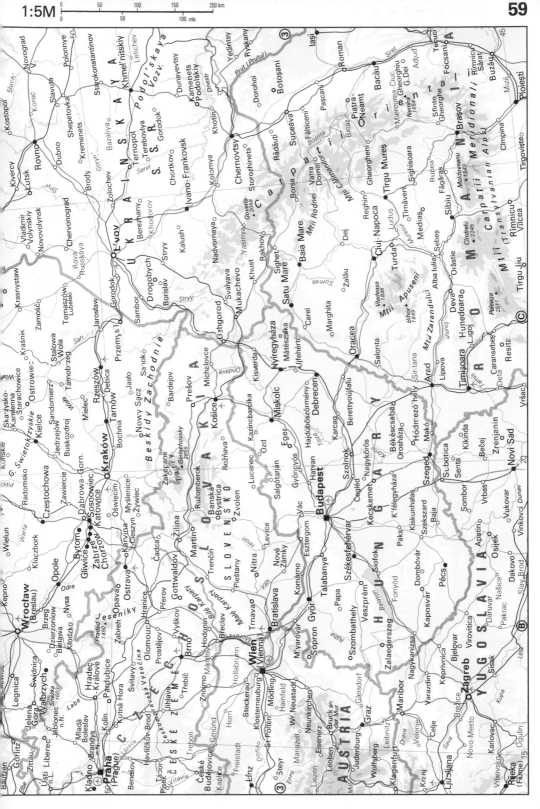

1:5M

0   50   100   150   200 km
0   50   100 mls

③

Kostopol
Novograd
Polonnye
Starokonstantinov
Khmel'nitskiy
Letichev
Vedintsy
Iaşi
Rimnicu
Sărat
Buzău
Ploieşti

Korec
Slavuta
Shepetovka
Polonnye
Dunayevtsy
Kamenets
Podol'skiy
Dorohoi
Botoşani
Roman
Bacău
G.Dej
Focşani
Mizil

Rovno
Dubno
Kremenets
Ternopol
Bazaliya
Gorodok
Khotin
Suceava
Fălticeni
Piatra-Neamţ
Sfîntu Gheorghe
Braşov
Cîmpina
Tîrgovişte

Lutsk
Kiverci
Brody
Zolochev
Seret
Chortkovo
Rădăuţi
Vatra Dornei
Bistriţa
Gheorgheni
Mercurea Ciuc
Rupea
Făgăraş

Vladimir
Volynskiy
Novovolynsk
Chervonograd
Ivano-Frankovsk
Kolomyya
Chernovtsy
Storozhinets
Borsa
Mţii Rodnei
Reghin
Tîrgu Mureş
Sighişoara
Mediaş
Sibiu
Orăştie
Tîrgu Jiu
Rîmnicu Vîlcea

Krasnystaw
Lvov
Stryy
Kalush
Nadvornaya
Yasinya
Rakhov
Sighet
Baia Mare
Dej
Cluj-Napoca
Turda
Alba Iulia
Sebes
Deva
Hunedoara

Tomaszów
Lubelski
Sambor
Drogobych
Borislav
Svalyava
Mukachevo
Khust
Satu Mare
Carei
Zalău
Ludus
Tîrnăveni

Zamość
Jaroslaw
Przemyśl
Sanok
Uzhgorod
Marghita
Oradea
Salonta

Krasnik
Rzeszów
Jaslo
Bardejov
Prešov
Michalovce
Kisvárda
Nyíregyháza
Mátészalka
Újfehértó
Berettyóújfalu
Lipova
Arad
Timişoara
Caransebeş
Reşiţa
Deta
Vršac

Stalowa Wola
Tarnobrzeg
Debica
Tarnów
Nowy Sącz
Zakopane
Ružomberok
Banská Bystrica
Rožňava
Košice
Kazincbarcika
Miskolc
Ózd
Eger
Gyöngyös
Hatvan
Debrecen
Hajdúböszörmény
Karcag
Nagykőrös
Békéscsaba
Orosháza
Hódmező'hely
Makó
Kikinda
Bečej
Zrenjanin
Novi Sad

Mielec
Bochnia
Martino
Zvolen
Lučenec
Salgótarján
Szolnok
Cegléd
Kecskemét
Szeged
Subotica
Senta
Vrbas

Oświęcim
Wadowice
Żilina
Čadca
Trenčín
Nitra
Nové Zámky
Levice
Vác
Budapest
Szolnok
Kiskunfélegyháza
Szekszárd
Baja
Sombor
Vrbas

Praha (Prague)
Kladno
Beroun
Benešov
Tábor
Písek
České Budějovice
Kaplice
Linz
Steyr
③
Mariazell
St Pölten
Stockerau
Klosterneuburg
Mödling
Wien (Vienna)
Bruck an der Mur
Leoben
Graz
Maribor
Zagreb
Rijeka (Fiume)
Ljubljana

Wrocław (Breslau)
Opole
Gliwice
Bytom
Zabrze
Chorzów
Sosnowiec
Katowice
Kraków
Ostrava
Karviná
Žilina
Čadca
Gottwaldov
Bílé Karpaty

Legnica
Jelenia Gora
Wałbrzych
Świdnica
Kłodzko
Bielawa
Dzierżoniów
Nysa
Jeseníky
Praděd 1490
Opava
Hranice
Přerov
Olomouc
Prostějov
Vyškov
Brno
Hodonín
Znojmo

Görlitz
Zittau
Ústí n.L.
Liberec
Jablonec n.N.
Mladá Boleslav
Hradec Králové
Pardubice
Kolín
Kutná Hora
Havlíčkův Brod
Jihlava
Třebíč
Znojmo
Horn

Kępno
Ostrów
Kluczbork
Częstochowa
Radomsko
Zawiercie
Dąbrowa-Górn.
Myślenice
Żywiec

Wieluń
Warta
Piotrków

UKRAINSKAYA S.S.R.

Podol'skaya Vozv.

Carpaţii Orientali

Carpaţii Meridionali (Transylvanian Alps)

Mţii Căliman

Mţii Apuseni
Bihor
Mţii Zarandului

Beskidy Zachodnie

SLOVENSKO
SLOVAKIA

ČESKÉ ZEMĚ
ČSR

HUNGARY

ROMANIA

YUGOSLAVIA

AUSTRIA

C

B

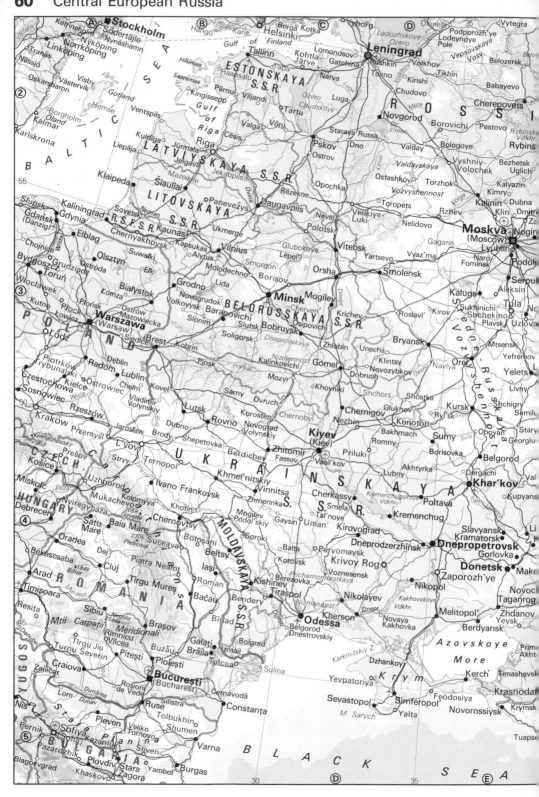

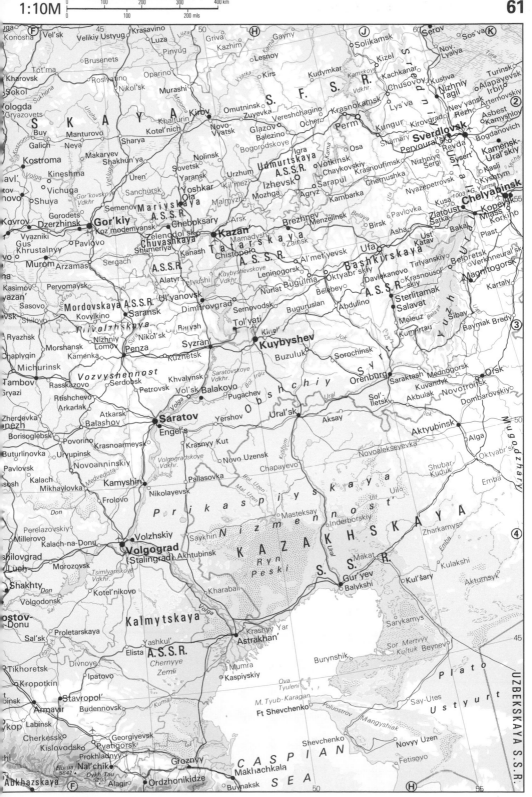

0 300 600 900 1200 1800mls
0 600 1200 1800

UNION OF SOVIET SOCIALIST REPUBLICS

ARCTIC OCEAN

INTERNATIONAL DATELINE

Bering Sea

Arctic Circle

Novosibirskiye Ostrova

Severnaya Zemlya

Zemlya Frantsa Iosifa

Svalbard (Nor.)

Novaya Zemlya

Barents Sea

Sea of Okhotsk

Sakhalin

Kuril'skiye Ostrova

Petropavlovsk-Kamchatskiy

Magadan

Norilsk

Yenisey

Ob'

Lena

Yakutsk

Vorkuta

Sergino

Krasnoyarsk

Novosibirsk

Barnaul

Irkutsk

Omsk

Karaganda

Aral Sea

Alma Ata

Tashkent

Sverdlovsk

Chelyabinsk

Ufa

Kuybyshev

Kazan'

Gor'kiy

Leningrad

Moskva

Saratov

Volgograd

Astrakhan'

Caspian Sea

Baku

Tbilisi

Yerevan

Rostov

Donetsk

Khar'kov

Dnepropetrovsk

Kiyev

Odessa

Minsk

Black Sea

Murmansk

Arkhangel'sk

Helsinki

Stockholm

Oslo

Riga

København

Warszawa

NORWAY

SWEDEN

FINLAND

DENMARK

UNITED KINGDOM

Edinburgh

Dublin

IRELAND

London

Paris

Færøerne (Den.)

NETH.

BEL.

LUX.

W. GERMANY

POLAND

CZECHOSLOVAKIA

AUSTRIA

HUNGARY

ROMANIA

București

YUGOSLAVIA

BULGARIA

Istanbul

Ankara

Adana

TURKEY

CYPRUS

SYRIA

Damascus

Halab

Beirut

LEB.

JOR.

Jerusalem

Amman

IRAQ

Baghdad

Basra

Mosul

KUWAIT

SAUDI ARABIA

The G

IRAN

Tehrān

Esfahān

Tabrīz

Mashhad

Ashkhabad

Herāt

AFGHANISTAN

Kābul

Kandahar

Islamabad

SINKING

MONGOLIA

Ulaanbaatar

Ürümci

INNER MONGOLIA

CHINA

Beijing

Tianjin

Taiyuan

Lanzhou

Xi'an

Zhengzhou

Huang He

Nanjing

Shanghai

Qingdao

Shenyang

Dalian

Yellow Sea

N. KOREA

Pyongyang

Sŏul

S. KOREA

Pusan

Kita-Kyūshū

Chŏngjin

Hābin

Changchun

Qiqihar

Vladivostok

Khabarovsk

Komsomol'sk

Sea of Japan

JAPAN

Hokkaidō

Sapporo

Tōkyō

Yokohama

Ōsaka

Honshū

Shikoku

Kyūshū

200 400 600 800 km
200 400 mils

ROSSIYSKAYA S.F.S.R.

SREDNESIBIRSKAYA PLOSKOGORYE

SAKHALIN

SIKHOTE Alin'

Khrebet Stanovoy

Aldanskoye Nagorye

SEA OF JAPAN

YELLOW SEA

KOREA

NORTH KOREA

Pyongyang

SOUTH KOREA

Taegu

Pusan

Beijing

Tianjin

Harbin

Changchun

Shenyang

Vladivostok

Khabarovsk

Komsomol'sk

Nikolayevsk

Ulaanbaatar

M O N G O L I A

Bayan Obo

Baotou

Datong

Hohhot

Erenhot

Chita

Ulan-Ude

Irkutsk

Angarsk

Bratsk

Krasnoyarsk

Kansk

Achinsk

Tomsk

Kemerovo

Novokuznetsk

Biysk

Abakan

Minusinsk

Kyzyl

Tuvinskaya A.S.S.R.

Buryatskaya A.S.S.R.

Baykal

Ürümqi

Turpan

Hami

Qitai

DZUNGARIA

ALTAY

Lena

Vilyuy

Olekma

Yenisey

1:20M

	R.S.F.S.R.
1	Chuvashskaya A.S.S.R.
2	Checheno-Ingushskaya A.S.S.R.
3	Severo-Osetinskaya A.S.S.R.
4	Kabardino-Balkarskaya A.S.S.R.
	GRUZINSKAYA S.S.R.
5	Abkhazskaya A.S.S.R.
6	Adzharskaya A.S.S.R.
	AZERBAYDZHANSKAYA S.S.R.
7	Nakhichevanskaya A.S.S.R.

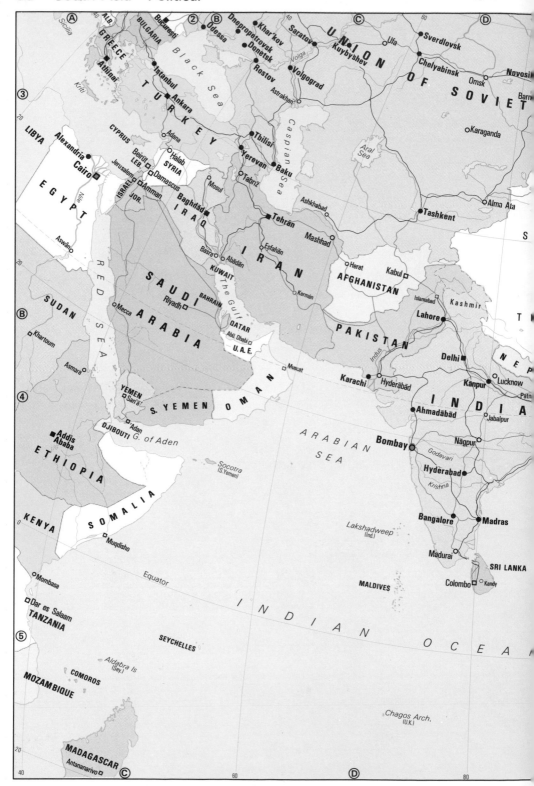

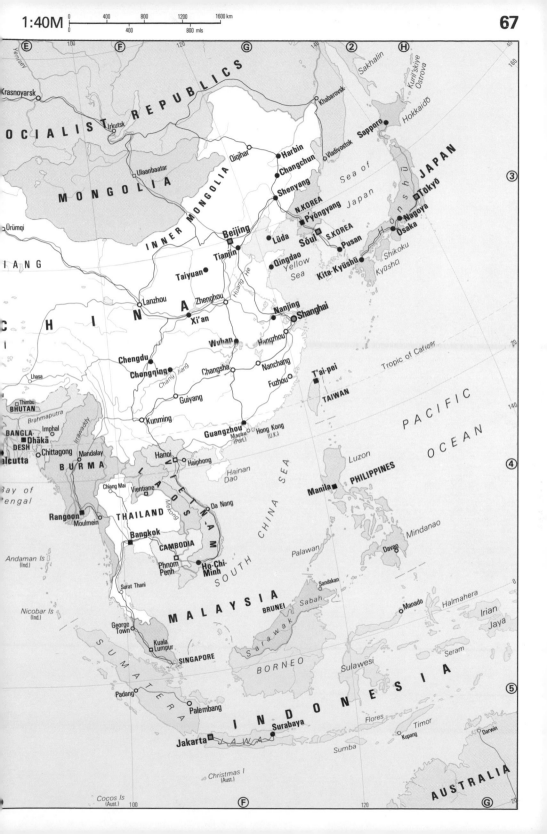

E F 120 G 140 ② H 160

Krasnoyarsk

Yenisey

Sakhalin

Kuril'skiye Ostrova

OCIALIST REPUBLICS

Irkutsk

Khabarovsk

Hokkaido

MONGOLIA

Ulaanbaatar

Qiqihar

Harbin

Changchun

Vladivostok

Sapporo

③

JAPAN

Ürümqi

INNER MONGOLIA

Shenyang

N.KOREA

Pyŏngyang

Sea of

Japan

Honshū

Tōkyō

Nagoya

Osaka

IANG

Beijing

Tianjin

Sŏul

S.KOREA

Pusan

Shikoku

CHINA

Lüda

Qingdao

Kita-Kyūshū

Kyūshū

Taiyuan

Lanzhou

Zhenghou

Huang He

Yellow
Sea

Xi'an

Nanjing

Shanghai

Lhasa

Wuhan

Hangzhou

Chengdu

Chang Jiang

Changsha

Nanchang

Chongqing

Fuzhou

Tropic of Cancer

20

Thimbu

BHUTAN

Brahmaputra

Guiyang

T'ai-pei

TAIWAN

PACIFIC

Imphal

Kunming

BANGLA-
DESH

Dhāka

OCEAN

140

alcutta

Chittagong

Mandalay

Guangzhou

Macau
(Port.)

Hong Kong
(U.K.)

Luzon

④

0

BURMA

Irrawaddy

Hanoi

Haiphong

Hainan
Dao

Manila

PHILIPPINES

Bay of
engal

Chiang Mai

Vientiane

LAOS

Da Nang

SOUTH

Mindanao

Rangoon

Moulmein

THAILAND

V
I
E
T
N
A
M

Mekong

CHINA

Davao

Andaman Is
(Ind.)

Bangkok

CAMBODIA

SEA

Palawan

Surat Thani

Phnom
Penh

Ho-Chi-
Minh

Sandakan

Nicobar Is
(Ind.)

MALAYSIA

BRUNEI

Sabah

Manado

Halmahera

George
Town

Kuala
Lumpur

Sarawak

Irian

Jaya

SUMATERA

SINGAPORE

BORNEO

Sulawesi

Seram

Padang

⑤

Palembang

INDONESIA

Flores

Timor

Darwin

Jakarta

JAWA

Surabaya

Kupang

Sumba

Christmas I
(Aust.)

Cocos Is
(Aust.)

AUSTRALIA

100 F 120 G 20

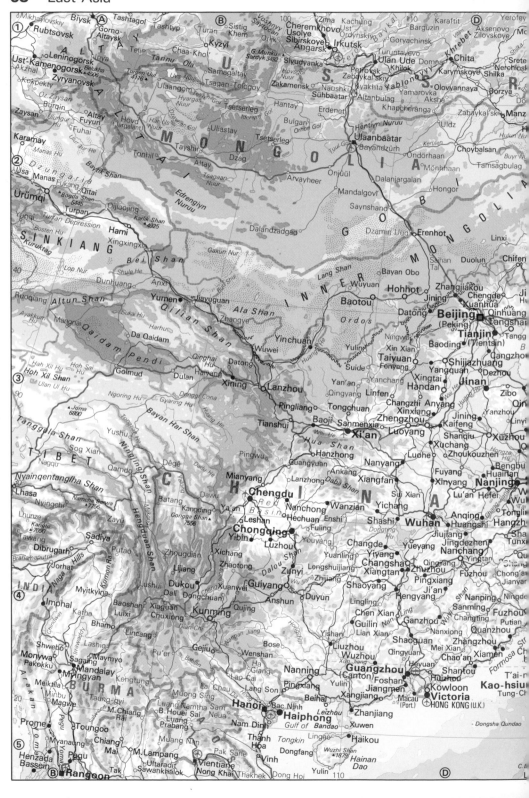

200 400 600 800 km
200 400 mls

SEA OF OKHOTSK

Skovorodino Zeya Tugur Moskal'vo Okha Opala
zhalinda Ovsyanka Ushumun Ekimchan Nikolayevsk-na-Amure Mys Lopatka
Tygda Poliny Bogorodskoye 150
Guqiqu Shimanovsk Ust-Umal'ta Osipenko De Kastri Katangli Paramushir 50
mangui Huma Norsk Oz. Chukchagirskoye Aleksandrovsk-Sakhalinskiy
Xinqu Kumara Svobodnyy Oz. Evoron Amgun Tymovskoye Onekotan
gun Zuoqi Belogorsk Chekunda Amgur SAKHALIN Shiashkotan
Blagoveshchensk Komsomol'sk Pobedino
Anhui Zavitinsk Bolon' na-Amure Poronaysk Rasshua
Nenjiang Bureya Litovko Oz. Bolon Vanino Zaliv
Obluch'ye Khabarovsk Sovetskaya Terpeniya Simushir
Butha Qi Bei'an Ling Birobidzhan Khor Gavan l'inskiy
Qiqihar Yichuno Hegang Vyazemskiy Gornozavodsk Yuzhno- Urup
Hailun Fujin Bikin Svetlaya Sakhalinsk Vityaz Depth
Anda Suihua Jiamusi Hulin Lesozavodsk Amgu Korsakov 10542
HARBIN Shuangyashan Dal'nerechensk Mys Aniva
hangchun Wuchang Jixi La Perouse Strait Wakkanai Iturup
liao Mudanjiang Oz. Khanka Spassk Turiy Rog Kunashir
Shuangliao Jilin Dal'niy Plastun Abashiri
Siping Liaoyuan Ussuriysk Rudnaya Rumoi Asahi Dake Nemuro
Yang Yanji Zaliv Pristan' Asahikawa 2290 Kushiro
Tieling Fushun Linjiang Nakhodka Olga Otaru HOKKAIDO
Yang Benxi Tonghua Hyesan Najin Sapporo Muroran Erimo-misaki
Anshan Dandong Huigh'on Songjin Ch'ongjin Hakodate Uchiura-wan
Manpo Samsu Soho-ri Aomori
Sinuiju Hamhung Hungnam NORTH Hirosaki Hachinohe
Korea Bay Anju KOREA Noshiro Morioka
Luda Wonsan Akita
shun P'yongyang SEA OF Sakata Ishinomaki
Haeju Ch'unch'on Yamagata Sendai
antai Kaesong Kangnung JAPAN Sado Niigata Fukushima
Chengshan Inch'on Ullung do Nagaoka
Jiao SOUL Tok-do Takaoka Utsunomiya
Chonan (Seoul) Kanazawa Mito
YELLOW Chongju SOUTH Oki Fukui Gifu Tokyo
Taejon KOREA Tottori Kyoto Yokohama
ang SEA Kunsan Chonji Matsue Nagoya Fuji-san
Chonju Taegu Osaka Shizuoka
Kwangju Masan Sakai Toyohashi
Mokp'o Pusan Kobe Wakayama Miyake
Korea Hiroshima Miyako
Cheju haehyop Shimonoseki Matsuyama Kochi Kir-suido Hachijo
Fukuoka Kita- Kyushu Shikoku
Cheju Sasebo Kumamoto Bungo-suido Myojin
Cheju do Nagasaki Miyazaki Sumisu
Shanghai Kyushu Tori
ngan Yang Kagoshima Osumi-kaikyo Sofu Gan
EAST Tanega
Ningbo Yaku
Tokara
CHINA SEA Retto Muko-jima Kazano Deep
nzhou Amami Chichi-jima 10374
Amami gunto Ogasawara Gunto
Tokuno Nishino-shima Haha-jima (Bonin Islands)
Okinawa (Jap.)
Chi-lung Okinawa Kitalo
T'ai-pei Sakishima gunto Naha gunto Iwo Jima Kazan Retto Fleming Deep
peh Shan Miyako (Volcano Is.) 8651
3884 Iriomote Ishigaki Daito Is (Jap.)
Hua-lien Tropic of Cancer
ai-tung (China Nat. Rep.) RYUKYU
-tung PACIFIC Farallon de Pajaros
Batan Is Maug Is 20
on Strait Asuncion
Babuyan Is Agrihan
130 Parece Vela 140 Pagan Alamagan
C. Engano OCEAN Guguan
Aparri Northern Sarigan
Marianas Anatahan

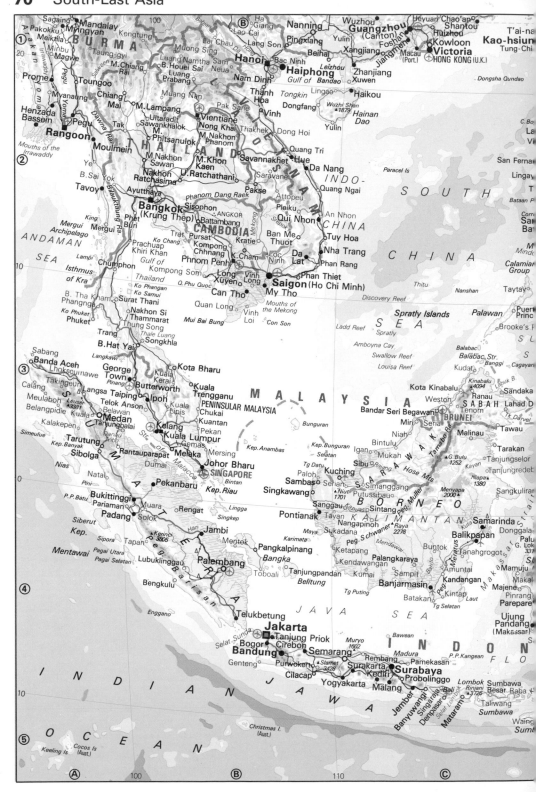

1:20M

200 400 600 800 km
200 400 mils

TAIWAN (FORMOSA) D
ai-tung (China Nat. Rep.)
-tung

P A C I F I C

130

E

140

F

C

20

Batan Is

on Strait

Babuyan Is

C. Engaño

Aparri

Tuguegarao

Ilagan

LUZON

Baler

abanatuan

uezon City
Polillo Is

Manila

PHILIPPINES

Daet Catanduanes

Naga

Boac Legazpi

Bulan

Catarman

Masbate Masbate

Samar

Catbalogan

Oras

Roxas Guiuan

Iloilo Tacloban Leyte 10497

Bacolod Dinaget 10265

egros Bohol Siargao

Siaton Bohol Sea Surigao

Manukan Butuan

Ozamiz Cagayan de Oro

amboanga Marawi Malanbang

ela L.Lanao Cotabato

silan Digos Davao

Jolo General Tinaca Pt
u Arch Santos

E B E S

Talaud Karakelong

Tahuna Sangine

Kepulauan
Sangihe

Manado

Buol Kuandang Molucca Sea

Gorontalo Belang

Kep.Togian

Luwuk Peleng Taliabu Mangole

Teluk
Tolo Kep. Banggai Obi

Danau
Towuti

Kendari Wowoni

Kolaka Butung

npone Muna

Baubau Kep.
Tukangbesi

S I A

Lomblen Alor

res

Ende

P A C I F I C

O C E A N

Farallon de Pajaros
Maug Is

Asuncion

Agrihan

Pagan

Northern Alamagan

Marianas Guguan

Sarigan

Anatahan Farallon
de Medinilla

Saipan 2

Tinian

Rota

Guam
(U.S.A.) Nero Deep
9637

10

Challenger Deep
11033

Mansyu Deep
9818

Ulithi Fais Gaferut

Yap Faraulep

Ngulu Sorol Lamotrek

Fais TERR. of the PACIFIC ISLANDS (USA)

Palau Woleai Ifalik
Islands Koror

Rep. of Belau Eauripik 3

C A R O L I N E I S L A N D S

Fed. States of
Micronesia

Sonsorol

Pulo Anna

Merir

Tobi

Helen Reef

Mapia Equator 0

Ninigo Group

Wuvulu

Waigeo Supiori

Selat Dampier Kwoka Biak Tg d'Urville

Morotai Manokwari Numfoor Sarmi

Tobelo Sorong Cendrawasih Yapen Jayapura Aitape Schouten Is

Ternate Halmahera Peg. Arfak
2939 Teluk
Cendrawasih

PAPUA Karkar

MOLUCCAS Misool Mamberamo Wewak 4
Sepik Long I.

Bacan IRIAN Dom NEW GUINEA Madang

Waigeo 1340 Angemuk Central Ramu Einschhafen

CERAM SEA Teluk Berau 3741 Mt. Kubor Goroka

Kep. Piru 3019 Bula Fakfak JAYA Pk Jaya Hagen 4359 Lae

Sula Namlea Kaimana 5029 Pk Mandala Mendi Bulolo

Seram Pegunungan Maoke 4702 Morobe

Buru Ambon Adi Kokonau Tanahmerah GUINEA Salamaua
3993

Kep. Banda PAPUA Albert Edward Kokoda
4073

BANDA Wokam Kikori Mt Victoria Port
Kep. Kobroor Kerema 4073 Moresby

SEA Kep.Kai Dobo Aru Digul Kapuri

Trangan Kai L. Murray

Nila Gulf of
Damar Teun Papua Daru

Wetar Romang Yamdena P. Kolepom

Selat Wetar Kep.Leti Babar Kepulauan Merauke Saibai

Dili Sermata Saumlaki Tanimbar Tg Vals Komoran

Atambua A R A F U R A S E A Mulgrave I. Banks I.
TIMOR Torres Strait Great

Kupang Thursday I. C. York Barrier Rf

Roti Pr.of Wales I. Somerset

CORAL

5

Savu Sea C. V. Diemen Wessel Is

Melville I. Dundas Str. C.Arnhem

Bathurst I. Croker I. Nhulunbuy Iron
Clarence Str Coburg Pen. Gove Range

Darwin A U S T R A L I A Albatross B. Weipa SEA

TIMOR D SEA Arnhem Land E Pen. 140 F

Philippine Sea (N E S E A)

Moro Gulf

Ceram Sea

Timor Sea

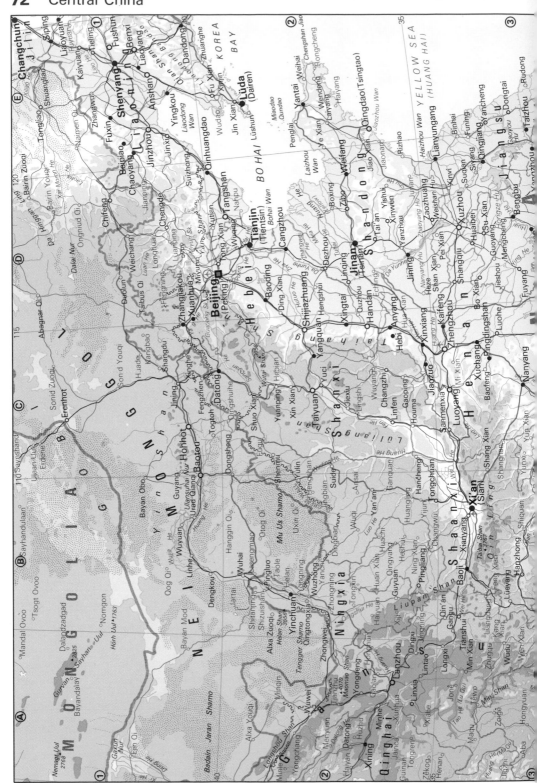

1:10M

0 100 200 300 400 km
0 100 200 mls

S O U T H   C H I N A   S E A

GULF OF TONGKIN

Shanghai Songjiang Suzhou Wuxi Jiaxing Zhoushan Qundao
Hangzhou Shaoxing Ningbo Linhai Huangyan Wenling Wenzhou
Z h e j i a n g
Wuhu Tongling Xuancheng Jiande Lishui Qingyuan
Wuhan Huangshi Anqing Jingdezhen Nanchang Fuzhou
H u b e i Jiujiang Poyang Hu Yingtan Shaocheng
Shashi Xianning Nanning F u j i a n Sanming
Changsha Yiyang Zhuzhou J i a n g x i Nanping Fuzhou (Foochow)
H u n a n Xiangtan Hengyang Ji'an Ganzhou Quanzhou Xiamen (Amoy)
Shaoyang Lengshuijiang Chaling Ruijin Shantou (Swatow)
Yongzhou Chen Xian G u a n g d o n g
Guilin Shaoguan **Guangzhou** (Canton) HONG KONG (U.K.)
G u a n g x i Wuzhou Foshan Shenzhen **Victoria** Kowloon
Liuzhou **Nanning** Zhanjiang Macau
G u i z h o u Hechi Beihai Haikou
Guiyang Du Xian Dongguan Maoming
Chongqing (Chungking) Zunyi Anshun Xingyi
S i c h u a n Y u n n a n
Chengdu Neijiang Zigong Yibin Luzhou **Kunming**
Leshan Yuxi

Hanoi **Haiphong**
V I E T N A M
L A O S
Red River Delta

Tai-pei T'ai-chung Kao-hsiung
T A I W A N (FORMOSA)
Peng-hu Lieh-tao (Pescadores)

D a x u e   S h a n
Daxue Shan Qionglai Shan

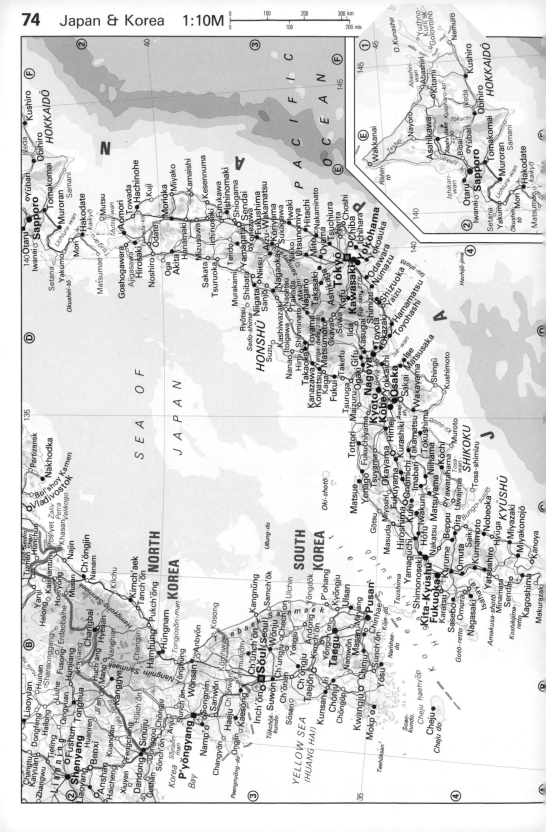

0 100 200 300 km
0 100 200 mls

PACIFIC OCEAN

SEA OF JAPAN

HOKKAIDŌ

HONSHŪ

TOKYO
Yokohama
Kawasaki
Nagoya
Osaka
Kyoto
Kobe

SHIKOKU

KYŪSHŪ

NORTH KOREA

SOUTH KOREA

Sŏul (Seoul)

Pusan

Taegu

P'yŏngyang

YELLOW SEA
(HUANG HAI)

Cheju do

Sapporo
Otaru
Muroran
Hakodate
Kushiro
Obihiro

Vladivostok

1:5M

| 0 | 50 | 100 | 150 | 200 km |
| 0 | 50 | | 100 mls | |

J A P A N

P A C I F I C   O C E A N

S E A   O F   J A P A N

Sendai · Higashine · Shiogama · Ishinomaki · Onagawa
Obanazawa · Murayama · Ayato · Natori · Kaminoyama
Tendo · Nagai · Yonezawa · Kamimachi
Yamagata · Aizu · **Fukushima** · Nihonmatsu
Iwaki · Hitachi · Hitachi-Ota · Katsuta
Shibata · Wakamatsu · **Kōriyama** · Naka · Ishioka · Tsuchiura
Niitsu · Nagaoka · Tokamachi · Shirakawa · Kuroiso · Yaita · Mito
Murakami · Niigata · Ojiya · Naoetsu · Nakanojō · Utsunomiya
Ryōtsu · Kashiwazaki · Takada · Nakano · Maebashi · Takasaki · Chichibu · Enzan · Kawagoe
Sado-shima · Aikawa · Mano-wan · Itoigawa · Arai · Nagano · Okaya · Suwa · Kōfu · **Tokyo** · **Chiba**
Nanao · Toyama · Matsumoto · Takayama · Ida · Iida · Shizuoka · **Yokohama** · **Kawasaki**
Wajima · Himi · Takaoka · Omachi · Nakatsugawa · Gifu · Nagoya · Hamamatsu · Numazu · Odawara
Noto-hantō · Kanazawa · Kaga · Ono · Katsuyama · Seto · **Nagoya** · Okazaki · Toyohashi · Shimoda · Itō
Komatsu · Fukui · Takefu · Tsuruga · Ogaki · Hikone · Kuwana · Suzuka · Tsu · Ise
Maizuru · Ōtsu · **Kyōto** · Nara · Yokkaichi · Matsusaka · Kumano · Shingū
Tottori · Fukuchiyama · Ashiya · **Ōsaka** · **Kōbe** · **Sakai** · Wakayama · Kainan · Tanabe · Kushimoto
Kurayoshi · Yonago · Himeji · Akashi · Kakogawa · Naruto · Tokushima · Anan · Aki
Okayama · Kurashiki · Tamano · Takamatsu · Sakaide · Marugame · **Kōchi** · Tosa · Nakamura
Hiroshima · Onomichi · Fukuyama · Imabari · **Matsuyama** · Susaki
Hamada · Masuda · Kure · Iwakuni · Hōjō · Uwajima
Hagi · Yamaguchi · Ube · **Shimonoseki** · Ōita · Beppu · Usuki
Kita-Kyūshū · **Fukuoka** · Tosu · Kurume · Ōmuta · Saiki · Nobeoka

KYŪSHŪ · **SHIKOKU**

Oki-shotō · Dōgo · Saigō

Suruga-wan · Sagami-wan · Ise-wan · Tosa-wan · Kii-suidō · Bungo-suidō

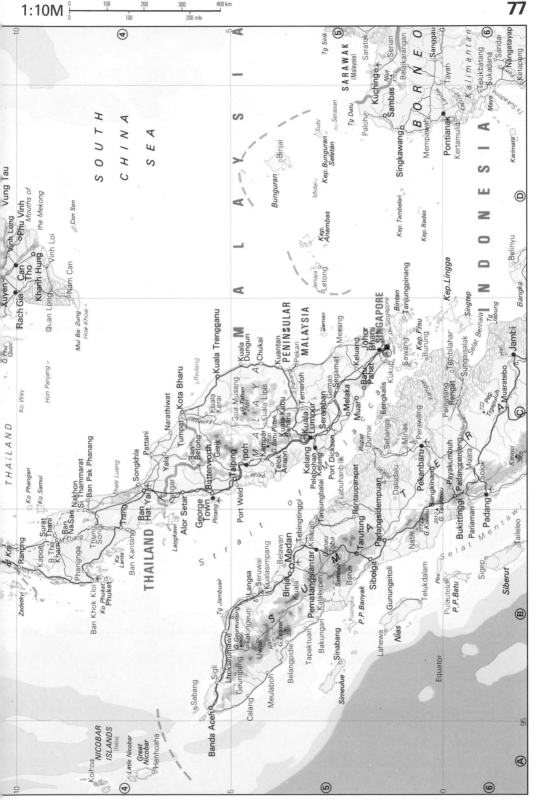

1:10M

0 100 200 300 400 km
0 100 200 300 mls

Celebes Sea

SULAWESI (CELEBES)

Flores Sea

Bali Sea

Java Sea

INDONESIA

BORNEO

SARAWAK (Mal.)

KALIMANTAN

JAWA

SUMATERA

MALAYSIA

SINGAPORE

BRUNEI

SABAH

Equator

Tarakan
Tanjungselor
Tanjungredeb
Sangkulirang
Samarinda
Balikpapan
Samboja
Bangsalsembera
Tenggarong
Tahahrogot
Kotabaru
Tanjung
Pagatan
Kintap
Jorong
Martapura
Banjarmasin
Kandangan
Amuntai
Barabai
Muaratewah
Buntok
Tewah
Palangkaraya
Kualakapuas
Sampit
Kumai
Sampito
Kotabaru
Kendawangan
Sukaraya
Sandai
Ketapang
Sukadana
Nangatayap
Telukbatang
Nangapinoh
Sintang
Kapit
Putussibau
Semitau
Lubok Antu
Sanggau
Balaikarangan
Serian
Tayan
Mempawah
Pontianak
Kertamulia
Singkawang
Sambas
Kuching
Sibu
Mukah
Bintulu
Belaga
Long
Batukelau
Longnawan
Merah
Tanjungselor

Pasangkayu
Karossa
Mamuju
Majene
Onang
Polewali
Ujung Pandang (Makassar)
(Pattallassang)

P.P. Postilyon
Kep. Sabalana
Kep. Kangean
P.P. Kangean

Sumenep
Pamekasan
Madura
Surabaya
Gresik
Mojokerto
Bangkalan
Pasuruan
Probolinggo
Situbondo
Banyuwangi
Jember
Malang
Kediri
Blitar
Tulungagung
Madiun
Surakarta
Magelang
Yogyakarta
Semarang
Kudus
Pekalongan
Tegal
Pemalang
Cirebon
Indramayu
Bandung
Garut
Tasikmalaya
Purwokerto
Cilacap
Sukabumi
Bogor
Cianjur
Jakarta
Tanjung Priok
Serang
Labuhan
Pameungpeuk

Palembang
Jambi
Pangkalpinang
Bangka
Belitung
Tanjungpandan
Manggar
Dendang
Toboali
Mentok
Belinyu
Koba
Sungaisalak
Rengat
Pematang
Pekanbaru
Dumai
Bengkalis
Perawang
Bengkulu
Lahat
Lubuklinggau
Muaraenim
Prabumulih
Kotabumi
Telukbetung
Kalianda
Kotaagung
Menggala
Sukadana
Kruio
Manna
Tais

Singapore
Johor Bahru
Melaka
Muar
Batu Pahat
Kluang
Segamat
Gemas
Seremban
Kuala Lumpur
Kelang
Kep. Riau
Tanjungpinang
Bintan
Kep. Lingga
Singtep
Kep. Anambas

Kota Kinabalu
Weston
Labuan
Beaufort
Tenom
Keningau
Salang

Enggano

:10M

| 0 | 100 | 200 | 300 | 400 km |
| 0 | | 100 | 200 mls | |

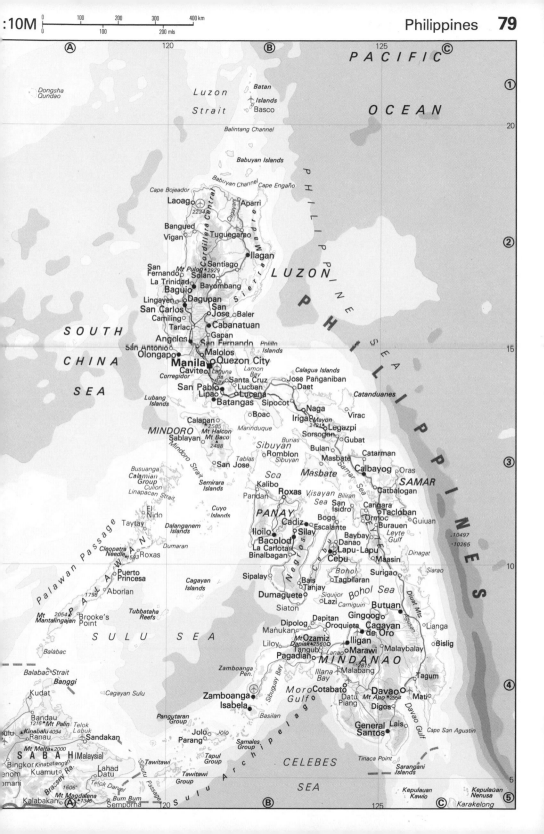

Ⓐ   120   Ⓑ   125   Ⓒ

① *Dongsha Qundao*

PACIFIC

Luzon Strait   *Batan Islands* ✈ Basco

OCEAN

20

Balintang Channel

Babuyan Islands

Babuyan Channel   *Cape Engaño*

Cape Bojeador   Laoag ✈ ▲2234   Aparri

Bangued   Tuguegarao   ●Ilagan

Vigan   ○Santiago   ②

San Fernando   Mt Pulog ▲2929   ●Solano

La Trinidad   Bayombang   LUZON

Baguio ●Dagupan   ○San Jose   Baler

Lingayen   Cabanatuan

San Carlos   Camiling   ○Gapan

Tarlac   Angeles○   ●San Fernando   *Polillo Islands*

San Antonio   ○Malolos

Olongapo   Quezon City   15

Corregidor   Manila   *Calagua Islands*

Cavite○   Santa Cruz   Jose Panganiban

Lubang Islands   San Pablo   Lucban   Daet

Lipao   Lucena   *Catanduanes*

Batangas   Sipocot   Naga   Virac

Calapan ○Boac   Iriga   ●Legazpi

MINDORO   ▲2595   Mayon ▲2421

Sablayan   Mt Halcon   *Marinduque*   Sorsogon   Gubat

○Mt Baco ▲2488   *Burias*   Bulan

Mindoro Strait   ○San Jose   *Sibuyan*   Masbate   Catarman

Busuanga   *Tablas*   Romblon   SAMAR   ③

Calamian Group   *Semirara Islands*   *Sibuyan Sea*   Masbate   Calbayog   Oras

Culion   Kalibo   *Visayan*   Catbalogan

Linapacan Strait   Pandan   Roxas   *Sea*   San Isidro   Carigara

Cuyo Islands   PANAY   Bogo   Ormoc   Tacloban

El Nido   Cadiz○   Escalante   Burauen   Guiuan

Taytay   *Dalanganem Islands*   Iloilo   Silay   Baybay   *Leyte Gulf*   .10497

Dumaran   Bacolod   Danao   .10265

Cleopatra Needle ▲1593   La Carlota   Lapu-Lapu   *Dinagat*

○Roxas   Binalbagan   Cebu   Maasin

PALAWAN   *Negros*   *Bohol*   Surigao   *Siargao*

Puerto Princesa   Sipalay   Bais   Tagbilaran   10

▲1798   *Cagayan Islands*   Tanjay   *Bohol Sea*

○Aborlan   Dumaguete   Lazi   *Camiguin*   Butuan

Siaton   Dapitan   Gingoog

Mt ▲2054   Dipolog   Oroquieta   Cagayan   ○Lianga

Mantalingajan   Brooke's Point   Manukan   Mt Ozamiz   de Oro

Tubbataha Reefs   Liloy   ▲2560   Iligan   Bislig

SULU SEA   Tangub   Marawi   Malaybalay

Balabac   Pagadian   MINDANAO   Tagum   ④

Balabac Strait   *Zamboanga Pen.*   Illana   Malabang

Banggi   Kudat   *Cagayan Sulu*   *Bay*   Cotabato   Davao

Bandau   Zamboanga   Moro   Datu   ▲2954

▲1216 Mt Palin   *Telok Labuk*   Isabela   Gulf   Piang   Mt Apo   ○Mati

Kinabalu ▲4094   Sandakan   *Basilan*   Digos

SABAH (Malaysia)   *Pangutaran Group*   General   Lais

Mt Melta ▲2000   Jolo   *Samales*   Santos   *Davao Gulf*   5

Bingkor *Kinabatangan*   *Tapul*   *Group*   *Capo San Agustin*

Kuamut   Jolo Parang   *Group*   *Sarangani*

Lahad Datu   *Tawitawi Group*   CELEBES   Tinaca Point   *Islands*

▲1606   *Telok Darvel*   SEA   *Kepulauan Kawio*   *Kepulauan Nenusa*

Mt Magdalena ▲1346   Ⓐ   *Bum Bum*   120   Ⓑ   125   Ⓒ   Karakelong   ⑤

South China Sea

Philippine Sea

Palawan Passage

Sulu Archipelago

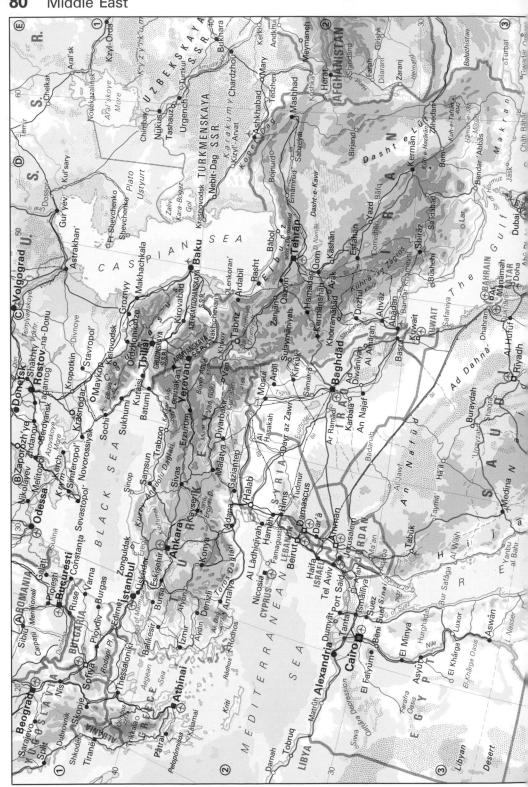

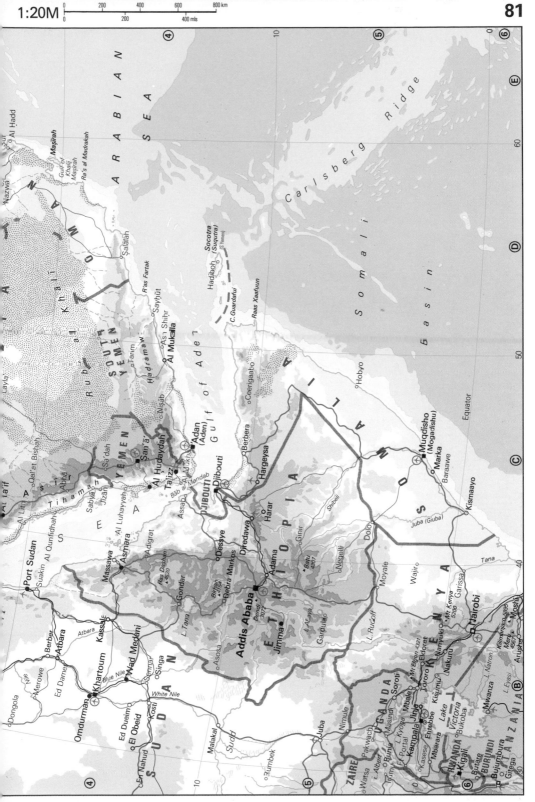

INNER MONGOLIA
ALTAI
MONGOLIA
SINKIANG
KAZAKHSKAYA S.S.R.
U.S.S.R.
KIRGIZSKAYA S.S.R.
TADZHIKSKAYA S.S.R.
UZBEKSKAYA S.S.R.
AFGHANISTAN
PAKISTAN
KASHMIR
TIBET
BHUTAN
BANGLADESH
INDIA
NEPAL

Qionglai Shan
Qiling Shan
Xiqing Shan
Bayan Har Shan
Ningjing Shan
Hoh Xil Shan
Tanggula Shan
Qing Zang
Gangdise Shan
Kunlun Shan
Altun Shan
Karakoram
Tarim Pendi
Dzungaria
Turfan Depression
Tien Shan
Pamir
Hindu Kush
Baluchistan
Kirthar Ra.
Naga Hills

Yinchuan
Wuwei
Lanzhou
Xining
Datong
Golmud
Da Qaidam
Mangnai
Dunhuang
Anxi
Yumen
Jiayuguan
Zhangye
Hami
Turpan
Ürümqi
Yining
Karamay
Kashi
Aksu
Kuqa
Korla
Hotan
Shache
Yarkand
Skardu
Gilgit
Chitral
Srinagar
Jammu
Lhasa
Nagqu
Qamdo
Yushu
Dêgê
Batang
Kangding
Baoshan
Dali
Tengchong
Bhamo
Myitkyina
Imphal
Shillong
Dhākā
Mymensingh
Sylhet
Gauhati
Jorhat
Dibrugarh
Sadiya
Thimphu
Darjeeling
Jalpaiguri
Rangpur
Purnia
Bhagalpur
Patna
Gaya
Baharampur
Mirzapur
Allahābād
Vārānasi
Kānpur
Lucknow
Faizābād
Gorakhpur
Kathmandu
Bareilly
Moradabad
Shāhjahānpur
Aligarh
Agra
Gwalior
Jhānsi
Kota
Jaipur
Ajmer
Bīkāner
Jodhpur
Delhi
Rohtak
Meerut
Saharanpur
Dehra Dun
Simla
Chandigarh
Ludhiana
Amritsar
Lahore
Sialkot
Gujrat
Rawalpindi
Islamabad
Peshawar
Mardan
Jalalabad
Kabul
Ghazni
Kandahar
Quetta
Sibi
Kalat
Hyderabad
Sukkur
Khairpur
Shikarpur
Bahawalpur
Multan
Faisalabad
Sahiwal
Khanewal
Dera Ghazi Khan
Dera Ismail Khan
Kohat
Khyber Pass
Herat
Farah
Zaranj
Mashhad
Tedzhen
Mary
Chardzhou
Bukhara
Samarkand
Dushanbe
Termez
Mazar-i-Sharif
Baghlan
Feyzabad
Tashkent
Namangan
Fergana
Andizhan
Frunze
Alma-Ata
Chimkent
Dzhambul
Balkhash
Aral'sk
Chelkar
Novokazalinsk
Kzyl-Orda
Turkestan
Ayaguz
Atasu
Dzhezkazgan

Mt. Everest
K2 (Godwin Austen) 8611
Nanga Parbat 8125
Muztagata 7546
Pik Pobedy 7439
Pik Kommunizma

Indus
Ganges
Yamuna
Brahmaputra
Mekong
Yangtze (Jinsha He)
Huang He
Irrawaddy
Amudar'ya
Syrdar'ya
Oz. Balkhash
Aral'skoye More
Lop Nor
Qinghai Hu
Bosten Hu
Nam Co

1:20M

0   200   400   600   800 km
0   200   400 mls

⑤ ⑥

Mentawai Trench

Banda Aceh
Lhokseumawe
Lhoksukon
Takingeun
Calang Leuser 3381
Meulaboh Belangpidie
Simeulue

ANDAMAN SEA

ⓓ

Chumphon
Isthmus
of Kra
Lambi
Mergui
Mergui
King
B. Sai Tok
Tavoy

Moulmein
G. of
Martaban
Rangoon
Bassein
Mouths of
the Irrawaddy
C. Negrais

ANDAMAN
ISLANDS
(India)

NICOBAR
ISLANDS
(India)

Ten Degree Channel

Carpenter   Ridge

90

ⓒ

80

B A Y   O F   B E N G A L

Balasore
Cuttack
Chilka Lake
Sambalpur
Raigan
Bilāspur
Raipur

Vizianagaram
Vishākhapatnam
Anakapalle
Kākināda
Rajahmundry
Warangal
Vijayawāda
Guntūr

Nellore

Madras

Kānchipuram
Pondicherry
Cuddalore
Nagapattinam

Chandrapur
Nāgpur
Hoshangabad

Hyderābād
Nizāmābād
Solāpur
Bijāpur
Raichūr
Kurnool
Bellāry
Anantapur
Chitradurga

Kānchipuram
Vellore
Salem
Coimbatore
Tiruchirāpalli
Palk Strait

Trincomalee
SRI LANKA
Jaffna
Batticaloa
Badulla
Kandy
Colombo
Galle
Matara
Dondra Head

O C E A N

ⓑ

80

I N D I A

Indore
Khandwa
Jālna
Jalgaon
Dhule
Pātbhāni
Aurangābād

Bangalore
Mysore
Shimoga
Mangalore
Calicut

Cochin
Madurai
Tuticorin
Trivandrum
Quilon
C. Comorin
G. of Mannar
Adam's
Bridge

Nine Degree Channel
Eight Degree Channel

I N D I A N

70

Ahmadābād
Rājkot
Jamnagar
Jūnāgadh
Kāthiāwar
Diu
G. of Khambhāt
Bhāvnagar
Vadodara
Surat
Damān
Bhusāwal

Bombay
Pune
Kolhāpur
Ratnāgiri
Panaji

LACCADIVE
ISLANDS
(India)

MALDIVES

One and Half Degree Channel

O C E A N

A R A B I A N   S E A

20

④

10

⑤

ⓐ

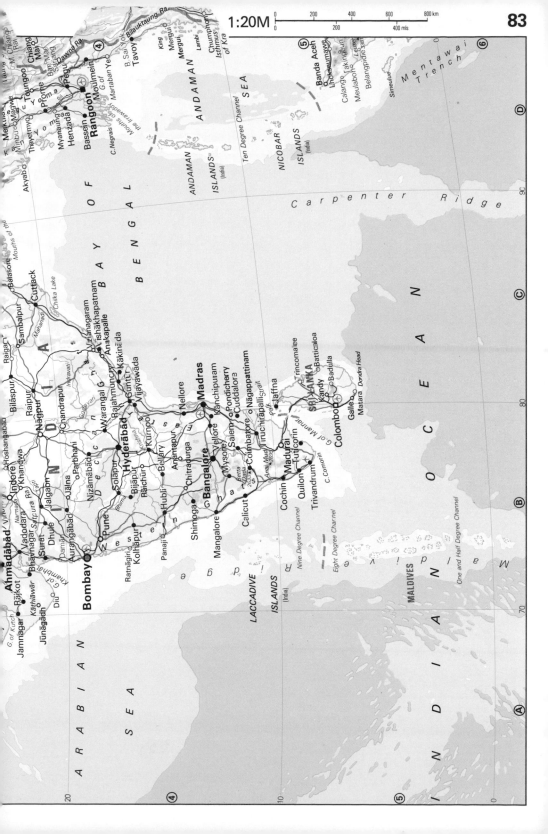

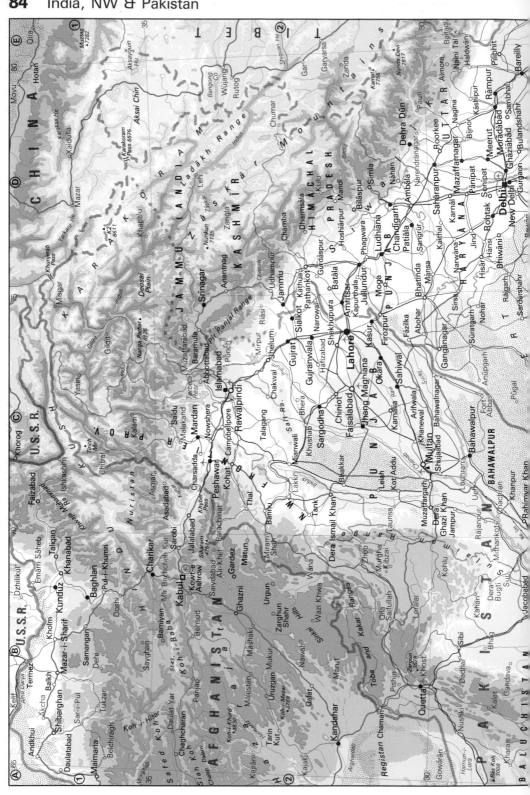

1:7.5M

0   100   200   300 km
0   50   100   150 mls

100 200 300 km
50 100 150 mils

TIBET · CHINA

BURMA

Ponnyadoung Ra.
Letha Range
Mt. Victoria 3053

NAGALAND
MANIPUR
MIZORAM
Mizo Hills
TRIPURA
MEGHALAYA
Khasi Jaintia Hills
ASSAM
ARUNACHAL Pradesh

Lhasa
Qüzü
Dagzê

HIMALAYA
GREAT RANGE
Mahabharat Range
Siwalik Range

Mt Everest (Qomolangma) 8848
Kangchenjunga 8586
Makalu 8475
Cho Oyu 8217
Annapurna 8078
Dhaulagiri 8172
Manaslu

SIKKIM
BHUTAN
NEPAL
Thimphu Punakha Tongsa Paro
Kathmandu Patan Bhadgaon

BANGLADESH
Dhaka Dacca
Chittagong
Cox's Bazar

WEST BENGAL
Calcutta
Haora
Diamond Harbour
Mouths of the Ganga (Ganges)
Sundarbans

BIHAR
Patna
Rajmahal Hills
Chota Nagpur Plateau
Ranchi Plateau

UTTAR PRADESH
Lucknow
Kanpur
Allahabad
Vārānasi

MADHYA PRADESH

Maikala Range

Raipur
Bhilai
Cuttack

BAY OF BENGAL

Tropic of Cancer

100   200   300 km
50   100   150 mls

hāne
Kalyān
Bombay Ⓐ
Lonāvale   80   Ⓒ
Pune **MAHARASHTRA**   Parbhani   Nānded   Nirmal   Belampalli   Jagdalpur   Kotapad
(Poona)   Bīr   Pūrna   Mancherāl   Sironcha   Dantewāra
bāg   Ahmadnajar   Bodhan   Nizāmābad   Jagtial   Bijāpur   Sukma
vardhān   Mahād   Daund   Udgir   Karīmnagar
Wai   Bārāmati   Lātūr   Siddipet   Yellandu   Bhadrāchalam
Mahād   Phaltan   Barsi   Bīdar   Warangal   Kottagūdem
Chiplūn   Sātāra   Pandharpur   Homnābād   Sangāreddi   Bhongir   Khammam   Rājahmundry
Karād   Vite   Akalkot   Gulbarga   Nalgonda   Suriāpet   Eluru   Kākināda ①
Sāngli   Shāhābād   Tāndūr   **Hyderābād**   **ANDHRA**   Yanam
Kolhāpur   Miraj   Bijāpur   Yādgir   Mahbūbnagar   Māchērla   Vijayawāda   Bhīmavaram
Ichalkaranji   Jamkhandi   Shorāpur   Nārāyanpet   Guntūr   Machilīpatnam
Mālvan   Belgaum   Bāgalkot   Rāichur   Wanparti   Narasarāopet   Tenāli
Vengurla   Guledagudda   **P R A D E S H**   Bāpatla
Panajī   Goa   Gajendragarh   Kurnool   Chilakalūrupet
Daman   **KARNATAKA**   Koppal   Adoni   Nandyāl   Chīrāla
Madgaon   S. Diu   Gadag   Bellary   Dhone   Kani   Ongole
Kārwār   Dandeli   Hubli   Hospet   Guntakal   Giddalūr   Giri   Kondukūr
Sirsi   Hāveri   Swāmihalli   Gooty   Tādpatri   Proddatūr   Kavali   15
Kumta   Rānibennur   Kottūru   Rāyadurg   Penner   Nellore
Bhatkal   Dāvangere   Hirihar   Kalyandurg   Anantapur   Gūdūr
Coondapoor   Chitradurga   Dhamavaram   Cuddapah   Venkatagiri   Sri Kālahasti
Udupi   Shimoga   Dhalavalli   Tarikere   Sira   Kadiri   Pulicat L.
Kārkal   Bhadrā Resr   Kādūr   Chik   Tirupati
Mangalore   Chikmagalūr   Arsikere   Tumkūr   Ballāpur   Chittoor   Arakkonam   **Madras**
Kāsaragod   Hassan   Tiptur   Dod Ballāpur   Kolar   Vellore   Kānchipuram ②
Hole Narsipur   Bangalore   Kolar   Amhūr
Cannanore   Madikeri   Mandya   Gold Fields   Javadi
Tellicherry   Mahe   Nanjangūd   Krishnagiri   Hills
Badagara   Chāmrājnagar   Mysore   Tiruppattūr   Tindivanam
Calicut   Doda Betta   Dharmapuri   Tiruvannāmalai   Pondicherry
(Kozhikode)   Ootacamund   2636   Erode   Villupuram   Cuddalore
Beypore   Nilgiri Hills   Coonoor   Salem   Vriddhāchalam   Chidambaram
Ponnāni   Coimbatore   **T A M I L   N Ā D U**
Trichūr   Palghāt   Tiruppur   Cauvery   Kumbakonam
Anaimalai   Tiruchchirāppalli   Kāraikāl
Androth   Pollāchi   Thanjāvūr   Nāgappattinam
Palani   Mannārgudi
Cochin   Bodināyakkanūr   Dindigul   Pudukkottai   Pt Calimera
Ernākulam   Kodikkarai
Kottayam   Kambam   Madurai   Pt Pedro
Alleppey   Virudunagar   Paramakkudi   Jaffna
Kāyankulam   Arūppukkottai   Rāmanāthapuram   Mullaittvu
Kalpeni   Puliyangudi   Rājapālaiyam   Talaimannar   Mannar   Vavuniya   Trincomalee
Quilon   Tenkāsi   Tuticorin   Adam's   Havankulam
Tirunelveli   Palayankottai   Gulf of   Bridge   Anurādhapura
Trivandrum   Tiruchchendūr   Mannār   Puttalam   Batticaloa ③
Nāgercoil   Dambulla
Kanniyākumari   C.Comorin   **SRI LANKA**   **CEYLON**   Matale
Chilaw   Kurunegala   Kandy
ight Degree Channel   Negombo   Gampola   Badulla
Colombo   Adam's Pk   Nuwara-Eliya
MALDIVES   Dehiwala-Mt Lavinia   2243   Ratnapura
Moratuwa   Opanake
Ambalangoda   Galle   Hambantota
Matara   Dondra Hd

Ⓐ   75   Ⓑ

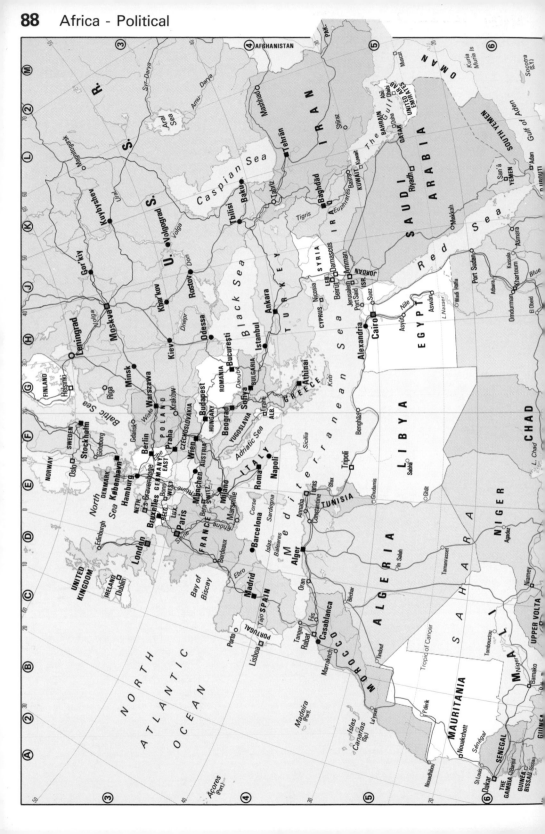

1:40M

0   400   800   1200   1600 km

0   400   800 mls

89

SOMALIA
ETHIOPIA
Addis Ababa
KENYA
UGANDA
RWANDA
BURUNDI
TANZANIA
ZAIRE
CONGO
GABON
EQUAT. GUINEA
CAMEROON
NIGERIA
CENTRAL AFRICAN REPUBLIC
ANGOLA
ZAMBIA
MALAWI
MOZAMBIQUE
ZIMBABWE
BOTSWANA
NAMIBIA (S.W. AFRICA)
SOUTH AFRICA
SWAZILAND
LESOTHO
MADAGASCAR
SEYCHELLES
COMOROS
GHANA
IVORY COAST
LIBERIA

INDIAN OCEAN
SOUTH ATLANTIC OCEAN
Gulf of Guinea
Mozambique Channel

Mogadishu
Kismaayo
Mombasa
Zanzibar
Dar es Salaam
Nairobi
Kampala
Entebbe
Kigali
Bujumbura
Dodoma
Arusha
Mwanza
Kigoma
Kalemie
Mbeya
Mbala
Lilongwe
Harare
Gweru
Bulawayo
Mutare
Beira
Sofala
Nampula
Lichinga
Lusaka
Ndola
Lubumbashi
Kitwe
Kabwe
Mansa
Hwange
Gaborone
Serowe
Keetmanshoop
Windhoek (S.A.)
Walvis Bay (S.A.)
Namibe
Lobito
Luanda
Cabinda (Ang.)
M'tadi
Kinshasa
Brazzaville
Kananga
Mbuji Mayi
Bandundu
Kikwit
Kananga
Ilebo
Mbandaka
Kisangani
Goma
Bukavu
Juba
Wau
Bambari
Bangui
Yaoundé
Douala
Malabo
Bata
Libreville
Lambaréné
Ngaoundéré
Onitsha
Port Harcourt
Ibadan
Lagos
Porto Novo
Lomé
Accra
Kumasi
Abidjan
Bouaké
Buchanan
Monrovia
Gulu
Jimma
Pretoria
Johannesburg
Mbabane
Maputo
Durban
East London
Port Elizabeth
Cape Town
Bloemfontein
Kimberley
Maseru
Upington
Gaborone
Ts.meb
Antananarivo
Antseranana
Mahajanga
Toamasina
Toliara

L. Turkana
L. Albert
L. Edward
L. Kivu
Lake Victoria
Lake Tanganyika
Lake Nyasa
L. Kariba
Lake Malawi

Zaire (Congo)
Congo
Kasai
Kwango
Kwilu
Lualaba
Lomami
Zambezi
Cubango
Limpopo
Orange
Kunene
Okavango
Ruvuma
Rufiji

Equator
Tropic of Capricorn

Seychelles Arch.
Amirante Is
Aldabra Is
Farquhar Is
Tromelin (Fr.)
Réunion (Fr.)
Mayotte (Fr.)
St Helena (U.K.)
Ascension (U.K.)
Tristan da Cunha (U.K.)
São Tomé & Príncipe
São Tomé (S.T. & P.)
Príncipe
Annobon
Bioko

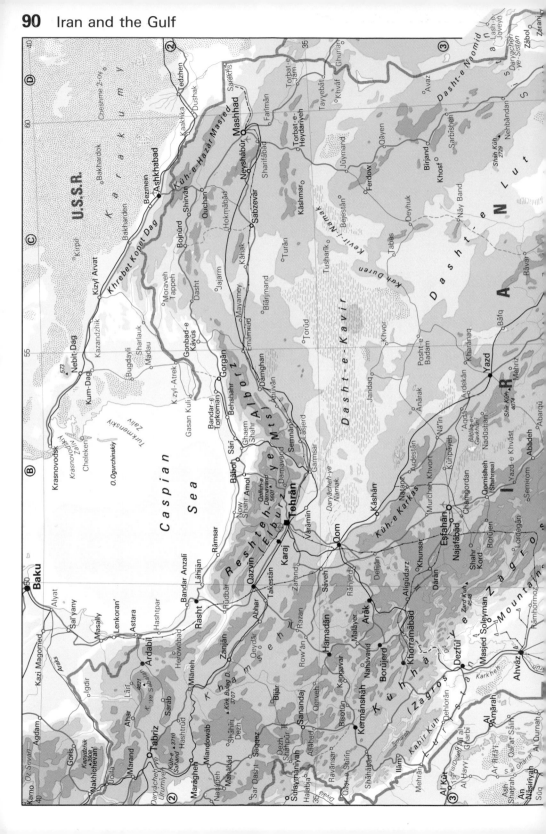

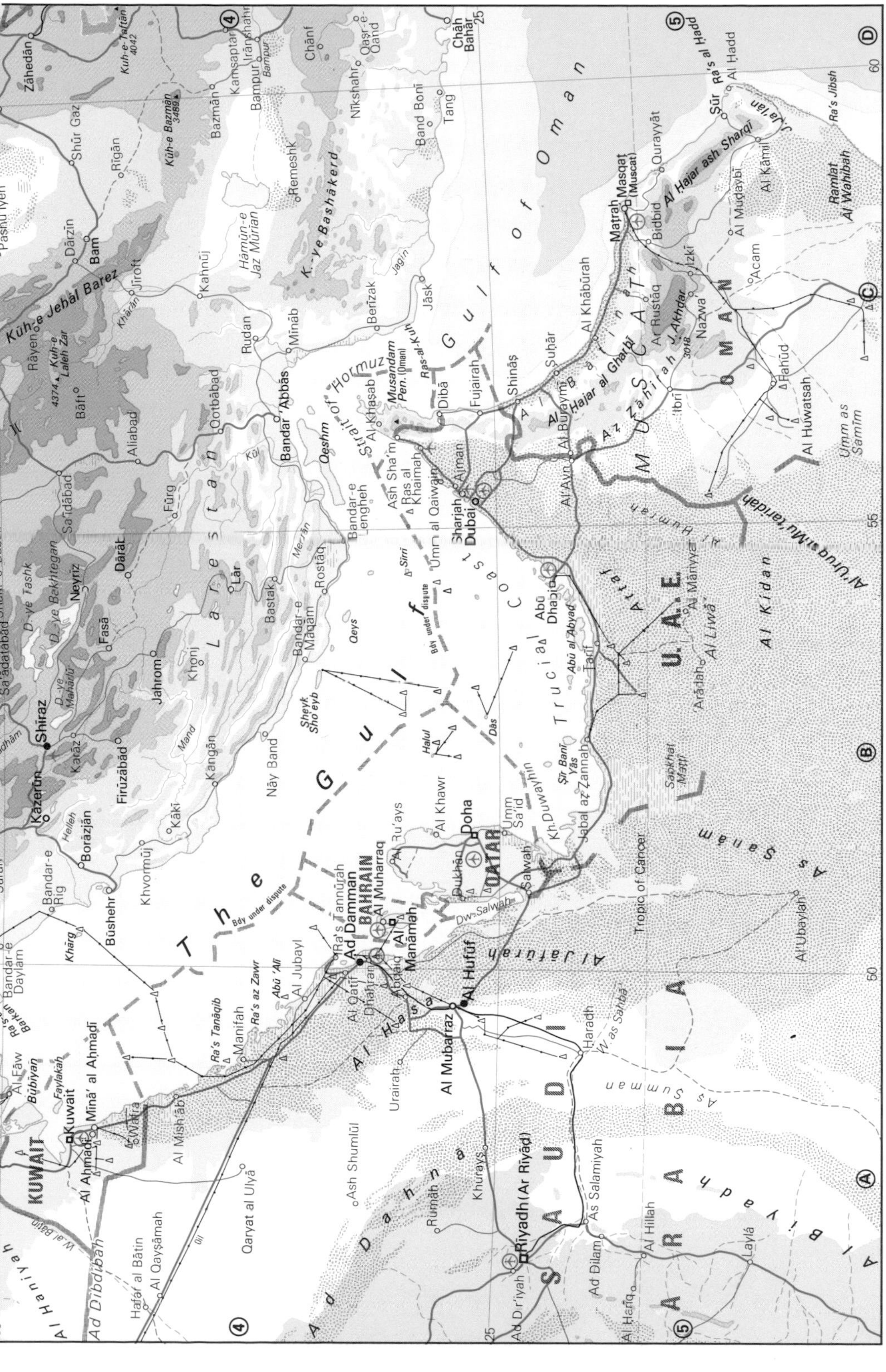

100
200
300 km
50
100
150 mls

30

Noşratābād
Zāhedān

④

Kūh-e Taftān
4042

Kamsaptar
Īrānshahr
Chānf
Qaşr-e Qand
Chāh Bahār 25

⑤

Ra's al Hadd
Al Hadd

D

60

Kerman
Pashū'īyeh
Shūr Gaz
Rīgān
Bampūr
Bazmān
Nīkshahr
Tang
Band Boni
Sūr
Quriyāt
Ra's al Jibsh

Dārzīn
Bam
Kūh-e Bazmān
3490

Remeshk
Jāsk
Masqat
(Muscat)
Bidbid
Al Hajar ash Sharqi
Al Kāmil
Ramlat
Al Wāhībah

Rāyen
Kūh-e Jehāl Barez
Kūh-e
Lāleh Zār
4374
Kahnūj
Mināb
Marrah
Ar Rustāq
Al Mudaybi

Şafāābād
Jīroft
Rudān
Rudbār
Ra's-al-Kūh
Al Khābūrah
J. Akhdar
3018
Izki
Acam

Bāghīn
Khānān
Qoṭbābād
Bandar 'Abbās
Gulf of Oman
Al Buraymi
Al 'Ayn
Nazwa
Al Huwatsah

D-ye Tashk
Shahr-e-Bābek
Aliabad
Qeshm
Strait of Hormuz
Musandam Pen.(Oman)
Shinās
Suḥār
Hajar al Gharbi
Ibri
Fahūd

Neyrīz
Fūrg
Kūl
Al Khasab
Ash Sha'm
Dibā
Fujairah
Al Buraymi
Umm as
Samīm

Fasā
Lār
Bandar-e-Lengheh
Ra's al Khaimah
Ajman
Şaqar

Jahrom
Khonj
Bastak
Mer'īn
Umm al Qaiwain
Sharjah
U.A.E.

Shīrāz
Kāvār
Bandar-e-Māqām
Sirrī
Dubai
Al Māmiyya
Al Kidan

Kāzerūn
Fīrūzābād
Kangān
Qeys
Bdy under dispute
Abū Dhabi
Abū al 'Abyad
Tarif

Nūrābād
Borāzjān
Kākī
Nāy Band
Sheyk Sho'eyb
Das
Abū al 'Abyad
Al Liwā
'Arādah

Gach Sārān
Bandar-e-Rīg
Khormūj
Halūl
Sīr Banī Yās
Jabal az Zannāh
As Sanam

Būshehr
Ru'ays
Al Khawr
Umm Sa'īd
Kh. Duwayhin

Bandar-e Daylam
Khārg
Bdy under dispute
Abū 'Alī
QATAR
Doha
Salwah
Sabkhat Maṭṭi
Tropic of Cancer

Ra's az Zawr
Ra's Tannūrah
BAHRAIN
Al Muharraq
Buhān
Salwah

Hendijan
Abū 'Alī
Ad Dammam
Al Muharraq
Manāmah
Dw. Salwah
Al Jafurah

KUWAIT
Ra's Tanāqib
Manifah
Al Qaṭīf
Dhahran
Al Hufūf

Al 'Ēw
Būbiyān
Faylakah
Ra's az Zawr
Al Jubayl
Bīdah
Al Mubarraz
Haradh
W. as Sahbā

Kuwait
Mīnā' al Ahmadī
Ash Shumlūl
Urairah
As Summan

Al Aḥmadī
Aş Şulaybīyah
Al Mish'āb
Al Mubarraz
SAUDI ARABIA

Şafwān
Al Busayyah
Qaryat al Ulyā
Ruhaiys
Khūrays
Riyadh (Ar Riyāḍ)
As Salamīyah

Al Hasā
Ad Dibdībah
Ḥafar al Bāṭin
Al Qaysūmah
Rumāh
Ad Dir'īyah
Al Ḥillah
Layla

Al Ḥanīyah
Ad Dahnā'
Ad Dir'īyah
Al Ḥarīq
Al Bilam
As Salamīyah

30
④
25
⑤

A
60
B
C
55

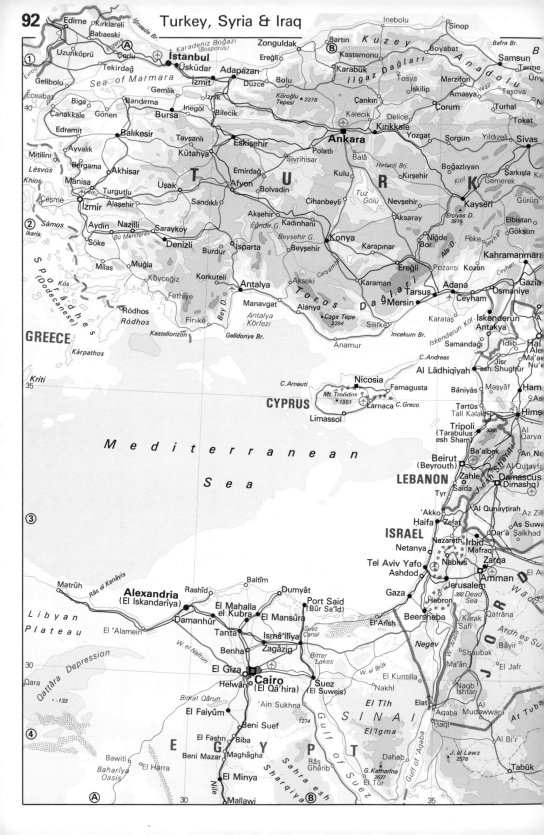

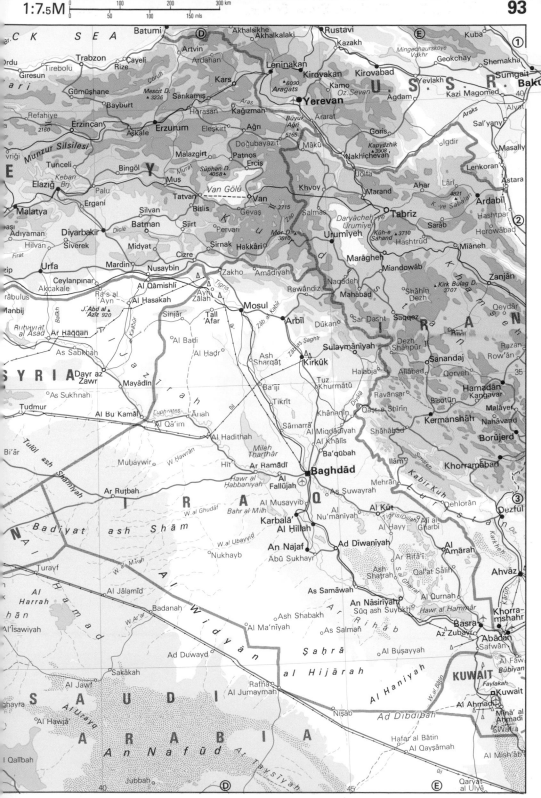

100   200   300 km
50   100   150 mls

BLACK SEA

Batumi
Ordu
Tirebolu
Giresun
Trabzon
Çayeli
Rize
Artvin
Ardahan
Akhalsikhe
Akhalkalaki
Rustavi
Kazakh
Kuba
Geokchay
Shemakha
Sumgait
Baku
Gümüşhane
Bayburt
Mescit D.
3236
Sarıkamış
Kars
Leninakan
Kirovakan
Kamo
Oz. Sevan
Kirovabad
Yevlakh
Agdam
Kazi Magomed
Alyat
Sal'yany
Masally
Lenkoran
Astara

Refahiye
Erzincan
2160
Erzurum
Aşkale
Horasan
Ağrı
Eleşkirt
Doğubayazıt
Aras
Aragats
6090
Yerevan
Ararat
Büyük
Ağrı
5165
Mākū
Goris
Kapydzhik
3908
Nakhichevan
Igdir
Kazi

Tunceli
Bingöl
Muş
Malazgirt
Patnos
Erciş
Süphan D.
4058
Van Gölü
Khvoy
Marand
Ahar
Lārī
K.-ye Sabalah
4821
Ardabīl
Hashtpar
Herowābād

Elazığ
Keban Brj.
Palu
Ergani
Silvan
Bitlis
Tatvan
Gevaş
Van
2715
Salmās
Daryācheh-ye Urumīye
Kūh-e Sāhand
3710
Tabrīz
Sarāb
Mīāneh

Malatya
Adıyaman
Hilvan
Diyarbakir
Siverek
Batman
Siirt
Midyat
Pervari
Şırnak
Hakkâri
Zap
Mor D.
3910
Urumīyeh
Marāgheh
Miandowāb
Hashtrūd

Urfa
Mardin
Nusaybin
Cizre
Zakho
Amādīyah
Rawāndiz
Naqadeh
Shāhīn Dezh
Zanjān
Kirk Bulag D.
3707
Qeydār

Ceylanpınar
Akçakale
Ra's al 'Ayn
Al Qāmishlī
'Ayn Zālah
Sinjār
Mosul
Mahābād
Saqqez
Bījār
Razan
Row'ān

Manbij
Ruhayrat al Asad
Ar Raqqah
As Sabkhah
J. 'Abd al 'Azīz 920
Tall 'Afar
Al Badī
Al Hadr
Arbīl
Dūkān
Sar Dasht
Dezh Shāhpūr
Sulaymānīyah
Sanandaj
Qorveh
Hamadān
Kangavar

SYRIA
Dayr az Zawr
As Sukhnah
Mayādīn
Ash Sharqāt
Ba'jī
Tuz Khurmātū
Kirkūk
Halabja
Allābād
Bīsotūn
Malāyer
Nahāvand
Borūjerd

Tudmur
Al Bu Kamāl
Al Qā'im
'Ānah
Tikrīt
Khānaqīn
Ravānsar
Qasr-e Shīrīn
Shāhābād
Kermānshāh
Khorramābād

Bi'ār
Al Hadithah
Muhaywir
Hīt
Ar Ramādī
Sāmarrā
Al Miqdādīyah
Ba'qūbah
Ilām
Mehrān

Ar Rutbah
Mileh Tharthār
Hawr al Habbānīyah
Al Fallūjah
Baghdād
As Suwayrah
Dehlorān
Dezfūl

Badiyat ash Shām
W. al Ghudāf
Bahr al Milh
Al Musayyib
Karbalā'
Al Hillah
An Nu'mānīyah
Al Kūt
Al Hayy
Ali al Gharbī
Al 'Amārah
Ahvāz

Turayf
Al Jālamīd
Nukhayb
W. al Ubayyid
Abū Sukhayr
An Najaf
Ad Dīwānīyah
Ar Rifā'ī
Qal'at Sālih
Khorramshahr

Al Harrah
Badanah
Ad Duwayd
As Samāwah
Ash Shatrah
Sūq ash Suyūkh
An Nāsirīyah
Al Qurnah
Hawr al Hammār
Basra
Az Zubayr
Abādān
Safwān

Al'Īsawiyah
Sakākah
Al Ma'nīyah
Ash Shabakh
As Salmān
Ar Rihāb
Al Busayyah
Al Fāw
Būbīyan
Faylakah

Al Jawf
Rafhā
Al Jumaymah
Nişāb
Şahrā al Hijārah
Al Haniyah
KUWAIT
Kuwait
Al Ahmadī
Mīnā' al Ahmadī
Al Wafra

Jubbah
An Nafūd
ARABIA
Hafar al Bātin
Ad Dibdibah
Al Qaysāmah
Al Mish'āb
Qaryat al Ulyā

SAUDI

0   25   50   75   100 km
0   25   50 mls

CYPRUS

Paleokhorio   Larnaca   34   C.Greco
Lefkara   Larnaca Bay
Zyyi   C.Kiti
Limassol
Akrotiri Bay   C.Gata

MEDITERRANEAN

SEA

Ras Burûn
Sabkhet el Bardawil
El 'Arîsh
Bir Lahfein
W. el Arish
W. Hareidin
Abu 'Aweigila
NIZANA
Queziot
El Quseima

EGYPT

G. Libni 463
G. Maghâra 735
Bir Gifgâfa
Bir Hasana
892 G. Halâl

Tartûs
Arwad
Duraykish
Kafrûn Bashûr
An Nasirah Tall Btsah
Hamîdîyah
Shaftâ Qal'at al Hisn
(KRAK-DES-CHEVALIERS)
Kleia
Kebir
Qoubayat Shinsi
Tall Kalakh
Al 'Ousayr
El Mîna
Zghorta
El Hermel
Jûsîy
Hisy
Tripoli
(Tarâbulus esh Sham)
Qornet es Saouda 3086
Bcharre
Batroun
Amioune
Laboue
Jab Halil 246
Jubail
BYBLOS
Kartaba
Deir el Ahmar
Dayr el 2659
An Nabl
Yabrûd
LEBANON
Rhazir
Ba'albek
El Beqa'a
Bikfaya 2628
Jounié
Baie de St Georges
Beirut
(Beyrouth)
Ba'abda
Zahle
Rayak
Qutayfah 1910
Al J.Ma'lûla
Dun
Aley
Az Zabdâni
Damour
Ayn al Fijah
At Tall
Dûma Adhrâ
Beit ed Dine
Machgharah
Barâda
Damascu
(Dimâshq)
Saïda (Sidon)
Jezzine
Rachaya
Qatana
Hâsbaiya
J.ash Shaykh (Mt Hermon)
A'waj Al Hijanat
Dayr 'Ali
Marjayoun
Al Kiswah
Tyr (Tyre, Sour)
Q.Shemona
Jouai'ya
Baniyas
Mas'adah
SYRIA
Ghabâghib
Burâq
Enn Nâqoûra
CEASE FIRE LINES 1974
Mismîyah
Benn
Jbail
Yesud
Al Qunaytirah
Al Sanamayn
Khabab
Nahariya
Ma'alot Tarshîhâ
1208 Har Meron
Hamâ'ala
Khushnîya
Al Lajâh 863
Shaq
'Akko (Acre)
Zefat (Safad)
Nawâ
Izra'
Shahbâ
Haifa (Hefa)
Rama
Sea of Galilee (Yam Kinneret)
Shaykh Miskin
Jabal 'Ar 17
B.of Haifa
Q. Yam
Shefar'am
Tiberias
Fiq
Ma'agan
As Suwayda
'Atlit
Q. Ata
Mt Carmel
Dishon
Nazareth
Yarmûk
W. al Ruqqâd
Dar'a
Zikhron Ya'aqov
Afula
Deir Abu Sa'id
Irbid
Ramtha
MEGIDDO ARMAGEDDON
Beyt Shean
W. az Zaydi
Buşrâ ash Shâm
CAESAREA
Jenin
Husn
Salk
Pardes Hanna
Qabatiya
Ajlûn
J. Um ed Dara 1247
Mafraq
Tisîyat
Hadera
Tubas
Jarash
Sabhâ
Netanya
Tulkarm
Farra
Es Samrâ
Sabastiya
Zarqa
Er Rummân
Herzliyya
Kefar Sava
Nablus
ISRAEL
Bat Yam
Petah Tiqwa
Suweilih
Qa Khanna
Yargon
Ramat Gan
Saridat
Ba'al Hazor 1016
Zarqa
Tel Aviv
Holon
Salt
Karama
Amman
Marka
Yafo (Jaffa)
Lod
Ramallah
Wadi es Sir
Sahâb
Rishon le Zion
Ramla
Jericho (Ariha)
Naur
Rehovot
Latrun
Sorek
Jerusalem (El Quds)
(Yerushalayim)
Jiza
Ashdod
Beit Jala
Bethlehem (Bayt Lahm)
Mâdabâ
Ashqelon
Qiryat Gat
Bet Guvrin
Hebron (El Khalil)
Dab'a
Qasr el Kharana
Jebel Mudeisisat
Wad 'adh Dha
Gaza
Sederot
Dura
En Gedi
Khan ez Zabîb
LACHISH
Gerar
Yatta
Gaza Strip
Edh Dhahiriya
Mazra
Rabba
Khan Yunis
Ofaqim
MEZADA
El Lisân
Qatrâna
Rafah
Be'er Sheva
Beersheba (Be'er Sheva)
Arad
Zeelim
Nevatim
Sedom
Karak 1253
Qa'el Hafira
HALUZA
Dimona
MAMSHIT
T.el Meise
Manzil
Revivim
Safi Ed Dabâb
Mazâr
QQeziot
SHIVTA
Yeroham
El Ghor
1305
Sede Boqer
Oron
Zin
W. el Hâsa
JORDA
AVEDAT
Hazeva
1356 J. Qasred Deir
Hâsâ
Mizpe Ramon
Rashâdîya
Danâ
Jurf ed Darâwîsh
1305 Har Ramon
Ein Yahav
1641 J. Atâ'ita
Jebel
Negev
Nijil
1615 Jum Suwwâna
Uneisa
Har Saggi 1006
Har Hakippa 467
1082
Shaubak

A   34   **B**   36   **C**

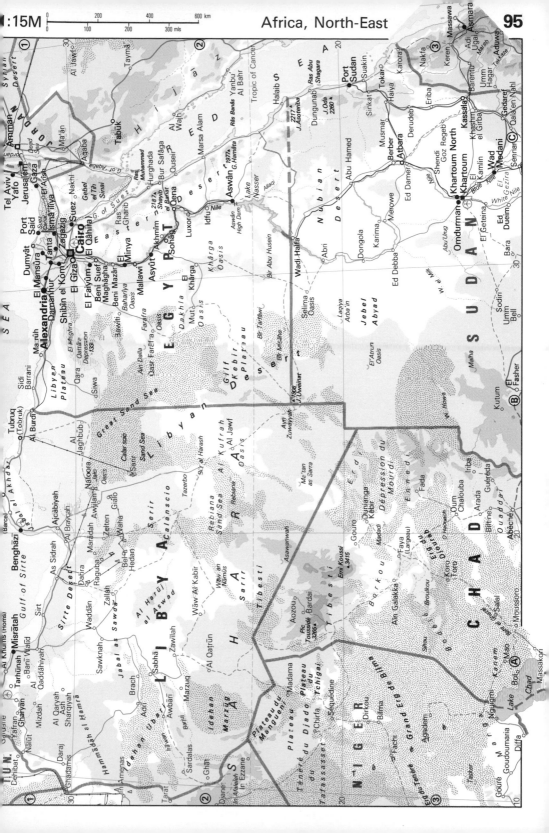

200 400 600 km
100 200 300 mls

JORDAN
Amman
Dead Sea
Ma'ān
Al Jawf
Taymā'

SYRIAN Desert

Tel Aviv-Yafo
Jerusalem
Gaza
El 'Arīsh
Suez Canal
Port Said
Dumyât
Damanhûr
Alexandria
Marûh
Sidi Barrâni
Tubruq (Tobruk)
Al Burdî
Al Akhdar

SEA

MEDITERRANEAN

Tabūk
'Aqaba
Gulf of 'Aqaba
Ras Muhammad
Gebel el Tih
Sinai
Nakhl
Ras Gharib
Hurghada
Bur Safâga
Quseir

HIJAZ

Yanbu' Al Bahr
Tropic of Cancer
Ras Banas
Marsa Alam
G.Hamīda 1971
Halâib
Ras Abu Shagara

RED SEA

Port Sudan
Suakin
Tokar
Nakfa
Karora
Massawa
Asmara
Adi Ugri
Keren
Barentu

Cairo
El Gîza
Ismâ'ilîya
Zagazig
Tanta
El Mansûra
Shibîn el Kôm
El Faiyûm
Beni Suef
El Minya
Mallawi
Asyût
Akhmîm
Sohâg
Qena
Luxor
Idfu
Aswân
Aswân High Dam
Lake Nasser

EGYPT

Bahariya Oasis
Farâfra Oasis
Bâwiti
Ain Dalla
Qasr Farâfra
Dâkhla Oasis
Mut
Khârga Oasis
El Khârga
Bîr Tarfâwi
Bîr Misâha
Selîma Oasis

Abû Hamed
Wadi Halfa
Abri
Dongola
Karima
Merowe
Ed Debba
Berber
Atbara
Ed Damer
Shendi
Khartoum North
Omdurman
Khartoum

SUDAN

Musmar
Haiya
Sinkat
Derudeb
Goz Regeb
Kassala
Khashm el Girba
Gedaref
Qala en Nahl

Wad Medani
Sennar
Ed Dueim
El Geteina
El Kamlin
Wâdi

Nubian Desert

Libyan Plateau
Qattâra Depression -133
Qâra
Siwa
Jaghbûb
Calanscio Sand Sea
Great Sand Sea

LIBYA

Benghâzî
Al Marj
Ajdâbiyah
As Sidrah
Marâdah
Zelten
Giâlo
Gulf of Sirte
Sirt
Misrâtah
Tarhûnah
Al Khums (Homs)
Banî Walîd
Zliten
Al Qaddâhiyah

Sirte Desert

Waddân
Sawknah
Al Qatrûn
Zallah
Zawilah

Al Harûj al Aswad

Waw al Kabir
Waw an Namûs

Marzûq
Sabhâ
Brach
Adri
Barjûj
Awbâri
Ubari

Idehan Marzûq

Ghat

Gilf Kebir Plateau

Aweinat
J. 'Uweinat 1908

Nahaggar

El'Atrun Oasis
Laqiya Arba'in
Bîr Abu Husein

Jebel Abyad

Sodiri
Umm Badr
Bara

Malha
Umm Keddada
Fasher
Kutum

CHAD

Dépression du Mourdi
Iriba
Guéréda
Bîltine
Abéché
Oum Chalouba
Arada
Fada
Fada
Ennedi
Borkou
Emi Koussi 3415
Faya (Largeau)
Koro Toro
Kora
Ati
Oum Hadjer
Biltine
Am Zoer
Dar

Aozou
Bardai
Pic Toussidé 3265
Tibesti
Zouar
Madama

NIGER

Dirkou
Bilma
Fachi
Agadem
Plateau du Diado
Plateau du Manguéni
Chirfa
Séguédine
Tchigai

Lake Chad
Bol
Massakori
Mao
Nguigmi
Diffa
Goudoumaria
Gouré
Tasker

TUN.
Dehibat
Nâlût
Gharyân
Mizdah
Al Qaryah Ash Sharqîyah
Ghadâmis
Ghat
Djanet
In Amenas
In Afaleh

Ed Débba

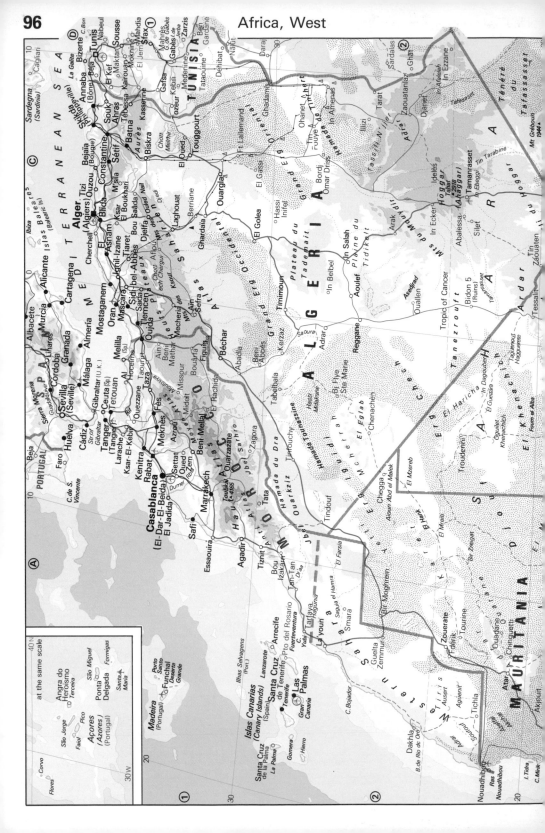

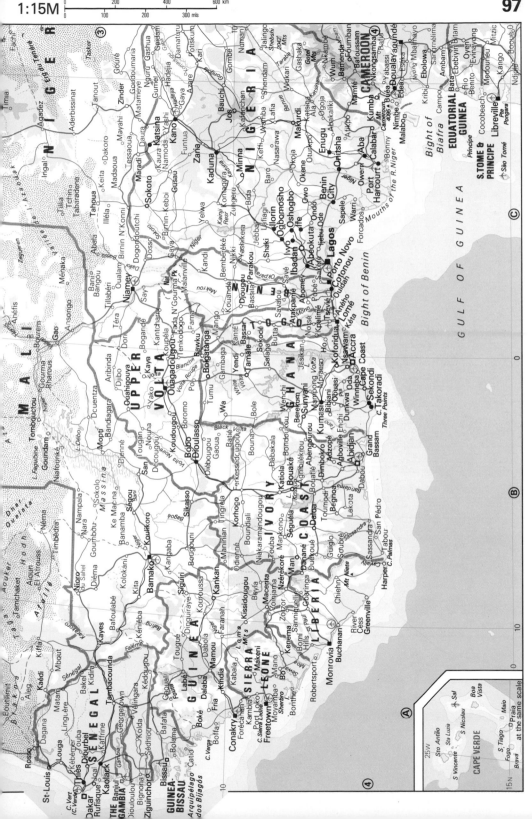

1:15M

200 400 600 km
100 200 300 mls

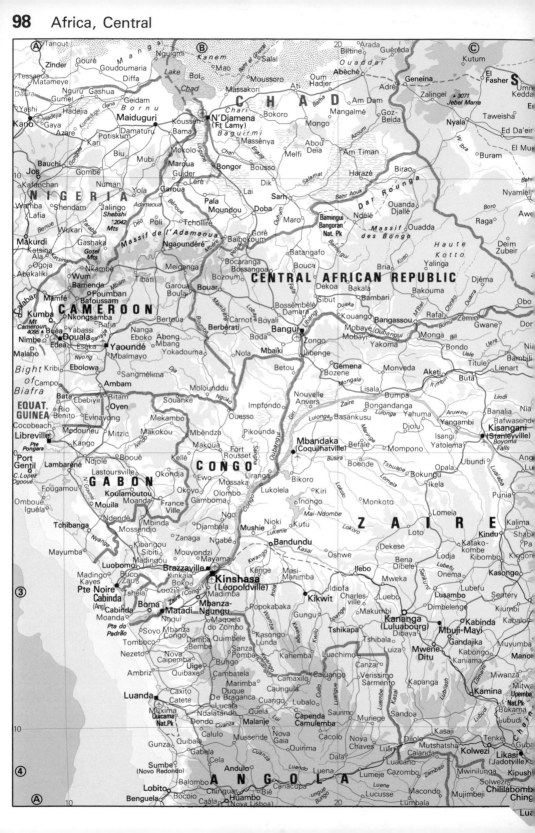

SUDAN · ETHIOPIA · SOMALIA · UGANDA · KENYA · TANZANIA · RWANDA · BURUNDI · DJIBOUTI · COMOROS · SEYCHELLES

Massawa · Keren · Asmara · Kassala · Adi Ugai · Marsa Fatma · Edd · Assab · Ta'izz · Al Mukha (Mocha) · Adan (Aden) · Shaykh Uthman

El Geteina · Wad Medani · El Gezira · Gedaref · Aduwa · Adigrat · Makale · Djibouti · Zeila · Berbera · Burco · Caynabo · Laas Caanood

El Obeid · Gondar · Debra Tabor · Dessye · Dire Dawa · Harar · Hargeysa · Damot · Galadi · Gaalkacyo

ETHIOPIA · Addis Ababa · Adama · Awash · Ahmar Mts · Ogaden · Warder

Jimma · Shashamanna · Goba · Ginir · Imi · Danan · Sinadogo · Ceelbuur

Juba · Lake Turkana · Moyale · Mega · Dolo · Luuq · Baardheere · Buur Hakaba · Markad · Muqdisho (Mugadishu) · Afgooye · Uarsciek · Jowhar

UGANDA · Kampala · Jinja · Entebbe · Lake Victoria · KENYA · Nairobi · Nakuru · Nyeri · Embu · Garissa · SOMALIA · Kismaayo · Giamame · Jilib · Baraawe

Kigali · RWANDA · BURUNDI · Bujumbura · Kigoma · TANZANIA · Dodoma · Arusha · Moshi · Kilimanjaro 5895 · Mombasa · Tanga · Zanzibar · Dar es Salaam · Bagamoyo

Mbeya · Iringa · Mikumi · Morogoro · Mafia I. · Kilwa Kivinje · Kilwa Kisiwani · Lindi · Mtwara · C. Delgado · Palma

SEYCHELLES · Aldabra Is · Assumption · Is Glorieuses · COMOROS · Moroni · Grande Comore · Mutsamudu · Anjouan · Mahéli · Mayotte (Fr.) · Dzaoudzi

SOMALIA · Alula · Candala · C. Guardafui · Boosaaso · Hordiyo · Ras Xaafuun · Bender Beyla · Qardho · Eyl · El Hamurre · Dabaro · Hobyo

Gulf of Aden · Str. of Bab al Mandeb

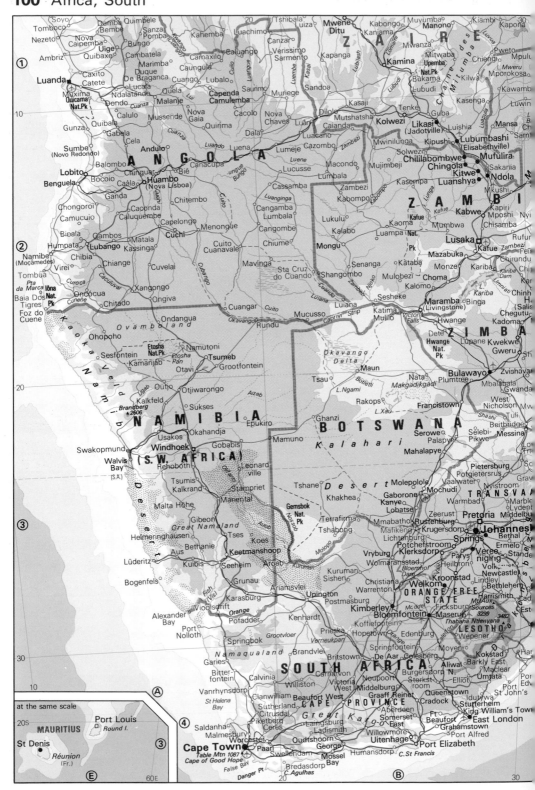

Tomboco · Soyo · Damba Quimbele · Tshibala · Mwene · Kabongo · Muyumba · Kiambi
Nezeto · Bembe · Sanza · Luachimo · Luiza · Ditu · Kaniama · Kapona
Ambriz · Uige · Pomba · Kahemba · Canzar · ZAIRE · Mwanza · Manono
Nova Caipemba · Bungo · Camaxilo · Verissimo · Kapanga · Kamina · Upemba · Chiengi · Mpulu
Luanda · Caxito · Quibaxe · Cambatela · Caungula · Sarmento · Kolwezi · Nat.Pk. · Bukama · L.Mweru · Mporokoso
Quicama · Ndalatando · Duque De Braganca · Cuango · Lubalo · Saurimo · Muriege · Sandoa · Tenke · Guba · Kasenga · Luwin
Nat.Pk. · Dondo · Lucala · Quela · Capenda · Mutshatsha · Kolwezi · Likasi · Lubudi · Kasenga
Gunza · Calulo · Malanje · Camulemba · Kasaji · Luishia · Mansa
Quibala · Mussende · Nova Gaia · Quirima · Dala · Cacolo · Nova Chaves · Dilolo · Solwezi · Kipushi · Lubumbashi · Sakania
Sumbe · Andulo · Bié · Canacupa · Lumeje · Cazombo · Mwinilunga · Chililabombwe · Chingola · Kitwe · Ndola
Lobito · Balombo · Chinguar · Huambo · Lucusse · Cassamba · Zambezi · Kasempa · Luanshya · Mufulira
Benguela · Bocoio · Caála · Lumbala · Kabompo · Kabwe · Mposhi · Chisamba
ANGOLA · ZAMBIA

MAURITIUS · Port Louis · Round I.
St Denis · Réunion (Fr.)
at the same scale

1:15M

0	200	400	600 km			
0	100	200	300 mls			

L. Rukwa
Sumbawanga
anga
Chunya
Mbeya Rungwe ▲2959
Iduma
Tukuyu
Karonga
Isoka
Chilumba
hinsali
Mbamba Bay
Rumphi
Shiwa
Ngandu
Mzuzu
Nkhata Bay
Apika Mzimba
Lundazi
Kasungu
hilongozi
Mchinji
hipata
Lilongwe
Dedza
Furancungo
Zomba
Chiçoa
Magoé
Blantyre
Teté
Chikwawa
Limbe

Ruaha Nat.Pk.
Mikumi
Iringa
Ifakara
Mahenge
Sao Hill
Njombe
Liwale
Manda
Nachingwea
Songea
Tunduru
Newala
Mecula
Lichinga
Maúa
Namuno
Mandimba
Mangoche
Salima
Malema Ribauè
Chilwa Alto Molócuè
Milange
Logela
Mocuba
Morrumbala

Kisiju
Mafia I.
Mohoro
Kilwa Kivinje
Kilwa Kisiwani
Lindi
Mtwara
Masasi
C.Delgado
Palma
Mocimboa da Praia
Ibo
Quissanga
Pemba
Mecufi
Namapa
Memba
Nacala
Moçambique
Nampula
Mogincual
Angoche
Gilé
Moma

SEYCHELLES
Aldabra Is
Assumption
Cosmoledo Is
Providence
Farquhar Is

Grande Comore
Moroni
Mutsamudu
Mahéli
COMOROS
Anjouan
Mayotte (Fr.)
Dzaoudzi

Is Glorieuses
Cap d'Ambre
C. St Sébastien
Antseranana
▲1478 Mgne d'Ambre
Ambilobe Nosy Bé
Ambanja
Vohimarina
Massif du Tsaratanana ▲2876
Sambava
Bealanana
B.Antongila
Analalava
Antsohiny
Antalaha
B. de Mahajamba
Befandriana
Maroantsetra
Mahajanga (Majunga)
Marovoay
Mampikony
Mandritsara
C.Masoala
Nosy Boraha
C. St André
Ambato Boeny
Tsaratanana
Ivongo
Soanierana
Ambodifototra
Fenoarivo Atsinanana
Besalampy
Juan de Nova (Fr.)
Morafenobe
Ankazobe
Anjozorobe
Toamasina (Tamatave)
Maintirano
Nosy Barren
Vohibinany

MADAGASCAR
(MALAGASY REP.)

Isoraromafiuluy
Murumanga
Ambatolampy ▲2643
Antananarivo (Tananarive)
Miandrivazo
Betafo
Antsirabe
Mahanoro
Morondava
Manabo
Atofinandrahana
Nosy Varika
Malaimbandy
Ambositra
Manja
Ambohimahasoa
Mananjary
Fianarantsoa
Ifahadiana
Ambalavao
Morombe
C.St Vincent
Ankazoabo
Massif de l'Isalo
Ivohibe
Manakara
Sakaraha
Ihosy
Farafangana
Tollara
Betroka
Vangaindrano
B.de St Augustin
Onilahy
Midongy Atsimo
Betioky
Bekily
Isoanala
Ampanihy
Amboasary
Beloha
Taolañaro
Tsihombe
Ambovombe
C. Ste Marie

Juan de Nova
Bassas da India (Fr.)
Europa (Fr.)

Mozambique Channel

1:7.5M

Swartruggens
Rustenburg
Brits
Middelburg
Waterval
Belfast Boven
Barberton
Marracuene
Maputo
Mafikeng
Koster
Pretoria
Witbank
Carolina
Komati
Namaacha
Matola
Baía de Maputo
Krugersdorp
Johannesburg
Germiston
Leslie
Breyten
Mbabane
SWAZILAND
Bela Vista
Carletonville
Heidelberg
Springs
Ermelo
Manzini
Stegi
Potchefstroom
Sasolburg
Vereeniging
Standerton
Amsterdam
Piet Retief
Nhlangano
Layumisa
Klerksdorp
Parys
Villiers
Morgenzon
Amersfoort
Usutu
Vryburg
Vaal Dam
Frankfort
Wilge
Paulpietersburg
Utrecht
Pongola
Sibayi L.
Ouaggablat
Bloemhof Dam
Heilbron
Vrede
Newcastle
Vryheid
Mkuzi
Warrenton
Christiana
Hoopstad
Odendaalsrus
Welkom
Lindley
Reitz
Warden
Drakensberg ▲2038
Dundee
Glencoe
Wasbank
Nongoma
Mtubatuba
L.St Lucia
ORANGE FREE STATE
Virginia
Ventersburg
Bethlehem
Harrismith
▲1905
Ladysmith
NATAL
Melmoth
Eshowe
Empangeni
Richard's Bay
Kimberley
Boshof
Brandfort
Ficksburg
Colenso
Weenen
Gingindlovu
Bloemfontein
Dealesville
Teyateyaneng
Maseru
Estcourt
Mooi River
Greytown
New Hanover
Stanger
Tongaat
Verulam
Durban
LESOTHO
Thaba Putsoa
Pietermaritzburg
Richmond

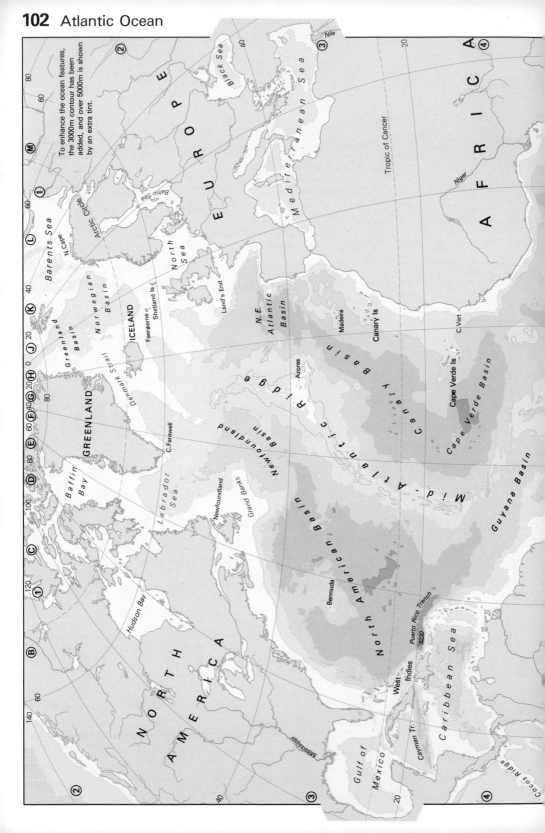

To enhance the ocean features, the 3000m contour has been added, and over 5000m is shown by an extra tint.

EUROPE

AFRICA

NORTH AMERICA

GREENLAND

ICELAND

Black Sea

Mediterranean Sea

Nile

Niger

Tropic of Cancer

Baltic Sea

Arctic Circle

N. Cape

Barents Sea

North Sea

Shetland Is

Faeröerne

Land's End

Norwegian Basin

Greenland Basin

Denmark Strait

Baffin Bay

C. Farewell

Labrador Sea

Hudson Bay

Newfoundland

Grand Banks

Newfoundland Basin

N.E. Atlantic Basin

Azores

Madeira

Canary Is

C. Vert

Cape Verde Is

Canary Basin

Cape Verde Basin

Mid-Atlantic Ridge

North American Basin

Guyana Basin

Bermuda

Puerto Rico Trench

9220

West Indies

Caribbean Sea

Cayman Tr.

Cocos Ridge

Gulf of Mexico

Mississippi

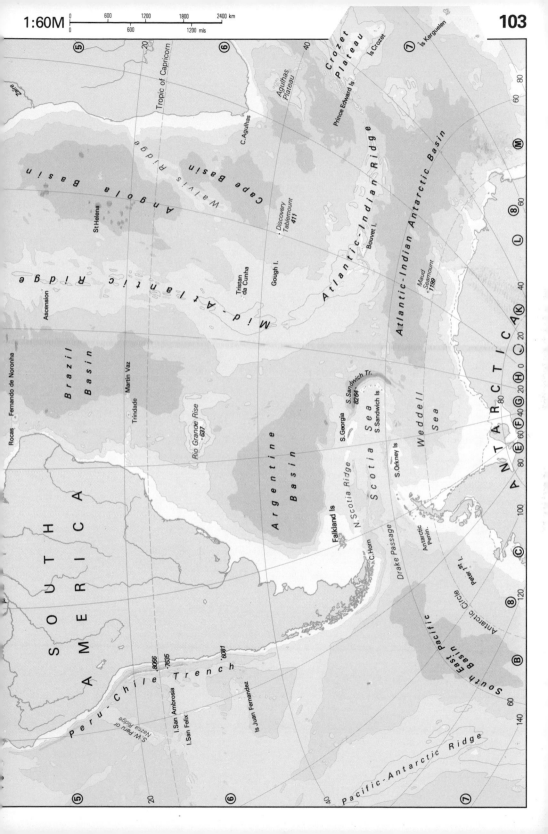

1:60M

0 — 600 — 1200 — 1800 — 2400 km
0 — 600 — 1200 mls

SOUTH AMERICA

Zaire

Tropic of Capricorn

Angola Basin

St Helena

Walvis Ridge

Cape Basin

Agulhas Plateau

C. Agulhas

Crozet Plateau

Is Crozet

Prince Edward Is

Is Kerguelen

Discovery Tablemount 411

Atlantic-Indian Ridge

Atlantic-Indian Antarctic Basin

Bouvet I.

Mid-Atlantic Ridge

Ascension

Tristan da Cunha

Gough I.

Maud Seamount 1159

Brazil Basin

Rocas

Fernando de Noronha

Martin Vaz

Trindade

Rio Grande Rise 637

Falkland Is

S. Georgia

S. Sandwich Tr. 8264

S. Sandwich Is

Scotia Sea

Weddell Sea

Argentine Basin

N. Scotia Ridge

Scotia Ridge

S. Orkney Is

Antarctic Penin.

Drake Passage

C. Horn

ANTARCTICA

Peter I. I.

Antarctic Circle

South East Pacific Basin

Peru-Chile Trench

8066
7635
6091

S.W. Peru or Nazca Ridge

I. San Ambrosia
I. San Felix

Is Juan Fernandez

Pacific-Antarctic Ridge

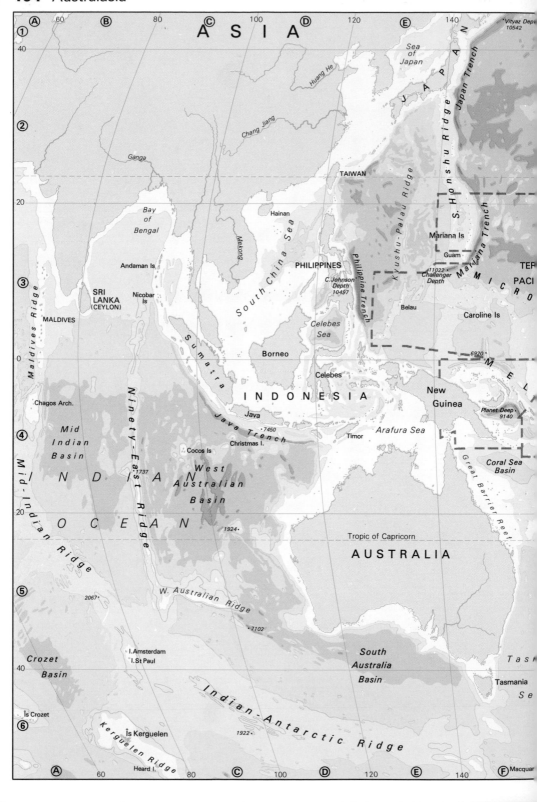

Ⓐ 60 Ⓑ 80 Ⓒ 100 Ⓓ 120 Ⓔ 140

①

*Vityaz Depth 10542

40

A S I A

Sea of Japan

Huang He

Chang Jiang

②

Ganga

J A P A N

Japan Trench

TAIWAN

20

S. Honshu Ridge

Mariana Trench

Bay of Bengal

Hainan

Kyushu-Palau Ridge

Mariana Is

Guam

TER
PACI

Andaman Is

Mekong

PHILIPPINES

Philippine Trench

11022
Challenger Depth

MICRO

③

Maldives Ridge

SRI
LANKA
(CEYLON)

Nicobar Is

C. Johnson Depth 10497

Belau

Caroline Is

MALDIVES

South China Sea

Celebes Sea

6920•

Chagos Arch.

Sumatra

Borneo

Celebes

New
Guinea

MEL

Mid-Indian Ridge

0

Mid
Indian
Basin

Ninety-East Ridge

Java Trench

I N D O N E S I A

Planet Deep• 9140

Java

•7450

④

N

D

Cocos Is

I

Christmas I.

A

West
Australian
Basin

Timor

Arafura Sea

Great Barrier Reef

Coral Sea
Basin

•1737

O

C

E

A

N

20

•1924

Tropic of Capricorn

A U S T R A L I A

Ta

W. Australian Ridge

⑤

2067•

•7102

I.Amsterdam
I.St Paul

40

Crozet
Basin

South
Australia
Basin

Tasmania

Se

Îs Crozet

Indian-Antarctic Ridge

⑥

Kerguelen Ridge

Îs Kerguelen

•1922

Ⓐ 60 Heard I. Ⓒ 100 Ⓓ 120 Ⓔ 140 Ⓕ Macquar

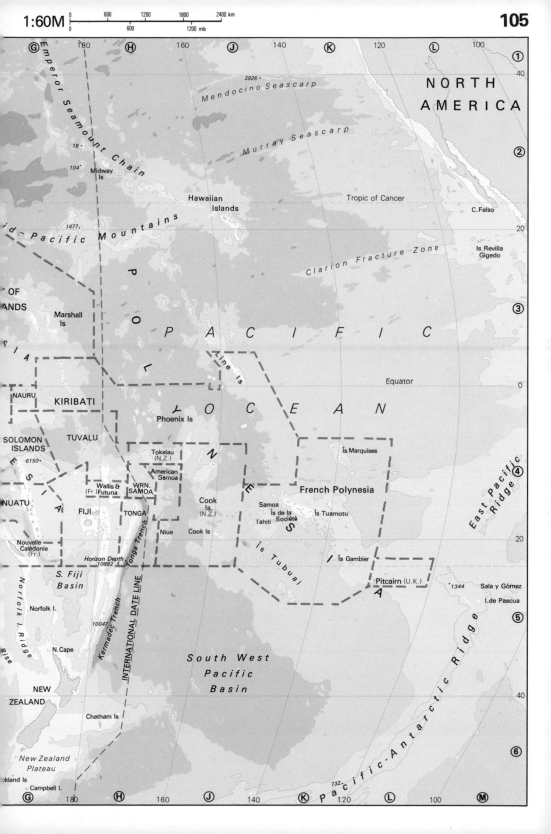

600 1200 1800 2400 km
600 1200 mls

G 180 H 160 J 140 K 120 L 100

① 40

Emperor Seamount Chain

Mendocino Seascarp

2926 ·

NORTH
AMERICA

②

Murray Seascarp

18 ·

104 · Midway Is

Hawaiian
Islands

Tropic of Cancer

C.Falso

20 ②

1477 ·

id- Pacific Mountains

Clarion Fracture Zone

Is Revilla
Gigedo

③

Y OF
ANDS

P
O
L
Y
N
E
S
I
A

Marshall
Is

P   A   C   I   F   I   C   C

Line Is

Equator 0

NAURU

KIRIBATI

Phoenix Is

O
C
E
A
N

Îs Marquises

East Pacific Ridge

④

SOLOMON
ISLANDS

6150 ·

TUVALU

Tokelau
(N.Z.)

American
Samoa

French Polynesia

NUATU

Wallis &
(Fr.)Futuna

WRN.
SAMOA

Cook
Is.
(N.Z.)

Samoa
Îs de la
Société

Îs Tuamotu

E
S
I
A

FIJI

TONGA

Niue

Cook Is

Tahiti

Îs Gambier

20

Nouvelle
Calédonie
(Fr.)

Horizon Depth
10082

Îs Tubuai

Pitcairn (U.K.)

· 1344

Sala y Gómez
I.de Pascua

Norfolk I. Ridge

Norfolk I.

10047

S. Fiji
Basin

INTERNATIONAL DATE LINE

Tonga Trench

⑤

N.Cape

Kermadec Trench

South West
Pacific

Pacific-Antarctic Ridge

40

NEW

Basin

ZEALAND

Chatham Is

New Zealand
Plateau

ckland Is

Campbell I.

732 ·

⑥

G 180 H 160 J 140 K 120 L 100 M

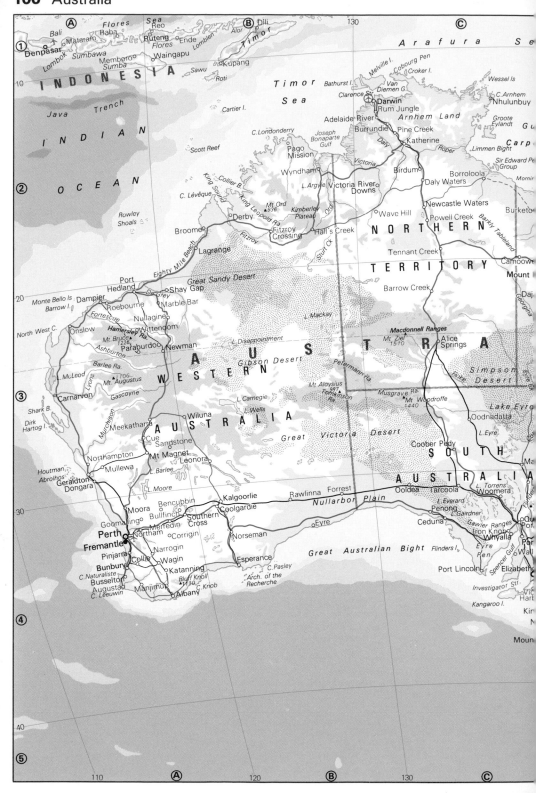

1:20M

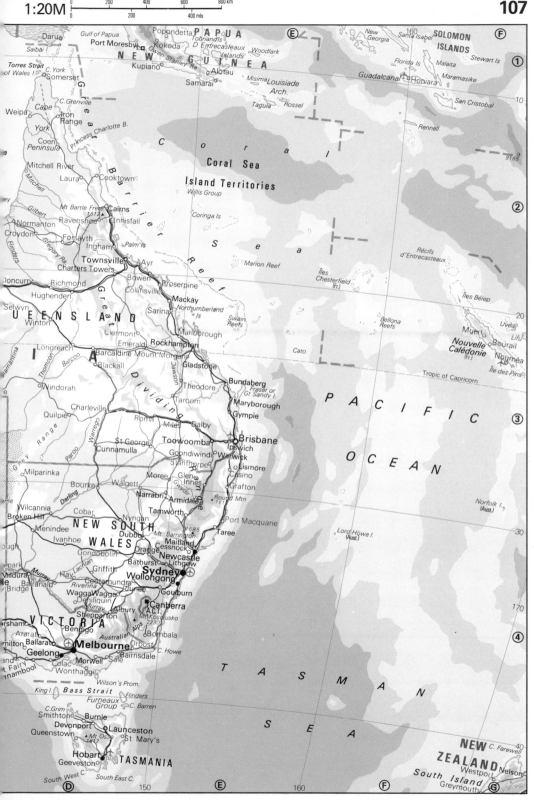

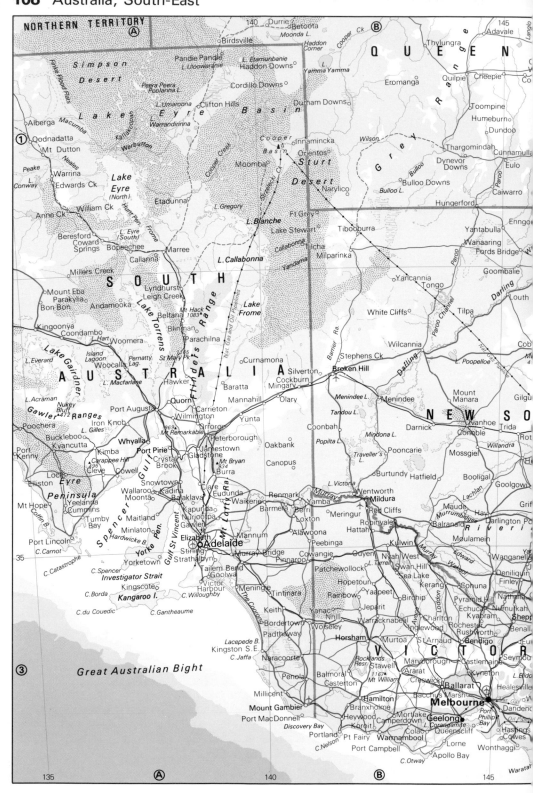

100 200 300 km
50 100 150 mils

Augathella C
LAND
Morven
Mungallala Mitchell
Muckadilla Roma Wallumbilla Miles
Mt Hutton Injune
Eurombah
Dawson
Taroom Mundubbera
Gayndah
Biggenden Maryborough
Double Island Pt
Goomeri
Murgon
Wondai
Gympie
Tewantin
Cooroy
Brooloo Nambour Maroochydore
Nanango Yarraman Caloundra
Kilcoy Caboolture
Toogoolawah
Crows Nest Redcliffe
Moreton I.
N. Stradbroke I.
Brisbane
Ipswich Beenleigh
Gold Coast
Beaudesert Tweed Heads
Boonah
Warwick Murwillumbah
Killarney Mullumbimby
C. Byron
Kyogle
Lismore
Casino Ballina
Woodburn
Yamba
Maclean
Grafton
Coff's Harbour

914 Mt Hutton
Wandoan
Guluguba
Kingaroy
Jandowae
Condamine Dalby
Tara
Meandarra
Glenmorgan
Oakey
Gatton
Pittsworth
Millmerran Clifton
Allora
Inglewood
Goondiwindi
Stanthorpe
Texas
Tenterfield
Ashford
Deepwater
Glen Innes
Glencoe
Glenreagh
Dorrigo Round Mtn
Bellingen
Nambucca Heads
Macksville
Smoky C.

Darling Downs
St George
Bollon
Dirranbandi
Thallon Talwood
Hebel Mungindi Boggabilla
Goodooga Garah
Lightning Ridge Ashley
Collarenebri Moree
Pokataroo Warialda
Rowena Bellata Bingara
Burren Jct Wee Waa Bundarra
Walgett Narrabri
Gwabegar Manilla
Boggabri
Baradine Guyra
Coonamble Coonabarabran Gunnedah Uralla Armidale
Walcha
Coolah Kempsey
Quirindi Tamworth Wauchope
Murrurundi Port Macquarie
Scone Kendall
Muswellbrook Gloucester Wingham
Merriwa Gulgong Forster
Dungog
Mudgee Singleton Maitland Port Stephens
Kandos Cessnock Raymond Terrace
Newcastle
L. Macquarie
Wyong Tuggerah L.
Lithgow
Richmond
Windsor
Parramatta Sydney
Campbelltown
Picton Wollongong
Camden Port Kembla
Bowral Shellharbour
Goulburn Nowra
Shoalhaven R.
Jervis B.
Ulladulla

PACIFIC OCEAN

Batemans Bay
Moruya
Canberra
A.C.T.
Queanbeyan
Cobargo
Bega
Merimbula
Eden

TASMANIA
Bass Strait
King I.
Flinders I.
Furneaux Group
Devonport
Launceston
Hobart

at the same scale

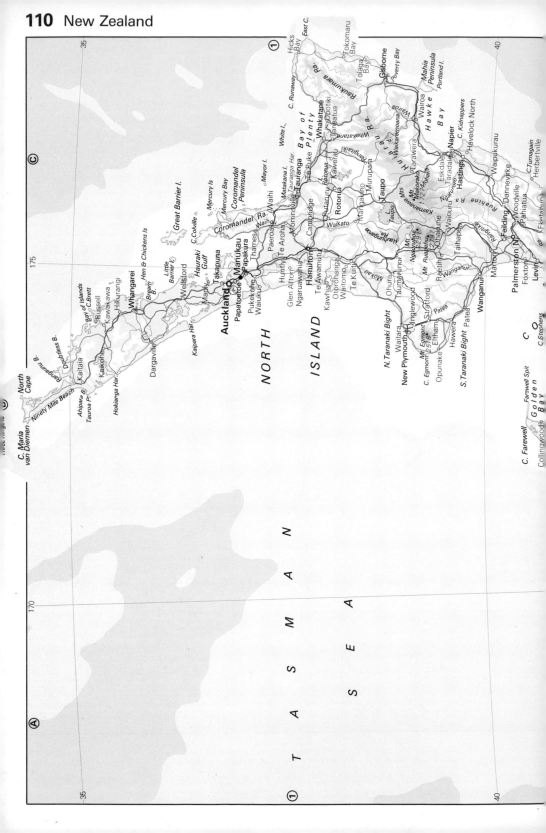

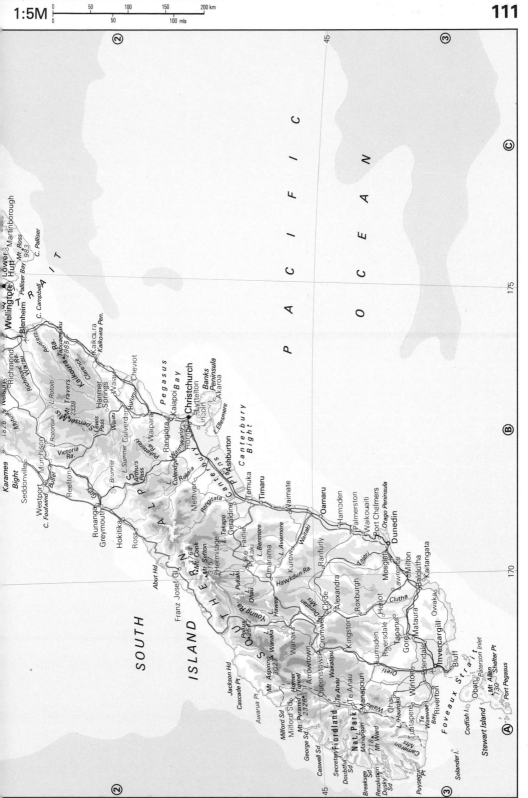

0 50 100 150 200 km
0   50   100 mls

② ③ ⓒ Ⓑ Ⓐ ② ③

SOUTH

ISLAND

SOUTHERN ALPS

P A C I F I C   O C E A N

45 175 170

Wellington
Lower Hutt
Martinborough
Palliser Bay
Mt Ross 983
C. Palliser
Blenheim
C. Campbell
Wairau
Tapuaenuku 2885
Kaikoura
Kaikoura Pen.
Clarence
Cheviot
Waiau
Hanmer Springs
Lewis Pass
Waipara
Rangiora
Kaiapoi
Pegasus Bay
Christchurch
Lyttelton
Banks Peninsula
Akaroa
Ellesmere
Lincoln
Homby
Waimakariri
Canterbury Bight
Rakaia
Ashburton
Temuka
Timaru
Waimate
Oamaru
Hamden
Palmerston
Waikouaiti
Port Chalmers
Otago Peninsula
Dunedin
Mosgiel
Milton
Balclutha
Kaitangata
Owaka
Clutha
Lawrence
Tapanui
Mataura
Gore
Clinton
Heriot
Roxburgh
Alexandra
Clyde
Cromwell
Ranfurly
Naseby
Kurow
Waitaki
Hawkdun Ra.
Omarama
L. Aviemore
L. Benmore
Fairlie
Lake Tekapo
L. Pukaki
Mt Cook 3764
Mt Sefton 3157
Hermitage
Geraldine
Methven
Rangitata
Mt Tasman
Franz Josef Gl.
Fox Gl.
Abut Hd
Ross
Hokitika
Greymouth
Runanga
Reefton
Westport
C. Foulwind
Seddonville
Karamea Bight
Buller
Murchison
Victoria Ra.
Brunner
Grey
Inangahua
Nelson 1826
Richmond
Richmond Ra.
Mt Travers 2338
Spenser Mts
Rotoiti
Rotoroa
Arnold
Hope
Waiau
Culverden
Hurunui
L. Sumner
Coleridge
Waimakariri
Arthurs Pass
Rakaia
Wanaka
L. Wanaka
L. Hawea
Hawea
Mt Aspiring 3027
Young Ra.
Pollux 2542
Ohau
Twizel
Kurow
Arrowtown
Queenstown
Frankton
Lumsden
Kingston
Riversdale
Wyndham
Winton
Balfour
Oreti
Invercargill
Bluff
Foveaux Strait
Obans
Mt Allen 730
Shelter Pt
Port Pegasus
Stewart Island
Codfish Island
Solander I.
Paysegur Pt
Dusky Sd
Resolution I.
Breaksea Sd
Doubtful Sd
George Sd
Caswell Sd
Secretary I.
Milford Sd
Milford Sd.
Mt Pyramid Tunnel 2326
Homer Tunnel
Te Anau
Lake Te Anau
L. Manapouri
Manapouri
Mt Ward 718
Cameron Mts
Waiau
Te Waewae Bay
Tuatapere
Riverton
Otautau
Wairaki
Mataura
Waikaia
Waipahi
Gore
Jackson Hd
Cascade Pt
Awarua Pt
Haast
Makarora
Lindis

Fiordland Nat. Park

Tararua
Ruahine

1:40M

0 400 800 1200 1600
0 400 800 mls

INDIAN OCEAN

Heard I. (Aust.)

Shackleton Ice Shelf
Knox Coast
C. Poinsett
Casey (Aust.)
Mirny (U.S.S.R.)
Queen Mary Land
C. Darnley
Davis (Aust.)
Amery Ice Shelf
Pt. Charles Gl.
Lambert Gl.
3355
American Highland
Mawson (Aust.)
Molodezhnaya (U.S.S.R.)
MacRobertson Land
Enderby Land
Syowa (Jap.)
Mizuho (Jap.)
Novolazarevskaya (U.S.S.R.)
Prinsesse Ragnhild Kyst
Prinsesse Astrid Kyst
Dronning Maud Land
Sanae (S.A.)
C. Norvegia
Coats Land
Halley (U.K.)

GREATER ANTARCTICA
Vostok (U.S.S.R.)
Wilkes Land
S. Magnetic Pole (1980)
Dumont d'Urville (Fr.)
Terre Adélie
George V Land
Oates Land
Leningradskaya (U.S.S.R.)
Sturge I.
Balleny Is
Scott I.

South Pole
Amundsen-Scott (U.S.)
Transantarctic Mts
Victoria Land
C. Adare
McMurdo (U.S.)
Scott (N.Z.)
C. Edare

Pensacola Mts
Q. Maud Mts
Mt Kirkpatrick 4528
Mt Markham 4351
Ross Ice Shelf
Roosevelt I.
C. Colbeck
Ross Sea
average minimum extent of sea ice

Grl Belgrano (Arg.)
Ronne Ice Shelf
Berkner I.
Ellsworth Land
5140 Vinson Massif
3022 Mt Seelig
LESSER ANTARCTICA
Marie Byrd Land
Mt Sidney 4181
Siple I.
Walgreen Coast
Siple (U.S.)
Palmer Land
Alexander I.
Charcot I.
Thurston I.
Peter I Øy (Nor.)
Amundsen Sea
Bellingshausen Sea

Graham Land
Antarctic Peninsula
Palmer Arch.
S. Shetland Is (U.K.)
S. Orkney Is (U.K.)
Orcadas (Arg.)
Signy (U.K.)
Scotia Sea
Falkland Is (U.K.)
ATLANTIC OCEAN
Weddell Sea
Drake Passage
Tierra del Fuego
ARGENTINA
CHILE

Antarctic Circle

PACIFIC OCEAN

Other Permanent Stations

1. Arctowski (Pol.)
2. Bellingshausen (U.S.S.R.)
3. Teniente Rodolfo Marsh (Ch.)
4. Arturo Prat (Ch.)
5. Petrel (Arg.)
6. Esperanza (Arg.)
7. Grl B.O'Higgins (Ch.)
8. Vice Marambio (Arg.)
9. T.Marienko (Arg.)
10. Almte Brown (Arg.)
11. Palmer (U.S.)
12. Faraday (U.K.)
13. Grl S.Martin (Arg.)

Index

In the index, the first number refers to the page, and the following letter and number to the section of the map in which the index entry can be found. For example, Paris 48C2 means that Paris can be found on page 48 where column C and row 2 meet.

Abbreviations used in the index

Adré

Adré *Chad*	98C1	Aïoun El Atrouss		Aksay *USSR*	61H3	Ålborg *Den*	39G7
Adri *Libya*	95A2	*Maur*	97B3	Aksayquin Hu, L		Al Brayqah *Libya*	95A1
Adria *Italy*	47E2	Aiquile *Bol*	30C2	*China*	84D1	Al Bū Kamāl *Syria*	93D3
Adrian, Michigan *USA*	14B2	Aïr, Desert Region		Akşehir *Turk*	92B2	Albula, R *Switz*	47C1
Adriatic S *Italy/Yugos*	52B2	*Niger*	97C3	Akseki *Turk*	92B2	Albuquerque *USA*	9C3
Aduwa *Eth*	99D1	Airdrie *Can*	13E2	Aksenovo Zilovskoye		Al Buraymi *Oman*	91C5
Adzopé *Ivory Coast*	97B4	Aire *France*	46B1	*USSR*	63D2	Al Burdi *Libya*	95B1
Aegean, S *Greece*	55B3	Aire, R *Eng*	42D3	Aksha *USSR*	68D1	Albury *Aust*	107D4
Afghanistan, Republic		Aire, R *France*	46C2	Aksu *China*	82C1	Al Buşayyah *Iraq*	93E3
Asia	80E2	Airforce I *Can*	6C3	Aktogay *USSR*	65J5	Alcalá de Henares	
Afgooye *Somalia*	99E2	Airolo *Switz*	47C1	Aktumsyk *USSR*	61J4	*Spain*	50B1
Afikpo *Nig*	97C4	Aishihik *Can*	4E3	Aktyubinsk *USSR*	65G4	Alcamo *Italy*	53B3
Åfjord *Nor*	38G6	Aishihik L *Can*	12G2	Akureyri *Iceland*	38B1	Alcaniz *Spain*	51B1
Aflou *Alg*	96C1	Aisne, Department		Akzhal *USSR*	65K5	Alcântara *Brazil*	31C2
Afmadu *Somalia*	99E2	*France*	46B2	Alabama, State *USA*	11B3	Alcaraz *Spain*	50B2
Afollé, Region *Maur*	97A3	Aisne, R *France*	49C2	Alabama, R *USA*	11B3	Alcázar de San Juan	
Afula *Israel*	94B2	Aitape *PNG*	71F4	Alabaster *USA*	17A1	*Spain*	50B2
Afyon *Turk*	92B2	Aiviekste, R *USSR*	58D1	Ala Dağlari, Mts *Turk*	92C2	Alcira *Spain*	51B2
Agadem *Niger*	95A3	Aixa Zuogi *China*	72B2	Alagir *USSR*	61F5	Alcobaça *Brazil*	35D1
Agadez *Niger*	97C3	Aix-en-Provence		Alagna *Italy*	47B2	Alcolea de Pinar	
Agadir *Mor*	96B1	*France*	49D3	Alagoas, State *Brazil*	31D3	*Spain*	50B1
Agar *India*	85D4	Aix-les-Bains *France*	47A2	Alagoinhas *Brazil*	31D4	Alcoy *Spain*	51B2
Agartala *India*	86C2	Aiyar Res *India*	86B2	Alagón *Spain*	51B1	Alcudia *Spain*	51C2
Agassiz *Can*	20B1	Aíyion *Greece*	55B3	Al Ahmadi *Kuwait*	93E4	Aldabra, Is *Indian O*	89J8
Agboville *Ivory Coast*	97B4	Aíyna, I *Greece*	55B3	Alajuela *Costa Rica*	25D3	Aldan *USSR*	63E2
Agdam *USSR*	93E1	Aïzawl *India*	86C2	Alakanuk *USA*	12B2	Aldanskoye Nagor'ye,	
Agematsu *Japan*	75B1	Aizu-Wakamatsu		Alakurtti *USSR*	38L5	Upland *USSR*	63E2
Agen *France*	48C3	*Japan*	74E3	Al Amärah *Iraq*	93E3	Aldeburgh *Eng*	43E3
Agha Järi *Iran*	90A3	Ajaccio *Corse*	52A2	Alameda *USA*	21A2	Alderney, I *UK*	48B2
Agno, R *Italy*	47D2	Ajalpan *Mexico*	23B2	Alamo *Mexico*	23B1	Aldershot *Eng*	43D4
Agordo *Italy*	47E1	Ajdabiyah *Libya*	95B1	Alamogordo *USA*	9C3	Aleg *Maur*	97A3
Agout, R *France*	48C3	Ajigasawa *Japan*	74E2	Alamosa *USA*	9C3	Alegrete *Brazil*	30E4
Ägra *India*	85D3	Ajlūn *Jordan*	94B2	Åland, I *Fin*	39H6	Alejandro Roca *Arg*	34C2
Ağri *Turk*	93D2	Ajman *UAE*	91C4	Alanya *Turk*	92B2	Alejandro Selkirk, I	
Agri, R *Italy*	53C2	Ajmer *India*	85C3	Alapaha, R *USA*	17B1	*Chile*	30H6
Agrigento *Italy*	53B3	Ajo *USA*	9B3	Alapayevsk *USSR*	65H4	Aleksandrovsk	
Agrínion *Greece*	55B3	Ajtos *Bulg*	54C2	Alaşehir *Turk*	92A2	Sakhalinskiy *USSR*	63G2
Agrio, R *Chile*	34A3	Ajuchitan *Mexico*	23A2	Ala Shan, Mts *China*	68C3	Alekseyevka *USSR*	65J4
Agropoli *Italy*	53B2	Ak, R *Turk*	55C3	Alaska, State *USA*	4C3	Aleksin *USSR*	60E3
Agryz *USSR*	61H2	Akaishi-sanchi, Mts		Alaska, G of *USA*	4D4	Älem *Sweden*	58B1
Agto *Greenland*	6E3	*Japan*	75B1	Alaska Pen *USA*	12C3	Além Paraíba *Brazil*	35C2
Aguadilla *Puerto Rico*	27D3	Akalkot *India*	87B1	Alaska Range, Mts		Alençon *France*	49C2
Agua Prieta *Mexico*	24B1	Akaroa *NZ*	111B2	*USA*	4C3	Alenuihaha Chan	
Aguascalientes		Akashi *Japan*	75A2	Alassio *Italy*	52A2	*Hawaiian Is*	21C4
Mexico	24B2	Akbulak *USSR*	61J3	Alatna, R *USA*	12D1	Alert *Can*	6D1
Aguascalientes, State		Akçakale *Turk*	93C2	Alatyr *USSR*	61G3	Alès *France*	49C3
Mexico	23A1	Akchar, Watercourse		Alawoona *Aust*	108B2	Alessandria *Italy*	52A2
Aguas Formosas *Brazil*	35C1	*Maur*	96A2	Al'Ayn *UAE*	91C5	Ålesund *Nor*	64B3
Agueda *Port*	50A1	Ak Dağ, Mt *Turk*	55C3	Alayskiy Khrebet, Mts		Aleutian Range, Mts	
Aguelhok *Mali*	96C3	Aketi *Zaïre*	98C2	*USSR*	82B2	*USA*	12C3
Agüenit, Well *Mor*	96A2	Akhalkalaki *USSR*	93D1	Alba *Italy*	49D3	Alexander Arch *USA*	4E4
Aguilas *Spain*	50B2	Akhalsikhe *USSR*	93D1	Al Bāb *Syria*	92C2	Alexander Bay *S	
Aguililla *Mexico*	23A2	Akharnái *Greece*	55B3	Albacete *Spain*	51B2	Africa*	100A3
Agulhas,C *S Africa*	100B4	Akhiok *USA*	12D3	Alba de Tormes *Spain*	50A1	Alexander City *USA*	17A1
Agusan, R *Phil*	79C4	Akhisar *Turk*	92A2	Al Badi *Iraq*	93D2	Alexander I *Ant*	112C3
Ahar *Iran*	93E2	Akhiste *USSR*	58D1	Alba Iulia *Rom*	54B1	Alexandra *NZ*	111A3
Ahipara B *NZ*	110B1	Akhmîm *Egypt*	95C2	Albania, Republic		Alexandra,C *South	
Ahmadäbäd *India*	85C4	Akhtubinsk *USSR*	61G4	*Europe*	54A2	Georgia*	29G8
Ahmadnagar *India*	87A1	Akhtyrka *USSR*	60D4	Albany *Aust*	106A4	Alexandra Fjord *Can*	6C2
Ahmar, Mts *Eth*	99E2	Aki *Japan*	75A2	Albany, Georgia *USA*	17B1	Alexandria *Egypt*	95B1
Ahr, R *W Germ*	46D1	Akimiski I *Can*	7B4	Albany, New York		Alexandria, Louisiana	
Ahrgebirge, Region *W		Akita *Japan*	74E3	*USA*	15D2	*USA*	11A3
Germ*	46D1	Akjoujt *Maur*	96A3	Albany, Oregon *USA*	8A2	Alexandria, Minnesota	
Ahuacatlán *Mexico*	23A1	'Akko *Israel*	94B2	Albany, R *Can*	7B4	*USA*	10A2
Ahualulco *Mexico*	23A1	Aklavik *Can*	4E3	Albardón *Arg*	34B2	Alexandria, Virginia	
Åhus *Sweden*	39G7	Aklé Aouana, Desert		Al Batinah, Region		*USA*	10C3
Åhuvän *Iran*	90B2	Region *Maur*	97B3	*Oman*	91C5	Alexandroúpolis	
Ahväz *Iran*	90A3	Akobo *Sudan*	99D2	Albatross B *Aust*	71F5	*Greece*	55C2
Aiajuela *Costa Rica*	26A4	Akobo, R *Sudan*	99D2	Al Baydā *Libya*	95B1	Alexis Creek *Can*	13C2
Aigle *Switz*	47B1	Akoha *Afghan*	84B1	Albemarle Sd *USA*	11C3	Aley *Leb*	94B2
Aiguille d'Arves, Mt		Akola *India*	85D4	Alberche, R *Spain*	50B1	Aleysk *USSR*	65K4
France*	47B2	Akot *India*	85D4	Alberga *Aust*	108A1	Al Fallūjah *Iraq*	93D3
Aiguille de la Grand		Akpatok I *Can*	6D3	Albert *France*	46B1	Alfaro *Spain*	51B1
Sassière, Mt *France*	47B2	Ákra Kafirévs, C		Alberta, Province *Can*	5G4	Alfatar *Bulg*	54C2
Aikawa *Japan*	75B1	*Greece*	55B3	Albert,L *Uganda/Zaïre*	99D2	Al Fāw *Iraq*	93E3
Aiken *USA*	17B1	Ákra Maléa, C *Greece*	55B3	Albert Lea *USA*	10A2	Alfensas *Brazil*	35B2
Ailao Shan, Upland		Akranes *Iceland*	38A2	Albert Nile, R *Uganda*	99D2	Alfiós, R *Greece*	55B3
China	73A5	Ákra Sídheros, C		Albertville *France*	49D2	Alfonsine *Italy*	47D2
Aimorés *Brazil*	35C1	*Greece*	55C3	Albi *France*	48C3	Alfonzo Cláudio *Brazil*	35C2
Ain Beni Mathar *Mor*	96B1	Ákra Spátha, C		Albia *USA*	18B1	Alfredo Chaves *Brazil*	35C2
Ain Dalla, Well *Egypt*	95B2	*Greece*	55B3	Albina *Suriname*	33G2	Alga *USSR*	61J4
Aïn el Hadjel *Alg*	51C2	Ákra Taínaron, C		Albion, Michigan *USA*	14B2	Algarrobo del Águila	
Aïn Galakka *Chad*	95A3	*Greece*	55B3	Albion, New York		*Arg*	34B3
Aïn Sefra *Alg*	96B1	Akron *USA*	10B2	*USA*	15C2	Algeciras *Spain*	50A2
'Ain Sukhna *Egypt*	92B4	Akrotiri B *Cyprus*	94A1	Al Bi'r *S Arabia*	92C4	Alger *Alg*	96C1
Aioi *Japan*	75A2	Aksai Chin, Mts *China*	84D1	Al Biyadh, Region *S		Algeria, Republic	
Aioun Abd el Malek,		Aksaray *Turk*	92B2	Arabia*	91A5	*Africa*	96B2
Well *Maur*	96B2			Alborán, I *Spain*	50B2	Alghero *Sardegna*	53A2

Andalucia

Andalucia, Region
Spain **50A2**
Andalusia USA **17A1**
Andaman Is Burma **83D4**
Andaman S Burma **83D4**
Andamooka Aust **108A2**
Andenes Nor **38H5**
Andermatt Switz **47C1**
Andernach W Germ **57B2**
Anderson, Indiana
USA **14A2**
Anderson, Missouri
USA **18B2**
Anderson, S Carolina
USA **17B1**
Anderson, R Can **4F3**
Andhra Pradesh, State
India **87B1**
Andikíthira, I Greece **55B3**
Andizhan USSR **65J5**
Andkhui USSR **65H6**
Andong S Korea **74B3**
Andorra, Principality
SW Europe **51C1**
Andorra-La-Vella
Andorra **51C1**
Andover Eng **43D4**
Andradina Brazil **35A2**
Andreafsky USA **12B2**
Andreas,C Cyprus **92B2**
Andria Italy **53C2**
Andros, I Bahamas **11C4**
Ándros, I Greece **55B3**
Androth, I India **87A2**
Andújar Spain **50B2**
Andulo Angola **100A2**
Anécho Togo **97C4**
Anéfis Mali **97C3**
Añelo Arg **34B3**
Angarsk USSR **63C2**
Ånge Sweden **38H6**
Angel de la Guarda, I
Mexico **24A2**
Angeles Phil **79B2**
Angelholm Sweden **39G7**
Angellala Creek, R
Aust **109C1**
Angels Camp USA **22B1**
Angemuk, Mt Indon **71E4**
Angers France **48B2**
Angkor, Hist Site
Camb **76C3**
Anglesey, I Wales **41C3**
Angleton USA **19A4**
Angmagssalik
Greenland **6G3**
Angoche Mozam **101D2**
Angol Chile **29B3**
Angola, Indiana USA **14B2**
Angola, Republic
Africa **100A2**
Angola Basin Atlantic
O **103H6**
Angoon USA **12H3**
Angoulême France **48C2**
Angra do Heroismo
Açores **96A1**
Angra dos Reis Brazil **35C2**
Anguil Arg **34C3**
Anguilla, I Caribbean **27E3**
Anguilla Cays, Is
Caribbean **26B2**
Angul India **86B2**
Angumu Zaïre **99C3**
Anholt, I Den **56C1**
Anhua China **73C4**
Anhui, Province China **72D3**
Aniak USA **12C2**
Anicuns Brazil **35B1**
Anizy-le-Château
France **46B2**
Anjak USA **4C3**
Anjou, Republic
France **48B2**
Anjouan, I Comoros **101D2**
Anjozorobe Madag **101D2**
Anju N Korea **74B3**
Ankang China **72B3**

Ankara Turk **92B2**
Ankaratra, Mt Madag **101D2**
Ankazoabo Madag **101D3**
Ankazobe Madag **101D2**
Anklam E Germ **56C2**
An Loc Viet **76D3**
Anlong China **73B4**
Anlu China **73C3**
Anna USA **18C2**
'Annaba Alg **96C1**
An Nabk S Arabia **92C3**
An Nabk Syria **92C3**
Anna Creek Aust **108A1**
An Najaf Iraq **93D3**
Annan Scot **42C2**
Annapolis USA **15C3**
Annapurna, Mt Nepal **86A1**
Ann Arbor USA **14B2**
An Nāsirah Syria **94C1**
An Nāsirīyah Iraq **93E3**
Annecy France **47B2**
Annemasse France **47B1**
An Nhon Viet **76D3**
Anning China **73A5**
Anniston USA **17A1**
Annonay France **49C2**
Annotto Bay Jamaica **27J1**
Anqing China **73D3**
Ansai China **72B2**
Ansbach W Germ **57C3**
Anse d'Hainault Haiti **26C3**
Anshan China **72E1**
Anshun China **73B4**
Ansongo Mali **97C3**
Ansted USA **14B3**
Antakya Turk **92C2**
Antalaha Madag **101E2**
Antalya Turk **92B2**
Antalya Körfezi, B
Turk **92B2**
Antananarivo Madag **101D2**
Antarctic Circle Ant **112C1**
Antarctic Pen Ant **112C3**
Antequera Spain **50B2**
Anti-Atlas, Mts Mor **96B2**
Anticosti I Can **7D5**
Antigua, I Caribbean **27E3**
Antioch USA **21A2**
Antlers USA **19A3**
Antofagasta Chile **30B3**
Antrim, County N Ire **45C1**
Antrim N Ire **45C1**
Antrim Hills N Ire **45C1**
Antseranana Madag **101D2**
Antsirabe Madag **101D2**
Antsohiny Madag **101D2**
An Tuc Viet **76D3**
Antwerpen Belg **46C1**
An Uaimh Irish Rep **45C2**
Anupgarh India **84C3**
Anuradhapura Sri
Lanka **87C3**
Anvik USA **4B3**
Anxi China **63B3**
Anyang China **72C2**
A'nyêmaqên Shan,
Upland China **72A3**
Anza, R Italy **47C2**
Anzac Can **13E1**
Anzhero-Sudzhensk
USSR **65K4**
Anzio Italy **53B2**
Aomori Japan **74E2**
Aosta Italy **52A1**
Aoukar, Desert Region
Maur **97B3**
Aoulef Alg **96C2**
Aozou Chad **95A2**
Apa, R Brazil/Par **30E3**
Apalachee B USA **11B4**
Apalachicola USA **17B2**
Apalachicola B USA **17A2**
Apan Mexico **23B2**
Apaporis, R Colombia **32C3**
Aparecida do
Taboado Brazil **35A2**
Aparri Phil **79B2**
Apatin Yugos **54A1**

Apatzingan Mexico **24B3**
Apeldoorn Neth **56B2**
Apiai Brazil **35B2**
Apo,Mt, Mt Phil **79C4**
Apollo Bay Aust **108B3**
Apopka,L USA **17B2**
Aporé, R Brazil **30F2**
Apostle Is USA **10A2**
Apostle L USA **10A2**
Apozol Mexico **23A1**
Appalachian Mts USA **11B3**
Appennino Abruzzese,
Mts Italy **52B2**
Appennino Ligure,
Mts Italy **52A2**
Appennino Lucano,
Mts Italy **53C2**
Appennino
Napoletano, Mts
Italy **53B2**
Appennino Tosco-
Emiliano, Mts Italy **52B2**
Appennino Tosco-
Emiliano, Mts Italy **52B2**
Appennino Umbro-
Marchigiano, Mts
Italy **52B2**
Appenzell Switz **47C1**
Appleby Eng **42C2**
Appleton, Wisconsin
USA **14A2**
Apucarana Brazil **30F3**
Apulco Mexico **23B1**
Apure, R Ven **32D2**
Apurimac, R Peru **32C6**
'Aqaba Jordan **92C4**
'Aqaba,G of Egypt/S
Arabia **92B4**
'Aqdā Iran **90B3**
Aquidauana Brazil **30E3**
Aquila Mexico **23A2**
Ara India **86A1**
Arab USA **17A1**
Arabian, S Asia/
Arabian Pen **81D4**
Aracajú Brazil **31D4**
Aracati Brazil **31D2**
Araçatuba Brazil **30F3**
Aracena Spain **50A2**
Araçuai Brazil **31C5**
Arad Israel **94B3**
Arad Rom **60B4**
Arada Chad **98C1**
'Arādah UAE **91B5**
Arafura S Indon/Aust **106C1**
Aragarças Brazil **30F2**
Aragón, Region Spain **51B1**
Aragon, R Spain **50B1**
Araguaia, R Brazil **33G6**
Araguaína Brazil **31B3**
Araguari Brazil **31B5**
Araguari, R Brazil **35B1**
Arai Japan **75B1**
Arak Alg **96C2**
Arāk Iran **90A3**
Arakan Yoma, Mts
Burma **76A2**
Arakkonam India **87B2**
Araks, R USSR **93E2**
Aral S USSR **62D3**
Aral'sk USSR **80E1**
Aral'skoye More, S
USSR **65G5**
Aran, I Irish Rep **40B2**
Aran, Is Irish Rep **41B3**
Aranda de Duero
Spain **50B1**
Arandas Mexico **23A1**
Aranjuez Spain **50B1**
Arao Japan **75A2**
Araouane Mali **97B3**
Arapey, R Urug **29E2**
Arapiraca Brazil **31D4**
Araporgas Brazil **35A2**
Ararangua Brazil **30G4**
Araraquara Brazil **31B6**
Araras Brazil **35B2**

Ararat Aust **107D4**
Ararat USSR **93D2**
Aras, R Turk **93D1**
Arato Japan **75C1**
Arauca, R Ven **32D2**
Arauco Chile **34A3**
Arauea Colombia **32C2**
Arävalli Range, Mts
India **85C4**
Araxá Brazil **31B5**
Arba Minch Eth **99D2**
Arbatax Sardegna **53A3**
Arbīl Iraq **93D2**
Arbois France **47A1**
Arbrå Sweden **39H6**
Arbroath Scot **44C3**
Arc France **47A1**
Arc, R France **47B2**
Arcachon France **48B3**
Arcadia USA **17B2**
Arcata USA **20B2**
Arcelia Mexico **23A2**
Archipiélago de
Camaguey, Arch
Cuba **26B2**
Archipiélago de la
Reina Adelaida,
Arch Chile **29B6**
Archipiélago de las
Chones, Arch Chile **29B4**
Archipiélago de las
Perlas, Arch Panama **32B2**
Arcos Brazil **35B2**
Arcos de la Frontera
Spain **50A2**
Arctic Circle **1C1**
Arctic Red Can **4E3**
Arctic Red R Can **4E3**
Arctic Village USA **4D3**
Arctowski, Base Ant **112C2**
Arda, R Bulg **54C2**
Ardabīl Iran **65F6**
Ardahan Turk **93D1**
Ardal Nor **39F6**
Ardar des Iforas,
Upland Alg/Mali **96C2**
Ardee Irish Rep **45C2**
Ardekān Iran **90B3**
Ardennes, Department
France **46C2**
Ardennes, Region
Belg **57A2**
Ardestan Iran **90B3**
Ardh es Suwwan,
Desert Region
Jordan **92C3**
Ardila, R Port **50A2**
Ardlethan Aust **109C2**
Ardmore USA **9D3**
Ardnamurchan, Pt
Scot **44A3**
Ardres France **46A1**
Ardrishaig Scot **44B3**
Ardrossan Scot **42B2**
Arecibo Puerto Rico **27D3**
Areia Branca Brazil **31D2**
Arena,Pt USA **21A2**
Arendal Nor **39F7**
Arequipa Peru **30B2**
Arezzo Italy **52B2**
Argenta Italy **52B2**
Argentan France **49C2**
Argenteuil France **46B2**
Argentina, Republic S
America **28C7**
Argentine Basin
Atlantic O **103F7**
Argenton-sur-Creuse
France **48C2**
Argeşul, R Rom **54C2**
Arghardab, R Afghan **84B2**
Argolikós Kólpos, G
Greece **55B3**
Argonne, Region
France **46C2**
Árgos Greece **55B3**
Argostólion Greece **55B3**
Arguello,Pt USA **22B3**

Argyle,L Aust	106B2	Arthurs P NZ	111B2
Århus Den	56C1	Artic Bay Can	6B2
Ariamsvlei Namibia	100A3	Artigas Urug	29E2
Arian zón, R Spain	50B1	Artillery L Can	4H3
Arias Arg	34C2	Artois, Region France	48C1
Aribinda Upper Volta	97B3	Arturo Prat, Base Ant	112C2
Arica Chile	30B2	Artvin Turk	93D1
Arifwala Pak	84C2	Aru Zaïre	99D2
Arima Trinidad	27L1	Aruanã Brazil	33G6
Arinos Brazil	35B1	Aruba, I Caribbean	27C4
Arinos, R Brazil	33F6	Arun, R Nepal	86B1
Ario de Rosales		Arunāchal Pradesh,	
Mexico	23A2	Union Territory India	86C1
Aripo,Mt Trinidad	27L1	Aruppukkottai India	87B3
Aripuana Brazil	33E5	Arusha Tanz	99D3
Aripuaná, R Brazil	33E5	Aruwimi, R Zaïre	98C2
Arisaig Scot	44B3	Arvayheer Mongolia	68C2
Ariskere India	87B2	Arve, R France	47B2
Aristazabal I Can	13B2	Arvida Can	7C5
Arizona Arg	34B3	Arvidsjaur Sweden	38H5
Arizona, State USA	9B3	Arvika Sweden	39G7
Årjäng Sweden	39G7	Arvin USA	21B2
Arkadak USSR	61F3	Arwad, I Syria	94B1
Arkadelphia USA	19B3	Arzamas USSR	61F2
Arkalya USSR	65H4	Asadabad Afghan	84C2
Arkansas, State USA	11A3	Asahi, R Japan	75A2
Arkansas, R USA	11A3	Asahi dake, Mt Japan	74E2
Arkansas City USA	18A2	Asahikawa Japan	74E2
Arkhangel'sk USSR	64F3	Asansol India	86B2
Arklow Irish Rep	41B3	Asawanwah, Well	
Arlberg P Austria	47D1	Libya	95A2
Arles France	49C3	Asbest USSR	61K2
Arlington, Texas USA	19A3	Asbury Park USA	15D2
Arlington, Virginia		Ascension, I Atlantic	
USA	15C3	O	103H5
Arlington, Washington		Aschaffenburg W	
USA	20B1	Germ	57B3
Arlit Niger	97C3	Aschersleben E Germ	56C2
Arlon Belg	57B3	Ascoli Piceno Italy	52B2
Armagh, County N Ire	45C1	Ascona Switz	47C1
Armagh N Ire	45C1	Asedjirad, Upland Alg	96C2
Armagós, I Greece	55C3	Asele Sweden	38H6
Armavir USSR	61F5	Aselle Eth	99D2
Armena Mexico	23A2	Asenovgrad Bulg	54B2
Armenia Colombia	32B3	Asfeld France	46C2
Armidale Aust	107E4	Asha USSR	61J2
Armstrong Can	13D2	Ashburn USA	17B1
Armyanskaya SSR,		Ashburton NZ	111B2
Republic USSR	65F5	Ashburton, R Aust	106A3
Arnaud, R Can	7C3	Ashdod Israel	92B3
Arnauti, C Cyprus	92B2	Ashdown USA	19B3
Arnhem Neth	56B2	Asheville USA	11B3
Arnhem,C Aust	106C2	Ashford Aust	109D1
Arnhem Land Aust	106C2	Ashford Eng	43E4
Arnold USA	22B1	Ashikaga Japan	74D3
Arnprior Can	15C1	Ashizuri-misaki, Pt	
Arnsberg W Germ	46E1	Japan	75A2
Aroab Namibia	100A3	Ashkhabad USSR	65G6
Arona Italy	47C2	Ashland, Kentucky	
Aropuk L USA	12B2	USA	10B3
Arosa Switz	52A1	Ashland, Nebraska	
Arquipélago dos		USA	18A1
Bijagós, Arch		Ashland, Ohio USA	14B2
Guinea-Bissau	97A3	Ashland, Oregon USA	8A2
Ar Ramādī Iraq	93D3	Ashley Aust	109C1
Arran, I Scot	42B2	Ashokan Res USA	16B2
Ar Raqqah Syria	93C2	Ashqelon Israel	94B3
Arras France	49C1	Ash Shabakh Iraq	93D3
Arrecife Canary Is	96A2	Ash Sha'm UAE	91C4
Arrecifes Arg	34C2	Ash Sharqāt Iraq	93D2
Arriaga Mexico	23A1	Ash Shatrah Iraq	93E3
Ar Rifā't Iraq	93E3	Ash Shihr S Yemen	81C4
Ar Rihāb, Desert		Ash Shumlul S Arabia	91A4
Region Iraq	93E3	Ashtabula USA	14B2
Arrochar Scot	44B3	Ashuanipi L Can	7D4
Arrowtown NZ	111A2	Asi, R Syria	92C3
Arroyo Seco Mexico	23B1	Asiago Italy	47D2
Ar Ru'ays Qatar	91B4	Asinara, I Medit S	53A2
Ar Rustaq Oman	91C5	Asino USSR	65K4
Ar Rutbah Iraq	93D3	Aşkale Turk	93D2
Arsiero Italy	47D2	Askorsund Sweden	39G7
Arsizio Italy	49D2	Asmar Afghan	84C1
Arsk USSR	61G2	Asmara Eth	95C3
Árta Greece	55B3	Aso Japan	75A2
Arteaga Mexico	23A2	Asosa Eth	99D1
Artemovsk USSR	63B2	Aspiring,Mt NZ	111A2
Artemovskiy USSR	63D2	Assab Eth	99E1
Artesia USA	9C3	As Sabkhah Syria	93C2

As Salamīyah S Arabia	91A5	Atoyac, R Mexico	23B2
As Salamīyah Syria	92C2	Atrato, R Colombia	32B2
As Salmān Iraq	93D3	Attaf, Region UAE	91B5
Assam, State India	86C1	At Tā'if S Arabia	81C3
As Samāwah Iraq	93E3	At Tall Syria	94C2
As Şanām, Region S		Attalla USA	17A1
Arabia	91B5	Attauapiskat Can	7B4
As Sanamayn Syria	94C2	Attauapiskat, R Can	7B4
Assen Neth	56B2	At Taysīyah, Desert	
Assens Den	56B1	Region S Arabia	93D3
As Sidrah Libya	95A1	Attica, Indiana USA	14A2
Assiniboia Can	5H5	Attigny France	46C2
Assiniboine,Mt Can	5G4	Attleboro,	
Assis Brazil	30F3	Massachusetts USA	15D2
As Sukhnah Syria	93C3	Attopeu Laos	76D3
As Summan, Region S		At Tubayq, Upland S	
Arabia	91A5	Arabia	92C4
Assumption, I		Atuel, R Arg	34B3
Seychelles	99E3	Atvidaberg Sweden	39H7
As Suwaydā' Syria	92C3	Atwater USA	22B2
As Suwayrah Iraq	93D3	Aubagne France	49D3
Astara USSR	93E2	Aube, Department	
Asti Italy	52A2	France	46C2
Astipálaia, I Greece	55C3	Aubenas France	49C3
Astorga Spain	50A1	Auburn, Alabama USA	17A1
Astoria USA	8A2	Auburn, California	
Astrakhan' USSR	61G4	USA	21A2
Asturias, Region Spain	50A1	Auburn, Indiana USA	14A2
Asunción Par	30E4	Auburn, Nebraska	
Aswa, R Uganda	99D2	USA	18A1
Aswân Egypt	80B3	Auburn, New York	
Aswân High Dam		USA	15C2
Egypt	95C2	Auburn, Washington	
Asyût Egypt	95C2	USA	20B1
As Zilaf Syria	92C3	Auch France	48C3
Atakpamé Togo	97C4	Auckland NZ	110D1
Atambua Indon	71D4	Auckland Is NZ	105G6
Atangmik Greenland	6E3	Aude, R France	48C3
Atar Maur	96A2	Auden Can	7B4
Atasu USSR	65J5	Audincourt France	47B1
Atbara Sudan	95C3	Augathella Aust	109C1
Atbasar USSR	65H4	Augsburg W Germ	57C3
Atchafalaya B USA	11A4	Augusta Italy	106A4
Atchison USA	10A3	Augusta, Georgia USA	11B3
Atco USA	16B3	Augusta, Kansas USA	18A2
Atenguillo Mexico	23A1	Augusta, Maine USA	10D2
Atessa Italy	52B2	Augustine I USA	12D3
Ath Belg	46B1	Augustow Pol	58C2
Athabasca Can	13E2	Augustus,Mt Aust	106A3
Athabasca, R Can	5G4	Aumale France	46A2
Athabasca L Can	5H4	Auraiya India	85D3
Athenry Irish Rep	45B2	Aurangābād India	85D5
Athens, Georgia USA	11B3	Aurès, Mts Alg	96C1
Athens, Ohio USA	14B3	Aurillac France	48C3
Athens, Texas USA	19A3	Aurora, Colorado USA	8C3
Athínai Greece	55B3	Aurora, Illinois USA	10B2
Athlone Irish Rep	41B3	Aurora, Indiana USA	14B3
Athol USA	16C1	Aurora, Mississippi	
Áthos, Mt Greece	55B2	USA	18B2
Athy Irish Rep	45C2	Aus Namibia	100A3
Ati Chad	98B1	Au Sable USA	14B2
Atikoken Can	7A5	Ausert, Well Mor	96A2
Atkarsk USSR	61F3	Austin, Minnesota	
Atkins USA	18B2	USA	10A2
Atlacomulco Mexico	23B2	Austin, Nevada USA	21B2
Atlanta, Georgia USA	11B3	Austin, Texas USA	9D3
Atlanta, Michigan		Australian Alps, Mts	
USA	14B2	Aust	107D4
Atlantic USA	18A1	Austria, Fed Republic	
Atlantic City USA	10C3	Europe	37E4
Atlantic Highlands		Authie, R France	46A1
USA	16B2	Autlán Mexico	24B3
Atlantic Indian Basin		Autun France	49C2
Atlantic O	103H8	Auvergne, Region	
Atlantic Indian Ridge		France	49C2
Atlantic O	103H7	Auxerre France	49C2
Atlas Saharien, Mts		Auxi-le-Château	
Alg	96C1	France	46B1
Atlin Can	4E4	Avallon France	49C2
Atlin L Can	4E4	Avalon USA	22C4
'Atlit Israel	94B2	Avalon Pen Can	7E5
Atlixco Mexico	23B2	Avaré Brazil	35B2
Atmore USA	11B3	Avaz Iran	90D3
Atofinandrahana		Avedat, Hist Site	
Madag	101D3	Israel	94B3
Atognak I USA	12D3	Aveíro Brazil	33F4
Atoka USA	19A3	Aveiro Port	50A1
Atotonilco Mexico	23A1	Avellaneda Arg	29E2

Avellino

6

Baluchistan, Region Pak	84B3
Bālurghāt India	86B1
Balykshi USSR	61H4
Bam Iran	91C4
Bama Nig	98B1
Bamako Mali	97B3
Bambari CAR	98C2
Bamberg USA	17B1
Bamberg W Germ	57C3
Bambili Zaïre	98C2
Bambui Brazil	35B2
Bamenda Cam	98B2
Bamfield Can	13C3
Bamingui, R CAR	98B2
Bamingui Bangoran, National Park CAR	98B2
Bamiyan Afghan	84B2
Bampur Iran	91D4
Bampur, R Iran	91D4
Banalia Zaïre	98C2
Banamba Mali	97B3
Ban Aranyaprathet Thai	76C3
Ban Ban Laos	76C2
Ban Betong Thai	77C4
Banbridge N Ire	45C1
Banbury Eng	43D3
Banchory Scot	44C3
Banco Chinchorro, Is Mexico	25D3
Bancroft Can	15C1
Bānda India	86A1
Banda Aceh Indon	70A3
Bandama, R Ivory Coast	97B4
Bandar Abbas Iran	91C4
Bandar Anzalī Iran	90A2
Bandar-e Daylam Iran	91B4
Bandar-e Lengheh Iran	91B4
Bandar-e Māqām Iran	91B4
Bandar-e Rig Iran	91B4
Bandar-e Torkoman Iran	90B2
Bandar Khomeynī Iran	91A3
Bandar Seri Begawan Brunei	78C2
Banda S Indon	71D4
Band Bont Iran	91C4
Bandeira, Mt Brazil	35C2
Bandiagara Mali	97B3
Bandirma Turk	60C5
Bandon Irish Rep	45B3
Bandundu Zaïre	98B3
Bandung Indon	78B4
Banes Cuba	25E2
Banff Can	13D2
Banff Scot	44C3
Banff, R Can	5G4
Banff Nat Pk Can	13D2
Bangalore India	87B2
Bangassou CAR	98C2
Banggi, I Malay	70C3
Bang Hieng, R Laos	76D2
Bangka, I Indon	78B3
Bangko Indon	78A3
Bangkok Thai	76C3
Bangladesh, Republic Asia	82C3
Bangong Co, L China	84D2
Bangor, Maine USA	10D2
Bangor N Ire	45D1
Bangor, Pennsylvania USA	16B2
Bangor Wales	42B3
Bangsalsembera Indon	78D3
Bang Saphan Yai Thai	76B3
Bangued Phil	79B2
Bangui CAR	98B2
Bangweulu, L Zambia	100C2
Ban Hat Yai Thai	77C4
Ban Hin Heup Laos	76C2
Ban Houei Sai Laos	76C1
Ban Hua Hin Thai	76B3
Bani, R Mali	97B3
Bani Bangou Niger	97C3
Banī Walīd Libya	95A1
Bāniyās Syria	92C3

Baniyas Syria	94B2
Banja Luka Yugos	52C2
Banjarmasin Indon	78C3
Banjul The Gambia	97A3
Ban Kantang Thai	77B4
Ban Khemmarat Laos	76D2
Ban Khok Kloi Thai	77B4
Banks I Aust	71F5
Banks I, British Columbia Can	5E4
Banks I, Northwest Territories Can	4F2
Banks L USA	20C1
Banks Pen NZ	111B2
Banks Str Aust	109C4
Bankura India	86B2
Ban Mae Sariang Thai	76B2
Ban Mae Sot Thai	76B2
Ban Me Thuot Viet	76D3
Bann, R N Ire	45C1
Ban Na San Thai	77B4
Bannu Pak	84C2
Baños Maule Chile	34A3
Ban Pak Neun Laos	76C2
Ban Pak Phanang Thai	77C4
Ban Ru Kroy Camb	76D3
Ban Sai Yok Thai	76B3
Ban Sattahip Thai	76C3
Banská Bystrica Czech	59B3
Bānswāra India	85C4
Ban Tha Kham Thai	77B4
Ban Thateng Laos	76D2
Ban Tha Tum Thai	76C2
Bantry Irish Rep	41B3
Bantry, B Irish Rep	41A3
Ban Ya Soup Viet	76D3
Banyuwangi Indon	78C4
Baofeng China	72C3
Bao Ha Viet	76C1
Baoji China	72B3
Bao Loc Viet	76D3
Baoshan China	68B4
Baotou China	72C1
Bāpatla India	87C1
Bapaume France	46B1
Ba'Qūbah Iraq	93D3
Baquerizo Morena Ecuador	32J7
Bar Yugos	54A2
Bara Sudan	99D1
Baraawe Somalia	99E2
Barabai Indon	78D3
Bāra Banki India	86A1
Barabinsk USSR	65J4
Barabinskaya Step, Steppe USSR	65J4
Baracaldo Spain	50B1
Baracoa Cuba	26C2
Baradá, R Syria	94C2
Baradine Aust	109C2
Bārāmati India	87A1
Baramula Pak	84C2
Bārān India	85D3
Barangas Phil	79B3
Baranof I USA	4E4
Baranovichi USSR	60C3
Baratta Aust	108A2
Barauni India	86B1
Barbacena Brazil	31C6
Barbados, I Caribbean	27F4
Barbastro Spain	51C1
Barberton S Africa	101H1
Barbezieux France	48B2
Barbòsa Colombia	32C2
Barbuda, I Caribbean	27E3
Barcaldine Aust	107D3
Barcellona Italy	53C3
Barcelona Spain	51C1
Barcelona Ven	33E1
Barcoo, R Aust	107D3
Barda del Medio Arg	34B3
Bardai Chad	95A2
Bardas Blancas Arg	29C3
Barddhamān India	86B2
Bardejov Czech	59C3
Bardi Italy	47C2
Bardonecchia Italy	47B2
Bardsey, I Wales	43B3

Bareilly India	84D3
Barentsøya, I Barents S	64D2
Barentu Eth	95C3
Bargarh India	86A2
Barge Italy	47B2
Barguzin USSR	63D2
Barguzin, R USSR	63D2
Barhi India	86B2
Bari Italy	53C2
Barika Alg	51D2
Barinas Ven	32C2
Baripāda India	86B2
Bari Sādri India	85C4
Barisal Bang	86C2
Barito, R Indon	78C3
Barjuj, Watercourse Libya	95A2
Barkam China	73A3
Barkley,L USA	18C2
Barkley Sd Can	13B3
Barkly East S Africa	100B4
Barkly Tableland, Mts Aust	106C2
Bar-le-Duc France	46C2
Barlee,L Aust	106A3
Barlee Range, Mts Aust	106A3
Barletta Italy	53C2
Barmer India	85C3
Barmera Aust	108B2
Barmouth Wales	43B3
Barnard Castle Eng	42D2
Barnaul USSR	65K4
Barnegat USA	16B3
Barnegat B USA	16B3
Barnes Icecap Can	6C2
Barnesville, Georgia USA	17B1
Barnesvillo, Ohio USA	14B3
Barnsley Eng	42D3
Barnstaple Eng	43B4
Baro Nig	97C4
Barpeta India	86C1
Barquisimeto Ven	32D1
Barra Brazil	31C4
Barra, I Scot	44A3
Barraba Aust	109D2
Barra de Navidad Mexico	23A2
Barra de Piraí Brazil	35C2
Barra do Garças Brazil	35A1
Barragem do Castelo do Bode, Res Port	50A2
Barragem do Maranhão Port	50A2
Barra Head, Pt Scot	44A3
Barra Mansa Brazil	31C6
Barranca Peru	32B6
Barrancabermeja Colombia	32C2
Barrancas Ven	33E2
Barranqueras Arg	30E4
Barranquilla Colombia	32C1
Barra,Sound of, Chan Scot	44A3
Barre USA	16C1
Barreal Arg	34B2
Barreiras Brazil	31C4
Barreiro Port	50A2
Barreiros Brazil	31D3
Barren,C Aust	107D5
Barren Is USA	12D3
Barretos Brazil	31B6
Barrhead Can	13E2
Barrie Can	14C2
Barrière Can	13C2
Barrier Range, Mts Aust	108B2
Barrington,Mt Aust	107E4
Barrouaillie St Vincent	27N2
Barrow USA	4C2
Barrow, R Irish Rep	45C2
Barrow Creek Aust	106C3
Barrow I Aust	106A3
Barrow-in-Furness Eng	42C2
Barrow,Pt USA	4C2
Barrow Str Can	6A2

Barry's Bay Can	15C1
Barsi India	87B1
Barstow USA	9B3
Bar-sur-Aube France	49C2
Bartica Guyana	33F2
Bartın Turk	92B1
Bartle Frere,Mt Aust	107D2
Bartlesville USA	9D3
Bartolomeu Dias Mozam	101C3
Bartoszyce Pol	58C2
Barung, I Indon	78C4
Barwāh India	85D4
Barwāni India	85C4
Barwon, R Aust	109C1
Barysh USSR	61G3
Basankusu Zaïre	98B2
Basavilbas Arg	34D2
Basco Phil	79B1
Basel Switz	52A1
Basento, R Italy	53C2
Bashaw Can	13E2
Bashi Chan Phil	79B1
Bashkirskaya ASSR, Republic USSR	61H3
Basilan, I Phil	79B4
Basildon Eng	43E4
Basingstoke Eng	43D4
Basin Region USA	8B2
Basra Iraq	93E3
Bas-Rhin, Department France	46D2
Bassac, R Camb	76D3
Bassano Can	13E2
Bassano Italy	52B1
Bassano del Grappa Italy	47D2
Bassari Togo	97C4
Bassas da India, I Mozam Chan	101C3
Bassein Burma	76A2
Basse Terre Guadeloupe	27E3
Bassila Benin	97C4
Bass Lake USA	22C2
Bass Str Aust	107D4
Båstad Sweden	39G7
Bastak Iran	91B4
Basti India	86A1
Bastia Corse	52A2
Bastogne Belg	57B3
Bastrop, Louisiana USA	19B3
Bastrop, Texas USA	19A3
Bata Eq Guinea	98A2
Batakan Indon	78C3
Batala India	84D2
Batang China	68B3
Batangafo CAR	98B2
Batan Is Phil	79B1
Batatais Brazil	35B2
Batavia USA	15C2
Batemans Bay Aust	109D3
Batesburg USA	17B1
Batesville, Arkansas USA	18B2
Batesville, Mississippi USA	19C3
Bath Eng	43C4
Bath, New York USA	15C2
Batha, R Chad	98B1
Bathurst Aust	107D4
Bathurst Can	7D5
Bathurst,C Can	4F2
Bathurst I Aust	106C2
Bathurst I Can	4H2
Bathurst Inlet, B Can	4H3
Bâtlāq-e-Gavkhūnī, Salt Flat Iran	90B3
Batlow Aust	109C3
Batman Turk	93D2
Batna Alg	96C1
Baton Rouge USA	11A3
Batroun Leb	94B1
Battambang Camb	76C3
Batticaloa Sri Lanka	87C3
Battle, R Can	13F2
Battle Creek USA	10B2

Battle Harbour

Battle Harbour *Can*	7E4
Battle Mountain *USA*	20C2
Batukelau *Indon*	78D2
Batumi *USSR*	65F5
Batu Pahat *Malay*	77C5
Baturaja *Indon*	78A3
Bat Yam *Israel*	94B2
Baubau *Indon*	71D4
Bauchi *Nig*	97C3
Bauges, Mts *France*	47B2
Bauld,C *Can*	7E4
Baumes-les-Dames *France*	47B1
Baunt *USSR*	63D2
Bauru *Brazil*	31B6
Baus *Brazil*	35A1
Bautzen *E Germ*	57C2
Baween, I *Indon*	78C4
Bawîti *Egypt*	95B2
Bawku *Ghana*	97B3
Bawlake *Burma*	76B2
Bawlen *Aust*	108A2
Baxley *USA*	17B1
Bayamo *Cuba*	25E2
Bayan *Indon*	78D4
Bayandalay *Mongolia*	72A1
Bayandzürh *Mongolia*	68C2
Bayan Har Shan, Mts *China*	68B3
Bayan Mod *China*	72A1
Bayan Obo *China*	72B1
Bayard, P *France*	47A2
Bayard,Mt *Can*	12J3
Baybay *Phil*	79B3
Bayburt *Turk*	93D1
Bay City, Michigan *USA*	10B2
Bay City, Texas *USA*	19A4
Bay Dağlari *Turk*	92B2
Baydaratskaya Guba, B *USSR*	64H3
Baydhabo *Somalia*	99E2
Bayeaux *France*	48B2
Bayerische Alpen, Mts *W Germ*	47D1
Bayern, State *W Germ*	57C3
Bâyir *Jordan*	92C3
Baykalskiy Khrebet, Mts *USSR*	68C1
Baykit *USSR*	63B1
Baylik Shan, Mts *China/Mongolia*	63B3
Baymak *USSR*	61J3
Bayombang *Phil*	79B2
Bayonne *France*	48B3
Bayreuth *W Germ*	57C3
Bay St Louis *USA*	19C3
Bay Shore *USA*	15D2
Bays,L of *Can*	15C1
Baytik Shan, Mts *China*	68A2
Baytown *USA*	19B4
Baza *Spain*	50B2
Bazaliya *USSR*	59D3
Bazas *France*	48B3
Bazhong *China*	73B3
Bazmān *Iran*	91D4
Bcharre *Leb*	94C1
Beach Haven *USA*	16B3
Beachy Head *Eng*	43E4
Beacon *USA*	16C2
Bealanana *Madag*	101D2
Beardstown *USA*	18B1
Bear Valley *USA*	22B1
Beatrice *USA*	8D2
Beatrice, Oilfield *N Sea*	44C2
Beatton, R *Can*	13C1
Beatton River *Can*	5F4
Beauchene Is *Falkland Is*	29E6
Beaudesert *Aust*	109D1
Beaufort S *Can*	1B5
Beaufort West *S Africa*	100B4
Beauharnois *Can*	15D1
Beauly *Scot*	44B3
Beaumont, California *USA*	21B3
Beaumont, Texas *USA*	11A3
Beaune *France*	49C2
Beauvais *France*	48C2
Beauval *Can*	13F1
Beaver, Alaska *USA*	12E1
Beaver, R, Saskatchewan *Can*	13F2
Beaver Creek *Can*	4D3
Beaver Creek *USA*	12E1
Beaver Dam, Kentucky *USA*	18C2
Beaverhill L *Can*	13E2
Beaver I *USA*	14A1
Beaver L *USA*	18B2
Beaverlodge *Can*	13D1
Beawar *India*	85C3
Beazley *Arg*	34B2
Bebedouro *Brazil*	35B2
Beccles *Eng*	43E3
Bečej *Yugos*	54B1
Béchar *Alg*	96B1
Becharof L *USA*	12C3
Beckley *USA*	11B3
Bedford, County *Eng*	43D3
Bedford *Eng*	43D3
Bedford, Indiana *USA*	14A3
Bedford Pt *Grenada*	27M2
Beechey, Pt *USA*	4D2
Beechworth *Aust*	109C3
Beenleigh *Aust*	109D1
Beersheba *Israel*	92B3
Beér Sheva, R *Israel*	94B3
Beeville *USA*	9D4
Befale *Zaïre*	98C2
Befandriana *Madag*	101D2
Bega *Aust*	109C3
Behbehān *Iran*	91B3
Behm Canal, Sd *USA*	12H3
Behshahr *Iran*	90B2
Behsud *Afghan*	84B2
Bei'an *China*	69E2
Beihai *China*	73B5
Beijing *China*	72D2
Beiliu *China*	76E1
Beipan Jiang, R *China*	73B4
Beipiao *China*	72E1
Beirut *Leb*	92C3
Bei Shan, Mts *China*	68B2
Beit ed Dîne *Leb*	94B2
Beit Jala *Israel*	94B3
Beja *Port*	50A2
Beja *Tunisia*	96C1
Bejaïa *Alg*	96C1
Béjar *Spain*	50A1
Bejestän *Iran*	90C3
Békéscsaba *Hung*	59C3
Bekily *Madag*	101D3
Bela *India*	86A1
Bela *Pak*	85B3
Belaga *Malay*	78C2
Bel Air *USA*	16A3
Belamoalli *India*	87B1
Belang *Indon*	71D3
Belangpidie *Indon*	70A3
Belau, Republic *Pacific O*	71E3
Belau, I *Pacific O*	104E3
Bela Vista *Mozam*	101C3
Belawan *Indon*	70A3
Belaya, R *USSR*	61J2
Belcher Chan *Can*	6A2
Belcher Is *Can*	7C4
Belchiragh *Afghan*	84B1
Belebey *USSR*	61H3
Belém *Brazil*	31B2
Belén *Colombia*	32B3
Belén *Urug*	34D2
Belen *USA*	9C3
Belet Uen *Somalia*	99E2
Belfast *N Ire*	45D1
Belfast *S Africa*	101H1
Belfast Lough, Estuary *N Ire*	45D1
Belfodio *Eth*	99D1
Belford *Eng*	42D2
Belfort *France*	49D2
Belgaum *India*	87A1
Belgium, Kingdom *N W Europe*	56A2
Belgorod *USSR*	60E3
Belgorod Dnestrovskiy *USSR*	60D4
Bel Hedan *Libya*	95A2
Belinyu *Indon*	78B3
Belitung, I *Indon*	78B3
Belize *Belize*	25D3
Belize, Republic *C America*	25D3
Bellac *France*	48C2
Bella Coola *Can*	5F4
Bellagio *Italy*	47C2
Bellaire *USA*	19A4
Bellano *Italy*	47C1
Bellary *India*	87B1
Bellata *Aust*	109C1
Belledonne, Mts *France*	47B2
Belle Fourche *USA*	8C2
Bellegarde *France*	49D2
Belle Glade *USA*	17B2
Belle I *Can*	7E4
Belle-Ile, I *France*	48B2
Belle Isle,Str of *Can*	7E4
Belleville *Can*	7C5
Belleville, Kansas *USA*	18A2
Bellevue, Washington *USA*	20B1
Bellin *Can*	7C3
Bellingen *Aust*	109D2
Bellingham *USA*	8A2
Bellingshausen, Base *Ant*	112C2
Bellingshausen S *Ant*	112C3
Bellinzona *Switz*	52A1
Bello *Colombia*	32B2
Bellona Reefs *Nouvelle Calédonie*	107E3
Bellota *USA*	22B1
Bellows Falls *USA*	15D2
Bell Pen *Can*	6B3
Belluno *Italy*	52B1
Bell Ville *Arg*	29D2
Belmonte *Brazil*	31D5
Belmopan *Belize*	25D3
Belmullet *Irish Rep*	45B1
Belogorsk *USSR*	69E1
Beloha *Madag*	101D3
Belo Horizonte *Brazil*	31C5
Beloit, Wisconsin *USA*	10B2
Belomorsk *USSR*	64E3
Beloretsk *USSR*	61J3
Belorusskaya SSR, Republic *USSR*	60C3
Belo-Tsiribihina *Madag*	101D2
Beloye More, S *USSR*	64E3
Beloye Ozero, L *USSR*	60E1
Belozersk *USSR*	60E1
Belpre *USA*	14B3
Beltana *Aust*	108A2
Belton *USA*	19A3
Bel'tsy *USSR*	59D3
Belvidere, New Jersey *USA*	16B2
Bembe *Angola*	98B3
Bembéréke *Benin*	97C3
Bemidji *USA*	10A2
Bena *Nor*	39G6
Bena Dibele *Zaïre*	98C3
Benalla *Aust*	108C3
Ben Attow, Mt *Scot*	44B3
Benavente *Spain*	50A1
Benbecula, I *Scot*	44A3
Bencubbin *Aust*	106A4
Bend *USA*	8A2
Ben Dearg, Mt *Scot*	44B3
Bender Beyla *Somalia*	99F2
Bendery *USSR*	60C4
Bendigo *Aust*	107D4
Benešov *Czech*	57C3
Benevento *Italy*	53B2
Bengal,B of *Asia*	83C4
Ben Gardane *Tunisia*	96D1
Bengbu *China*	72D3
Benghāzī *Libya*	95B1
Bengkalis *Indon*	78A2
Bengkulu *Indon*	78A3
Benguela *Angola*	100A2
Benha *Egypt*	92B3
Ben Hope, Mt *Scot*	44B2
Beni *Zaïre*	99C2
Béni, R *Bol*	32D6
Beni Abbes *Alg*	96B1
Benicarló *Spain*	51C1
Benidji *USA*	7A5
Benidorm *Spain*	51B2
Beni Mansour *Alg*	51C2
Beni Mazar *Egypt*	95C2
Beni Mellal *Mor*	96B1
Benin, Republic *Africa*	97C4
Benin City *Nig*	97C4
Beni Suef *Egypt*	95C2
Ben Kilbreck, Mt *Scot*	44B2
Ben Lawers, Mt *UK*	44B3
Ben Lomond, Mt *Aust*	109C4
Ben Macdui, Mt *Scot*	44C3
Ben More Assynt, Mt *Scot*	44B2
Benmore,L *NZ*	111B2
Ben Nevis, Mt *Scot*	44B3
Bennington *USA*	15D2
Bennt Jbail *Leb*	94B2
Bénoué, R *Cam*	98B2
Benson, Arizona *USA*	9B3
Bentiu *Sudan*	99C2
Benton, Arkansas *USA*	19B3
Benton, Kentucky *USA*	18C2
Benton Harbor *USA*	14A2
Benue, R *Nig*	97C4
Benwee Hd, C *Irish Rep*	45B1
Ben Wyvis, Mt *Scot*	44B3
Benxi *China*	72E1
Beograd *Yugos*	54B2
Beohāri *India*	86A2
Beppu *Japan*	74C4
Berat *Alb*	55A2
Berber *Sudan*	95C3
Berbera *Somalia*	99E1
Berbérati *CAR*	98B2
Berck *France*	46A1
Berdichev *USSR*	60C4
Berdyansk *USSR*	60E4
Berekum *Ghana*	97B4
Berenda *Aust*	22B2
Berens, R *Can*	5J4
Berens River *Can*	5J4
Beresford *Aust*	108A1
Berettyoûjfalu *Hung*	59C3
Bereza *USSR*	58D2
Berezhany *USSR*	59C3
Berezniki *USSR*	65G4
Berezovka *USSR*	60D4
Berezovo *USSR*	64H3
Bergama *Turk*	92A2
Bergamo *Italy*	52A1
Bergen *Nor*	39F6
Bergen op Zoom *Neth*	46C1
Bergerac *France*	48C3
Bergisch-Gladbach *W Germ*	46D1
Bering Gl *USA*	12F2
Bering Str *USSR/USA*	1C6
Berîzak *Iran*	91C4
Berja *Spain*	50B2
Berkeley *USA*	8A3
Berkner I *Ant*	112B2
Berkshire, County *Eng*	43D4
Berkshire Hills *USA*	16C1
Berland, R *Can*	13D2
Berlin *E Germ*	56C2
Berlin, New Hampshire *USA*	15D2
Bermejo *Bol*	30D3
Bermejo, R *Arg*	30D3
Bermuda, I *Atlantic O*	3M5
Bern *Switz*	52A1
Bernardsville *USA*	16B2
Bernasconi *Arg*	34C3
Bernburg *E Germ*	56C2

Berner Orberland, Mts	
Switz	47B1
Bernier B Can	6B2
Berounka, R Czech	57C3
Berri Aust	108B2
Berriane Alg	96C1
Berry, Region France	48C2
Berryessa,L USA	22A1
Berry Is Bahamas	11C4
Bertoua Cam	98B2
Bertraghboy B Irish	
Rep	45B2
Berwick USA	15C2
Berwick-upon-Tweed	
Eng	42C2
Berwyn, Mts Wales	43C3
Besalampy Madag	101D2
Besançon France	49D2
Beskidy Zachodnie,	
Mts Pol	59C3
Besni Turk	93C2
Besor, R Israel	94B3
Bessemer USA	11B3
Betafo Madag	101D2
Betanzos Spain	50A1
Bet Guvrin Israel	94B3
Bethal S Africa	101G1
Bethanie Namibia	100A3
Bethany, Missouri	
USA	18B1
Bethany, Oklahoma	
USA	18A2
Bethel, Alaska USA	4B3
Bethel, Connecticut	
USA	16C2
Bethel Park USA	14B2
Bethesda USA	15C3
Bethlehem Israel	94B3
Bethlehem S Africa	101G1
Bethlehem USA	15C2
Bethune France	48C1
Betioky Madag	101D3
Betoota Aust	108B1
Betou Congo	98B2
Betpak Dala, Steppe	
USSR	82A1
Betroka Madag	101D3
Betsiamites Can	7D5
Bettiah India	86A1
Bettles USA	12D1
Béttola Italy	47C2
Betul India	85D4
Betwa, R India	85D3
Betzdorf W Germ	46D1
Beverley,L USA	12C3
Beverly USA	16D1
Beverly Hills USA	21B3
Beyla Guinea	97B4
Beypore India	87B2
Beyşehir Turk	92B2
Beysehir Gölü, L Turk	92B2
Beyt Shean Israel	94B2
Bezau Austria	47C1
Bezhetsk USSR	60E2
Béziers France	49C3
Bezmein USSR	90C2
Beznosova USSR	63C2
Bhadgaon Nepal	86B1
Bhadrachalam India	87C1
Bhadrakh India	86B2
Bhadra Res India	87B2
Bhadrävati India	87B2
Bhag Pak	84B3
Bhägalpur India	86B1
Bhakkar Pak	84C2
Bhamo Burma	82D3
Bhandära India	85D4
Bharatpur India	85D3
Bharüch India	85C4
Bhätiäpära Ghat Bang	86B2
Bhatinda India	84C2
Bhatkal India	87A2
Bhätpära India	86B2
Bhävnagar India	85C4
Bhera Pak	84C2
Bheri, R Nepal	86A1
Bhilai India	86A2
Bhilwära India	85C3

Bhīmavaram India	87C1
Bhind India	85D3
Bhiwäni India	84D3
Bhongir India	87B1
Bhopäl India	85D4
Bhubaneshwar India	86B2
Bhuj India	85B4
Bhusäwal India	85D4
Bhutan, Kingdom Asia	82C3
Biak, I Indon	71E4
Biala Podlaska Pol	58C2
Bialograd Pol	58B2
Bialystok Pol	58C2
Biargtangar, C Iceland	38A1
Biarjmand Iran	90C2
Biarritz France	48B3
Biasca Switz	47C1
Biba Egypt	92B4
Bibai Japan	74E2
Bibala Angola	100A2
Biberach W Germ	57B3
Bibiani Ghana	97B4
Bicaz Rom	54C1
Bida Nig	97C4
Bidar India	87B1
Bidbid Oman	91C5
Bideford Eng	43B4
Bideford B Eng	43B4
Bidon 5 Alg	96C2
Bié Angola	100A2
Biebrza Pol	58C2
Biel Switz	52A1
Bielawa Pol	59B2
Bielefeld W Germ	56B2
Bieler See, L Switz	47B1
Biella Italy	52A1
Bielsk Podlaski Pol	58C2
Bien Hoa Viet	76D3
Biferno, R Italy	53B2
Biga Turk	92A1
Bigadiç Turk	55C3
Big Black, R USA	19C3
Big Blue, R USA	18A1
Big Cypress Swamp	
USA	17B2
Big Delta USA	4D3
Bigent W Germ	49D2
Biggar Can	13F2
Biggar Kindersley Can	5H4
Biggenden Aust	109D1
Bigger,Mt Can	12G3
Bighorn, R USA	8C2
Bight of Bangkok, B	
Thai	76C3
Bight of Benin, B W	
Africa	97C4
Bight of Biafra, B Cam	97C4
Big I Can	6C3
Bignasco Switz	47C1
Bignona Sen	97A3
Big Pine USA	21B2
Big Pine Key USA	17B2
Big Pine Mt USA	22C3
Big Rapids USA	14A2
Big River Can	5H4
Big Spring USA	9C3
Big Trout L Can	7A4
Big Trout Lake Can	7B4
Bihač Yugos	52C2
Bihär India	86B1
Bihar, State India	86B2
Biharamulo Tanz	99D3
Bihor, Mt Rom	60B4
Bijäpur India	87B1
Bijäpur India	87C1
Bijär Iran	90A2
Bijauri Nepal	86A1
Bijeljina Yugos	54A2
Bijie China	73B4
Bijnor India	84D3
Bijnot Pak	84C3
Bikäner India	84C3
Bikfaya Leb	94B2
Bikin USSR	69F2
Bikoro Zaïre	98B3
Bilara India	85C3
Bilaspur India	84D2
Bilaspur India	86A2

Bilauktaung Range,	
Mts Thai	76B3
Bilbao Spain	50B1
Bilé, R Czech	59B3
Bileća Yugos	54A2
Bilecik Turk	92B1
Bili, R Zaïre	98C2
Biliran, I Phil	79B3
Billings USA	8C2
Bilma Niger	95A3
Biloxi USA	11B3
Biltine Chad	98C1
Bina-Etawa India	85D4
Binalbagan Phil	79B3
Bindura Zim	101C2
Binga Zim	100B2
Binga, Mt Zim	101C2
Bingara Aust	109D1
Bingen W Germ	57B3
Binghamton USA	10C2
Bingkor Malay	78D1
Bingöl Turk	93D2
Binhai China	72D3
Bintan, I Indon	78A2
Bintuhan Indon	78A3
Bintulu Malay	78C2
Bió Bió, R Chile	29B3
Bioko, I Atlantic O	102J4
Bīr India	87B1
Bīr Abu Husein, Well	
Egypt	95B2
Bi'r al Harash, Well	
Libya	95B2
Birao CAR	98C1
Biratnagar Nepal	86B1
Birch Creek USA	12E1
Birchip Aust	108B3
Birch Mts Can	5G4
Bird Can	7A4
Birdsville Aust	106C3
Birdum Aust	106C2
Birganj Nepal	86A1
Bīr Gifgåfa, Well	
Egypt	94A3
Bīr Hasana, Well	
Egypt	94A3
Birigui Brazil	35A2
Birjand Iran	90C3
Birkat Qarun, L Egypt	92B4
Birkenfeld W Germ	46D2
Birkenhead Eng	42C3
Bīrlad Rom	60C4
Bir Lahfân, Well Egypt	94A3
Birmingham Eng	43C3
Birmingham USA	11B3
Bīr Misâha, Well	
Egypt	95B2
Bir Moghrein Maur	96A2
Birnin Kebbi Nig	97C3
Birni N'Konni Nig	97C3
Birobidzhan USSR	69F2
Birr Irish Rep	45C2
Bir Rabalou Alg	51C2
Birrie, R Aust	109C1
Birsay Scot	44C2
Birsk USSR	61J2
Bīr Tarfâwi, Well	
Egypt	95B2
Biryusa USSR	63B2
Birzai USSR	39J7
Bir Zreigat, Well Maur	96B2
Biscay,B of Spain/	
France	48A2
Biscayne B USA	17B2
Bischwiller France	46D2
Bishan China	73B4
Bishop USA	8B3
Bishop Auckland Eng	42D2
Bishop's Stortford Eng	43E4
Bishrämpur India	86A2
Biskra Alg	96C1
Bislig Phil	79C4
Bismarck USA	8C2
Bīsotūn Iran	90A3
Bissau Guinea-Bissau	97A3
Bissett Can	10A1
Bistcho L Can	5G4
Bistrita, R Rom	54C1

Bitam Gabon	98B2
Bitburg W Germ	57B3
Bitche France	46D2
Bitlis Turk	93D2
Bitola Yugos	55B2
Bitterfeld E Germ	56C2
Bitterfontein S Africa	100A4
Bitter Lakes Egypt	92B3
Bitteroot Range, Mts	
USA	8B2
Biwa-ko, L Japan	74D3
Biyo Kaboba Eth	99E1
Biysk USSR	65K4
Bizerte Tunisia	96C1
Bj bou Arréridj Alg	51C2
Bjelovar Yugos	52C1
Bj Flye Ste Marie Alg	96B2
Bjørnøya, I Barents S	64C2
Black, R USA	12F1
Black, R USA	18B2
Blackall Aust	107D3
Blackburn Eng	42C3
Blackburn,Mt USA	4D3
Black Diamond Can	13E2
Black Hills USA	5H5
Black Isle, Pen Scot	44B3
Blackman's Barbados	27R3
Black Mts Wales	43C4
Blackpool Eng	43C3
Black River Jamaica	27H1
Black Rock Desert	
USA	8B2
Black S USSR/Europe	65E5
Blacksod B Irish Rep	45A1
Black Sugarloaf, Mt	
Aust	109D2
Black Volta, R Ghana	97B3
Blackwater, R Irish	
Rep	41B3
Blackwell USA	18A2
Blagoevgrad Bulg	54B2
Blagoveshchensk	
USSR	63E2
Blaine USA	20B1
Blair Atholl Scot	44C3
Blairgowrie Scot	44C3
Blakely USA	17B1
Blanche,L Aust	108A1
Blanco, R Arg	34A2
Blanco, R Arg	34B1
Blanco,C USA	8A2
Blanc Sablon Can	7E4
Blandford Forum Eng	43C4
Blangy-sur-Bresle	
France	46A2
Blankenberge Belg	46B1
Blantyre Malawi	101C2
Blaye France	48B2
Blayney Aust	109C2
Blenheim NZ	111B2
Blida Alg	96C1
Blind River Can	14B1
Blinman Aust	108A2
Blitar Indon	78C4
Block I USA	15D2
Block Island Sd USA	16D2
Bloemfontein S Africa	101G1
Bloemhof S Africa	101G1
Bloemhof Dam, Res S	
Africa	101G1
Blommesteinmeer, L	
Surinam	33F3
Blonduós Iceland	38A1
Bloody Foreland, C	
Irish Rep	45B1
Bloomfield, Indiana	
USA	14A3
Bloomfield, Iowa USA	18B1
Bloomington, Illinois	
USA	10B2
Bloomington, Indiana	
USA	14A3
Bloomsburg USA	16A2
Blora Indon	78C4
Blosseville Kyst, Mts	
Greenland	6H3
Bludenz Austria	57B3
Bluefield USA	11B3

Bluefields

Bluefields *Nic*	32A1
Blue Mountain Peak, Mt *Jamaica*	26B3
Blue Mt *USA*	16A2
Blue Mts *Aust*	109D2
Blue Mts *Jamaica*	27J1
Blue Mts *USA*	8A2
Blue Nile, R *Sudan*	99D1
Bluenose L *Can*	4G3
Blue Ridge Mts *USA*	11B3
Blue River *Can*	13D2
Blue Stack, Mt *Irish Rep*	45B1
Bluff *NZ*	111A3
Bluff Knoll, Mt *Aust*	106A4
Blumenau *Brazil*	30G4
Blundez *Austria*	49D2
Bly *USA*	20B2
Blying Sd *USA*	12E3
Blyth *Eng*	42D2
Blythe *USA*	9B3
Blytheville *USA*	11B3
Bo *Sierra Leone*	97A4
Boac *Phil*	79B3
Boading *China*	72D2
Boardman *USA*	14B2
Boatou *China*	63C3
Boa Vista *Brazil*	33E3
Boa Vista, I *Cape Verde*	97A4
Bobai *China*	76E1
Bóbbio *Italy*	47C2
Bobo Dioulasso *U Volta*	97B3
Bobruysk *USSR*	60C3
Boca Chica Key, I *USA*	17B2
Bôca do Acre *Brazil*	32D5
Bocaiúva *Brazil*	35C1
Bocaranga *CAR*	98B2
Boca Raton *USA*	17B2
Bochnia *Pol*	59C3
Bocholt *W Germ*	56B2
Bochum *W Germ*	46D1
Bocoio *Angola*	100A2
Boda *CAR*	98B2
Bodaybo *USSR*	63D2
Bodega Head, Pt *USA*	21A2
Bodélé, Region *Chad*	95A3
Boden *Sweden*	38J5
Bodensee, L *Switz/W Germ*	47C1
Bodhan *India*	87B1
Bodinâyakkanür *India*	87B2
Bodmin *Eng*	43B4
Bodmin Moor, Upland *Eng*	43B4
Bodø *Nor*	38G5
Bodorodskoye *USSR*	63G2
Bodrum *Turk*	55C3
Boende *Zaïre*	98C3
Boffa *Guinea*	97A3
Bogale *Burma*	76B2
Bogalusa *USA*	19C3
Bogan, R *Aust*	109C2
Bogandé *U Volta*	97B3
Bogarnes *Iceland*	6H3
Boğazliyan *Turk*	92C2
Bogdanovich *USSR*	61K2
Bogda Shan, Mt *China*	68A2
Bogenfels *Namibia*	100A3
Boggabilla *Aust*	109D1
Boggabri *Aust*	109C2
Boggeragh Mts *Irish Rep*	45B2
Bogo *Phil*	79B3
Bogong,Mt *Aust*	109C3
Bogor *Indon*	78B4
Bogorodskoye *USSR*	61H2
Bogotá *Colombia*	32C3
Bogotol *USSR*	63A2
Bogra *Bang*	86B2
Bo Hai, B *China*	72D2
Bohain-en-Vermandois *France*	46B2
Bohai Wan, B *China*	72D2
Böhmer-Wald, Upland *W Germ*	57C3

Bohol, I *Phil*	79B4
Bohol S *Phil*	79B4
Bois, R *Brazil*	35A1
Bois Blanc I *USA*	14B1
Boise *USA*	8B2
Bojador,C *Mor*	96A2
Bojeador,C *Phil*	79B2
Bojnürd *Iran*	90C2
Boké *Guinea*	97A3
Bokhara, R *Aust*	109C1
Boknafjord, Inlet *Nor*	39F7
Boko *Congo*	98B3
Bokor *Camb*	76C3
Bokungu *Zaïre*	98C3
Bol *Chad*	98B1
Bolaänos *Mexico*	23A1
Bolama *Guinea-Bissau*	97A3
Bolanos, R *Mexico*	23A1
Bolbec *France*	48C2
Bole *Ghana*	97B4
Boleslawiec *Pol*	59B2
Bolgatanga *Ghana*	97B3
Bolgrad *USSR*	60C4
Bolívar *Arg*	34C3
Bolivar, Missouri *USA*	18B2
Bolivar, Tennessee *USA*	18C2
Bolivia, Republic *S America*	30C2
Bollnas *Sweden*	38H6
Bollon *Aust*	109C1
Bollvar, Mt *Ven*	32C2
Bologna *Italy*	52B2
Bologoye *USSR*	60D2
Bolon *USSR*	69F2
Bol'shoy Irgiz, R *USSR*	61G3
Bol'shoy Kamen *USSR*	74C2
Bol'shoy Kavkaz, Mts *USSR*	65F5
Bol'shoy Uzen, R *USSR*	61G4
Bolson de Mapimi, Desert *Mexico*	9C4
Bolton *Eng*	43C3
Bolu *Turk*	92B1
Bolungarvik *Iceland*	38A1
Bolvadin *Turk*	92B2
Bolzano *Italy*	52B1
Boma *Zaïre*	98B3
Bombala *Aust*	107D4
Bombay *India*	87A1
Bombo *Uganda*	99D2
Bom Despacho *Brazil*	35B1
Bomdila *India*	86C1
Bomi Hills *Lib*	97A4
Bom Jesus da Lapa *Brazil*	31C4
Bomnak *USSR*	63E2
Bomokandi, R *Zaïre*	99C2
Bomu, R *CAR/Zaïre*	98C2
Bonaire, I *Caribbean*	27D4
Bona,Mt *USA*	12F2
Bonanza *Nic*	25D3
Bonavista *Can*	7E5
Bon Bon *Aust*	108A2
Bondo *Zaïre*	98C2
Bondoukou *Ivory Coast*	97B4
Bonfim *Guyana*	33E3
Bongandanga *Zaïre*	98C2
Bongor *Chad*	98B1
Bonham *USA*	19A3
Bonifacio *Corse*	53A2
Bonifacio,Str of, Chan *Medit S*	52A2
Bonita Springs *USA*	17B2
Bonn *W Germ*	57B2
Bonners Ferry *USA*	20C1
Bonnet Plume, R *Can*	12H1
Bonnyville *Can*	13E2
Bonthe *Sierra Leone*	97A4
Booaaso *Somalia*	99E1
Booligal *Aust*	108B2
Boonah *Aust*	109D1
Boonville *USA*	15C2
Boorowa *Aust*	109C2
Boothia,G of *Can*	6A2
Boothia Pen *Can*	6A2

Booué *Gabon*	98B3
Bopeechee *Aust*	108A1
Bor *Sudan*	99D2
Bor *Turk*	92B2
Bor *Yugos*	54B2
Borah Peak, Mt *USA*	8B2
Borås *Sweden*	39G7
Borãzjan *Iran*	91B4
Borda,C *Aust*	108A3
Bordeaux *France*	48B3
Borden I *Can*	4G2
Borden Pen *Can*	6B2
Bordentown *USA*	16B2
Borders, Region *Scot*	42C2
Bordertown *Aust*	108B3
Bordi Omar Dris *Alg*	96C2
Borens River *Can*	8D1
Borgå *Fin*	39K6
Borgarnes *Iceland*	38A2
Borger *USA*	9C3
Borgholm *Sweden*	39H7
Borgosia *Italy*	47C2
Borgo Valsugana *Italy*	47D1
Borislav *USSR*	59C3
Borisoglebsk *USSR*	61F3
Borisov *USSR*	60C3
Borisovka *USSR*	60E3
Borkou, Region *Chad*	95A3
Borlänge *Sweden*	39H6
Bormida *Italy*	47C2
Bormio *Italy*	47D1
Borneo, I *Malaysia/Indon*	67F5
Bornholm, I *Den*	39H7
Bornova *Turk*	55C3
Boro, R *Sudan*	98C2
Boromo *U Volta*	97B3
Borovichi *USSR*	60D2
Borroloola *Aust*	106C2
Borsa *Rom*	54B1
Borüjed *Iran*	90A3
Borüjen *Iran*	90B3
Bory Tucholskie, Region *Pol*	58B2
Borzya *USSR*	63D2
Bose *China*	73B5
Boshof *S Africa*	101G1
Bosna, R *Yugos*	54A2
Bōsō-hantō, B *Japan*	75C1
Bosquet *Alg*	51C2
Bossangoa *CAR*	98B2
Bossèmbélé *CAR*	98B2
Bossier City *USA*	19B3
Bosten Hu, L *China*	65K5
Boston *Eng*	43D3
Boston *USA*	10C2
Boston Mts *USA*	11A3
Botãd *India*	85C4
Botevgrad *Bulg*	54B2
Bothaville *S Africa*	101G1
Bothnia,G of *Sweden/Fin*	64C3
Botletli, R *Botswana*	100B3
Botosani *Rom*	60C4
Botswana, Republic *Africa*	100B3
Botte Donato, Mt *Italy*	53C3
Bottrop *W Germ*	46D1
Botucatu *Brazil*	35B2
Botwood *Can*	7E5
Bouaflé *Ivory Coast*	97B4
Bouaké *Ivory Coast*	89D7
Bouar *CAR*	98B2
Bouârfa *Mor*	96B1
Bouca *CAR*	98B2
Boufarik *Alg*	51C2
Bougouni *Mali*	97B3
Bouillon *France*	46C2
Bou Izakarn *Mor*	96B2
Boulay-Moselle *France*	46D2
Boulder, Colorado *USA*	8C2
Boulder City *USA*	9B3
Boulder Creek *USA*	22A2
Boulogne *France*	48C1
Boumba, R *CAR*	98B2
Bouna *Ivory Coast*	97B4

Boundary Peak, Mt *USA*	8B3
Boundiali *Ivory Coast*	97B4
Bourail *Nouvelle Calédonie*	107F3
Bourem *Mali*	97B3
Bourg *France*	49D2
Bourg de Péage *France*	49D2
Bourges *France*	48C2
Bourg-Madame *France*	48C3
Bourgogne, Region *France*	49C2
Bourg-St-Maurice *France*	47B2
Bourke *Aust*	108C2
Bournemouth *Eng*	43D4
Bou Saâda *Alg*	96C1
Bousso *Chad*	98B1
Boutilmit *Maur*	97A3
Bouvet I *Atlantic O*	103J7
Bovril *Arg*	34D2
Bow, R *Can*	13E2
Bowen *Aust*	107D2
Bowie, Texas *USA*	19A3
Bow Island *Can*	13E2
Bowling Green, Kentucky *USA*	11B3
Bowling Green, Missouri *USA*	18B2
Bowling Green, Ohio *USA*	14B2
Bowling Green, Virginia *USA*	15C3
Bowmanville *Can*	15C2
Bowral *Aust*	109D2
Bowron, R *Can*	13C2
Bo Xian *China*	72D3
Boxing *China*	72D2
Boyabat *Turk*	92B1
Boyali *CAR*	98B2
Boyd *Can*	5J4
Boyertown *USA*	16B2
Boyle *Can*	13E2
Boyle *Irish Rep*	41B3
Boyne, R *Irish Rep*	45C2
Boynoton Beach *USA*	17B2
Boyoma Falls *Zaïre*	98C2
Bozcaada, I *Turk*	55C3
Boz Dağlari, Mts *Turk*	55C3
Bozeman *USA*	8B2
Bozene *Zaïre*	98B2
Bozoum *CAR*	98B2
Bra *Italy*	47B2
Brač, I *Yugos*	52C2
Bracebridge *Can*	15C1
Brach *Libya*	95A2
Bräcke *Sweden*	38H6
Bradenton *USA*	17B2
Bradford *Eng*	42D3
Brae *Scot*	44E1
Braemar *Scot*	44C3
Braga *Port*	50A1
Bragado *Arg*	34C3
Bragana *Port*	50A1
Bragança *Brazil*	31B2
Bragança Paulista *Brazil*	35B2
Brahman-Baria *Bang*	86C2
Brāhmani, R *India*	86B2
Brahmaputra, R *India*	86C1
Braie Verte *Can*	7E5
Brăila *Rom*	60C4
Brainerd *USA*	10A2
Brakna, Region *Maur*	97A3
Bralorne *Can*	5F4
Brampton *Can*	14C2
Branco, R *Brazil*	33E3
Brandberg, Mt *Namibia*	100A3
Brandenburg *E Germ*	56C2
Brandfort *S Africa*	101G1
Brandon *Can*	8D2
Brandvlei *S Africa*	100B4
Brandys nad Lebem *Czech*	57C2
Braniewo *Pol*	58B2
Brantford *Can*	10B2

Burrinjuck Res

Burrinjuck Res *Aust*	109C2
Bursa *Turk*	60C5
Bur Safâga *Egypt*	80B3
Burton *USA*	14B2
Burton upon Trent *Eng*	43D3
Burtrask *Sweden*	38J6
Burtundy *Aust*	108B2
Buru *Indon*	71D4
Burundi, Republic *Africa*	99C3
Burung *Indon*	78A2
Buryatskaya ASSR, Republic *USSR*	63D2
Burye *Eth*	99D1
Burynshik *USSR*	61H4
Bury St Edmunds *Eng*	43E3
Büshehr *Iran*	91B4
Busira, R *Zaïre*	98B3
Buskozdroj *Pol*	58C2
Busrá ash Shām *Syria*	94C2
Busselton *Aust*	106A4
Busto *Italy*	49D2
Busto Arsizio *Italy*	52A1
Busuanga, I *Phil*	79A3
Buta *Zaïre*	98C2
Buta Ranquil *Arg*	34B3
Butare *Rwanda*	99C3
Bute, I *Scot*	42B2
Butha Qi *China*	69E2
Butler *USA*	14C2
Butte *USA*	8B2
Butterworth *Malay*	77C4
Butt of Lewis, C *Scot*	40B2
Button Is *Can*	6D3
Butuan *Phil*	79C4
Butung, I *Indon*	71D4
Buturlinovka *USSR*	61F3
Butwal *Nepal*	86A1
Buulo Barde *Somalia*	99E2
Buur Hakaba *Somalia*	99E2
Buy *USSR*	61F2
Buyant Ovvo *Mongolia*	72B1
Buynaksk *USSR*	61G5
Buyr Nuur, L *Mongolia*	63D3
Büyük Ağri, Mt *Turk*	93D2
Büyük Menderes, R *Turk*	92A2
Buzâu *Rom*	54C1
Buzau, R *Rom*	54C1
Buzuluk *USSR*	61H3
Buzzards B *USA*	16D2
Byala *Bulg*	54C2
Byala Slatina *Bulg*	54B2
Byam Martin, Chan *Can*	4H2
Byam Martin I *Can*	4H2
Bydgoszcz *Pol*	58B2
Bygland *Nor*	39F7
Bylot I *Can*	6C2
Byrock *Aust*	109C2
Byron *USA*	22B2
Byron,C *Aust*	109D1
Bytom *Pol*	59B2

C

Caacupé *Par*	30E4
Caála *Angola*	100A2
Caamano Sd *Can*	13B2
Caazapá *Par*	30E4
Cabanatuan *Phil*	79B2
Cabedelo *Brazil*	31E3
Cabeza del Buey *Spain*	50A2
Cabildo *Arg*	34C3
Cabildo *Chile*	34A2
Cabimas *Ven*	32C1
Cabinda *Angola*	98B3
Cabinda, Province *Angola*	98B3
Cabo Beata *Dom Rep*	27C3
Cabo Binibeca, C *Spain*	51C2
Cabo Carbonara, C *Sardegna*	53A3

Cabo Carranza, C *Chile*	34A3
Cabo Carvoeiro, C *Port*	50A2
Cabo Colnett, C *Mexico*	9B3
Cabo Corrientes, C *Colombia*	32B2
Cabo Corrientes, C *Mexico*	24B2
Cabo Cruz, C *Cuba*	26B3
Cabo de Ajo, C *Spain*	50B1
Cabo de Caballeria, C *Spain*	51C1
Cabo de Creus, C *Spain*	51C1
Cabo de Gata, C *Spain*	50B2
Cabo de Hornos, C *Chile*	29C7
Cabo de la Nao, C *Spain*	51C2
Cabo de Peñas, C *Spain*	50A1
Cabo de Roca, C *Port*	50A2
Cabo de Salinas, C *Spain*	51C2
Cabo de São Tomé, C *Brazil*	35C2
Cabo de São Vicente, C *Port*	50A2
Cabo de Sines, C *Port*	50A2
Cabo de Tortosa, C *Spain*	51C1
Cabo Dos Bahias, C *Arg*	29C4
Cabo Espichel, C *Port*	50A2
Cabo Falso, C *Mexico*	9B4
Cabo Ferrat, C *Alg*	51B2
Cabo Finisterre, C *Spain*	50A1
Cabo Formentor, C *Spain*	51C1
Cabo Frio *Brazil*	35C2
Cabo Frio, C *Brazil*	35C2
Cabo Gracias à Dios *Honduras*	26A4
Cabo Maguarinho, C *Brazil*	31B2
Cabo Negro, C *Mor*	50A2
Cabonga,Résr *Can*	10C2
Caboolture *Aust*	109D1
Cabo Orange, C *Brazil*	33G3
Cabo Punta Banda, C *Mexico*	21B3
Cabora Bassa Dam *Mozam*	101C2
Caborca *Mexico*	24A1
Cabo Rojo, C *Mexico*	24C2
Cabos *Mexico*	23B1
Cabo San Diego, C *Arg*	29C6
Cabo San Lorenzo, C *Ecuador*	32A4
Cabo Teulada, C *Sardegna*	53A3
Cabo Trafalgar, C *Spain*	50A2
Cabo Tres Forcas, C *Mor*	50B2
Cabo Tres Puntas, C *Arg*	29C5
Cabot Str *Can*	7D5
Cabra *Spain*	50B2
Cabreira, Mt *Port*	50A1
Cabrera, I *Spain*	51C2
Cabrero *Chile*	34A3
Cabriel, R *Spain*	51B2
Cacahuamilpa *Mexico*	23B2
Čačak *Yugos*	54B2
C A Carillo *Mexico*	23B2
Cáceres *Brazil*	30E2
Caceres *Spain*	50A2
Cache, R *USA*	18B2
Cache Creek *Can*	13C2
Cachi *Arg*	30C4
Cachimbo *Brazil*	33G5
Cachoeira *Brazil*	31D4

Cachoeira Alta *Brazil*	35A1
Cachoeira de Paulo Alfonso, Waterfall *Brazil*	31D3
Cachoeira do Sul *Brazil*	29F2
Cachoeiro de Itapemirim *Brazil*	31C6
Cachuma,L *USA*	22C3
Cacolo *Angola*	100A2
Caconda *Angola*	100A2
Caçu *Brazil*	35A1
Caculuvar, R *Angola*	100A2
Čadca *Czech*	59B3
Cader Idris, Mts *Wales*	43C3
Cadillac *USA*	10B2
Cadiz *Phil*	79B3
Cadiz *Spain*	50A2
Caen *France*	48B2
Caernarfon *Wales*	42B3
Caernarfon B *Wales*	43B3
Caesarea, Hist Site *Israel*	94B2
Caetité *Brazil*	31C4
Cafayate *Arg*	30C4
Caga Tepe *Turk*	92B2
Cagayan, R *Phil*	79B2
Cagayan de Oro *Phil*	79B4
Cagayan Is *Phil*	79B4
Cagayan Sulu, I *Phil*	79A4
Cagliari *Sardegna*	53A3
Caguas *Puerto Rico*	27D3
Caha Mts *Irish Rep*	45B3
Cahersiveen *Irish Rep*	45A3
Cahir *Irish Rep*	45C2
Cahone Pt *Irish Rep*	45C2
Cahors *France*	48C3
Caia *Mozam*	101C2
Caianda *Angola*	100B2
Caiapó, R *Brazil*	35A1
Caiapônia *Brazil*	35A1
Caicó *Brazil*	31D3
Caicos Is *Caribbean*	26C2
Caicos Pass *Bahamas*	11C4
Cairn Mt *USA*	12C2
Cairngorms, Mts *Scot*	44C3
Cairns *Aust*	107D2
Cairo *Egypt*	92B3
Cairo *USA*	11B3
Caiwarro *Aust*	108B1
Cajabamba *Peru*	32B5
Cajamarca *Peru*	32B5
Calabozo *Ven*	27D5
Calafat *Rom*	54B2
Calafate *Arg*	29B6
Calagua Is *Phil*	79B3
Calahorra *Spain*	51B1
Calais *France*	48C1
Calama *Chile*	30C3
Calamar *Colombia*	32C3
Calamian Group, Is *Phil*	79A3
Calang *Indon*	70A3
Calanscio Sand Sea *Libya*	95B2
Calapan *Phil*	79B3
Calarasi *Rom*	54C2
Calatayud *Spain*	51B1
Calaveras Res *USA*	22B2
Calbayog *Phil*	79B3
Calcasieu L *USA*	19B4
Calcutta *India*	86B2
Caldas da Rainha *Port*	50A2
Caldas Novas *Brazil*	31B5
Caldera *Chile*	30B4
Caldwell *USA*	8B2
Caleta Olivia *Arg*	29C5
Calexico *USA*	9B3
Calgary *Can*	5G4
Calhoun *USA*	17B1
Calhoun Falls *USA*	17B1
Cali *Colombia*	32B3
Calicut *India*	87B2
Caliente, Nevada *USA*	8B3
California, State *USA*	8A3
California Aqueduct *USA*	22C3

Calimera,Pt *India*	87B2
Calingasta *Arg*	34B2
Calistoga *USA*	22A1
Callabonna, R *Aust*	108B1
Callabonna,L *Aust*	108A1
Callander *Can*	15C1
Callander *Scot*	44B3
Callanna *Aust*	108A1
Callao *Peru*	32B6
Calling L *Can*	13E1
Calnali *Mexico*	23B1
Caloosahatchee, R *USA*	17B2
Caloundra *Aust*	109D1
Calpulalpan *Mexico*	23B2
Caltanissetta *Italy*	53B3
Caluango *Angola*	98B3
Calulo *Angola*	100A2
Caluquembe *Angola*	100A2
Calvert I *Can*	13B2
Calvi *Corse*	52A2
Calvillo *Mexico*	23A1
Calvinia *S Africa*	100A4
Camagüey *Cuba*	25E2
Camagüey,Arch de, Is *Cuba*	25E2
Camaná *Peru*	30B2
Camargo *Bol*	30C3
Camarillo *USA*	22C3
Camarones *Arg*	29C4
Camas *USA*	20B1
Camaxilo *Angola*	98B3
Cambatela *Angola*	98B3
Cambodia, Republic *S E ASia*	76C3
Camborne *Eng*	43B4
Cambrai *France*	49C1
Cambrian Mts *Wales*	43C3
Cambridge *Can*	14B2
Cambridge, County *Eng*	43D3
Cambridge *Eng*	43E3
Cambridge *Jamaica*	27H1
Cambridge, Maryland *USA*	15C3
Cambridge, Massachussets *USA*	15D2
Cambridge *NZ*	110C1
Cambridge, Ohio *USA*	14B2
Cambridge Bay *Can*	4H3
Cam Burun, Pt *Turk*	60E5
Camden, Arkansas *USA*	11A3
Camden *Aust*	109D2
Camden, New Jersey *USA*	15D3
Camden, South Carolina *USA*	17B1
Cameron, Missouri *USA*	18B2
Cameron, Texas *USA*	19A3
Cameron I *Can*	4H2
Cameron Mts *NZ*	111A3
Cameroon, Federal Republic *Africa*	98A2
Cameroun, Mt *Cam*	98A2
Cametá *Brazil*	31B2
Camiguin, I *Phil*	79B4
Camiling *Phil*	79B2
Camilla *USA*	17B1
Camino *USA*	22B1
Camiri *Bol*	30D3
Camocim *Brazil*	31C2
Camooweal *Aust*	106C2
Campana *Arg*	34D2
Campana, I *Chile*	29A5
Campania I *Can*	13B2
Campbell,C *NZ*	111B2
Campbell I *Can*	13B2
Campbell I *NZ*	105G6
Campbell,Mt *Can*	4E3
Campbellpore *Pak*	84C2
Campbell River *Can*	5F5
Campbellton *Can*	7D5
Campbelltown *Aust*	109D2
Campbeltown *Scot*	42B2
Campeche *Mexico*	25C3
Camperdown *Aust*	108B3

Campina Grande Brazil	31D3
Campinas Brazil	31B6
Campina Verde Brazil	35B1
Campo Cam	98A2
Campobasso Italy	53B2
Campo Belo Brazil	35B2
Campo Florido Brazil	35B1
Campo Gallo Arg	30D4
Campo Grande Brazil	30F3
Campo Maior Brazil	31C2
Campo Mourão Brazil	30F3
Campos Brazil	35C2
Campos Altos Brazil	35B1
Campo Tures Italy	47D1
Cam Ranh Viet	76D3
Camrose Can	5G4
Camucuio Angola	100A2
Canaan Tobago	27K1
Canaan USA	16C1
Canacupa Angola	100A2
Canada, Dominion N America	2F3
Cañada de Gomez Arg	29D2
Canadian, R USA	9C3
Canakkale Turk	60C5
Canalejas Arg	34B3
Canal Flats Can	13D2
Cananea Mexico	24A1
Canary Basin Atlantic O	102G3
Canas Mexico	23A2
Canatlán Mexico	24B2
Canaveral,C USA	11B4
Canavieiras Brazil	31D5
Canberra Aust	107D4
Canby, California USA	20B2
Candala Somalia	99F1
Çandarli Körfezi, B Turk	55C3
Candlewood,L USA	16C2
Canelones Urug	29E2
Caney USA	18A2
Cangamba Angola	100A2
Cangombe Angola	100B2
Cangzhou China	72D2
Caniapiscau, R Can	7D4
Caniapiscau,L Can	7D4
Canicatti Italy	53B3
Canindé Brazil	31D2
Çankırı Turk	92B1
Canmore Can	13D2
Canna,I Scot	44A3
Cannanore India	87B2
Cannes France	49D3
Cann River Aust	109C3
Canoas Brazil	30F4
Canoe L Can	13F1
Canon City USA	9C3
Canopus Aust	108B2
Canora Can	5H4
Canowindra Aust	109C2
Cansore Pt Irish Rep	45C2
Canterbury Eng	43E4
Canterbury Bight, B NZ	111B2
Canterbury Plains NZ	111B2
Can Tho Viet	77D4
Canton, Mississippi USA	19C3
Canton, Missouri USA	18B1
Canton, Ohio USA	10B2
Cantwell USA	12E2
Canyon City USA	20C2
Canyon Range, Mts Can	12J2
Canyonville USA	20B2
Canzar Angola	98C3
Cao Bang Viet	76D1
Capanema Brazil	31B2
Capão Bonito Brazil	35B2
Capbreton France	48B3
Cap Corrientes, C Mexico	24B2
Cap Corse, C Corse	52A2
Cap d'Ambre, C Madag	101D2
Cap de la Hague, C France	48B2
Cap-de-la-Madeleine Can	15D1
Cap de Nouvelle-France, C Can	6C3
Capdepera Spain	51C2
Cap de Tancitiario, C Mexico	23A2
Cape Barren I Aust	109C4
Cape Basin Atlantic O	103J6
Cape Breton I Can	7E5
Cape Coast Ghana	97B4
Cape Cod B USA	15D2
Cape Dorset Can	6C3
Cape Fear, R USA	17C1
Cape Girardeau USA	18C2
Cape Henrietta Maria Can	6B3
Cape Johnston Depth Pacific O	104E3
Capelinha Brazil	35C1
Cape Lisburne USA	4B3
Capelongo Angola	100A2
Cape May USA	15D3
Cape Mendocino USA	5F5
Capenda Camulemba Angola	98B3
Cape Perry Can	4F2
Cape Province S Africa	100B4
Cape Tatnam Can	7A4
Cape Town S Africa	100A4
Cape Verde, Is Atlantic O	102G4
Cape Verde Basin Atlantic O	102G4
Cape Yakataga USA	12F3
Cape York Pen Aust	107D2
Cap Gris Noz, C France	46A1
Cap-Haitien Haiti	26C3
Capim, R Brazil	31B2
Cap Moule à Chique, C St Lucia	27P2
Capo Isola di Correnti C Italy	53C3
Capo Rizzuto, C Italy	53C3
Capo Santa Maria di Leuca, C Italy	55A3
Capo San Vito Italy	53B3
Capo Spartivento, C Italy	53C3
Cap Pt St Lucia	27P2
Capri,I Italy	53B2
Caprivi Strip, Region Namibia	100B2
Cap Rosso, C Corse	52A2
Cap Vert, C Sen	97A3
Caquetá, R Colombia	32C4
Caracal Rom	54B2
Caracaraí Brazil	33E3
Caracas Ven	32D1
Caraguatatuba Brazil	35B2
Carahue Chile	29B3
Caraí Brazil	35C1
Carandaí Brazil	35C2
Carangola Brazil	31C6
Caransebes Rom	54B1
Carappee Hill, Mt Aust	108A2
Caratasca Honduras	26A3
Caratinga Brazil	35C1
Caravaca Spain	51B2
Caravelas Brazil	35D1
Carbondale, Illinois USA	18C2
Carbonia Sardegna	53A3
Carboear Can	7E5
Carcaion Can	5G4
Carcar Mts Somalia	99E1
Carcassonne France	48C3
Carcross Can	4E3
Cardel Mexico	23B2
Cardenas Cuba	25D2
Cárdenas Mexico	23B1
Cardiff Wales	43C4
Cardigan Wales	43B3
Cardigan B Wales	43B3
Cardston Can	13E2
Carei Rom	54B1
Careiro Brazil	33F4
Carén Chile	34A2
Carey USA	14B2
Carhaix-Plouguer France	48B2
Carhué Arg	29D3
Cariacica Brazil	31C6
Caribou Can	5J4
Caribou Mts, Alberta Can	5G4
Caribou Mts, British Columbia Can	5F4
Carigara Phil	79B3
Carignan France	46C2
Caripito Ven	33E1
Carleton Place Can	15C1
Carletonville S Africa	101G1
Carlinville USA	18C2
Carlisle Eng	42C2
Carlisle USA	15C2
Carlos Arg	34C3
Carlos Chagas Brazil	35C1
Carlow, County Irish Rep	45C2
Carlow Irish Rep	45C2
Carlsbad, California USA	21B3
Carlsbad, New Mexico USA	9C3
Carlyle Can	5H5
Carmacks Can	12G2
Carmagnola Italy	47B2
Carmarthen Wales	43B4
Carmarthen Wales	43B4
Carmel, California USA	22B2
Carmel, New York USA	16C2
Carmel,Mt Israel	94B2
Carmelo Urug	34D2
Carmel Valley USA	22B2
Carmen, I Mexico	9B4
Carmen de Patagones Arg	29D4
Carmi USA	18C2
Carmichael USA	21A2
Carmo do Paranaiba Brazil	35B1
Carmona Spain	50A2
Carnarvon Aust	106A3
Carnarvon S Africa	100B4
Carncacá Brazil	35D1
Carndonagh Irish Rep	45C1
Carnegi,L Aust	106B3
Carnot CAR	98B2
Carnot,C Aust	108A2
Carol City USA	17B2
Carolina Brazil	31B3
Carolina S Africa	101H1
Carolina Beach USA	17C1
Caroline Is Pacific O	104F3
Carpathians, Mts E Europe	60B4
Carpatii Orientali, Mts Rom	59D3
Carpentaria,G of Aust	106C2
Carpenter Ridge Indian O	83C5
Carpentras France	49D3
Carpi Italy	52B2
Carpinteria USA	22C3
Carrabelle USA	17B2
Carrara Italy	52B2
Carrauntoohill, Mt Irish Rep	41B3
Carrickmacross Irish Rep	45C2
Carrick on Shannon Irish Rep	45B2
Carrick-on-Suir Irish Rep	45C2
Carrieton Aust	108A2
Carrington USA	8D2
Carrión, R Spain	50B1
Carroll USA	10A2
Carrollton, Georgia USA	17A1
Carrollton, Kentucky USA	14A3
Carrollton, Missouri USA	18B2
Carruthersville USA	18C2
Carsamba Turk	60E5
Carsamba, R Turk	92B2
Carson City USA	8B3
Carsonville USA	14B2
Cartagena Colombia	26B4
Cartagena Spain	51B2
Cartago Colombia	32B3
Cartago Costa Rica	25D4
Carterton NZ	111C2
Carthage, Missouri USA	18B2
Carthage, New York USA	15C2
Carthage, Texas USA	19B3
Cartier I Timor S	106B2
Cartwright Can	7E4
Caruaru Brazil	31D3
Carúpano Ven	33E1
Carvin France	46B1
Casablanca Chile	34A2
Casablanca Mor	96B1
Casa Branca Brazil	35B2
Casa Grande USA	9B3
Casale Monferrato Italy	52A1
Casalmaggiore Italy	47D2
Casares Arg	34C3
Cascade Mts Can/ USA	13C3
Cascade Pt NZ	111A2
Cascade Range, Mts USA	8A2
Cascavel Brazil	30F3
Caserta Italy	53B2
Casey, Base Ant	112C9
Cashel Irish Rep	45C2
Casilda Arg	34C2
Casino Aust	107E3
Casma Peru	32B5
Caspe Spain	51B1
Casper USA	8C2
Caspian S USSR	65G6
Cass USA	14C3
Cassamba Angola	100B2
Cassel France	46B1
Cassiar Can	12J3
Cassiar Mts Can	4E3
Cassilândia Brazil	35A1
Cassino Italy	53B2
Castaic USA	22C3
Castaño, R Arg	34B2
Castelfranco Italy	47D2
Castellane France	49D3
Castelli Arg	34D3
Castellon de la Plana Spain	51B2
Castelo Brazil	31C3
Castelo Branco Port	50A2
Castelsarrasin France	48C3
Castelvetrano Italy	53B3
Casterton Aust	108B3
Castilla La Nueva, Region Spain	50B2
Castilla La Vieja, Region Spain	50B1
Castlebar Irish Rep	41B3
Castlebay Scot	44A3
Castle Douglas Scot	42C2
Castlegar Can	20C1
Castleisland Irish Rep	45B2
Castlemain Aust	108B3
Castlerea Irish Rep	45B2
Castlereagh Aust	109C2
Castres-sur-l'Agout France	48C3
Castries St Lucia	27E4
Castro Arg	29B4
Castro Brazil	30F3
Castro Alves Brazil	31D4
Castrovillari Italy	53C3
Castroville USA	22B2

Caswell Sd

Chattanooga *USA* 11B3
Chauk *Burma* 76A1
Chaumont *France* 49D2
Chauny *France* 46B2
Chau Phu *Viet* 77D3
Chaves *Port* 50A1
Chazaouet *Alg* 50B2
Chazón *Arg* 34C2
Chcontá *Colombia* 32C2
Cheb *Czech* 57C2
Cheboksary *USSR* 65F4
Cheboygan *USA* 10B2
Chech'on *S Korea* 74B3
Chechro *Pak* 85C3
Checotah *USA* 18A2
Cheduba, I *Burma* 76A2
Cheepie *Aust* 108B1
Chegga *Maur* 96B2
Chegutu *Zim* 100C2
Chehalis *USA* 20B1
Cheju *S Korea* 74B4
Cheju do, I *S Korea* 74B4
Cheju-haehyŏp, Str *S Korea* 74B4
Chekunda *USSR* 03F2
Chelan,L *USA* 20B1
Cheleken *USSR* 90B2
Chelforo *Arg* 34B3
Chelkar *USSR* 80D1
Chelm *Pol* 59C2
Chelmno *Pol* 58B2
Chelmsford *Eng* 43E4
Cheltenham *Eng* 43C4
Chelyabinsk *USSR* 65H4
Chemba *Mozam* 101C2
Chenab, R *India/Pak* 84D2
Chenachen *Alg* 96B2
Cheney *USA* 20C1
Cheney Res *USA* 18A2
Chongda *China* 72D1
Chengdu *China* 73A3
Chengshan Jiao, Pt *China* 72E2
Chenxi *China* 73C4
Chen Xian *China* 73C4
Cheo Xian *China* 73D3
Chopén *Peru* 32B5
Chepes *Arg* 34B2
Cher, R *France* 48C2
Cheran *Mexico* 23A2
Cheraw *USA* 17C1
Cherbourg *France* 48B2
Cherchell *Alg* 96C1
Cheremkhovo *USSR* 63C2
Cherepovets *USSR* 60E2
Cherkassy *USSR* 60D4
Cherkessk *USSR* 61F5
Chernigov *USSR* 60D3
Chernobyl *USSR* 60D2
Chernovtsy *USSR* 60C4
Chernushka *USSR* 61J2
Chernyakhovsk *USSR* 60B3
Chernyye Zemli, Region *USSR* 61G4
Cherokees,L o'the *USA* 18A2
Cherquenco *Chile* 34A3
Cherrapunji *India* 86C1
Cherven' *USSR* 60C3
Chervonograd *USSR* 59C2
Chesapeake, B *USA* 10C3
Cheshire, County *Eng* 42C3
Cheshire *USA* 16C1
Chëshskaya Guba, B *USSR* 64F3
Chester, California *USA* 21A1
Chester *Eng* 42C3
Chester, Illinois *USA* 18C2
Chester, Massachusets *USA* 16C1
Chester, Pennsylvania *USA* 15C3
Chester, S Carolina *USA* 17B1
Chester, R *USA* 16A3
Chesterfield *Eng* 42D3
Chesterfield Inlet *Can* 6A3

Chestertown *USA* 16A3
Chetumal *Mexico* 25D3
Chetwynd *Can* 13C1
Chevak *USA* 12A2
Cheviot *NZ* 111B2
Cheviots, Hills *Eng/Scot* 40C2
Chewelah *USA* 13D3
Cheyenne *USA* 8C2
Chhapra *India* 86A1
Chhātak *Bang* 86C1
Chhatarpur *India* 85D4
Chhindwāra *India* 85D4
Chhuka *Bhutan* 86B1
Chia'i *Taiwan* 73E5
Chiange *Angola* 100A2
Chiang Kham *Thai* 76C2
Chiang Mai *Thai* 76B2
Chiavenna *Italy* 47C1
Chiba *Japan* 74E3
Chībāsa *India* 86B2
Chibia *Angola* 100A2
Chibougamou *Can* 7C4
Chiburi-jima, I *Japan* 75A1
Chibuto *Mozam* 101C3
Chicago *USA* 10B2
Chicago Heights *USA* 14A2
Chichagof I *USA* 12G3
Chichester *Eng* 43D4
Chichibu *Japan* 75B1
Chichi-jima, I *Japan* 69G4
Chickamauga L *USA* 11B3
Chickasawhay, R *USA* 19C3
Chickasha *USA* 9D3
Chicken *USA* 12F2
Chiclayo *Peru* 32A5
Chico *USA* 8A3
Chico, R *Arg* 29C4
Chicoa *Mozam* 101C2
Chicopee *USA* 15D2
Chicoutimi *Can* 7C5
Chicualacuala *Mozam* 101C3
Chidambaram *India* 87B2
Chidley,C *Can* 6D3
Chiefland *USA* 17B2
Chiehn *Lib* 97B4
Chiengi *Zambia* 99C3
Chieri *Italy* 47B2
Chiers, R *France* 46C2
Chiesa *Italy* 47C1
Chiese, R *Italy* 47D2
Chieti *Italy* 52B2
Chifeng *China* 72D1
Chiginigak,Mt *USA* 12C3
Chigmit Mts *USA* 4C3
Chignahuapán *Mexico* 23B2
Chignik *USA* 12C3
Chihuahua *Mexico* 24B2
Chik Ballāpur *India* 87B2
Chikmagalūr *India* 87B2
Chikuminuk L *USA* 12C2
Chikwawa *Malawi* 101C2
Chi-kyaw *Burma* 76A1
Chilakalūrupet *India* 87C1
Chilapa *Mexico* 23B2
Chilaw *Sri Lanka* 87B3
Chile, Republic 28B6
Chilecito, Mendoza *Arg* 34B2
Chililabombwe *Zambia* 100B2
Chilka, L *India* 86B2
Chilko, R *Can* 13C2
Chilko L *Can* 5F4
Chilkotin, R *Can* 13C2
Chillán *Chile* 34A3
Chillar *Arg* 34D3
Chillicothe, Missouri *USA* 18B2
Chillicothe, Ohio *USA* 14B3
Chilliwack *Can* 13C3
Chilmari *India* 86B1
Chilongozi *Zambia* 101C2
Chiloquin *USA* 20B2
Chilpancingo *Mexico* 24C3
Chiltern Hills, Upland *Eng* 43D4
Chilton *USA* 14A2
Chilumba *Malawi* 101C2

Chi-lung *Taiwan* 69E4
Chilwa, L *Malawi* 101C2
Chimay *Belg* 46C1
Chimbay *USSR* 65G5
Chimborazo, Mt *Ecuador* 32B4
Chimbote *Peru* 32B5
Chimkent *USSR* 65H5
Chimoio *Mozam* 101C2
China, Republic *Asia* 67E3
Chinandega *Nic* 25D3
Chincha Alta *Peru* 32B6
Chinchilla *Aust* 109D1
Chinde *Mozam* 101C2
Chindwin, R *Burma* 86C2
Chingola *Zambia* 100B2
Chinguar *Angola* 100A2
Chinguetti *Maur* 96A2
Chinhae *S Korea* 74B3
Chinhoyi *Zim* 100C2
Chiniak,C *USA* 12D3
Chiniot *Pak* 84C2
Chinju *S Korea* 74B3
Chinko, R *CAR* 98C2
Chīrāla *India* 87C1
Chiredzi *Zim* 101C3
Chirfa *Niger* 95A2
Chiriqui, Mt *Panama* 32A2
Chirpan *Bulg* 54C2
Chirripo Grande, Mt *Costa Rica* 32A2
Chirundu *Zim* 100B2
Chisamba *Zambia* 100B2
Chishui He, R *China* 73B4
Chisone, R *Italy* 47B2
Chita *USSR* 68D1
Chitado *Angola* 100A2
Chitembo *Angola* 100A2
Chitina *USA* 12F2
Chitina, R *USA* 12F2
Chitradurga *India* 87B2
Chitral *Pak* 84C1
Chitré *Panama* 32A2
Chittagong *Bang* 86C2
Chittaurgarh *India* 85C4
Chittoor *India* 87B2
Chiume *Angola* 100B2
Chiusa *Italy* 47D1
Chivasso *Italy* 47B2
Chivilcoy *Arg* 29D2
Chivu *Zim* 100C2
Chizu *Japan* 75A1
Choele Choel *Arg* 29C3
Choique *Arg* 34C3
Choix *Mexico* 24B2
Chojnice *Pol* 58B2
Choke, Mts *Eth* 99D1
Cholet *France* 48B2
Cholula *Mexico* 23B2
Choma *Zambia* 100B2
Chomo Yummo, Mt *China/India* 86B1
Chomutov *Czech* 57C2
Chona, R *USSR* 63C1
Ch'ŏnan *S Korea* 74B3
Chon Buri *Thai* 76C3
Chone *Ecuador* 32A4
Ch'ŏngjin *N Korea* 74B2
Chongju *N Korea* 74B3
Ch'ŏngju *S Korea* 74B3
Chongoroi *Angola* 100A2
Chongqing *China* 73B4
Chŏngŭp *S Korea* 74B3
Chŏnju *S Korea* 74B3
Chooyu, Mt *China/Nepal* 86B1
Chortkov *USSR* 59D3
Ch'ŏrwŏn *N Korea* 74B3

Chorzow *Pol* 59B2
Choshi *Japan* 74E3
Chos-Malal *Arg* 34A3
Choszczno *Pol* 58B2
Chotanāgpur, Region *India* 86A2
Chott Melrhir *Alg* 96C1
Chowchilla *USA* 22B2
Choybalsan *Mongolia* 63D3
Chrantrey Inlet, B *Can* 6A3
Chraykovskiy *USSR* 61H2
Christchurch *NZ* 111B2
Christiana *S Africa* 101G1
Christian,C *Can* 6D2
Christian Sd *USA* 12H3
Christianshab *Greenland* 6E3
Christmas I *Indian O* 104D4
Christopol *USSR* 61G2
Chu *USSR* 65J5
Chu, R *USSR* 65J5
Chubut, State *Arg* 29C4
Chubut, R *Arg* 29C4
Chudovo *USSR* 60D2
Chudskoye Ozer, L *USSR* 64D4
Chugach Mts *USA* 4D3
Chugiak *USA* 12E2
Chūgoku-sanchi, Mts *Japan* 75A1
Chuí *Brazil* 29F2
Chuillán *Chile* 29B3
Chukai *Malay* 77C5
Chu Lai *Viet* 76D2
Chula Vista *USA* 21B3
Chulitna *USA* 12E2
Chulman *USSR* 63E2
Chulucanas *Peru* 32A5
Chulumani *Bol* 30C2
Chulym *USSR* 65K4
Chulym, R *USSR* 63A2
Chuma, R *USSR* 63B2
Chumar *India* 84D2
Chumikan *USSR* 63F2
Chumphon *Thai* 77B3
Chunchura *India* 86B2
Ch'ungju *S Korea* 74B3
Chunya *Tanz* 99D3
Chunya, R *USSR* 63C1
Chupara Pt *Trinidad* 27L1
Chuquicamata *Chile* 30C3
Chur *Switz* 52A1
Churāchāndpur *India* 86C2
Churchill *Can* 7A4
Churchill, R, Labrador *Can* 7D4
Churchill, R, Manitoba *Can* 7A4
Churchill,C *Can* 7A4
Churchill Falls *Can* 7D4
Churchill L *Can* 5H4
Chūru *India* 84C3
Churumuco *Mexico* 23A2
Chusovoy *USSR* 61J2
Chuvashkaya ASSR, Republic *USSR* 61G2
Chuxiong *China* 68B4
Chu Yang Sin, Mt *Viet* 76D3
Cianjur *Indon* 78B4
Ciano d'Enza *Italy* 47D2
Cianorte *Brazil* 35A2
Ciechanow *Pol* 58C2
Ciego de Avila *Cuba* 25E2
Ciénaga *Colombia* 32C1
Cienfuegos *Cuba* 25D2
Cieszyn *Pol* 59B3
Cieza *Spain* 51B2
Cihanbeyli *Turk* 92B2
Cihuatlán *Mexico* 23A2
Cijulung *Indon* 78B4
Cilacap *Indon* 78B4
Cîmpina *Rom* 54C1
Cinca, R *Spain* 51C1
Cincinnati *USA* 10B3
Cindrelu, Mt *Rom* 54B1
Cine, R *Turk* 55C3

Ciney

Comeragh, Mts *Irish Rep*	45C2
Comilla *Bang*	86C2
Comitán *Mexico*	25C3
Commercy *France*	46C2
Committees B *Can*	6B3
Como *Italy*	52A1
Comodoro Rivadavia *Arg*	29C5
Comonfort *Mexico*	23A1
Comorin,C *India*	87B3
Comoros, Is *Indian O*	101D2
Compiègne *France*	49C2
Compostela *Mexico*	23A1
Comte Salas *Arg*	34B2
Cona *China*	86C1
Conakry *Guinea*	97A4
Concarán *Arg*	34B2
Concarneau *France*	48B2
Conceiçao da Barra *Brazil*	35D1
Conceição do Araguaia *Brazil*	31B3
Conceiçao do Mato Dentro *Brazil*	35C1
Concepción *Chile*	29B3
Concepción *Par*	30E3
Concepción, R *Arg*	29E2
Concepcion del Oro *Mexico*	24B2
Concepcion del Uruguay *Arg*	34D2
Conception,Pt *USA*	9A3
Conchas *Brazil*	35B2
Conchos, R *Mexico*	9C4
Concord, California *USA*	21A2
Concord, New Hampshire *USA*	10C2
Concordia *Arg*	29E2
Concordia *USA*	8D3
Concrete *USA*	20B1
Condamine *Aust*	109D1
Condobolin *Aust*	107D4
Condon *USA*	20B1
Condroz, Mts *Belg*	46C1
Conecuh, R *USA*	17A1
Conegliano *Italy*	47E2
Congo, Republic *Africa*	89F8
Congo, R *Congo*	89F8
Coniston *Can*	14B1
Connaught, Region *Irish Rep*	45B2
Conneaut *USA*	14B2
Connecticut, State *USA*	10C2
Connecticut, R *USA*	15D2
Connellsville *USA*	15C2
Connemara,Mts of *Irish Rep*	45B2
Connersville *USA*	14A3
Conoble *Aust*	108B2
Conroe *USA*	19A3
Conselheiro Lafaiete *Brazil*	35C2
Con Son, Is *Viet*	77D4
Constanta *Rom*	60C5
Constantine *Alg*	96C1
Constantine,C *USA*	12C3
Constitución *Chile*	29B3
Consul *Can*	13F3
Contarina *Italy*	47E2
Contas, R *Brazil*	31C4
Contreras *Mexico*	23B2
Contuoyto L *Can*	4H3
Conway, Arkansas *USA*	11A3
Conway, New Hampshire *USA*	15D2
Conway, South Carolina *USA*	17C1
Conway,L *Aust*	108A1
Conwy *Wales*	42C3
Coober Pedy *Aust*	106C3
Cook *NZ*	110B2
Cook,C *Can*	13B2
Cook Inlet, B *USA*	4C3

Cook Is *Pacific O*	105H4
Cook,Mt *NZ*	111B2
Cooktown *Aust*	107D2
Coolabah *Aust*	109C2
Cooladdi *Aust*	108C1
Coolah *Aust*	109C2
Coolamon *Aust*	109C2
Coolgardie *Aust*	106B4
Cooma *Aust*	109C3
Coonabarabran *Aust*	109C2
Coonambie *Aust*	109C2
Coonbah *Aust*	108B2
Coondambo *Aust*	108A2
Coondapoor *India*	87A2
Coongoola *Aust*	108C1
Coonoor *India*	87B2
Cooper Basin *Aust*	108B1
Cooper Creek *Aust*	106C3
Cooper Creek, R *Aust*	108B1
Coorong,The *Aust*	108A3
Cooroy *Aust*	109D1
Coos B *USA*	20B2
Coos Bay *USA*	20B2
Cootamundra *Aust*	107D4
Cootehill *Irish Rep*	45C1
Copala *Mexico*	23B2
Copalillo *Mexico*	23B2
Copiapó *Chile*	30B4
Copparo *Italy*	47D2
Copper, R *USA*	12F2
Copper Centre *USA*	4D3
Copper Cliff *Can*	14B1
Coppermine *Can*	4G3
Coppermine, R *Can*	4G3
Coquimbo *Chile*	30B4
Corabia *Rom*	54D2
Coral Gables *USA*	17B2
Coral Harbour *Can*	6B3
Coral S *Aust/PNG*	107D2
Coral Sea Basin *Pacific O*	104F4
Coral Sea Island Territories *Aust*	107E2
Corangamite,L *Aust*	108B3
Corantijn, R *Surinam/Guyana*	33F3
Corbeil-Essonnes *France*	46B2
Corcubíon *Spain*	50A1
Cordele *USA*	11B3
Cordillera Cantabrica, Mts *Spain*	50A1
Cordillera Central, Mts *Dom Rep*	26C3
Cordillera Central, Mts *Phil*	79B2
Cordillera de Ansita, Mts *Arg*	34B2
Cordillera de los Andes, Mts *Peru*	32B5
Cordillera del Toro, Mt *Arg*	30C4
Cordillera de Mérida *Ven*	32C2
Cordillera de Viento, Mts *Arg*	34A3
Cordillera Isabelia, Mts *Nicaragua*	25D3
Cordillera Occidental, Mts *Colombia*	32B3
Cordillera Oriental, Mts *Colombia*	32B3
Cordillo Downs *Aust*	108B1
Córdoba *Arg*	29D2
Córdoba *Mexico*	24C3
Córdoba *Spain*	50B2
Córdoba, State *Arg*	29D2
Cordova *USA*	4D3
Coricudgy,Mt *Aust*	109D2
Corigliano Calabro *Italy*	53C3
Corinth, Mississippi *USA*	11B3
Corinto *Brazil*	31C5
Cork, County *Irish Rep*	45B2
Cork *Irish Rep*	41B3
Çorlu *Turk*	92A1

Cornel Fabriciano *Brazil*	31C5
Cornelio Procópio *Brazil*	35A2
Corner Brook *Can*	7E5
Corner Inlet, B *Aust*	109C3
Corning *USA*	15C2
Cornwall *Can*	7C5
Cornwall, County *Eng*	43B4
Cornwall,C *Eng*	43B4
Cornwall I *Can*	4H2
Cornwallis I *Can*	6A2
Coro *Ven*	32D1
Coroatá *Brazil*	31C2
Coroico *Bol*	30C2
Coromandel *Brazil*	35B1
Coromandel Coast *India*	87C2
Coromandel Pen *NZ*	110C1
Coromandel Range, Mts *NZ*	110C1
Corona, California *USA*	22D4
Coronation *Can*	13E2
Coronation G *Can*	4G3
Coronda *Arg*	34C2
Coronel *Chile*	29B3
Coronel Brandsen *Arg*	34D3
Coronel Dorrego *Arg*	34C3
Coronel Fabriciano *Brazil*	35C1
Coronel Oviedo *Par*	30E4
Coronel Pringles *Arg*	29D3
Coronel Suárez *Arg*	34C3
Coronel Vidal *Arg*	34D3
Coropuna, Mt *Peru*	30B2
Corowa *Aust*	109C3
Corps *France*	49D3
Corpus Christi *USA*	9D4
Corpus Christi,L *USA*	9D4
Corregidor, I *Phil*	79B3
Corrente, R, Mato Grosso *Brazil*	35A1
Corrientes *Arg*	30E4
Corrientes, State *Arg*	30E4
Corrigan *USA*	19B3
Corrigin *Aust*	106A4
Corringe Is *Aust*	107E2
Corryong *Aust*	109C3
Corse, I *Medit S*	52A2
Corsewall, Pt *Scot*	42B2
Corsicana *USA*	9D3
Corte *Corse*	52A2
Cortez *USA*	9C3
Cortina d'Ampezzo *Italy*	52B1
Cortland *USA*	15C2
Coruca de Catalan *Mexico*	23A2
Çoruh, R *Turk*	93D1
Çorum *Turk*	60E5
Corumbá *Brazil*	30E2
Corumba, R *Brazil*	35B1
Corumbaiba *Brazil*	35B1
Corvallis *USA*	20B2
Corvo, I *Açores*	96A1
Corwen *Wales*	43C3
Coscomatopec *Mexico*	23B2
Cosenza *Italy*	53C3
Cosmoledo, Is *Seychelles*	101D1
Cosquín *Arg*	34C2
Costa Blanca, Region *Spain*	51B2
Costa Brava, Region *Spain*	51C1
Costa de la Luz, Region *Spain*	50B2
Costa del Sol, Region *Spain*	50B2
Costa Mesa *USA*	22D4
Costa Rica, Republic *C America*	25D3
Cotabato *Phil*	79B4
Cotagaita *Bol*	30C3
Côte d'Azur, Region *France*	49D3

Côtes de Meuse, Mts *France*	46C2
Cotonou *Benin*	97C4
Cotopaxi, Mt *Ecuador*	32B4
Cotswold Hills, Upland *Eng*	43C4
Cottage Grove *USA*	20B2
Cottbus *E Germ*	56C2
Couedic,C du *Aust*	108A3
Couer d'Alene L *USA*	20C1
Coulommiers *France*	46B2
Coulonge, R *Can*	15C1
Coulterville *USA*	22B2
Council *USA*	4B3
Council Bluffs *USA*	8D2
Courmayeur *Italy*	47B2
Courtenay *Can*	13B3
Coutances *France*	48B2
Coventry *Eng*	43D3
Covilhã *Spain*	50A1
Covington, Georgia *USA*	17B1
Covington, Louisiana *USA*	19B3
Cowal,L *Aust*	109C2
Cowangie *Aust*	108B3
Cowansville *Can*	15D1
Coward Springs *Aust*	108A1
Cowell *Aust*	108A2
Cowes *Aust*	108C3
Cowichan L *Can*	20B1
Cowiltz, R *USA*	20B1
Cowra *Aust*	109C2
Coxim *Brazil*	30F2
Coxsackie *USA*	16C1
Cox's Bazar *Bang*	86C2
Coyote *USA*	22B2
Coyuca de Benitez *Mexico*	23A2
Cradock *S Africa*	100B4
Craig *USA*	8C2
Crailsheim *W Germ*	57C3
Craiova *Rom*	54B2
Cranberry L *USA*	15D2
Cranbrook *Can*	5G5
Crane, Oregon *USA*	20C2
Cranston *USA*	16D2
Crater L *USA*	20B2
Crater Lake Nat Pk *USA*	20B2
Crateus *Brazil*	31C3
Crato *Brazil*	31D3
Crawfordsville *USA*	14A2
Crawfordville *USA*	17B1
Crawley *Eng*	43D4
Cree L *Can*	5H4
Creil *France*	46B2
Crema *Italy*	47C2
Cremona *Italy*	52B1
Crépy-en-Valois *France*	46B2
Cres, I *Yugos*	52B2
Crescent City *USA*	20B2
Crespo *Arg*	34C2
Creston *Can*	13D3
Creston *USA*	18B1
Crestview *USA*	17A1
Creswick *Aust*	108B3
Crêt de la Neige, Mt *France*	47A1
Crete *USA*	18A1
Crete,S of *Greece*	55B3
Creuse, R *France*	48C2
Crewe *Eng*	43C3
Crianlarich *Scot*	44B3
Criciuma *Brazil*	30G4
Crieff *Scot*	44C3
Crillon,Mt *USA*	12G3
Cristalina *Brazil*	35B1
Croatia, Region *Yugos*	52C1
Crocker Range, Mts *Malay*	78D1
Crockett *USA*	19A3
Croker I *Aust*	106C2
Cromarty *Scot*	44C3
Cromer *Eng*	43E3
Cromwell *NZ*	111A3
Crooked, I *Bahamas*	11C4

Crooked

Djenné

Djenné *Mali*	97B3
Djibo *Upper Volta*	97B3
Djibouti *Djibouti*	99E1
Djibouti, Republic *E Africa*	99E1
Djolu *Zaïre*	98C2
Djougou *Benin*	97C4
Djugu *Zaïre*	99D2
Djúpivogur *Iceland*	38C2
Djurdjura, Mts *Alg*	51C2
Dmitrov *USSR*	60E2
Dnepr, R *USSR*	60D4
Dneprodzerzhinsk *USSR*	60D4
Dnepropetrovsk *USSR*	60E4
Dneprovskaya Nizmennost', Region *USSR*	60C3
Dnestr, R *USSR*	60B4
Dno *USSR*	60D2
Doba *Chad*	98B2
Dobele *USSR*	58C1
Doblas *Arg*	34C3
Dobo *Indon*	71E4
Doboj *Yugos*	54A2
Dobrush *USSR*	60D3
Doce, R *Brazil*	31C5
Doctor R P Peña *Arg*	30D3
Dod *India*	87B2
Doda Betta, Mt *India*	87B2
Dodge City *USA*	9C3
Dodoma *Tanz*	99D3
Dôgo, I *Japan*	75A1
Dogondoutchi *Niger*	97C3
Doğubayazit *Turk*	93D2
Doha *Qatar*	91B4
Dolbeau *Can*	7C5
Dôle *France*	49D2
Dolgellau *Wales*	43C3
Dolo *Eth*	99E2
Dolomitche, Mts *Italy*	47D1
Dolores *Arg*	29E3
Dolores *Urug*	34D2
Dolores Hidalgo *Mexico*	23A1
Dolphin and Union Str *Can*	4G3
Dolphin,C *Falkland Is*	29E6
Dom, Mt *Indon*	71E4
Dombarovskiy *USSR*	65G4
Dombas *Nor*	38F6
Dombasle-sur-Meurthe *France*	46D2
Dombóvár *Hung*	54A1
Domfront *France*	48B2
Dominica, I *Caribbean*	27E3
Dominican Republic *Caribbean*	27C3
Dominion,C *Can*	6C3
Domino *Can*	7E4
Domna *USSR*	68D1
Domodossola *Italy*	52A1
Dompu *Indon*	78D4
Domuyo, Mt *Arg*	29B3
Domville,Mt *Aust*	109D1
Dom-yanskoya *USSR*	65H4
Don, R *Scot*	44C3
Don, R *USSR*	61F4
Donaghadee *N Ire*	45C1
Donau, R *W Germ*	57C3
Donauwörth *W Germ*	57C3
Don Benito *Spain*	50A2
Doncaster *Eng*	42D3
Dondo *Angola*	98B3
Dondo *Mozam*	101C2
Dondra Head. C *Sri Lanka*	87C3
Donegal, County *Irish Rep*	45B1
Donegal *Irish Rep*	40B3
Donegal, B *Irish Rep*	40B3
Donegal, Mts *Irish Rep*	45B1
Donetsk *USSR*	60E4
Dong'an *China*	73C4
Dongara *Aust*	106A3
Dongchuan *China*	73A4
Dongfang *China*	76D2
Dongfeng *China*	74B2
Donggala *Indon*	70C4
Donggi Cona, L *China*	68B3
Donggou *China*	74A3
Donghai Dao, I *China*	73C5
Dong He, R *China*	72A1
Dong Hoi *Viet*	76D2
Dong Jiang, R *China*	73C5
Dongola *Sudan*	95C3
Dongshan *China*	73D5
Dongsha Qundao, I *China*	68D4
Dongsheng *China*	72C2
Dongtai *China*	72E3
Dongting Hu, L *China*	73C4
Dongxing *China*	73B5
Dongzhi *China*	73D3
Doniphan *USA*	18B2
Donji Vakuf *Yugos*	52C2
Dönna, I *Nor*	38G5
Donner, P *USA*	21A2
Donnersberg, Mt *W Germ*	46D2
Donnybrook *S Africa*	101G1
Don Pedro Res *USA*	22B2
Doonerak,Mt *USA*	12D1
Dopolong *Phil*	79B4
Do Qu, R *China*	73A3
Dora Baltea, R *Italy*	47B2
Dorbirn *Austria*	49D2
Dorchester *Eng*	43C4
Dorchester,C *Can*	6C3
Dordogne, R *France*	48C2
Dordrecht *Neth*	56A2
Dorle, L *Can*	13F2
Dorle Lake *Can*	13F2
Dori *Upper Volta*	97B3
Dormans *France*	46B2
Dornbirn *Austria*	57B3
Dornoch *Scot*	44B3
Dornoch Firth, Estuary *Scot*	44B3
Dorotea *Sweden*	38H6
Dorrigo *Aust*	109D2
Dorris *USA*	20B2
Dorset, County *Eng*	43C4
Dorsten *W Germ*	46D1
Dortmund *W Germ*	56B2
Doruma *Zaïre*	98C2
Dosatuy *USSR*	63D2
Doshi *Afghan*	84B1
Dos Palos *USA*	22B2
Dosso *Niger*	97C3
Dossor *USSR*	65G5
Dothan *USA*	11B3
Douai *France*	49C1
Douala *Cam*	98A2
Double Island Pt *Aust*	109D1
Doubs, R *France*	49D2
Doubtful Sd *NZ*	111A3
Douentza *Mali*	97B3
Douglas, Arizona *USA*	9C3
Douglas *Eng*	42B2
Douglas, Georgia *USA*	17B1
Douglas, Wyoming *USA*	8C2
Douglas,C *USA*	12A1
Douglas Chan *Can*	13B2
Douglas,Mt *USA*	12D3
Doullens *France*	46B1
Doun, County *N Ire*	45C1
Dourados *Brazil*	30F3
Douro, R *Port*	50A1
Dover, Delaware *USA*	15C3
Dover *Eng*	43E4
Dover, New Hampshire *USA*	15D2
Dover, New Jersey *USA*	16B2
Dover, Ohio *USA*	14B2
Dover, R *Eng*	43D3
Dover,Str of *UK/France*	41D3
Downington *USA*	16B3
Downpatrick *N Ire*	42B2
Downton,Mt *Can*	13C2
Doylestown *USA*	16B2
Dözen, I *Japan*	75A1
Dr'aa, R *Mor*	96A2
Dracena *Brazil*	35A2
Dracut *USA*	16D1
Draguignan *France*	49D3
Drakensberg, Mts *S Africa*	101C3
Drakensberg, Mt *S Africa*	101G1
Drake Pass *Pacific/ Atlantic O*	103E7
Dráma *Greece*	55B2
Drammen *Nor*	39G7
Drangajökull *Iceland*	38A1
Drava, R *Yugos*	52C1
Drayton Valley *Can*	13D2
Dreaux *France*	49C2
Dresden *E Germ*	57C2
Dreux *France*	48C2
Drewsey *USA*	20C2
Drin, R *Alb*	54B2
Drina, R *Yugos*	54A2
Drissa, R *USSR*	58D1
Drogheda *Irish Rep*	45C2
Drogobych *USSR*	59C3
Dronning Maud Land, Region *Ant*	112B12
Dr P.P. Pená *Par*	30D3
Drumheller *Can*	5G4
Drummond I *USA*	14B1
Drummondville *Can*	15D1
Druskininksi *USSR*	58C2
Dry B *USA*	12G3
Dryden *Can*	7A5
Dry Harbour Mts *Jamaica*	27H1
Duang, I *Burma*	76B3
Dubai *UAE*	91C4
Dubawnt, R *Can*	5H3
Dubawnt L *Can*	4H3
Dubbo *Aust*	107D4
Dublin, County *Irish Rep*	45C2
Dublin *Irish Rep*	45C2
Dublin *USA*	17B1
Dubna *USSR*	60E2
Dubno *USSR*	60C3
Du Bois *USA*	15C2
Dubose,Mt *Can*	13B2
Dubrovica *USSR*	58D2
Dubrovnik *Yugos*	54A2
Dubuque *USA*	10A2
Dudelange *Lux*	46D2
Dudinka *USSR*	1C10
Dudley *Eng*	43C3
Duekoué *Ivory Coast*	97B4
Duero, R *Spain*	50B1
Dufftown *Scot*	44C3
Dugi Otok, I *Yugos*	52B2
Duisburg *W Germ*	56B2
Dükan *Iraq*	93E3
Duk Faiwil *Sudan*	99D2
Dukhān *Qatar*	91B4
Dukou *China*	73A4
Dulan *China*	68B3
Dulce, R *Arg*	34C2
Dulit Range, Mts *Malay*	78C2
Dullabchara *India*	86C2
Duluth *USA*	10A2
Dümä *Syria*	94C2
Dumai *Indon*	78A2
Dumaran, I *Phil*	79A3
Dumas *USA*	9C3
Dumayr *Syria*	94C2
Dumbarton *Scot*	42B2
Dumfries *Scot*	42C2
Dumfries and Galloway, Region *Scot*	42B2
Dumka *India*	86B2
Dumoine,L *Can*	15C1
Dumont d'Urville, Base *Ant*	112C8
Dumyat *Egypt*	95C1
Dunărea, R *Rom*	54C2
Dunary Head, Pt *Irish Rep*	45C2
Dunav, R *Bulg*	54B2
Dunayevtsy *USSR*	59D3
Duncan *Can*	13C3
Duncannon *USA*	16A2
Duncansby Head, Pt *Scot*	44C2
Dundalk *Irish Rep*	45C1
Dundalk *USA*	16A3
Dundalk B *Irish Rep*	45C2
Dundas *Greenland*	6D2
Dundas Pen *Can*	4G2
Dundas Str *Aust*	71E5
Dundee *S Africa*	101H1
Dundee *Scot*	44C3
Dundoo *Aust*	108B1
Dundrum, B *N Ire*	42B2
Dunedin *NZ*	111B3
Dunedin *USA*	17B2
Dunedoo *Aust*	109C2
Dunfermline *Scot*	44C3
Dungarpur *India*	85C4
Dungarvan *Irish Rep*	45C2
Dungeness *Eng*	43E4
Dungog *Aust*	109D2
Dungu *Zaïre*	99C2
Dungunab *Sudan*	95C2
Dunhuang *China*	68B2
Dunkerque *France*	46B1
Dunkirk *USA*	10C2
Dunkur *Eth*	99D1
Dunkwa *Ghana*	97B4
Dun Laoghaire *Irish Rep*	41B3
Dunmanway *Irish Rep*	45B3
Dunmore Town *Bahamas*	26B1
Dunnet Head, Pt *Scot*	44C2
Duns *Scot*	42C2
Dunsmuir *USA*	20B2
Dunstan Mts *NZ*	111A2
Dun-sur-Meuse *France*	46C2
Duolun *China*	72D1
Duque de Bragança *Angola*	98B3
Du Quoin *USA*	18C2
Dura *Israel*	94B3
Durance, R *France*	49D3
Durango *Mexico*	24B2
Durango *Spain*	50B1
Durango *USA*	9C3
Durano *Urug*	29E2
Durant *USA*	9D3
Duraykīsh *Syria*	94C1
Durban *S Africa*	101H1
Duren *W Germ*	46D1
Durg *India*	86A2
Durgapur *India*	86B2
Durham, County *Eng*	42D2
Durham *Eng*	42D2
Durham, N Carolina *USA*	11C3
Durham, New Hampshire *USA*	16D1
Durham Downs *Aust*	108B1
Durmitor, Mt *Yugos*	54A2
Durness *Scot*	44B2
Durrës *Alb*	55A2
Durrie *Aust*	108B1
Dursey, I *Irish Rep*	45A3
Dursunbey *Turk*	55C3
D'Urville I *NZ*	110B2
Dushak *USSR*	90D2
Dushan *China*	73B4
Dushanbe *USSR*	82A2
Dusky Sd *NZ*	111A3
Düsseldorf *W Germ*	56B2
Duyun *China*	73B4
Düzce *Turk*	92B1
Dvina, R *USSR*	60C2
Dwārka *India*	85B4
Dyer,C *Can*	6D3
Dyersburg *USA*	11B3
Dyfed, County *Wales*	43B3
Dykh Tau Dağlari, Mt *USSR*	61F5
Dynevor Downs *Aust*	108B1
Dzag *Mongolia*	68B2
Dzamin Uüd *USSR*	63C3
Dzaoudzi *Mayotte*	101D2

Dzarnïn Üüd *Mongolia*	68C2
Dzavhan Gol, R	
Mongolia	68B2
Dzehezkazgan *USSR*	80E1
Dzerzhinsk *USSR*	61F2
Dzhalinda *USSR*	63E2
Dzhambul *USSR*	65J5
Dzhankoy *USSR*	60D4
Dzhezkazgan *USSR*	65H4
Dzhilikul' *USSR*	84B1
Dzhungarskiy Alatau,	
Mts *USSR*	65J5
Dzierzoniow *Pol*	59B2
Dzungaria, Basin	
China	82C1

E

Eabamet L *Can*	7B4
Eagle, Alaska *USA*	12F2
Eagle L, California	
USA	20B2
Eagle Mountain L	
USA	19A3
Eagle Pass *USA*	9C4
Eagle Plain *Can*	4E3
Eagle River *USA*	12E2
Earlimart *USA*	21B2
Easley *USA*	17B1
East Aurora *USA*	15C2
Eastbourne *Eng*	43E4
East Chicago *USA*	14A2
East China Sea *China/*	
Japan	69E3
Eastern Ghats, Mts	
India	87B4
East Falkland, I	
Falkland Is	29E6
East Fork, R *USA*	12E1
Eastgate *USA*	21B2
East Germany,	
Republic *Europe*	56C2
Easthampton *USA*	16C1
East Hampton *USA*	16C2
East Lake *USA*	14A2
East Liverpool *USA*	14B2
East London *S Africa*	100B4
Eastmain *Can*	7C4
Eastmain, R *Can*	7C4
Eastman *USA*	17B1
Easton, Maryland *USA*	15C3
Easton, Pennsylvania	
USA	15C2
East Orange *USA*	16B2
East Pacific Ridge	
Pacific O	105L4
East Point *USA*	17B1
East Retford *Eng*	42D3
East St Louis *USA*	11A3
East Siberian S *USSR*	1B7
East Sussex, County	
Eng	43E4
Eatonton *USA*	17B1
Eau Claire *USA*	10A2
Eauripik, I *Pacific O*	71F3
Ebano *Mexico*	23B1
Ebebiyin *Eq Guinea*	98B2
Eberswalde *E Germ*	56C2
Ebian *China*	73A4
Ebinur, L *China*	65K5
Eboli *Italy*	53C2
Ebolowa *Cam*	98B2
Ebro, R *Spain*	51B1
Eceabat *Turk*	92A1
Eching *China*	72D2
Echo *USA*	20C1
Echo Bay *Can*	4G3
Echternach *Lux*	46D2
Echuca *Aust*	108B3
Ecija *Spain*	50A2
Eclipse Sd *Can*	6B2
Ecuador, Republic *S*	
America	32B4
Eday, I *Scot*	44C2
Edd *Eth*	99E1
Ed Da'ein *Sudan*	98C1
Ed Damer *Sudan*	95C3
Ed Debba *Sudan*	95C3

Eddrachillis, B *Scot*	44B2
Ed Dueim *Sudan*	99D1
Eddystone Pt *Aust*	109C4
Edea *Cam*	98A2
Eden *Aust*	109C3
Eden, R *Eng*	42C2
Edenburg *S Africa*	101G1
Edendale *NZ*	111A3
Edenkoben *W Germ*	46E2
Eder, R *W Germ*	46E1
Edgell I *Can*	6D3
Edgeøya, I *Barents S*	64D2
Edgewood *USA*	16A3
Edh Dhahiriya *Israel*	94B3
Edhessa *Greece*	55B2
Edinburgh *Scot*	44C3
Edirne *Turk*	60C5
Edisto, R *USA*	17B1
Edith Cavell,Mt *Can*	13D2
Edmonds *USA*	20B1
Edmonton *Can*	5G4
Edmundston *Can*	7D5
Edna *USA*	19A4
Edna Bay *USA*	12H3
Edolo *Italy*	52B1
Edom, Region *Jordan*	94B3
Edremit *Turk*	92A2
Edremit Körfezi, B	
Turk	55C3
Edrengiyn Nuruu, Mts	
Mongolia	68B2
Edson *Can*	5G4
Eduardo Castex *Arg*	34C3
Eduni,Mt *Can*	12J2
Edward, R *Aust*	108B3
Edward,L *Zaïre/*	
Uganda	99C3
Edwards Creek *Aust*	108A1
Edwards Plat *USA*	9C3
Edwardsville *USA*	18C2
Edziza,Mt *Can*	12H3
Eek *USA*	12B2
Eeklo *Belg*	46B1
Effingham *USA*	10B3
Egedesminde	
Greenland	6E3
Egegik *USA*	12C3
Eger *Hung*	59C3
Egersund *Nor*	39F7
Egg Harbor City *USA*	16B3
Eglinton I *Can*	4G2
Egmont,C *NZ*	110B1
Egmont,Mt *NZ*	110B1
Eğridir Gölü, L *Turk*	92B2
Egypt, Republic *Africa*	95B2
Eibar *Spain*	50B1
Eibeuf *France*	49C2
Eifel, Region *W Germ*	46D1
Eigg, I *Scot*	44A3
Eight Degree Chan	
Indian O	83B5
Eighty Mile Beach	
Aust	106B2
Eildon,L *Aust*	108C3
Eindhoven *Neth*	56B2
Einsiedeln *Switz*	47C1
Ein Yahav *Israel*	94B3
Eisenach *E Germ*	57C2
Eisenerz *Austria*	57C3
Eitorf *W Germ*	46D1
Ejin qi *China*	72A1
Ejutla *Mexico*	23B2
Eketahuna *NZ*	110C2
Ekibastuz *USSR*	65J4
Ekimchan *USSR*	63F2
Ek Mahalla el Kubra	
Egypt	92B3
Eksjo *Sweden*	39H7
Ekwen, R *Can*	10B1
El'Alamein *Egypt*	92A3
El'Arîsh *Egypt*	92B3
El Asnam *Alg*	96C1
Elat *Israel*	92B4
El'Atrun Oasis *Sudan*	95B3
Elazig *Turk*	93C2
Elba, I *Italy*	52B2
El Balyana *Egypt*	95C2

El Banco *Colombia*	32C2
Elbasan *Alb*	55B2
El Baúl *Ven*	27D5
Elbe, R *E Germ/W*	
Germ	57C2
El Bega'a, R *Leb*	94C1
Elberta *USA*	14A2
Elbert,Mt *USA*	8C3
Elberton *USA*	17B1
Elbistan *Turk*	92C2
Elblag *Pol*	58B2
El Bolson *Arg*	29B4
Elbrus, Mt *USSR*	61F5
El Cajon *USA*	21B3
El Campo *USA*	19A4
Elche *Spain*	51B2
Elda *Spain*	51B2
El Diviso *Colombia*	32B3
El Djouf, Desert	
Region *Maur*	96B2
Eldon *USA*	18B2
El Dorado, Arkansas	
USA	11A3
Eldorado *Brazil*	35B2
El Dorado, Kansas	
USA	9D3
El Dorado *Mexico*	24B2
El Dorado *Ven*	33E2
Eldoret *Kenya*	99D2
Eleanor,L *USA*	22C1
El Eglab, Region *Alg*	96B2
El Escorial *Spain*	50B1
Eleşkirt *Turk*	93D2
Eleuthera, I *Bahamas*	11C4
El Faiyûm *Egypt*	92B4
El Fasher *Sudan*	98C1
El Fashn *Egypt*	92B4
El Ferrol del Caudillo	
Spain	50A1
El Fula *Sudan*	99C1
El Gassi *Alg*	96C1
El Geteina *Sudan*	99D1
El Gezira, Region	
Sudan	99D1
El Ghor, V *Israel/*	
Jordan	94B3
Elgin, Illinois *USA*	10B2
Elgin *Scot*	44C3
El Gîza *Egypt*	92B3
El Golea *Alg*	96C1
Elgon,Mt *Uganda/*	
Kenya	99D2
El Goran *Eth*	99E2
El Grullo *Mexico*	23A2
El Guettara, Well *Mali*	96B2
El Hamurre *Somalia*	99E2
El Haricha, Desert	
Region *Mali*	96B2
El Harra *Egypt*	92A4
El Harrach *Alg*	51C2
El Hawata *Sudan*	99D1
El Higo *Mexico*	23B1
El Huecu *Arg*	34A3
El'Igma, Desert	
Region *Egypt*	92B4
Elim *USA*	12B2
Elira,C *Can*	4H2
Elisenvaara *Fin*	39K6
Elista *USSR*	61F4
Elizabeth *Aust*	106C4
Elizabeth *USA*	15D2
Elizabeth City *USA*	11C3
Elizabethtown, N	
Carolina *USA*	17C1
Elizabethtown,	
Pennsylvania *USA*	16A2
El Jadida *Mor*	96B1
El Jafr *Jordan*	92C3
El Jebelein *Sudan*	99D1
El Jem *Tunisia*	96D1
Elk *Pol*	58C2
Elk, R, Maryland *USA*	16B3
Elk, R, W Virginia	
USA	14B3
El Kamlin *Sudan*	95C3
El Kef *Tunisia*	96C1
Elk Grove *USA*	22B1

El Khârga *Egypt*	80B3
El-Khârga Oasis *Egypt*	80B3
Elkhart *USA*	14A2
El Khenachich, Desert	
Region *Mali*	96B2
Elkhovo *Bulg*	54C2
Elkins *USA*	14C3
Elko *USA*	8B2
Elkton *USA*	16B3
El Kuntilla *Egypt*	92B3
El Lagowa *Sudan*	99C1
Ellef Ringnes I *Can*	4H2
Ellensburg *USA*	8A2
Ellenville *USA*	16B2
Ellesmere I *Can*	6B2
Ellesmere,L *NZ*	111B2
Ellicott City *USA*	16A3
Elliot *S Africa*	100B4
Elliot Lake *Can*	7B5
El Lisan, Pen *Jordan*	94B3
Ellsworth Land,	
Region *Ant*	112B3
El Maghra, L *Egypt*	95B1
El Manûra *Egypt*	92B3
Elmer *USA*	16B3
El Merelé, Desert	
Region *Maur*	96B3
El Milagro *Arg*	34B2
El Mina *Leb*	94B1
El Minya *Egypt*	92B4
Elmira, California *USA*	22B1
Elmira, New York *USA*	10C2
El Mreitl, Well *Maur*	96B2
Elmsborn *W Germ*	56B2
El Muglad *Sudan*	98C1
El Mzereb, Well *Mali*	96B2
El Nido *Phil*	79A3
El Obeid *Sudan*	99D1
El Oro *Mexico*	23A2
El Oued *Alg*	96C1
El Paso *USA*	9C3
El Porta *USA*	21A2
El Portal *USA*	22C2
El Puerto del Sta	
Maria *Spain*	50A2
El Quseima *Egypt*	94B3
El Reno *USA*	9D3
Elsa *Can*	4E3
El Salvador, Republic	
C America	25D3
Elsinore L *USA*	22D4
El Sosneade *Arg*	34B3
Elsterwerde *E Germ*	57C2
El Teleno, Mt *Spain*	50A1
Eltham *NZ*	110B1
El Tigre *Ven*	33E2
El Tîh, Desert Region	
Egypt	92B4
El Tio *Arg*	34C2
Eltopia *USA*	20C1
El Tûr *Egypt*	92B4
Elūru *India*	87C1
Elvas *Port*	50A2
Elvira *Brazil*	32C5
El Volcán *Chile*	34A2
Elwood *USA*	14A2
Ely *Eng*	43E3
Ely, Minnesota *USA*	10A2
Ely, Nevada *USA*	8B3
Elyria *USA*	14B2
Emämrüd *Iran*	90B2
Emäm Säheb *Afghan*	84B1
Eman, R *Sweden*	58B1
Emba *USSR*	61J4
Emba, R *USSR*	61J4
Embalse Cerros	
Colorados, L *Arg*	29C3
Embalse de Alarcón,	
Res *Spain*	51B2
Embalse de Alcántarà,	
Res *Spain*	50A2
Embalse de Almendra,	
Res *Spain*	50A1
Embalse de Garcia de	
Sola, Res *Spain*	50A2
Embalse de Guri, L	
Ven	33E2

Embalse de Mequinenza

Falkenberg *Sweden*	39G7
Falkirk *Scot*	42C2
Falkland Is, Dependency *S Atlantic*	29D6
Falkland Sd *Falkland Is*	29E6
Fallbrook *USA*	22D4
Fallon *USA*	8B3
Fall River *USA*	15D2
Falls City *USA*	18A1
Falmouth *Eng*	43B4
Falmouth *Jamaica*	27H1
Falmouth, Massachusetts *USA*	16D2
False B *S Africa*	100A4
Falso,C *Mexico*	24A2
Falster, I *Den*	56C2
Fălticeni *Rom*	54C1
Falun *Sweden*	39H6
Famagusta *Cyprus*	92B2
Famenne, Region *Belg*	46C1
Fang *Thai*	76B2
Fangak *Sudan*	99D2
Fang liao *Taiwan*	73E5
Fano *Italy*	52B2
Faraday, Base *Ant*	112C3
Faradje *Zaïre*	99C2
Farafangana *Madag*	101D3
Farafra Oasis *Egypt*	95B2
Farah *Afghan*	80E2
Farallon de Medinilla, I *Pacific O*	71F2
Faranah *Guinea*	97A3
Faraulep, I *Pacific O*	71F3
Fareham *Eng*	43D4
Farewell,C *NZ*	107G5
Farewell Spit, Pt *NZ*	110B2
Fargo *USA*	8D2
Fari'a, R *Israel*	94B2
Faribault *USA*	10A2
Faridpur *Bang*	86B2
Farīmān *Iran*	90C2
Farmington, Missouri *USA*	18B2
Farmington, New Mexico *USA*	9C3
Farmington Res *USA*	22B2
Farne Deep *N Sea*	42D2
Farnham,Mt *Can*	13D2
Faro *Can*	12H2
Faro *Port*	50A2
Fåro, I *Sweden*	39H7
Farquhar, Is *Indian O*	89K9
Farrar, R *Scot*	44B3
Farrell *USA*	14B2
Fársala *Greece*	55B3
Fasā *Iran*	91B4
Fastnet Rock *Irish Rep*	45B3
Fastov *USSR*	60C3
Fatehpur *India*	86A1
Father *Can*	13D1
Fatima du Sul *Brazil*	30F2
Fauresmith *S Africa*	101G1
Faverges *France*	47B2
Fawn, R *Can*	7B4
Fax, R *Sweden*	38H6
Faxaflói, B *Iceland*	38A2
Faya *Chad*	95A3
Fayetteville, Arkansas *USA*	11A3
Fayetteville, N Carolina *USA*	11C3
Faylakah, I *Kuwait*	93E4
Fāzilka *India*	84C2
Fdérik *Maur*	96A2
Fear,C *USA*	11C3
Feather Middle Fork, R *USA*	21A2
Fécamp *France*	48C2
Federación *Arg*	34D2
Federal *Arg*	34D2
Federated States of Micronesia, Is *Pacific O*	71F3
Fehmarn, I *W Germ*	56C2
Feijó *Brazil*	32C5
Feilai Xai Bei Jiang, R *China*	73C5
Feilding *NZ*	110C2
Feira *Zambia*	100C2
Feira de Santan *Brazil*	31D4
Feke *Turk*	92C2
Feldkirch *Austria*	57B3
Feliciano, R *Arg*	34D2
Felixstowe *Eng*	41D3
Feltre *Italy*	47D1
Femund, L *Nor*	38G6
Fengcheng *China*	74A2
Fengdu *China*	73B4
Fenging *China*	72D1
Fengjie *China*	73B3
Feng Xian *China*	72B3
Fengzhen *China*	72C1
Fen He, R *China*	72C2
Fenoarivo Atsinanana *Madag*	101D2
Feodosiya *USSR*	60E5
Ferdow *Iran*	90C3
Fère-Champenoise *France*	46B2
Fergana *USSR*	82B2
Fermanagh, County *N Ire*	45C1
Fermoy *Irish Rep*	45B2
Fern, Mt *Austria*	47D1
Fernandina, I *Ecuador*	32J7
Fernandina Beach *USA*	17B1
Fernando de Noronha, I *Atlantic O*	103G5
Fernandópolis *Brazil*	35A2
Ferndale *USA*	20B1
Fernley *USA*	21B2
Ferrara *Italy*	52B2
Ferreñafe *Peru*	32B5
Ferriday *USA*	19B3
Fès *Mor*	96B1
Festus *USA*	18B2
Feteşti *Rom*	54C2
Fethiye *Turk*	92A2
Fetisovo *USSR*	61H5
Fetlar, I *Scot*	44D1
Feyzabad *Afghan*	65J6
Fianarantsoa *Madag*	101D3
Fiche *Eth*	99D2
Ficksburg *S Africa*	101G1
Fidonza *Italy*	47D2
Fier *Alb*	55A2
Fiera Di Primeiro *Italy*	47D1
Fife, Region *Scot*	44C3
Fife Ness, Pen *Scot*	44C3
Figeac *France*	48C3
Figueira da Foz *Port*	50A1
Figueras *Spain*	51C1
Figuig *Mor*	96B1
Fiji, Is *Pacific O*	105G4
Filadelfia *Par*	30D3
Filiaşi *Rom*	54B2
Filiatrá *Greece*	55B3
Filicudi, I *Italy*	53B3
Fillmore, California *USA*	21B3
Findhorn, R *Scot*	44B3
Findlay *USA*	10B2
Findlay,Mt *Can*	13D2
Finger Lakes *USA*	15C2
Fingoè *Mozam*	101C2
Finike *Turk*	92B2
Finke, R *Aust*	106C3
Finke Flood Flats *Aust*	108A1
Finland, Republic *N Europe*	64D3
Finland,G of *N Europe*	39J7
Finlay, R *Can*	5F4
Finlay Forks *Can*	5F4
Finley *Aust*	108C3
Finnsnes *Nor*	38H5
Finschhafen *PNG*	71F4
Finsteraarhorn, Mt *Switz*	47C1
Finsterwalde *E Germ*	56C2
Fintona *N Ire*	45C1
Fiordland Nat Pk *NZ*	111A3
Fiq *Syria*	94B2
Firat, R *Turk*	93C2
Firebaugh *USA*	22B2
Firenze *Italy*	52B2
Firmat *Arg*	34C2
Firozābād *India*	85D3
Firozpur *India*	84C2
Firspång *Sweden*	39H7
Firth of Clyde, Estuary *Scot*	42B2
Firth of Forth, Estuary *Scot*	44C3
Firth of Lorn, Estuary *Scot*	44A3
Firth of Tay, Estuary *Scot*	40C2
Firūzābād *Iran*	91B4
Fish, R *Namibia*	100A3
Fish Camp *USA*	22C2
Fishers I *USA*	16C2
Fisher Str *Can*	6B3
Fishguard *Wales*	43B4
Fiskenaesset *Greenland*	6E3
Fismes *France*	46B2
Fitchburg *USA*	15D2
Fitful Head, Pt *Scot*	44D2
Fitzgerald *USA*	17B1
Fitzroy, R *Aust*	106B2
Fitzroy Crossing *Aust*	106B2
Fitzwilliam I *Can*	14B1
Fizi *Zaïre*	99C3
Flagstaff *USA*	9B3
Flamborough Head, C *Eng*	42D2
Flaming Gorge Res *USA*	8C2
Flannan Isles, Is *Scot*	44A2
Flat, R *Can*	12J2
Flathead, R *USA*	13E3
Flathead L *USA*	8B2
Flat River *USA*	18B2
Flattery,C *USA*	8A2
Fleetwood *Eng*	42C3
Flekkefjord *Nor*	39F7
Fleming Deep *Pacific Oc*	69G4
Flemington *USA*	16B2
Flensburg *W Germ*	56B2
Fleurier *Switz*	47B1
Flinders, I *Aust*	106C4
Flinders, I *Aust*	107D4
Flinders, R *Aust*	107D2
Flinders Range, Mts *Aust*	106C4
Flin Flon *Can*	5H4
Flint *USA*	10B2
Flint *Wales*	42C3
Flint, R *USA*	11B3
Flixecourt *France*	46B1
Florala *USA*	17A1
Florence, Alabama *USA*	11B3
Florence, Kansas *USA*	18A2
Florence, Oregon *USA*	20B2
Florence, S Carolina *USA*	11C3
Florencia *Colombia*	32B3
Florenville *Belg*	46C2
Flores *Guatemala*	25D3
Flores, I *Açores*	96A1
Flores, I *Indon*	106B1
Flores, R *Indon*	34D3
Flores S *Indon*	70C4
Floriano *Brazil*	31C3
Florianópolis *Brazil*	30G4
Florida, State *USA*	25D2
Florida *Urug*	29E2
Florida B *USA*	17B2
Florida City *USA*	17B2
Florida Is *Solomon Is*	107E1
Florida Keys, Is *USA*	11B4
Florida,Strs of *USA*	11B4
Flórina *Greece*	55B2
Florø *Nor*	38F6
Fluchthorn, Mt *Austria*	47D1
Focsani *Rom*	54C1
Foggia *Italy*	53C2
Fogo, I *Cape Verde*	97A4
Foix *France*	48C3
Foley I *Can*	6C3
Foligno *Italy*	52B2
Folkestone *Eng*	43E4
Folkston *USA*	17B1
Follonica *Italy*	52B2
Folsom *USA*	22B1
Folsom L, L *USA*	22B1
Fond-du-Lac *Can*	5H4
Fond du Lac *USA*	10B2
Fontainebleau *France*	48C2
Fontenac *USA*	18B2
Fontenay-le-Comte *France*	48B2
Fonyód *Hung*	52C1
Foraker,Mt *USA*	12D2
Forbach *France*	46D2
Forbes *Aust*	109C2
Forcados *Nig*	97C4
Forde *Nor*	38F6
Fords Bridge *Aust*	108C1
Fordyce *USA*	19B3
Forécarian *Guinea*	97A4
Forel,Mt *Greenland*	6G3
Forest *Can*	14B2
Forest Park *USA*	17B1
Forestville *USA*	22A1
Forfar *Scot*	44C3
Forges-les-Eaux *France*	46A2
Forks *USA*	20B1
Forlì *Italy*	52B2
Formentera, I *Spain*	51C2
Formia *Italy*	53B2
Formigas, I *Açores*	96A1
Formosa *Arg*	30F4
Formosa *Brazil*	31B5
Formosa, State *Arg*	30D3
Formosa Str *Taiwan/ China*	73D5
Fornovo di Taro *Italy*	47D2
Forres *Scot*	44C3
Forrest *Aust*	106B4
Forrest City *USA*	11A3
Forsayth *Aust*	107D2
Forssa *Fin*	39J6
Forster *Aust*	109D2
Forsyth, Missouri *USA*	18B2
Fort Abbas *Pak*	84C3
Fort Albany *Can*	7B4
Fortaleza *Brazil*	31D2
Fort Augustus *Scot*	44B3
Fort Beaufort *S Africa*	100B4
Fort Bragg *USA*	21A2
Fort Collins *USA*	8C2
Fort Coulogne *Can*	15C1
Fort de France *Martinique*	27E4
Fort Deposit *USA*	17A1
Fort Dodge *USA*	10A2
Fortescue, R *Aust*	106A3
Fort Frances *Can*	7A5
Fort Franklin *Can*	4F3
Fort George *Can*	7C4
Fort Good Hope *Can*	4F3
Fort Grey *Aust*	108B1
Forth, R *Scot*	44B3
Fort Hope *Can*	7B4
Fortin Uno *Arg*	34B3
Fort Laird *Can*	4F3
Fort Lallemant *Alg*	96C1
Fort Lauderdale *USA*	11B4
Fort Liard *Can*	4F3
Fort Mackay *Can*	5G4
Fort Macleod *Can*	5G5
Fort McMurray *Can*	5G4
Fort McPherson *Can*	4E3
Fort Madison *USA*	18B2
Fort Morgan *USA*	8C2
Fort Myers *USA*	11B4
Fort Nelson *Can*	5F4
Fort Norman *Can*	4F3
Fort Payne *USA*	17A1
Fort Peck Res *USA*	8C2
Fort Pierce *USA*	11B4
Fort Providence *Can*	4G3
Fort Resolution *Can*	5G3
Fort Rousset *Congo*	98B3

Fort Rupert

Fort Rupert *Can*	7C4
Fort St James *Can*	5F4
Fort St John *Can*	13C1
Fort Saskatchewan *Can*	13E2
Fort Scott *USA*	18B2
Fort Selkirk *Can*	4E3
Fort Severn *Can*	7B4
Fort Shevchenko *USSR*	61H5
Fort Simpson *Can*	4F3
Fort Smith *Can*	5G3
Fort Smith *USA*	11A3
Fort Stockton *USA*	9C3
Fortuna, California *USA*	20B2
Fort Vermillion *Can*	5G4
Fort Walton Beach *USA*	17A1
Fort Wayne *USA*	10B2
Fort William *Scot*	44B3
Fort Worth *USA*	9D3
Fortymile, R *USA*	12F2
Fort Yukon *USA*	12E1
Foshan *China*	73C5
Fossano *Italy*	47B2
Foster,Mt *USA*	12G3
Fougamou *Gabon*	98B3
Fougères *France*	48B2
Foulness I *Eng*	43E4
Foulwind,C *NZ*	111B2
Foumban *Cam*	98B2
Fourmies *France*	49C1
Foúrnoi, I *Greece*	55C3
Fouta Djallon, Mts *Guinea*	97A3
Foveaux, Str *NZ*	111B2
Fowey *Eng*	43B4
Fox Creek *Can*	13D2
Foxe Basin, G *Can*	6B3
Foxe Chan *Can*	6B3
Foxe Pen *Can*	6C3
Foxton *NZ*	110C2
Fox Valley *Can*	13F2
Foynes *Irish Rep*	45B2
Foz do Cuene *Angola*	100A2
Foz do Iguaçu *Brazil*	30F4
Frackville *USA*	16A2
Fraga *Arg*	34B2
Framingham *USA*	16D1
Franca *Brazil*	31B6
France, Republic *Europe*	49C2
Frances *Can*	10A2
Frances, R *Can*	12J2
France Ville *Gabon*	98B3
Franche Comté, Region *France*	49D2
Francistown *Botswana*	100B3
Francois L *Can*	13B2
Frankfort, Indiana *USA*	14A2
Frankfort, Kentucky *USA*	11B3
Frankfort *S Africa*	101G1
Frankfurt *W Germ*	57B2
Frankfurt am Main *W Germ*	46E1
Frankfurt-an-der-Oder *E Germ*	56C2
Fränkischer Alb, Upland *W Germ*	57C3
Franklin, Indiana *USA*	14A3
Franklin, Louisiana *USA*	19B4
Franklin, Massachusetts *USA*	16D1
Franklin, New Jersey *USA*	16B2
Franklin, Pennsylvania *USA*	14C2
Franklin, Region *Can*	4G2
Franklin B *Can*	4F2
Franklin D Roosevelt, L *USA*	20C1
Franklin Mts *Can*	4F3
Franklin Str *Can*	4J2
Frankovsk *USSR*	64D5
Franz Josef Glacier *NZ*	111B2
Fraser, R *Can*	5F5
Fraserburgh *Scot*	44C3
Fraser I *Aust*	109D1
Fraser L *Can*	13B2
Frasne *France*	47B1
Frauenfeld *Switz*	47C1
Fray Bentos *Urug*	34D2
Frazerburgh *Scot*	40C2
Frederica *USA*	16B3
Fredericia *Den*	56B1
Frederick, Maryland *USA*	15C3
Fredericksburg, Virginia *USA*	15C3
Frederick Sd *USA*	12H3
Fredericktown *USA*	18B2
Fredericton *Can*	7D5
Frederikshab *Greenland*	6E3
Frederikshavn *Den*	39G7
Fredonia *USA*	15C2
Fredrikstad *Nor*	39G7
Freehold *USA*	16B2
Freeport *Bahamas*	26B1
Freeport, Texas *USA*	19A4
Freetown *Sierra Leone*	97A4
Freiburg *W Germ*	57B3
Freistadt *Austria*	57C3
Fremantle *Aust*	106A4
Fremont, California *USA*	22B2
Fremont, Nebraska *USA*	18A1
Fremont, Ohio *USA*	14B2
French Guiana, Dependency *S America*	33G3
Frenchmans Cap, Mt *Aust*	109C4
French Polynesia, Is *Pacific O*	105J4
Fresnillo *Mexico*	24B2
Fresno *USA*	8B3
Fresno, R *USA*	22C2
Fretigney *France*	47A1
Frévent *France*	46B1
Freycinet Pen *Aust*	109C4
Fria *Guinea*	97A3
Friant *USA*	22C2
Friant Dam *USA*	22C2
Fribourg *Switz*	52A1
Friedrichshafen *W Germ*	57B3
Frobisher B *Can*	6D3
Frobisher Bay *Can*	6D3
Frobisher L *Can*	5H4
Frolovo *USSR*	61F4
Frome *Eng*	43C4
Frome, R *Aust*	108A1
Frome, R *Eng*	43C4
Frome,L *Aust*	106C4
Frontera *Mexico*	25C3
Front Royal *USA*	15C3
Frosinone *Italy*	53B2
Frunze *USSR*	82B1
Fuchuan *China*	73C5
Fuding *China*	73E4
Fuerte, R *Mexico*	24B2
Fuerte Olimpo *Par*	30E3
Fuerteventura, I *Canary Is*	96A2
Fugu *China*	72C2
Fuhai *China*	68A2
Fujairah *UAE*	91C4
Fujian, Province *China*	73D4
Fujin *China*	69F2
Fujinomiya *Japan*	75B1
Fuji-san, Mt *Japan*	74D3
Fujisawa *Japan*	75B1
Fuji-Yoshida *Japan*	75B1
Fukang *China*	63A3
Fukuchiyima *Japan*	74C3
Fukui *Japan*	74D3
Fukuoka *Japan*	74C4
Fukushima *Japan*	74E3
Fukuyama *Japan*	74C4
Fulda *W Germ*	57B2
Fulda, R *W Germ*	57B2
Fuling *China*	73B4
Fullarton *Trinidad*	27L1
Fullerton *USA*	22D4
Fulton, Kentucky *USA*	18C2
Fulton, New York *USA*	15C2
Fumay *France*	46C1
Funabashi *Japan*	75C1
Funchal *Medeira*	96A1
Fundão *Brazil*	35C1
Fundy,B of *Can*	7D5
Funhalouro *Mozam*	101C3
Funing *China*	72D3
Funing *China*	73B5
Funtua *Nig*	97C3
Fuqing *China*	73D4
Furancungo *Mozam*	101C2
Fürg *Iran*	91C4
Furka, P *Switz*	47C1
Furneaux Group, Is *Aust*	107D5
Fürstenwalde *E Germ*	56C2
Fürth *W Germ*	57C3
Furukawa *Japan*	74D3
Fury and Hecla St *Can*	6B3
Fushun, Liaoning *China*	74A2
Fushun, Sichuan *China*	73A4
Fusong *China*	74B2
Füssen *W Germ*	57C3
Fu Xian *China*	72E2
Fuxin *China*	72E1
Fuyang *China*	72D3
Fuyuan, Liaoning *China*	72E1
Fuyuan, Yunnan *China*	73A4
Fuyun *China*	68A2
Fuzhou *China*	73D4
Fyn, I *Den*	56C1

G

Gaalkacyo *Somalia*	99E2
Gabbs *USA*	21B2
Gabela *Angola*	100A2
Gabe's *Tunisia*	96D1
Gabilan Range, Mts *USA*	22B2
Gabon, Republic *Africa*	98B3
Gaborone *Botswana*	100B3
Gabrovo *Bulg*	54C2
Gach Sārān *Iran*	91B3
Gadsden, Alabama *USA*	17A1
Gads L *Can*	10A1
Gaeta *Italy*	53B2
Gaferut, I *Pacific O*	71F3
Gafsa *Tunisia*	96C1
Gagarin *USSR*	60D2
Gagnon *Can*	7D4
Gagra *USSR*	61F5
Gaibanda *India*	86B1
Gaimán *Arg*	29C4
Gainesville, Florida *USA*	17B2
Gainesville, Georgia *USA*	17B1
Gainesville, Texas *USA*	19A3
Gainsborough *Eng*	42D3
Gairdner,L *Aust*	108A2
Gairloch *Scot*	44B3
Gaithersburg *USA*	16A3
Gajendragarh *India*	87B1
Ga Jiang, R *China*	73D4
Galadi *Eth*	99E2
Galana, R *Kenya*	99D3
Galapagos Is *Pacific O*	103D5
Galashiels *Scot*	42C2
Galaţi *Rom*	54C1
Galena, Alaska *USA*	4C3
Galena, Kansas *USA*	18B2
Galeota Pt *Trinidad*	27L1
Galera Pt *Trinidad*	27L1
Galesburg *USA*	10A2
Galeton *USA*	15C2
Galich *USSR*	61F2
Galicia, Region *Spain*	50A1
Galina Pt *Jamaica*	27J1
Gallabat *Sudan*	99D1
Gallarate *Italy*	47C2
Galle *Sri Lanka*	87C3
Gállego, R *Spain*	51B1
Gallipoli *Italy*	55A2
Gällivare *Sweden*	38J5
Galloway, District	42B2
Galloway,Mull of, C *Scot*	42B2
Gallup *USA*	8C3
Galt *USA*	22B1
Galveston *USA*	25C2
Galveston B *USA*	11A4
Galvez *Arg*	34C2
Galvi *Corse*	49D3
Galway, County *Irish Rep*	45B2
Galway *Irish Rep*	41B3
Galway, B *Irish Rep*	41B3
Gamba *China*	86B1
Gambaga *Ghana*	97B3
Gambell *USA*	4A3
Gambia, R *The Gambia/Sen*	97A3
Gambia,The, Republic *Africa*	97A3
Gamboma *Congo*	98B3
Gambos *Angola*	100A2
Gampola *Sri Lanka*	87C3
Ganale Dorya, R *Eth*	99E2
Gananoque *Can*	15C2
Ganda *Angola*	100A2
Gandajika *Zaïre*	98C3
Gandava *Pak*	84B3
Gander *Can*	7E5
Gāndhidhām *India*	85C4
Gāndhinagar *India*	85C4
Gāndhi Sāgar, L *India*	85D4
Gandia *Spain*	51B2
Ganga, R *India*	86B2
Ganganar *India*	85C3
Gangaw *Burma*	86C2
Gangca *China*	72A2
Gangdise Shan, Mts *China*	82C2
Gangtok *India*	86B1
Gangu *China*	72B3
Gannett Peak, Mt *USA*	8C2
Ganquan *China*	72B2
Gantheaume, C *Aust*	108A3
Gantseviohi *USSR*	39K8
Ganzhou *China*	73D4
Gao *Mali*	97C3
Gaolan *China*	72A2
Gaoping *China*	72C2
Gaoua *U Volta*	97B3
Gaoual *Guinea*	97A3
Gaoyou Hu, L *China*	72D3
Gaozhou *China*	73C5
Gap *France*	49D3
Gapan *Phil*	79B2
Gar *China*	84D2
Garah *Aust*	109C1
Garanhuns *Brazil*	31D3
Garberville *USA*	21A1
Garça *Brazil*	35B2
Garcias *Brazil*	35A2
Garda *Italy*	47D2
Garden City *USA*	9C3
Garden Pen *USA*	14A1
Gardey *Arg*	34D3
Gardez *Afghan*	84B2
Gardiners I *USA*	16C2
Gardner *USA*	16D1
Gardone *Italy*	47D2
Gardula *Eth*	99D2
Gargano *Italy*	47D2
Garhākota *India*	85D4
Gari *USSR*	61K2
Garies *S Africa*	100A4
Garissa *Kenya*	99D3
Garland *USA*	19A3

Golconda

Golconda *USA*	20C2
Gold Beach *USA*	20B2
Gold Coast *Aust*	109D1
Golden *Can*	13D2
Golden B *NZ*	110B2
Goldendale *USA*	20B1
Golden Gate, Chan *USA*	22A2
Golden Meadow *USA*	19B4
Goldfield *USA*	21B2
Gold River *Can*	13B3
Goleniów *Pol*	56C2
Goleta *USA*	22C3
Golfe d'Ajaccio, G *Corse*	52A2
Golfe de Gabes, G *Tunisia*	96D1
Golfe de St Florent, G *Corse*	52A2
Golfe de St-Malo, B *France*	48B2
Golfe du Lion, G *France*	49C3
Golfo Corcovado, G *Chile*	29B4
Golfo de Almeira, G *Spain*	50B2
Golfo de Ancud, G *Chile*	29B4
Golfo de Batabano, G *Cuba*	25D2
Golfo de Cadiz, G *Spain*	50A2
Golfo de Cagliari, G *Sardegna*	53A3
Golfo de California, G *Mexico*	24A1
Golfo de Chiriqui, G *Panama*	25D4
Golfo de Fonseca *Honduras*	25D3
Golfo de Guacanayabo, G *Cuba*	26B2
Golfo de Guayaquil, G *Ecuador*	32A4
Golfo del Darien, G *Colombia/Panama*	26B5
Golfo de los Mosquitos, G *Panama*	32A2
Golfo del Papagaya, G *Nic*	25D3
Golfo de Mazarrón, G *Spain*	51B2
Golfo de Nicoya, G *Costa Rica*	25D4
Golfo de Oristano, G *Sardegna*	53A3
Golfo de Panamá, G *Panama*	25E4
Golfo de Papagayo, G *Costa Rica*	25D3
Golfo de Paria, G *Ven*	27E4
Golfo de Penas, G *Chile*	29B5
Golfo de St Florent *Corse*	49D3
Golfo de San Jorge, G *Spain*	51C1
Golfo de Tehuantepec G *Mexico*	24C3
Golfo de Torugas, G *Colombia*	32B3
Golfo de Uraba, G *Colombia*	32B2
Golfo de Valencia, G *Spain*	51C2
Golfo de Venezuela, G *Ven*	27C4
Golfo di Genova, G *Italy*	52A2
Golfo di Policastro, G *Italy*	53C3
Golfo di Squillace, G *Italy*	53C3
Golfo di Taranto, G *Italy*	53C2
Golfo di Venezia, G *Italy*	52B1
Golfo Dulce, G *Costa Rica*	25D4
Golfo San Jorge, G *Arg*	29C5
Golfo San Matías, G *Arg*	29D4
Golmud *China*	68B3
Golocha *Eth*	99E2
Golovin B *USA*	12B2
Golovnino *USSR*	74F2
Goma *Zaïre*	99C3
Gombe *Nig*	97D3
Gomel *USSR*	60D3
Gomera, I *Canary Is*	96A2
Gómez Palacio *Mexico*	24B2
Gonam, R *USSR*	63E2
Gonbad-e Kāvūs *Iran*	90C2
Gonda *India*	86A1
Gondal *India*	85C4
Gondar *Eth*	99D1
Gönen *Turk*	92A1
Gonen, R *Turk*	55C3
Gongga Shan, Mt *China*	73A4
Gonghe *China*	72A2
Gongola, R *Nig*	97D3
Gonzales, California *USA*	22B2
Gonzales, Texas *USA*	19A4
Gonzalez Chaves *Arg*	34C3
Good Hope Mt *Can*	13C2
Goodland *USA*	8C2
Goodnews Bay *USA*	12B3
Goodooga, R *Aust*	109C1
Goole *Eng*	42D3
Goolgowi *Aust*	108C2
Goolwa *Aust*	108A3
Goomalling *Aust*	106A4
Goombalie *Aust*	108C2
Goomer *Aust*	109D1
Goomeri *Aust*	109D1
Goondiwindi *Aust*	109D1
Goose Bay *Can*	7E4
Goose Creek *USA*	17C1
Goose L *USA*	20B2
Gooty *India*	87B1
Gora Munku Sardyk, Mt *USSR*	63C2
Goražde *Yugos*	54A2
Gordon *USA*	4D3
Gordon L *Can*	13E1
Gordonsville *USA*	15C3
Goré *Chad*	98B2
Gore *Eth*	99D2
Gore *NZ*	111A3
Gore Topko, Mt *USSR*	63F2
Gorey *Irish Rep*	45C2
Gorgān *Iran*	90B2
Goris *USSR*	93E2
Gorizia *Italy*	52B1
Gor'kiy *USSR*	65F4
Gor'kovskoye Vodokhranilishche, Res *USSR*	61F2
Görlitz *E Germ*	57C2
Gorlovka *USSR*	60E4
Gorman *USA*	22C3
Gorna Orjahovica *Bulg*	54C2
Gorno-Altaysk *USSR*	68A1
Gornozavodsk *USSR*	69G2
Gorodets *USSR*	61F2
Gorodok, Ukrainskaya S.S.R. *USSR*	59C3
Gorodok, Ukrainskaya S.S.R. *USSR*	59D3
Goroka *PNG*	71F4
Gorokhpur *India*	86A1
Gorongosa *Mozam*	101C2
Gorontalo *Indon*	71D3
Goro Yurma, Mt *USSR*	61K2
Gort *Irish Rep*	45B2
Goryachinsk *USSR*	63C2
Goryn', R *USSR*	59D3
Góry Świetokrzyskie, Upland *Pol*	59C2
Gory Tel'pos-iz', Mt *USSR*	64G3
Gorzow Wielkopolski *Pol*	39H8
Goshogawara *Japan*	74E2
Gospić *Yugos*	52C2
Gostivar *Yugos*	54B2
Gostynin *Pol*	58B2
Göteborg *Sweden*	39G7
Gotel, Mts *Nig*	98B2
Gotland, I *Sweden*	39H7
Gotō-retto, I *Japan*	74B4
Gotska Sandön, I *Sweden*	39H7
Götsu *Japan*	74C3
Gottwaldov *Czech*	59B3
Goudoumaria *Niger*	98B1
Gough I *Atlantic O*	103H7
Goulburn *Aust*	109C2
Goumbou *Mali*	97B3
Goundam *Mali*	97B3
Gouré *Niger*	98B1
Gourma Rharous *Mali*	97B3
Gournay-en-Bray *France*	46A2
Gouro *Chad*	95A3
Gove Pen *Aust*	71E5
Goverla, Mt *USSR*	60B4
Governador Valadares *Brazil*	35C1
Govind Ballabh Paht Sāgar, L *India*	86A2
Gowanda *USA*	15C2
Gowārān *Afghan*	84B3
Goya *Arg*	30E4
Goz-Beïda *Chad*	98C1
Gozo, I *Medit S*	53B3
Goz Regeb *Sudan*	95C3
Graaff-Reinet *S Africa*	100B4
Gracefield *Can*	15C1
Grafton *Aust*	109D1
Grafton, N Dakota *USA*	8D2
Grafton, W Virginia *USA*	14B3
Graham, I *Can*	5E4
Graham, R *Can*	13C1
Graham L *Can*	13E1
Grahamstown *S Africa*	100B4
Grajaú *Brazil*	31B3
Grajewo *Pol*	58C2
Grámmos, Mt *Greece/ Alb*	55B2
Grampian, Region *Scot*	44C3
Grampian, Mts *Scot*	44B3
Granada *Colombia*	32C3
Granada *Nic*	25D3
Granada *Spain*	50B2
Granby *Can*	15D1
Gran Canaria, I *Canary Is*	96A2
Gran Chaco, Region *Arg*	30D4
Grand, R, Michigan *USA*	14A2
Grand, R, Missouri *USA*	18B1
Grand B *Dominica*	27Q2
Grand Bahama, I *Bahamas*	11C4
Grand Bank *Can*	7E5
Grand Banks *Atlantic O*	102F2
Grand Bassam *Ivory Coast*	97B4
Grand Canyon *USA*	9B3
Grand Cayman, I *Caribbean*	26A3
Grand Centre *Can*	13E2
Grand Coulee *USA*	20C1
Grande, R *Arg*	34B3
Grande, R, Bahia *Brazil*	31C4
Grande, R, Minas Gerais/São Paulo *Brazil*	35B1
Grande Cache *Can*	13D2
Grande Chartreuse, Region *France*	47A2
Grande Comore, I *Comoros*	101D2
Grande Prairie *Can*	13D1
Grande Prairie *USA*	19A3
Grand Erg de Bilma, Desert *Niger*	95A3
Grand erg Occidental, Mts *Alg*	96B2
Grand erg Oriental, Mts *Alg*	96C2
Grande Rivière de la Baleine, R *Can*	7C4
Grande Ronde, R *USA*	20C1
Grand Falls, New Brunswick *Can*	7D5
Grand Falls, Newfoundland *Can*	7E5
Grand Forks *Can*	20C1
Grand Forks *USA*	8D2
Grand Gorge *USA*	16B1
Grand Haven *USA*	14A2
Grand Isle *USA*	19C3
Grand L *USA*	19B4
Grand Mere *Can*	15D1
Grândola *Port*	50A2
Grand Rapids *Can*	5J4
Grand Rapids, Michigan *USA*	14A2
Grand Rapids, Minnesota *USA*	10A2
Grand St Bernard, P *Italy/Switz*	47B2
Grand Teton, Mt *USA*	8B2
Grand Teton Nat Pk *USA*	8B2
Grandvilliers *France*	46A2
Grangeburg *USA*	25D1
Granollérs *Spain*	51C1
Gran Paradiso, Mt *Italy*	52A1
Gran Pilastro, Mt *Austria/Italy*	47D1
Grantham *Eng*	43D3
Grant,Mt *USA*	21B2
Grantown-on-Spey *Scot*	44C3
Grants *USA*	9C3
Grants Pass *USA*	20B2
Granville *France*	48B2
Granville L *Can*	5H4
Grão Mogol *Brazil*	35C1
Grasse *France*	49D3
Grass Valley *USA*	21A2
Gravelbourg *Can*	5H5
Gravelines *France*	46B1
Gravelotte *S Africa*	100C3
Gravenhurst *Can*	15C2
Gravesend *Aust*	109D1
Gravina I *USA*	12H3
Grayling *USA*	12B2
Grays Harbor, B *USA*	20B1
Grayson *USA*	14B3
Grayville *USA*	18C2
Graz *Austria*	59B3
Great, R *Jamaica*	27H1
Great Abaco, I *Bahamas*	11C4
Great Australian Bight, G *Aust*	106B4
Great B, New Jersey *USA*	16B3
Great Bahama Bank *Bahamas*	25E2
Great Barrier I *NZ*	110C1
Great Barrier Reef, Is *Aust*	107D2
Great Barrington *USA*	16C1
Great Bear L *Can*	4F3
Great Bend *USA*	9D2
Great Dividing Range, Mts *Aust*	107D3
Great Driffield *Eng*	42D2
Great Egg Harbor, B *USA*	16B3
Greater Antarctic, Region *Ant*	112B10

Greater Antilles, Is *Caribbean*	26B2	Greenwood, Mississippi *USA*	19B3
Greater London, Metropolitan County *Eng*	43D4	Greenwood, S Carolina *USA*	17B1
Greater Manchester, Metropolitan County *Eng*	43C3	Greers Ferry L *USA*	18B2
Great Exuma, I *Bahamas*	25E2	Gregory,L *Aust*	108A1
Great Falls *USA*	8B2	Gregory Range, Mts *Aust*	107D2
Great Glen, V *Scot*	44B3	Greifswald *E Germ*	56C2
Great Himalayan Range, Mts *Asia*	86B1	Gremikha *USSR*	64F3
Great Inagua, I *Bahamas*	11C4	Grenå *Den*	56C1
Great Karroo, Mts *S Africa*	100B4	Grenada *USA*	19C3
Great L *Aust*	109C4	Grenada, I *Caribbean*	27E4
Great Namaland, Region *Namibia*	100A3	Grenadines,The, Is *Caribbean*	27E4
Great Ormes Head, C *Wales*	42C3	Grenfell *Aust*	109C2
Groat Ragged, I *Bahamas*	11C4	Grenoble *France*	49D2
Great Ruaha, R *Tanz*	99D3	Grenville *Grenada*	27M2
Great Sacandaga L *USA*	15D2	Grenville,C *Aust*	107D2
Great Salt L *USA*	8B2	Gresham *USA*	20B1
Great Sand Sea *Libya/Egypt*	95B2	Gresik, Jawa *Indon*	78C4
Great Sandy Desert *Aust*	106B3	Gresik, Sumatera *Indon*	78A3
Great Sandy Desert *USA*	8A2	Gretna *USA*	19B4
Great Slave L *Can*	4G3	Grey, R *NZ*	111B2
Great South B *USA*	16C2	Grey Hunter Pk, Mt *Can*	12G2
Great Victoria Desert *Aust*	106B3	Grey Is *Can*	7E4
Great Wall *China*	72B2	Greylock,Mt *USA*	16C1
Great Yarmouth *Eng*	43E3	Greymouth *NZ*	111B2
Greco,C *Cyprus*	94B1	Grey Range, Mts *Aust*	107D3
Greece, Republic *Europe*	55B3	Greystones *Irish Rep*	45C2
Greece *USA*	15C2	Greytown *S Africa*	101H1
Greeley *USA*	8C2	Griekwastad *S Africa*	101F1
Greely Fjord *Can*	6B1	Griffin *USA*	17B1
Green B *USA*	14A1	Griffith *Aust*	108C2
Green Bay *USA*	14A2	Grim,C *Aust*	107D5
Greencastle, Indiana *USA*	14A3	Grimsby *Can*	15C2
Greenfield, Massachusetts *USA*	16C1	Grimsby *Eng*	42D3
Greenfield, Wisconsin *USA*	14A2	Grimsey, I *Iceland*	38B1
Green Lake *Can*	13F2	Grimshaw *Can*	13D1
Greenland, Dependency *N Atlantic*	6F2	Grimstad *Nor*	39F7
Greenland Basin *Greenland S*	102H1	Grindelwald *Switz*	47C1
Greenland S *Greenland*	1B1	Grinnell Pen *Can*	6A2
Greenock *Scot*	42B2	Grise Fjord *Can*	6B2
Greenport *USA*	16C2	Griva *USSR*	61H1
Greensboro, Maryland *USA*	16B3	Grobina *USSR*	39J7
Greensboro, N Carolina *USA*	11C3	Grodno *USSR*	58C2
Greensburg, Pennsylvania *USA*	15C2	Gromati, R *India*	86A1
Greenstone, Pt *Scot*	44B3	Groningen *Neth*	56B2
Greenup *USA*	18C2	Groote Eylandt, I *Aust*	106C2
Greenville, Alabama *USA*	17A1	Grootfontein *Namibia*	100A2
Greenville *Lib*	97B4	Grootvloer, Salt L *S Africa*	100B3
Greenville, Mississippi *USA*	19B3	Gros Islet *St Lucia*	27P2
Greenville, N Hampshire *USA*	16D1	Grosser Feldberg, Mt *W Germ*	46E1
Greenville, Ohio *USA*	14B2	Grosseto *Italy*	52B2
Greenville S Carolina *USA*	17B1	Gross-Gerau *W Germ*	46E2
Greenville, Texas *USA*	19A3	Grossglockner, Mt *Austria*	57C3
Greenwich *Eng*	43E4	Gross Venediger, Mt *Austria*	47E1
Greenwich *USA*	16C2	Grosvenor,L *USA*	12C3
Greenwood, Delaware *USA*	16B3	Groveland *USA*	22B2
		Grover City *USA*	21A2
		Groveton *USA*	15D2
		Groznyy *USSR*	61G5
		Grudziadz *Pol*	58B2
		Grünau *Namibia*	100A3
		Grutness *USSR*	44D2
		Gruzinskaya SSR, Republic *USSR*	65F5
		Gryazi *USSR*	61F3
		Gryazovets *USSR*	61E2
		Grytviken *South Georgia*	29G8
		Gt Blasket, I *Irish Rep*	45A2
		Guaçuí *Brazil*	35C2
		Guadalajara *Mexico*	23A1
		Guadalajara *Spain*	50B1
		Guadalcanal, I *Solomon Is*	107E1
		Guadalimar, R *Spain*	50B2
		Guadalope, R *Spain*	51B1
		Guadalqivir, R *Spain*	50B2
		Guadalupe *Mexico*	24B2
		Guadalupe, I *Mexico*	3G6

Guadeloupe, I *Caribbean*	27E3	Guinea Basin *Atlantic O*	102H4
Guadian, R *Spain*	50B2	Guinea-Bissau, Republic *Africa*	97A3
Guadiana, R *Port*	50A2	Guinea,G of *W Africa*	97C4
Guadix *Spain*	50B2	Güines *Cuba*	26A2
Guajará Mirim *Brazil*	32D6	Guir, Well *Mali*	97B3
Guajira,Pen de *Colombia*	32C1	Guiranwala *Pak*	84C2
Gualaceo *Ecuador*	32B4	Güiria *Ven*	33E1
Gualeguay *Arg*	34D2	Guise *France*	46B2
Gualeguaychú *Arg*	34D2	Guiuan *Phil*	79C3
Guam, I *Pacific O*	71F2	Gui Xian *China*	73B5
Guamini *Arg*	34C3	Guiyang *China*	73B4
Gua Musang *Malay*	77C5	Guizhou, Province *China*	73B4
Guanajuato *Mexico*	23A1	Gujarat, State *India*	85C4
Guanajuato, State *Mexico*	23A1	Gujrat *Pak*	84C2
Guanare *Ven*	32D2	Gulbarga *India*	87B1
Guane *Cuba*	25D2	Gulbene *USSR*	58D1
Guangdong, Province *China*	73C5	Guledagudda *India*	87B1
Guanghan *China*	73A3	Gulf,The *S W Asia*	80D3
Guanghua *China*	72C3	Gulgong *Aust*	109C2
Guangmao Shan, Mt *China*	73A4	Gulin *China*	73B4
Guangnan *China*	73B5	Gulkana *USA*	12E2
Guangyuan *China*	72B3	Gulkana, R *USA*	12E2
Guangze *China*	73D4	Gull L *Can*	13E2
Guangzhou *China*	67F3	Gull Lake *Can*	13F2
Guanhães *Brazil*	35C1	Gulu *Uganda*	99D2
Guania, R *Colombia*	32D3	Guluguba *Aust*	109C1
Guanipa, R *Ven*	27E5	Gumel *Nig*	97C3
Guantánamo *Cuba*	26B2	Gummersbach *W Germ*	46D1
Guanting Shuiku, Res *China*	72D1	Gumpla *India*	86A2
Guanxi, Province *China*	73B5	Gümüshane *Turk*	93C1
Guan Xian *China*	73A3	Guna *India*	85D4
Guapa *Colombia*	32B2	Guña, Mt *Eth*	99D1
Guaporé, R *Brazil/Bol*	33E6	Gundagai *Aust*	109C3
Guaquí *Bol*	30C2	Gungu *Zaïre*	98B3
Guaranda *Ecuador*	32B4	Gunnedah *Aust*	109D2
Guarapuava *Brazil*	30F4	Guntakal *India*	87B1
Guaratinguetá *Brazil*	35B2	Guntersville *USA*	17A1
Guarda *Port*	50A1	Guntersville L *USA*	17A1
Guardafui,C *Somalia*	99F1	Guntür *India*	87C1
Guarda Mor *Brazil*	35B1	Gunung Batu Putch, Mt *Malay*	77C5
Guasave *Mexico*	9C4	Gunung Besar, Mt *Indon*	78D3
Guastalla *Italy*	47D2	Gunung Bulu, Mt *Indon*	78D2
Guatemala *Guatemala*	25C3	Gunung Gedang, Mt *Indon*	78A3
Guatemala, Republic *C America*	25C3	Gunung Lawit, Mt *Malay*	78C2
Guatraché *Arg*	34C3	Gunung Lawu, Mt *Indon*	78C4
Guavrare, R *Colombia*	32C3	Gunung Menyapa, Mt *Indon*	78D2
Guaxupé *Brazil*	35B2	Gunung Niapa, Mt *Indon*	78D2
Guayaguayare *Trinidad*	27L1	Gunung Patah, Mt *Indon*	78A3
Guayaquil *Ecuador*	32A4	Gunung Raung, Mt *Indon*	78C4
Guaymas *Mexico*	24A2	Gunung Resag, Mt *Indon*	78A3
Guayquiraro, R *Arg*	34D2	Gunung Sarempaka, Mt *Indon*	78D3
Guba *Eth*	99D2	Gunung Sumbing, Mt *Indon*	78C4
Guba *Zaïre*	100B2	Gunung Tahan, Mt *Malay*	77C5
Guban, Region *Somalia*	99E2	Gunung Talakmau, Mt *Indon*	78A2
Gubat *Phil*	79B3	Gunza *Angola*	100A2
Gubin *Pol*	56C2	Guoyang *China*	72D3
Güdür *India*	87B2	Gurdàspur *India*	84D2
Guelpho *Can*	14B2	Gurgaon *India*	84D3
Guelta Zemmur *Mor*	96A2	Gurkha *Nepal*	86A1
Guenabacoa *Cuba*	26A2	Gürün *Turk*	92C2
Guéréda *Chad*	98C1	Gurupi, R *Brazil*	31B2
Guéret *France*	48C2	Gurvan Sayhan Uul, Upland *Mongolia*	72A1
Guernsey, I *UK*	48B2	Gur'yev *USSR*	61H4
Guerrero, State *Mexico*	23A2	Gurzinskaya, Republic *USSR*	65F5
Gughe, Mt *Eth*	99D2	Gusau *Nig*	97C3
Gugigu *China*	63E2	Gusev *USSR*	58C2
Guguan, I *Pacific O*	71F2	Gushan *China*	74A3
Guiargambone *Aust*	109C2		
Guidong *China*	73C4		
Guiglo *Ivory Coast*	97B4		
Gui Jiang, R *China*	73C5		
Guildford *Eng*	43D4		
Guilin *China*	73C4		
Guillestre *France*	47B2		
Guinan *China*	72A2		
Guinea, Republic *Africa*	97A3		

Gus'khrustalnyy

28

Igoumenítsa *Greece* 55B3
Igra *USSR* 61H2
Iguala *Mexico* 23B2
Iguape *Brazil* 31B6
Iguape *Brazil* 35B2
Iguatama *Brazil* 35B2
Iguatu *Brazil* 31D3
Iguéla *Gabon* 98A3
Ihosy *Madag* 101D3
Iida *Japan* 74D3
Iide-san, Mt *Japan* 75B1
Iisalmi *Fin* 38K6
Iizuka *Japan* 75A2
Ijebu Ode *Nig* 97C4
Ijsselmeer, S *Neth* 56B2
Ikaría, I *Greece* 55C3
Ikeda *Japan* 74E2
Ikela *Zaïre* 98C3
Ikhtiman *Bulg* 54B2
Ikolik,C *USA* 12D3
Ikopa, R *Madag* 101D2
Ilagan *Phil* 79B2
Ilām *Iran* 90A3
Ilanz *Switz* 47C1
Île à la Crosse *Can* 13F1
Île à la Crosse,L *Can* 13F1
Ilebo *Zaire* 89G8
Île de Jerba, I *Tunisia* 96D1
Ile de Noirmoutier, I *France* 48B2
Ile de Ré, I *France* 48B2
Île des Pins, I *Nouvelle Calédonie* 107F3
Ile d'Ouessant, I *France* 48A2
Ilu d'Yeu, I *France* 48B2
Ilek, R *USSR* 61J3
Îles Bélèp *Nouvelle Calédonie* 107F2
Îles Chesterfield *Nouvelle Calédonie* 107E2
Iles d'Hyleres, Is *France* 49D3
Ilfracombe *Eng* 43B4
Ilgaz Dağları, Mts *Turk* 92B1
Ilha Bazaruto, I *Mozam* 101C3
Ilha De Maracá, I *Brazil* 33G3
Ilha de Marajó, I *Brazil* 33G4
Ilha de São Sebastião, I *Brazil* 35B2
Ilha do Bananal, Region *Brazil* 33G6
Ilha Grande, I *Brazil* 35C2
Ilha Santo Amaro, I *Brazil* 35B2
Ilhas Selvegens, I *Atlantic O* 96A1
Ilhéus *Brazil* 31D4
Iliamna L *USA* 12C3
Iliamna V *USA* 12D2
Iligan *Phil* 79B4
Il'inskiy *USSR* 63G3
Iliodhrómia, I *Greece* 55B3
Illana B *Phil* 79B4
Illapel *Chile* 34A2
Iller, R *Chile* 34A2
Illéla *Niger* 97C3
Iller, R *W Germ* 47D1
Illiamna L *USA* 4C4
Illinois, State *USA* 10A2
Illinois, R *USA* 18B2
Illizi *Alg* 96C2
Ilo *Peru* 30B2
Iloilo *Phil* 79B3
Ilomantsi *Fin* 38L6
Ilorin *Nig* 97C4
Imabari *Japan* 75A2
Imalchi *Japan* 75B1
Imatra *Fin* 60C1
Imbituba *Brazil* 30G4
Imi *Eth* 99E2
Imlay *USA* 20C2
Immenstadt *W Germ* 47D1
Imola *Italy* 52B2
Imperatriz *Brazil* 31B3
Imperia *Italy* 52A2

Impfondo *Congo* 98B2
Imphäl *India* 86C2
Imst *Austria* 47D1
Imuruk L *USA* 12B1
Ina *Japan* 75B1
In Afahleleh, Well *Alg* 96C2
Inamba-jima, I *Japan* 75B2
In Amenas *Alg* 96C2
Inari *Fin* 38K5
Inarijärvi, L *Fin* 38K5
Inawashiro-ko, L *Japan* 75C1
In Belbel *Alg* 96C2
Ince Burun, Pt *Turk* 60E5
Incekum Burun, Pt *Turk* 92B2
Inch'ŏn *S Korea* 74B3
In Dagouber, Well *Mali* 96B2
Indaia, R *Brazil* 35B1
Indals, R *Sweden* 38H6
Independence, California *USA* 21B2
Independence, Kansas *USA* 18A2
Independence, Missouri *USA* 18B2
Inderagiri, R *Indon* 78A3
Inderborskly *USSR* 61H4
India, Federal Republic *Asia* 83B3
Indiana, State *USA* 14A2
Indiana *USA* 15C2
Indian-Antarctic Ridge *Indian O* 104C6
Indianapolis *USA* 14A3
Indian Harbour *Can* 7E4
Indian O 104B4
Indianola, Iowa *USA* 18B1
Indianola, Mississippi *USA* 19B3
Indianópolis *Brazil* 35B1
Indo China, Region *S E Asia* 76D2
Indonesia, Republic *S E Asia* 70C4
Indore *India* 85D4
Indramayu *Indon* 78B4
Indre, R *France* 48C2
Indus, R *Pak* 85B3
Inebdu *Turk* 60D5
In Ebeggi, Well *Alg* 96C2
In Ecker *Alg* 96C2
Inegöl *Turk* 92A1
In Ézzane *Alg* 96D2
Ingal *Niger* 97C3
Ingersoll *Can* 14B2
Ingham *Aust* 107D2
Inglefield Land, Region *Can* 6D2
Inglewood *NZ* 110B1
Inglewood, Queensland *Aust* 109D1
Inglewood *USA* 22C4
Inglewood, Victoria *Aust* 108B3
Ingólfshöfði, I *Iceland* 38B2
Ingolstadt *W Germ* 57C3
Ingräj Bäzär *India* 86B2
In-Guezzam, Well *Alg* 96C3
Inhambane *Mozam* 101C3
Inharrime *Mozam* 101C3
Inhumas *Brazil* 35B1
Inirida, R *Colombia* 32D3
Inishbofin, I *Irish Rep* 45A2
Inishkea, I *Irish Rep* 45A1
Inishmaan, I *Irish Rep* 45B2
Inishmore, I *Irish Rep* 45B2
Inishmurray, I *Irish Rep* 45B1
Inishowen, District *Irish Rep* 45C1
Inishshark, I *Irish Rep* 45A2
Inishturk, I *Irish Rep* 45A2
Injune *Aust* 109C1
Inklin *Can* 12H3
Inklin, R *Can* 12H3
Inland L *USA* 12C1

Inn, R *Austria* 47D1
Innamincka *Aust* 108B1
Inner Mongolia, Autonomous Region *China* 68C2
Innisfail *Aust* 107D2
Innoko, R *USA* 12C2
Innsbruck *Austria* 57C3
Inongo *Zaïre* 98B3
Inowrocław *Pol* 58B2
In Salah *Alg* 96C2
Interlaken *Switz* 47B1
Intepec *Mexico* 24C3
Intra *Italy* 47C2
Intu *Indon* 78D3
Inubo-saki, C *Japan* 75C1
Inukjuac *Can* 7C4
Inuvik *Can* 4E3
Inveraray *Scot* 44B3
Invercargill *NZ* 111A3
Inverell *Aust* 109D1
Invermere *Can* 13D2
Inverness *Scot* 44B3
Inverurie *Scot* 44C3
Investigator Str *Aust* 108A3
Inya *USSR* 68A1
Inyanga *Zim* 101C2
Inyokern *USA* 21B2
Inzia, R *Zaïre* 98B3
Ioánnina *Greece* 55B3
Iola *USA* 18A2
Iona, I *Scot* 44A3
Iôna Nat Pk *Angola* 100A2
Ione *USA* 20C1
Ionian S *Italy/Greece* 55A3
Ionfor Nison, Is *Greece* 55B3
Íos, I *Greece* 55C3
Iowa, R *USA* 10A2
Iowa City *USA* 10A2
Ipameri *Brazil* 35B1
Ipanema *Brazil* 35C1
Ipatovo *USSR* 61F4
Ipiales *Colombia* 32B3
Ipoh *Malay* 77C5
Iporá *Brazil* 30F2
Ipsala *Turk* 55C2
Ipswich *Aust* 109D1
Ipswich *Eng* 43E3
Ipswich *USA* 16D1
Iquique *Chile* 30B3
Iquitos *Peru* 32C4
Iráklion *Greece* 55C3
Iran, Republic *S W Asia* 80D2
Iränshahr *Iran* 91D4
Irapuato *Mexico* 23A1
Iraq, Republic *S W Asia* 93D3
Irã Wan, Watercourse *Libya* 95A2
Irbid *Jordan* 94B2
Irbit *USSR* 61K2
Ireland, Republic *NW Europe* 36C3
Ireng, R *Guyana* 33F3
Iri *S Korea* 74B3
Irian Jaya, Province *Indon* 71E4
Iriba *Chad* 95B3
Iriga *Phil* 79B3
Iringa *Tanz* 99D3
Iriri, R *Brazil* 33G5
Irish S *Eng/Irish Rep* 42B3
Irkillik, R *USA* 12D1
Irkutsk *USSR* 63C2
Irlysh *USSR* 65J4
Iron Knob *Aust* 108A2
Iron Mountain *USA* 14A1
Iron Range *Aust* 107D2
Iron River *USA* 14A1
Irontown *USA* 14B3
Ironwood *USA* 10A2
Iroquois Falls *Can* 10B2
Iro-zaki, C *Japan* 75B2
Irrawaddy,Mouths of the *Burma* 76A2
Irtysh, R *USSR* 65H4

Irun *Spain* 51B1
Irvine *Scot* 42B2
Irving *USA* 19A3
Isabela *Phil* 79B4
Isabela, I *Ecuador* 32J7
Isachsen *Can* 4H2
Isachsen,C *Can* 4H2
Isafjörður *Iceland* 6H3
Isahaya *Japan* 74C4
Isangi *Zaïre* 98C2
Isar, R *W Germ* 47D1
Isarco, R *Italy* 47D1
Isbister *Scot* 44D1
Ischgl *Austria* 47D1
Ischia, I *Italy* 53B2
Ise *Japan* 75B2
Iseo *Italy* 47D2
Iserlohn *W Germ* 46D1
Isernia *Italy* 53B2
Ise-wan, B *Japan* 75B2
Ishigaki, I *Japan* 69E4
Ishikari, R *Japan* 74E2
Ishikari-wan, B *Japan* 74E2
Ishim *USSR* 65H4
Ishim, R *USSR* 65H4
Ishinomaki *Japan* 74E3
Ishioka *Japan* 75C1
Ishkashim *Afghan* 84C1
Ishpeming *USA* 14A1
Isil'kul *USSR* 65J4
Isiolo *Kenya* 99D2
Isiro *Zaïre* 98C2
Iskenderun *Turk* 92C2
Iskenferun Körfezi, B *Turk* 92C2
İskilip *Turk* 92B1
Iskitim *USSR* 65K4
Iskur, R *Bulg* 54B2
Iskut, R *Can/USA* 12H3
Isla *Mexico* 23B2
Isla Bermejo, I *Arg* 34C3
Isla Blanquilla *Ven* 27E4
Isla Coiba, I *Panama* 32A2
Isla de Cedros, I *Mexico* 9B4
Isla de Chiloé, I *Chile* 29B4
Isla de Cozumel, I *Mexico* 25D2
Isla de la Gonâve *Cuba* 26C3
Isla de la Juventud, I *Cuba* 26A2
Isla de las Lechiguanas, I *Arg* 34D2
Isla del Coco, I *Costa Rica* 3K8
Isla del Maiz, I *Caribbean* 25D3
Isla de Lobos, I *Mexico* 23B1
Isla de los Estados, I *Arg* 29D6
Isla de Marajó, I *Brazil* 28E2
Isla de Pascua, I *Pacific O* 105L5
Isla de Providencia, I *Caribbean* 26A4
Isla de San Andres, I *Caribbean* 26A4
Isla de Santa Catarina, I *Brazil* 30G4
Isla du Diable, I *French Guiana* 33G2
Isla Fernando de Noronha, I *Brazil* 31E2
Isla Grande de Tierra del Fuego, I *Arg/Chile* 29C6
Isla la Tortuga, I *Ven* 27D4
Islamabad *Pak* 84C2
Isla Magdalena, I *Mexico* 24A2
Isla Margarita *Ven* 27E4
Isla Mocha *Chile* 34A3
Islamorada *USA* 17B2
Island L *Can* 10A1
Island Lg *Aust* 108A2
Islands,B of *NZ* 110B1

Isla Puná

Jebel esh Sharqi, Mts Leb/Syria 92C3
Jebel Ithriyat, Mt Jordan 94C3
Jebel Ja'lan, Mt Oman 91C5
Jebel Liban, Mts Leb 94B2
Jebel Ma'lūlā, Mt Syria 94C2
Jebel Marra, Mt Sudan 98C1
Jebel Mudeisisat, Mt Jordan 94C3
Jebel Oda, Mt Sudan 95C2
Jebel Qasr ed Deir, Mt Jordan 94B3
Jebel Um ed Daraj, Mt Jordan 94B2
Jebel Uweinat, Mt Sudan 95B2
Jedburgh Scot 42C2
Jedrzejów Pol 59C2
Jefferson, Texas USA 19B3
Jefferson City USA 11A3
Jefferson,Mt USA 8B3
Jeffersonville USA 14A3
Jekabpils USSR 60C2
Jelena Gora Pol 59B2
Jelgava USSR 60B2
Jember Indon 78C4
Jena E Germ 57C2
Jenaja, I Indon 78B2
Jenbach Austria 47D1
Jenin Israel 94B2
Jennings USA 19B3
Jenseniky, Upland Czech 59B2
Jensen Nunatakker, Mt Greenland 6F3
Jens Munk, I Can 6B3
Jeparit Aust 108B3
Jequié Brazil 31D4
Jequital, R Brazil 35C1
Jequitinhonha Brazil 35C1
Jequitinhonha, R Brazil 31C5
Jerez de la Frontera Spain 50A2
Jerez de los Caballeros Spain 50A2
Jericho Israel 94B3
Jerilderie Aust 108C3
Jersey, I UK 48B2
Jersey City USA 10C2
Jersey Shore USA 15C2
Jerseyville USA 18B2
Jerusalem Israel 92C3
Jervis B Aust 109D3
Jervis Inlet, Sd Can 13C2
Jesenice Yugos 52B1
Jessore Bang 86B2
Jesup USA 11B3
Jesus Maria Arg 34C2
Jewett City USA 16D2
Jezerce, Mt Alb 54A2
Jezioro Mamry, L Pol 58C2
Jezioro Śniardwy, L Pol 58C2
Jezzine Leb 94B2
Jhābua India 85C4
Jhālāwār India 85D4
Jhang Maghiana Pak 84C2
Jhānsi India 85D3
Jhārsuguda India 86A2
Jhelum Pak 84C2
Jhelum, R Pak 84C2
J H Kerr L USA 11C3
Jhunjhunūn India 84D3
Jiamusi China 69F2
Ji'an, Jiangxi China 73C4
Ji'an, Jilin China 74B2
Jiande China 73D4
Jiang'an China 73B4
Jiangbiancun China 73D4
Jiangcheng China 73A5
Jiang Jiang, R China 73B3
Jiangmen China 73C5
Jiangsu, Province China 72D3

Jiangxi, Province China 73C4
Jiangyou China 73A3
Jianping China 72D1
Jianshui China 73A5
Jian Xi, R China 73D4
Jianyang China 73D4
Jiaonan China 72E2
Jiao Xian China 72E2
Jiaozhou Wan, B China 72E2
Jiaozuo China 72C2
Jiaxiang China 73E3
Jiayuguan China 68B3
Jiddah S Arabia 81B3
Jieshou China 72D3
Jiexiu China 72C2
Jigzhi China 72A3
Jihlava Czech 59B3
Jilib Somalia 99E2
Jilin China 69E2
Jiloca, R Spain 51B1
Jiménez, Coahuila Mexico 9C4
Jimma Eth 99D2
Jinan China 72D2
Jind India 84D3
Jingbian China 72B2
Jingdezhen China 73D4
Jinghong China 76C1
Jingmen China 73C3
Jingning China 72B2
Jing Xiang China 73B4
Jinhua China 73D4
Jining, Nei Monggol China 72C1
Jining, Shandong China 72D2
Jinja Uganda 99D2
Jinping China 76C1
Jinsha Jiang, R China 73A4
Jinshi China 73C4
Jinxi China 72E1
Jin Xian China 72E2
Jinzhou China 72E1
Jiparaná, R Brazil 33E5
Jipijapa Ecuador 32A4
Jiquilpan Mexico 23A2
Jiroft Iran 91C4
Jishou China 73B4
Jisr ash Shughūr Syria 92C2
Jiu, R Rom 54B2
Jiujiang China 73D4
Jiulong China 73A4
Jiulong Jiang, R China 73D4
Jixi China 69F2
Jiza Jordan 94B3
Jizan S Arabia 81C4
Joal Sen 97A3
João Monlevade Brazil 35C1
João Pessoa Brazil 31E3
João Pirheiro Brazil 35B1
Jocoli Arg 34B2
Jodhpur India 85C3
Joensuu Fin 38K6
Joeuf France 46C2
Joffre,Mt Can 13D2
Jogbani India 86B1
Jog Falls India 87A2
Johannesburg S Africa 101G1
Johannesburg USA 21B2
Johan Pen Can 6C2
John, R USA 12D1
John Day USA 20C2
John Day, R USA 20B1
John O'Groats Scot 44C2
John Redmond Res USA 18A2
Johnson City, Tennessee USA 11B3
Johnston USA 17B1
Johnston Pt St Vincent 27N2
Johnstown, Pennsylvania USA 15C2
Johor Bharu Malay 77C5
Joigny France 49C2
Joinville Brazil 30G4

Jok, R USSR 61H3
Jokkmokk Sweden 38H5
Jolfa Iran 93E2
Joliet USA 10B2
Joliette Can 7C5
Jolo Phil 79B4
Jolo, I Phil 79B4
Joma, Mt China 82D2
Jonava USSR 58C1
Jonê China 72A3
Jonesboro, Arkansas USA 11A3
Jonesboro, Louisiana USA 19B3
Jones Sd Can 6B2
Joniškis USSR 58C1
Jönköping Sweden 39G7
Joplin USA 11A3
Jordan, Kingdom S W Asia 92C3
Jordan, R Israel 94B2
Jordan Valley USA 20C2
Jorhāt India 86C1
Jörn Sweden 38J5
Jorong Indon 78C3
Jørpeland Nor 39F7
Jose Pañganiban Phil 79B3
Joseph Bonaparte G Aust 106B2
Jotunheimen, Mt Nor 64B3
Jouai'ya Leb 94B2
Jounié Leb 94B2
Jowal India 86C1
Jowhar Somalia 99E2
Joy,Mt Can 12H2
Juan de Fuca,Str of USA/Can 5F5
Juan de Nova, I Mozam Chan 101D2
Juàrez Arg 34D3
Juàzeiro Brazil 31C3
Juazeiro do Norte Brazil 31D3
Juba Sudan 99D2
Juba, R Somalia 99E2
Jubail Leb 94B1
Jubbah S Arabia 93D3
Jucar, R Spain 51B2
Juchatengo Mexico 23B2
Juchipila, R Mexico 23A1
Juchitlan Mexico 23A1
Judenburg Austria 57C3
Juilaca Peru 30B2
Juiling Shan, Hills China 73C4
Juiz de Fora Brazil 31C6
Jujuy, State Arg 30C3
Juli Peru 30C2
Julianatop, Mt Surinam 33F3
Julianehab Greenland 6F3
Jülich W Germ 46D1
Jullundur India 84D2
Jumla Nepal 86A1
Jum Suwwāna, Mt Jordan 94B3
Jūnāgadh India 85C4
Junan China 72D2
Junction City USA 9D3
Jundiaí Brazil 31B6
Juneau USA 4E4
Junee Aust 107D4
June Lake USA 22C2
Jungfrau, Mt Switz 52A1
Juniata, R USA 16A2
Junín Arg 29D2
Junlian China 73A4
Juquiá Brazil 31B6
Jur, R Sudan 99C2
Jura, I Scot 42B2
Jura, Mts France 49D2
Jura,Sound of, Chan Scot 44B3
Jurf ed Darāwīsh Jordan 94B3
Jūrmala USSR 60B2
Juruá, R Brazil 32D4
Juruena, R Brazil 33F6

Jūsīyah Syria 94C1
Justo Daract Arg 34B2
Jutai, R Brazil 32D4
Juticalpa Honduras 25D3
Jüymand Iran 90C3
Jylland, Pen Den 56B1
Jyväskyla Fin 38K6

K

K2, Mt China/India 82B2
Kaakhka USSR 90C2
Kaapmuiden S Africa 101H1
Kabaena, I Indon 71D4
Kabala Sierra Leone 97A4
Kabale Rwanda 99D3
Kabalo Zaïre 98C3
Kabambare Zaïre 98C3
Kabarole Uganda 99D2
Kabinda Zaïre 98C3
Kabir Kuh, Mts Iran 90A3
Kabompo Zambia 100B2
Kabompo, R Zambia 100B2
Kabongo Zaïre 98C3
Kabul Afghan 84B2
Kachchh,G of India 85B4
Kachkanar USSR 61J2
Kachug USSR 63C2
Kadan Burma 76B3
Kadapongan, I Indon 78D3
Kadi India 85C4
Kadina Aust 108A2
Kadinhanı Turk 92B2
Kadiri India 87B2
Kadiyevka USSR 60E4
Kadoma Zim 100B2
Kadugli Sudan 99C1
Kaduna Nig 97C3
Kaduna, R Nig 97C3
Kadur India 87B2
Kaédi Maur 97A3
Kaena Pt Hawaiian Is 21C4
Kaesŏng N Korea 74B3
Kafanchan Nig 97C4
Kaffrine Sen 97A3
Kafrün Bashūr Syria 94C1
Kafue Zambia 100B2
Kafue, R Zambia 100B2
Kafue Nat Pk Zambia 100B2
Kaga Japan 74D3
Kagan USSR 65H6
Kağızman Turk 93D1
Kagoshima Japan 74C4
Kāhak Iran 90C2
Kahama Tanz 99D3
Kahan Pak 84B3
Kahayan, R Indon 78C3
Kahemba Zaïre 98B3
Kahler Asten, Mt W Germ 46E1
Kahnūj Iran 91C4
Kahoka USA 18B1
Kahoolawe, I Hawaiian Is 21C4
Kahramanmaraş Turk 92C2
Kahuku Pt Hawaiian Is 21C4
Kaiapoi NZ 111B2
Kaieteur Fall Guyana 33F2
Kaifeng China 72C3
Kaikohe NZ 110B1
Kaikoura NZ 111B2
Kaikoura Pen NZ 111B2
Kaikoura Range, Mts NZ 111B2
Kaili China 73B4
Kailua Hawaiian Is 21C4
Kaimana Indon 71E4
Kainan Japan 75B2
Kainji Res Nig 97C3
Kaipara Harbour, B NZ 110B1
Kaiping China 73C5
Kairouan Tunisia 96D1
Kaiser Peak, Mt USA 22C2
Kaiserslautern W Germ 57B3
Kaishantun China 74B2
Kaisiadorys USSR 58D2
Kaitaia NZ 110B1

Kaitangata

Kaitangata *NZ*	111A3	Kamanawa Mts *NZ*	110C1	Kansas, R *USA*	18A2	Karesvando *Sweden*	38J5
Kaithal *India*	84D3	Kamanjab *Namibia*	100A2	Kansas City *USA*	10A3	Karet, Desert Region	
Kaiwi Chan *Hawaiian*		Kamat, Mt *India*	84D2	Kansk *China*	73D5	*Maur*	96B2
Is	21C4	Kamban *India*	87B3	Kansk *USSR*	63B2	Kargasok *USSR*	65K4
Kai Xian *China*	73B3	Kambarka *USSR*	61H2	Kantchari *U Volta*	97C3	Kari *Nig*	97D3
Kaiyuan, Liaoning		Kambia *Sierra Leone*	97A4	Kanthi *India*	86B2	Kariba *Zim*	100B2
China	73A5	Kamenets Podolskiy		Kantishna *USA*	12D2	Kariba, L *Zim/Zambia*	100B2
Kaiyuan, Yunnan		*USSR*	59D3	Kantishna, R *USA*	12D2	Kariba Dam *Zim/*	
China	74A2	Kamenka *USSR*	61F3	Kanye *Botswana*	100B3	*Zambia*	100B2
Kaiyuh Mts *USA*	12C2	Kamen-na-Obi *USSR*	65K4	Kao-hsiung *Taiwan*	68D4	Karima *Sudan*	95C3
Kajaani *Fin*	38K6	Kamensk-Ural'skiy		Kaoka Veld, Plain		Karimata, I *Indon*	78B3
Kajaki *Afghan*	84B2	*USSR*	61K2	*Namibia*	100A2	Karimganj *Bang*	86C2
Kajiado *Kenya*	99D3	Kamilukuak L *Can*	5H3	Kaolack *Sen*	97A3	Karīmnagar *India*	87B1
Kajrān *Afghan*	84B2	Kamina *Zaïre*	98C3	Kaoma *Zambia*	100B2	Karin *Somalia*	99E1
Kaka *Sudan*	99D1	Kaminak L *Can*	7A3	Kapaau *Hawaiian Is*	21C4	Karis *Fin*	39J6
Kakamega *Kenya*	99D2	Kaminoyama *Japan*	75C1	Kapanga *Zaïre*	98C3	Karishimbe, Mt *Zaïre*	99C3
Kake *Japan*	75A2	Kamloops *Can*	5F4	Kap Cort Adelaer, C		Káristos *Greece*	55B3
Kake *USA*	12H3	Kamo *USSR*	93E1	*Greenland*	6F3	Kärkal *India*	87A2
Kakhonak *USA*	12D3	Kamogawa *Japan*	75C1	Kap Dalton, C		Karkar, I *PNG*	71F4
Kakhovskoye		Kampala *Uganda*	99D2	*Greenland*	6H3	Karkheh, R *Iran*	90A3
Vodokhranilishche,		Kampar *Malay*	77C5	Kapellskär *Sweden*	39H7	Karkinitskiy Zaliv, B	
Res *USSR*	65E5	Kampar, R *Indon*	78A2	Kap Farvel, C		*USSR*	60D4
Kākī *Iran*	91B4	Kampen *Neth*	56B2	*Greenland*	6F3	Karlik Shan, Mt *China*	63B3
Kākināda *India*	87C1	Kamphaeng Phet *Thai*	76B2	Kap Gustav Holm, C		Karlino *Pol*	58B2
Kakogawa *Japan*	75A2	Kampot *Camb*	77C3	*Greenland*	6G3	Karl Marx Stadt *E*	
Kaktovik *USA*	4D2	Kamsaptar *Iran*	91D4	Kapiri *Zambia*	100B2	*Germ*	57C2
Kakuda *Japan*	75C1	Kamskoye		Kapit *Malay*	78C2	Karlobag *Yugos*	52C2
Kalabáka *Greece*	55B3	Vodokhranilishche,		Kaplan *USA*	19B3	Karlovac *Yugos*	52C1
Kalabakan *Malay*	78D1	Res *USSR*	61J2	Kaplice *Czech*	57C3	Karlovo *Bulg*	54B2
Kalabo *Zambia*	100B2	Kāmthi *India*	85D4	Kapoe *Thai*	77B4	Karlovy Vary *Czech*	57C2
Kalach *USSR*	61F3	Kamyshin *USSR*	61G3	Kapona *Zaïre*	99C3	Karlshamn *Sweden*	39G7
Kalach-na-Donu *USSR*	61F4	Kamyshlov *USSR*	61K2	Kaposvár *Hung*	52C1	Karlskoga *Sweden*	39G7
Kaladan, R *Burma*	86C2	Kanaaupscow, R *Can*	7C4	Kap Parry, C *Can*	6C2	Karlskrona *Sweden*	39H7
Ka Lae, C *Hawaiian Is*	21C4	Kananga *Zaïre*	98C3	Kap Ravn, C		Karlsruhe *W Germ*	57B3
Kalahari Desert		Kanash *USSR*	61G2	*Greenland*	6H3	Karlstad *Sweden*	39G7
Botswana	100B3	Kanayama *Japan*	75B1	Kapsukas *USSR*	60B3	Karluk *USA*	12D3
Kalajoki *Fin*	38J6	Kanazawa *Japan*	74D3	Kapuas, R *Indon*	78B3	Karnafuli Res *Bang*	86C2
Kalakan *USSR*	63D2	Kanbisha *USA*	4C3	Kapunda *Aust*	108A2	Karnal *India*	84D3
Kalakepen *Indon*	70A3	Kānchipuram *India*	87B2	Kapurthala *India*	84D2	Karnataka, State *India*	87A1
Kalam *Pak*	84C1	Kandahar *Afghan*	84B2	Kapuskasing *Can*	7B5	Karnobat *Bulg*	54C2
Kalámai *Greece*	55B3	Kandalaksha *USSR*	64E3	Kaputar, Mt *Aust*	109D2	Karoi *Zim*	100B2
Kalamazoo *USA*	10B2	Kandalakshskaya Guba		Kapydzhik, Mt *USSR*	93E2	Karonga *Malawi*	99D3
Kalat *Pak*	84B3	B *USSR*	38L5	Kap York, C		Karora *Sudan*	95C3
Kalecik *Turk*	92B1	Kandi *Benin*	97C3	*Greenland*	6D2	Karossa *Indon*	78D3
Kalembau, I *Indon*	78D3	Kandos *Aust*	109C2	Karabük *Turk*	92B1	Kárpathos, I *Greece*	55C3
Kalémié *Zaïre*	99C3	Kandy *Sri Lanka*	87C3	Karacabey *Turk*	55C2	Karrats Fjord	
Kalevala *USSR*	38L5	Kane *USA*	15C2	Karachi *Pak*	85B4	*Greenland*	6E2
Kalewa *Burma*	86C2	Kane Basin, B *Can*	6C1	Karād *India*	87A1	Kars *Turk*	93D1
Kalgin I *USA*	12D2	Kanem, Desert Region		Kara Daglari, Mt *Turk*	60E5	Karsakpay *USSR*	65H4
Kalgoorlie *Aust*	106B4	*Chad*	98B1	Karadeniz Boğazi, Sd		Kärsava *USSR*	58D1
Kalianda *Indon*	78B4	Kangaba *Mali*	97B3	*Turk*	60C5	Karshi *USSR*	80E2
Kalibo *Phil*	79B3	Kangal *Turk*	92C2	Karaftit *USSR*	68D1	Karstula *Fin*	38J6
Kalima *Zaïre*	98C3	Kangâmiut *Greenland*	6E3	Karaganda *USSR*	65J5	Kartaba *Leb*	94B1
Kalimantan, Province		Kangān *Iran*	91B4	Karagayly *USSR*	65J5	Kartal *Turk*	54C2
Indon	78C3	Kangar *Malay*	77C4	Kāraikāl *India*	87B2	Kartaly *USSR*	61K3
Kálimnos, I *Greece*	55C3	Kangaroo I *Aust*	106C4	Karaj *Iran*	90B2	Kārūn, R *Iran*	90A3
Kálimpang *India*	86B1	Kanga'tsiaq *Greenland*	6E3	Karak *Jordan*	92C3	Karwa *India*	86A1
Kalinin *USSR*	60E2	Kangavar *Iran*	90A3	Kara Kalpakskaya,		Kārwār *India*	87A2
Kaliningrad *USSR*	60B3	Kangbao *China*	72C1	Republic *USSR*	65G5	Karymskoye *USSR*	68D1
Kalinkovichi *USSR*	60C3	Kangchenjunga, Mt		Karakax He, R *China*	84D1	Kasai, R *Zaïre*	98B3
Kalispell *USA*	8B2	*Nepal*	82C3	Karakelong, I *Indon*	71D3	Kasaji *Zaïre*	100B2
Kalisz *Pol*	58B2	Kangding *China*	73A4	Karakoram, Mts *India*	84D1	Kasama *Zambia*	101C2
Kaliua *Tanz*	99D3	Kangerdlugssuaq, B		Karakoram, P *India/*		Kasanga *Tanz*	99D3
Kalix, R *Sweden*	38J5	*Greenland*	6G3	*China*	84D1	Kāsaragod *India*	87A2
Kalkfeld *Namibia*	100A3	Kangerdlugssvatsaiq,		Karakoro, R *Maur/Sen*	97A3	Kasba L *Can*	5H3
Kalkrand *Namibia*	100A3	B *Greenland*	6G3	Karakumy, Desert		Kasempa *Zambia*	100B2
Kallakoopah, R *Aust*	108A1	Kangetet *Kenya*	99D2	*USSR*	65G6	Kasenga *Zaïre*	100B2
Kallávesi, L *Fin*	38K6	Kanggye *N Korea*	74B2	Karaman *Turk*	92B2	Kasese *Uganda*	99D2
Kallonis Kólpos, B		Kangiqsualujjuaq *Can*	7D4	Karamay *China*	65K5	Kāshān *Iran*	90B3
Greece	55C3	Kangiqsujuaq *Can*	6C3	Karamea *NZ*	111B2	Kashegelok *USA*	12C2
Kalmar *Sweden*	39H7	Kangnŭng *S Korea*	74B3	Karamea Bight, B *NZ*	111B2	Kashi *China*	82B2
Kalmytskaya ASSR,		Kango *Gabon*	98B2	Kāranja *India*	85D4	Kāshipur *India*	84D3
Republic *USSR*	61G4	Kangto, Mt *China*	68B4	Karapınar *Turk*	92B2	Kashiwazaki *Japan*	74D3
Kalomo *Zambia*	100B2	Kang Xian *China*	72B3	Kara S *USSR*	64H2	Kashmar *Iran*	90C2
Kalona *USA*	18B1	Kanh Hung *Viet*	77D4	Karasuk *USSR*	65J4	Kashmir, State *India*	66D3
Kalone Peak, Mt *Can*	13B2	Kaniama *Zaïre*	98C3	Karataş *Turk*	92C2	Kasimov *USSR*	61F3
Kalpeni, I *India*	87A2	Kani Giri *India*	87B1	Kara Tau, Mts *USSR*	65H5	Kaskaskia, R *USA*	18C2
Kálpi *India*	85D3	Kanin Nos, Pt *USSR*	64F3	Karathuri *Burma*	76B3	Kasko *Fin*	38J6
Kalskag *USA*	12B2	Kankaanpää *Fin*	39J6	Karatsu *Japan*	74B4	Kasli *USSR*	61K2
Kaltag *USA*	12C2	Kankakee *USA*	14A2	Karāz *Iran*	91B4	Kaslo *Can*	5G5
Kaluga *USSR*	60E3	Kankakee, R *USA*	14A2	Karbalā' *Iraq*	93D3	Kasonga *Zaïre*	98C3
Kalush *USSR*	59C3	Kankan *Guinea*	97B3	Karcag *Hung*	59C2	Kasongo-Lunda *Zaïre*	98B3
Kalyandurg *India*	87B2	Känker *India*	86A2	Kardhítsa *Greece*	55B3	Kásos, I *Greece*	55C3
Kalyazin *USSR*	60E2	Kanniyākuman *India*	87B3	Karel'skaya ASSR,		Kaspiyskiy *USSR*	61G4
Kama, R *USSR*	61H1	Kano *Nig*	97C3	Republic *USSR*	64E3	Kassala *Sudan*	95C3
Kamaishi *Japan*	74E3	Kanoya *Japan*	74C4			Kassel *W Germ*	56B2
Kamalia *Pak*	84C2	Kānpur *India*	86A1			Kasserine *Tunisia*	96C1
		Kansas, State *USA*	9D3			Kassinga *Angola*	100A2

Khrebet Dzhugdzhur, Mts *USSR*	63F2
Khrebet Kopet Dag, Mts *USSR*	90C2
Khrebet Pay-khoy, Mts *USSR*	64H3
Khrebet Tarbagatay, Mts *USSR*	82C1
Khrebet Tukuringra, Mts *USSR*	63E2
Khulna *Bang*	86B2
Khunjerab, P *China/India*	84D1
Khunsar *Iran*	90B3
Khurays *S Arabia*	91A4
Khurda *India*	86B2
Khurja *India*	84D3
Khushab *Pak*	84C2
Khushnīyah *Syria*	94B2
Khust *USSR*	59C3
Khuwei *Sudan*	99C1
Khuzdar *Pak*	85B3
Khvāf *Iran*	90D3
Khvalynsk *USSR*	61G3
Khvor *Iran*	90C3
Khvormūj *Iran*	91B4
Khvoy *Iran*	93D2
Khwaja Muhammad, Mts *Afghan*	84C1
Khyber P *Afghan/Pak*	84C2
Kiambi *Zaïre*	99C3
Kiamichi, R *USA*	19A3
Kiana *USA*	12B1
Kibangou *Congo*	98B3
Kibaya *Tanz*	99D3
Kibombo *Zaïre*	98C3
Kibondo *Tanz*	99D3
Kibungu *Rwanda*	99D3
Kičevo *Yugos*	55B2
Kicking Horse P *Can*	5G4
Kidal *Mali*	97C3
Kidderminster *Eng*	43C3
Kidira *Sen*	97A3
Kidnappers,C *NZ*	110C1
Kiel *W Germ*	56C2
Kielce *Pol*	59C2
Kieler Bucht, B *W Germ*	56C2
Kifab *USSR*	80E2
Kiffa *Maur*	97A3
Kigali *Rwanda*	89H8
Kigluaik Mts *USA*	12A2
Kigoma *Tanz*	99C3
Kii-sanchi, Mts *Japan*	75B2
Kii-suido, B *Japan*	74C4
Kikinda *Yugos*	54B1
Kikládhes, Is *Greece*	55B3
Kikori *PNG*	71F4
Kikwit *Zaïre*	98B3
Kilauea Crater, Mt *Hawaiian Is*	21C4
Kilbuck Mts *USA*	4C3
Kilchu *N Korea*	74B2
Kilcoy *Aust*	109D1
Kildare, County *Irish Rep*	45C2
Kildare *Irish Rep*	45C2
Kilgore *USA*	19B3
Kilifi *Kenya*	99D3
Kilimanjaro, Mt *Tanz*	99D3
Kilindoni *Tanz*	99D3
Kilis *Turk*	92C2
Kilkee *Irish Rep*	45B2
Kilkenny, County *Irish Rep*	45C2
Kilkenny *Irish Rep*	45C2
Kilkieran B *Irish Rep*	45B2
Kilkís *Greece*	55B2
Killala B *Irish Rep*	45B1
Killaloe *Irish Rep*	45B2
Killarney *Aust*	109D1
Killarney *Irish Rep*	41B3
Killeen *USA*	19A3
Killik, R *USA*	12D1
Killin *Scot*	44B3
Killíni, Mt *Greece*	55B3
Killybegs *Irish Rep*	45B1
Kilmarnock *Scot*	42B2
Kil'mez *USSR*	61H2
Kilosa *Tanz*	99D3
Kilrush *Irish Rep*	41B3
Kilwa *Zaïre*	99C3
Kilwa Kisiwani *Tanz*	99D3
Kilwa Kivinje *Tanz*	99D3
Kimba *Aust*	108A2
Kimball,Mt *USA*	12F2
Kimberley *Can*	13D3
Kimberley *S Africa*	101F1
Kimberley Plat *Aust*	106B2
Kimch'aek *N Korea*	74B2
Kimch'ŏn *S Korea*	74B3
Kími *Greece*	55B3
Kimry *USSR*	60E2
Kinabalu, Mt *Malay*	70C3
Kinabatangan, R *Malay*	78D1
Kincardine *Can*	14B2
Kincolith *Can*	13B1
Kinder *USA*	19B3
Kindersley *Can*	13F2
Kindia *Guinea*	97A3
Kindu *Zaïre*	98C3
Kinel' *USSR*	61H3
Kineshma *USSR*	61F2
Kingaroy *Aust*	109D1
King City *USA*	21A2
Kingcome Inlet *Can*	5F4
King George Is *Can*	7C4
King I *Aust*	107D4
King I *Can*	13B2
Kingissepp *USSR*	60B2
King Leopold Range, Mts *Aust*	106B2
Kingman *USA*	9B3
Kingombe *Zaïre*	98C3
Kingoonya *Aust*	108A2
Kingsburg *USA*	22C2
Kings Canyon Nat Pk *USA*	21B2
Kingscote *Aust*	108A3
King Sd *Aust*	106B2
Kingsford *USA*	14A1
Kingsland *USA*	17B1
King's Lynn *Eng*	43E3
Kings Park *USA*	16C2
Kings Peak, Mt *USA*	8B2
Kingston *Aust*	107C4
Kingston *Can*	7C5
Kingston *Jamaica*	25E3
Kingston, New York *USA*	15D2
Kingston *NZ*	111A3
Kingstown *St Vincent*	27E4
Kingsville *USA*	9D4
Kingussie *Scot*	44B3
King William I *Can*	4J3
King William's Town *S Africa*	100B4
Kinkala *Congo*	98B3
Kinna *Sweden*	39G7
Kinnairds Head, Pt *Scot*	44D3
Kinomoto *Japan*	75B1
Kinross *Scot*	44C3
Kinsale *Irish Rep*	45B3
Kinshasa *Zaïre*	98B3
Kintap *Indon*	78D3
Kintyre, Pen *Scot*	42B2
Kinuso *Can*	13D1
Kinyeti, Mt *Sudan*	99D2
Kiparissía *Greece*	55B3
Kiparissiakós Kólpos, G *Greece*	55B3
Kipawa,L *Can*	15C1
Kipili *Tanz*	99D3
Kipnuk *USA*	12B3
Kippure, Mt *Irish Rep*	45C2
Kipushi *Zaïre*	100B2
Kirensk *USSR*	63C2
Kirgizskaya SSR, Republic *USSR*	65J5
Kirgizskiy Khrebet, Mts *USSR*	82B1
Kiri *Zaïre*	98B3
Kiribati, Is *Pacific O*	105G4
Kırıkkale *Turk*	92B2
Kirishi *USSR*	60D2
Kirithar Range, Mts *Pak*	85B3
Kirkağaç *Turk*	55C3
Kirk Bulāg Dāgh, Mt *Iran*	90A2
Kirkby *Eng*	42C2
Kirkcaldy *Scot*	44C3
Kirkcudbright *Scot*	42B2
Kirkenes *Nor*	38K5
Kirkland Lake *Can*	7B5
Kirkpatrick,Mt *Ant*	80E
Kirksville *USA*	10A2
Kirkūk *Iraq*	93D2
Kirkwall *Scot*	44C2
Kirkwood *USA*	18B2
Kirov *USSR*	60D3
Kirov *USSR*	61G2
Kirovabad *USSR*	65F5
Kirovakan *USSR*	93D1
Kirovgrad *USSR*	61J2
Kirovograd *USSR*	60D4
Kirovsk *USSR*	64E3
Kirs *USSR*	61H2
Kirşehir *Turk*	92B2
Kiruna *Sweden*	56C2
Kiryū *Japan*	75B1
Kisangani *Zaïre*	98C2
Kisarazu *Japan*	75B1
Kishanganj *India*	86B1
Kishangarh *India*	85C3
Kishinev *USSR*	60C4
Kishiwada *Japan*	75B2
Kisii *Kenya*	99D3
Kisiju *Tanz*	99D3
Kiskunhalas *Hung*	59B3
Kislovodsk *USSR*	65F5
Kismaayo *Somalia*	99E3
Kiso-sammyaku, Mts *Japan*	75B1
Kissidougou *Guinea*	97A4
Kissimmee,L *USA*	17B2
Kisumu *Kenya*	99D3
Kisvárda *Hung*	59C3
Kita *Mali*	97B3
Kitab *USSR*	65H6
Kitakata *Japan*	75C1
Kita-Kyūshū *Japan*	74C4
Kitale *Kenya*	99D2
Kitalo, I *Japan*	69G4
Kitami *Japan*	74E2
Kitchener *Can*	7B5
Kitgum *Uganda*	99D2
Kíthira, I *Greece*	55B3
Kíthnos, I *Greece*	55B3
Kiti,C *Cyprus*	94A1
Kitimat *Can*	5F4
Kitnen, R *Fin*	38K5
Kitsuki *Japan*	75A2
Kittanning *USA*	15C2
Kittilä *Fin*	38J5
Kitunda *Tanz*	99D3
Kitwanga *Can*	13B1
Kitwe *Zambia*	100B2
Kitzbühel *Austria*	57C3
Kitzbühler Alpen, Mts *Austria*	47E1
Kitzingen *W Germ*	57C3
Kiumbi *Zaïre*	98C3
Kivalina *USA*	12B1
Kivercy *USSR*	59D2
Kivu,L *Zaïre/Rwanda*	99C3
Kiwalik *USA*	4B3
Kiyev *USSR*	60D3
Kizel *USSR*	61J2
Kizil, R *Turk*	92C2
Kizil-Arvat *USSR*	80D2
Kizil-Atrek *USSR*	90B2
Kladno *Czech*	57C2
Klagenfurt *Austria*	57C3
Klaipėda *USSR*	60B2
Klamath *USA*	8A2
Klamath, R *USA*	20B2
Klamath Falls *USA*	8A2
Klamath Mts *USA*	20B2
Klatovy *Czech*	57C3
Klawak *USA*	12H3
Kleiat *Leb*	94B1
Klerksdorp *S Africa*	101G1
Klin *USSR*	60E2
Klintehamn *Sweden*	58B1
Klintsy *USSR*	60D3
Ključ *Yugos*	52C2
Kłodzko *Pol*	59B2
Klondike, R *USA/Can*	12G2
Klondike Plat *USA/Can*	4D3
Klosterneuburg *Austria*	59B3
Kluane, R *Can*	12G2
Kluane L *Can*	12G2
Kluane Nat Pk *Can*	12G2
Kluczbork *Pol*	59B2
Klukwan *USA*	12G3
Klutina L *USA*	12E2
Knight I *USA*	12E2
Knighton *Wales*	43C3
Knin *Yugos*	52C2
Knob,C *Aust*	106A4
Knokke-Heist *Belg*	46B1
Knox Coast *Ant*	112C9
Knoxville, Tennessee *USA*	11B3
Knud Ramsussens Land, Region *Greenland*	6H3
Koba *Indon*	78B3
Kobbermirebugt *Greenland*	6F3
Kobe *Japan*	74D4
København *Den*	56C1
Koblenz *W Germ*	57B2
Kobrin *USSR*	60B3
Kobroör, I *Indon*	71E4
Kobuk, R *USA*	12C1
Kočani *Yugos*	54B2
Ko Chang, I *Thai*	76C3
Koch Bihār *India*	86B1
Kochel *W Germ*	47D1
Koch I *Can*	6C3
Kōchi *Japan*	74C4
Kodiak *USA*	12D3
Kodiak I *USA*	12D3
Kodikkarai *India*	87B2
Kodok *Sudan*	99D2
Koes *Namibia*	100A3
Koffiefontein *S Africa*	101G1
Koforidua *Ghana*	97B4
Kōfu *Japan*	74D3
Koga *Japan*	75B1
Køge *Den*	39G7
Kohat *Pak*	84C2
Koh-i-Baba, Mts *Afghan*	84B2
Koh-i-Hisar, Mts *Afghan*	84B1
Koh-i-Khurd, Mt *Afghan*	84B2
Kohīma *India*	86C1
Koh-i-Mazar, Mt *Afghan*	84B1
Kohlu *Pak*	84B3
Kohtla Järve *USSR*	60C2
Koide *Japan*	75B1
Koidern *Can*	12F2
Koihoa, Is *Nicobar Is*	77A4
Kōje-do, I *S Korea*	74B4
Kokchetav *USSR*	65H4
Kokemaki, L *Fin*	39J6
Kokkola *Fin*	38J6
Kokoda *PNG*	107D1
Kokomo *USA*	14A2
Kokonau *Indon*	71E4
Kokpekty *USSR*	65K5
Koksoak, R *Can*	7D4
Kokstad *S Africa*	100B4
Ko Kut, I *Thai*	76C3
Kola *USSR*	38L5
Kolaka *Indon*	71D4
Ko Lanta, I *Thai*	77B4
Kolār *India*	87B2
Kolār Gold Fields *India*	87B2
Kolda *Sen*	97A3
Kolding *Den*	39F7
Kolhāpur *India*	87A1
Koliganek *USA*	12C3

Kolín Czech	59B2
Köln W Germ	57B2
Kolo Pol	58B2
Kolobrzeg Pol	58B2
Kolokani Mali	97B3
Kolomna USSR	60E2
Kolomyya USSR	60C4
Kolpashevo USSR	65K4
Kolpekty USSR	68A2
Kólpos Merabéllou, B Greece	55C3
Kólpos Singitikós, G Greece	55B2
Kólpos Strimonikós, G Greece	55B2
Kólpos Toronaíos, G Greece	55B2
Kol'skiy Poluostrov, Pen USSR	38L5
Kolvereid Nor	38G6
Kolwezi Zaïre	100B2
Kolyma, R USSR	1C7
Kom, Mt Bulg/Yugos	54B2
Koma Eth	99D2
Komaduga Gana, R Nig	97D3
Komárno Czech	59B3
Komati, R S Africa	101H1
Komatsu Japan	74D3
Komatsushima Japan	75A2
Komi, Republic USSR	64G3
Komodo, I Indon	70C4
Komoran, I Indon	71E4
Komoro Japan	75B1
Komotiní Greece	55C2
Kompong Cham Camb	76D3
Kompong Chhnang, Mts Camb	76C3
Kompong Som Camb	77C3
Kompong Thom Camb	76C3
Kompong Trabek Camb	76D3
Komsomol'sk na Amure USSR	63F2
Konda, R USSR	65H4
Kondoa Tanz	99D3
Kondukür India	87B1
Kong Christian IX Land, Region Greenland	6G3
Kong Frederik VI Kyst, Mts Greenland	6F3
Kong Karls Land, Is Barents S	64C2
Kongkemul, Mt Indon	78D2
Kongolo Zaïre	98C3
Kongsberg Den	39F7
Kongsvinger Nor	39G6
Konin Pol	58B2
Konjic Yugos	54A2
Konosha USSR	61F1
Konosu Japan	75B1
Konotop USSR	60D3
Konsk USSR	63B2
Konstanz W Germ	49D2
Kontagora Nig	97C3
Kontum Viet	76D3
Konya Turk	92B2
Kootenay, R Can	13D3
Kopargaon India	85C5
Kópasker Iceland	6J3
Kópavogur Iceland	38A2
Koper Yugos	52B1
Kopet Dag, Mts Iran/ USSR	80D2
Kopeysk USSR	61K2
Ko Phangan, I Thai	77C4
Ko Phuket, I Thai	77B4
Köping Sweden	39H7
Koppal India	87B1
Koprivnica Yugos	52C1
Korangi Pak	85B4
Koraput India	87C1
Korba India	86A2
Korbach W Germ	57B2
Korbuk, R USA	4B3
Korçë Alb	55B2
Korčula, I Yugos	52C2
Korea B China/Korea	72E2
Korea Str S Korea/ Japan	74B4
Korec USSR	59D2
Körğlu Tepesi, Mt Turk	92B1
Korhogo Ivory Coast	97B4
Kori Creek India	85B4
Korinthiakós Kólpos, G Greece	55B3
Kórinthos Greece	55B3
Kóriyama Japan	74E3
Korkino USSR	61K3
Korkuteli Turk	92B2
Korla China	82C1
Kornat, I Yugos	52C2
Köroğlu Tepesi, Mt Turk	60D5
Korogwe Tanz	99D3
Koroit Aust	108B3
Koror, Palau Is Pacific O	71E3
Körös, R Hung	59C3
Korosten USSR	60C3
Koro Toro Chad	95A3
Korovin, I USA	12B3
Korsakov USSR	69G2
Korsør Den	39G7
Kortrijk Belg	56A2
Kós, I Greece	55C3
Ko Samui, I Thai	77C4
Koscierzyna Pol	58B2
Kosciusko, Mt Aust	107D4
Kosciusko I USA	12H3
Koshikijima-retto, I Japan	74B4
Košice Czech	59C3
Kosong N Korea	74B3
Kosovska Mitrovica Yugos	54B2
Kossou, L Ivory Coast	97B4
Koster S Africa	101G1
Kosti Sudan	99D1
Kostopol' USSR	59D2
Kostroma USSR	61F2
Kostrzyn Pol	56C2
Koszalin Pol	39H8
Kota India	85D3
Kotaagung Indon	78A4
Kotabaharu Indon	78C3
Kotabaru Indon	78D3
Kota Bharu Malay	77C4
Kotabum Indon	78A3
Kot Addu Pak	84C2
Kota Kinabulu Malay	78D1
Kotapad India	87C1
Kotel'nich USSR	61G2
Kotel'nikovo USSR	61F4
Kotka Fin	39K6
Kotlas USSR	64F3
Kotlik USA	12B2
Kotor Yugos	54A2
Kotovsk USSR	60C4
Kotri Pak	85B3
Kottagüdem India	87C1
Kottayam India	87B3
Kotto, R CAR	98C2
Kottüru India	87B2
Kotzebue USA	12B1
Kotzebue Sd USA	4B3
Kouande Benin	97C3
Kouango CAR	98C2
Koudougou U Volta	97B3
Koulamoutou Gabon	98B3
Koulikoro Mali	97B3
Koupéla U Volta	97B3
Kourou French Guiana	33G2
Kouroussa Guinea	97B3
Kousséri Cam	98B1
Kouvola Fin	39K6
Kovel USSR	60B3
Kovrov USSR	61F2
Kovylkino USSR	61F3
Kovzha, R USSR	60E1
Ko Way, I Thai	77C4
Kowloon Hong Kong	73C5
Kowt-e-Ashrow Afghan	84B2
Köyceğğiz Turk	92A2
Koydor USSR	38L5
Koyna Res India	87A1
Koyuk USA	12B2
Koyuk, R USA	12B1
Koyukuk USA	12C2
Koyukuk, R USA	12C1
Kozan Turk	92C2
Kozañi Greece	55B2
Koz'modemyansk USSR	61G2
Koztroma USSR	61F2
Közu-shima, I Japan	75B2
Kragerø Nor	39F7
Kragujevac Yugos	54B2
Kra,Isthmus of Burma/ Malay	77B3
Krak des Chevaliers, Hist Site Syria	94C1
Kraków Pol	59B2
Kraljevo Yugos	54B2
Kramatorsk USSR	60E4
Kramfors Sweden	38H6
Kranj Yugos	52B1
Krapotkin USSR	61F4
Krasavino USSR	61G1
Krashnokamsk USSR	61J2
Krasino USSR	64G2
Kraśnik Pol	59C2
Krasnoarmeysk USSR	61G3
Krasnodar USSR	60E5
Krasnotur'insk USSR	61K2
Krasnoufimsk USSR	61J2
Krasnoustol'skiy USSR	61J0
Krasnovishersk USSR	65G3
Krasnovodsk USSR	65G5
Krasnoyarsk USSR	63B2
Krasnystaw Pol	59C2
Krasnyy Kut USSR	61G3
Krasnyy Luch USSR	60E4
Krasnyy Yar USSR	61G4
Kratie Camb	76D3
Kraulshavn Greenland	6E2
Krefeld W Germ	56B2
Kremenchug USSR	60D4
Kremenchugskoye Vodokhranilische, Res USSR	60D4
Kremenets USSR	59D2
Kribi Cam	98A2
Krichev USSR	60D3
Krimml Austria	47E1
Krinstinestad Fin	38J6
Krishna, R India	87B1
Krishnagiri India	87B2
Krishnangar India	86B2
Kristiansand Nor	39F7
Kristianstad Sweden	39G7
Kristiansund Nor	64B3
Kristinehamn Sweden	39G7
Kríti, I Greece	55B3
Krivoy Rog USSR	60D4
Krk, I Yugos	52B1
Kronpris Frederik Bjerge, Mts Greenland	6G3
Kronshtadt USSR	39K7
Kroonstad S Africa	101G1
Kropotkin USSR	65F5
Krugersdorp S Africa	101G1
Krui Indon	78A4
Kruje Alb	55A2
Krupki USSR	58D2
Krusenstern,C USA	12B1
Kruševac Yugos	54B2
Krustpils USSR	39K7
Kruzof I USA	12G3
Krym, Pen USSR	65E5
Krym, R USSR	60D5
Krymsk USSR	60E5
Krzyz Pol	58B2
Ksar El Boukhari Alg	96C1
Ksar el Kebir Mor	96B1
Kuala Indon	70A3
Kuala Dungun Malay	77C5
Kuala Kerai Malay	77C4
Kuala Kubu Baharu Malay	77C5
Kuala Lipis Malay	77C5
Kuala Lumpur Malay	77C5
Kuala Trengganu Malay	77C4
Kuamut Malay	78D1
Kuandian China	74A2
Kuantan Malay	77C5
Kuba USSR	93E1
Kubar PNG	71F4
Kuching Malay	78C2
Kudat Malay	70C3
Kudus Indon	78C4
Kudymkar USSR	61H2
Kufstein Austria	57C3
Kuh Duren, Upland Iran	90C3
Küh e Bazmān, Mt Iran	91C4
Küh-e Dinar, Mt Iran	90B3
Küh-e-Hazār Masjed, Mts Iran	90C2
Küh-e Jebāl Barez, Mts Iran	91C4
Küh-e Karkas, Mts Iran	90B3
Kuh-e Laleh Zar, Mt Iran	91C4
Küh-e Sahand, Mt Iran	90A2
Kuh e Taftān, Mt Iran	91D4
Kühhaye Sabalan, Mts Iran	90A2
Kühjä-ye Zāgros, Mts Iran	90A3
Kuhmo Fin	38K6
Kühpāyeh Iran	90B3
Kühpäyeh, Mt Iran	90C3
Küh ye Bashäkerd, Mts Iran	91C4
Küh ye Sabalan, Mt Iran	90A2
Kuibis Namibia	100A3
Kuigillingok USA	4B4
Kuiu I USA	12H3
Kuji Japan	74E2
Kuju-san, Mt Japan	75A2
Kukaklek L USA	12C3
Kukës Alb	54B2
Kukup Malay	77C5
Kül, R Iran	91C4
Kula Turk	55C3
Kulakshi USSR	61J4
Kulal,Mt Kenya	99D2
Kulata Bulg	55B2
Kuldiga USSR	60B2
Kul'sary USSR	61H4
Kulu India	84D2
Kulu Turk	92B2
Kulunda USSR	65J4
Kulwin Aust	108B2
Kuma, R USSR	61G5
Kumagaya Japan	75B1
Kumai Indon	78C3
Kumamoto Japan	74C4
Kumano Japan	75B2
Kumanovo Yugos	54B2
Kumara China	63E2
Kumasi Ghana	97B4
Kumba Cam	98A2
Kumbakonam India	87B2
Kumertau USSR	61J3
Kümhwa S Korea	74B3
Kumla Sweden	39H7
Kumta India	87A2
Kümüx China	82C1
Kunar, R Afghan	84C2
Kunda USSR	39K7
Kundla India	85C4
Kunduz Afghan	84B1
Kunene, R Angola	89F9
Kungsbacka Sweden	39G7
Kungur USSR	61J2
Kunhing Burma	76B1
Kunlun Shan, Mts China	82B2
Kunming China	73A4
Kunsan S Korea	74B3
Kuopio Fin	38K6

Kupa

Lake City, S Carolina USA	17C1
Lake District, Region Eng	42C2
Lake Elsinore USA	22D4
Lake Eyre Basin Aust	106C3
Lakefield Can	15C2
Lake Harbour Can	6D3
Lake Hughes USA	22C3
Lakehurst USA	16B2
Lake Jackson USA	19A4
Lake la Biche Can	13E2
Lakeland USA	17B2
Lake of the Woods Can	7A5
Lake Oswego USA	20B1
Lakeport USA	21A2
Lake Providence USA	19B3
Lake Pukaki NZ	111B2
Lakes Entrance Aust	109C3
Lakeshore USA	22C2
Lake Stewart Aust	108B1
Lake Traverse Can	15C1
Lakeview USA	8A2
Lakeview Mt Can	20B1
Lake Village USA	19B3
Lake Wales USA	17B2
Lakewood, California USA	22C4
Lakewood, New Jersey USA	16B2
Lakewood, Ohio USA	14B2
Lake Worth USA	17B2
Lakhimpur India	86A1
Lakhpat India	85B4
Lakki Pak	84C2
Lakonikós Kólpos, G Greece	55B3
Lakota Ivory Coast	97B4
Laksefjord, Inlet Nor	38K4
Lakselv Nor	38K4
La Laguna Arg	34C2
La Libertad Ecuador	32A4
La Ligua Chile	34A2
La Linea Spain	50A2
Lalitpur India	85D4
La Loche Can	5H4
la Loche,L Can	13F1
La Louvière Belg	46C1
La Luz Nic	26A4
La Malbaie Can	7C5
La Malinche, Mt Mexico	23B2
La Mancha, Region Spain	50B2
Lamar, Colorado USA	9C3
Lamar, Missouri USA	18B2
La Marque USA	19A4
Lambaréné Gabon	98B3
Lambayeque Peru	32A5
Lambert Gl Ant	112B10
Lambertville USA	16B2
Lamblon,C Can	4F2
Lambro, R Italy	47C2
Lam Chi, R Thai	76C2
Lamego Port	50A1
La Meije, Mt France	47B2
La Merced Peru	32B6
La Mesa USA	21B3
Lamía Greece	55B3
Lammermuir Hills Scot	42C2
Lammhult Sweden	39G7
Lamon B Phil	79B3
Lamoni USA	18B1
Lamotrek, I Pacific O	71F3
Lampeter Wales	43B3
Lamu Kenya	99E3
Lana Italy	47D1
Lanai, I Hawaiian Is	21C4
Lanai City Hawaiian Is	21C4
Lanark Scot	42C2
Lanbi, I Burma	76B3
Lancang, R China	76C1
Lancashire, County Eng	42C3
Lancaster, California USA	21B3
Lancaster Eng	42C2
Lancaster, Mississippi USA	18B1
Lancaster, New Hampshire USA	15D2
Lancaster, Ohio USA	14B3
Lancaster, Pennsylvania USA	10C3
Lancaster, S Carolina USA	17B1
Lancaster Sd Can	6B2
Landak, R Indon	78B3
Landan W Germ	46E2
Landeck Austria	57C3
Lander USA	8C2
Landeta Arg	34C2
Landsberg W Germ	57C3
Lands End, C Can	4F2
Land's End, Pt Eng	43B4
Landshut W Germ	57C3
Làndskrona Sweden	39G7
Lanett USA	17A1
Langenhagen W Germ	56B2
Langenthal Switz	47B1
Langholm Scot	42C2
Langjökull, Mts Iceland	38A2
Langkawi, I Malay	77B4
Langley Can	13C3
Langlo, R Aust	108C1
Langnau Switz	47B1
Langres France	49D2
langsa Indon	70A3
Lang Shan, Mts China	68C2
Lang Son Viet	76D1
Languedoc, Region France	48C3
Lanin, Mt Arg	29B3
Lanoa,L, L Phil	79B4
Lansdale USA	16B2
Lansdowne House Can	7B4
Lansford USA	16B2
Lansing USA	10B2
Lanslebourg France	47B2
Lanzarote, I Canary Is	96A2
Lanzhou China	72A2
Lanzo Torinese Italy	47B2
Laoag Phil	79B2
Lao Cai Viet	76C1
Laoha He, R China	72D1
Laois, County Irish Rep	45C2
Laon France	46B2
La Oroya Peru	32B6
Laos, Republic S E Asia	76C2
Lapalisse France	49C2
La Palma Panama	32B2
La Palma, I Canary Is	96A2
La Pampa, State Arg	34B3
La Paragua Ven	33E2
La Paz Arg	29E2
La Paz Arg	34B2
La Paz Bol	30C2
La Paz Mexico	24A2
La Perouse, Str USSR/Japan	69G2
La Piedad Mexico	23A1
La Pine USA	20B2
Laplace USA	19B3
la Placita Mexico	23A3
La Plata Arg	29E2
La Plonge,L Can	13F1
La Porte USA	14A2
Lappeenranta Fin	39K6
Lappland, Region Sweden/Fin	38H5
Lapua Fin	38J6
Lapu-Lapu Phil	79B3
La Purisma Mexico	9B4
Laqiya Arba'in, Well Sudan	95B2
La Quiaca Arg	30C3
L'Aquila Italy	52B2
Làr Iran	91B4
Larache Mor	96B1
Laramie USA	8C2
Laramie Range, Mts USA	8C2
Larca Spain	50B2
Laredo USA	9D4
Larestan, Region Iran	91B4
L'Argentière France	47B2
Largo USA	17B2
Largs Scot	42B2
Lári Iran	90A2
La Rioja Arg	30C4
La Rioja, State Arg	30C4
Lárisa Greece	55B3
Larkana Pak	85B3
Larnaca Cyprus	92B3
Larnaca B Cyprus	94A1
Larne N Ire	45D1
La Robla Spain	50A1
La Roche-en-Ardenne Belg	46C1
La Rochelle France	48B2
La Roche-sur-Foron France	47B1
La Roche-sur-Yon France	48B2
La Roda Spain	51B2
La Romana Dom Rep	27D3
La Ronge Can	5H4
La Ronge,L Can	5H4
Larvik Nor	39F7
Lar'yak USSR	65J3
La Sagra, Mt Spain	50B2
La Salle Can	15D1
La Salle USA	18C1
La Sarre Can	7C5
Las Avispas Arg	34C1
Las Cabras Chile	34A2
Lascombe Can	5G4
Las Cruces USA	9C3
La Solle, Mt Haiti	26C3
Lasengmia China	72B2
La Serena Chile	30B4
Las Flores Arg	29E3
Lashio Burma	76B1
La Sila, Mts Italy	53C3
Làsjerd Iran	90B2
Las Lajas Chile	34A3
Las Marismas, Marshland Spain	50A2
Las Palmas de Gran Canaria Canary Is	96A2
La Spezia Italy	52A2
Las Plumas Arg	29C4
Las Rosas Arg	34C2
Lassen Peak, Mt USA	20B2
Lassen Volcanic Nat Pk USA	20B2
las Tinai Mexico	23B2
Lastoursville Gabon	98B3
Lastovo, I Yugos	52C2
Las Tres Marias, Is Mexico	24B2
Las Varillas Arg	34C2
Las Vegas USA	9C3
Latina Italy	53B2
La Toma Arg	34B2
La Tortuga, I Ven	32D1
La Trinidad Phil	79B2
Latrobe Aust	109C4
Latrun Israel	94B3
La Tuque Can	7C5
Làtũr India	87B1
Latviyskaya SSR, Republic USSR	60B2
Launceston Aust	107D5
Launceston Eng	43B4
La Unión Chile	29B4
La Union El Salvador	25D3
La Union Mexico	23A2
La Unión Peru	32B5
Laura Aust	107D2
Laurel, Delaware USA	15C3
Laurel, Maryland USA	16A3
Laurel, Mississippi USA	11B3
Laurens USA	17B1
Laurinburg USA	17C1
Lausanne Switz	52A1
Laut, I Indon	78D3
Lautaro, Mt Chile	29B5
Lauterecken W Germ	46D2
Laval Can	15D1
Laval France	48B2
Laveaga Peak, Mt USA	22B2
Laveno Italy	47C2
Lavras Brazil	31B6
Lavrentiya USSR	4A3
Lavumisa Swaziland	101H1
Lawas Malay	78D1
Lawksawk Burma	76B1
Lawrence, Kansas USA	18A2
Lawrence, Massachusetts USA	15D2
Lawrence NZ	111A3
Lawrenceville, Illinois USA	14A3
Lawton USA	9D3
Layla S Arabia	91A5
Laylo Sudan	99D2
La'youn Mor	96A2
Lázaro Cárdenas Mexico	23A2
Laz Daua Somalia	99E1
Lazi Phil	79B4
Lead USA	8C2
Leader Can	13F2
Leavenworth USA	18A2
Leba Pol	58B2
Lebanon, Missouri USA	18B2
Lebanon, Oregon USA	20B2
Lebanon, Pennsylvania USA	15C2
Lebanon, Republic S W Asia	92C3
Lebombo, Mts Mozam/S Africa/Swaziland	101C3
Lebork Pol	58B2
Le Bourg-d'Oisans France	47A2
Le Brassus Switz	47B1
Lebu Chile	29B3
Le Buet, Mt France	47B1
Le Cateau France	46B1
Lecce Italy	55A2
Lecco Italy	52A1
Lech, R Austria	47D1
Lechtaler Alpen, Mts Austria	47D1
Le Creusot France	49C2
Ledbury Eng	43C3
Leduc Can	13E2
Lee USA	16C1
Lee, R Irish Rep	45B3
Leeds Eng	41C3
Leek Eng	43C3
Leer W Germ	56B2
Leesburg, Florida USA	17B2
Leesburg, Virginia USA	16A3
Leesville USA	19B3
Leeton Aust	109C2
Leeuwarden Neth	56B2
Leeuwin,C Aust	106A4
Lee Vining USA	22C2
Leeward Is Caribbean	27E3
Lefkara Cyprus	94A1
Legazpi Phil	79B3
Legnago Italy	47D2
Legnica Pol	59B2
Leguan Inlet Guyana	33F2
Leguizamo Colombia	32C4
Leh India	84D2
Le Harve France	48C2
Lehigh, R USA	16B2
Lehighton USA	16B2
Leiah Pak	84C2
Leibnitz Austria	59B3
Leicester, County Eng	43D3
Leicester Eng	43D3
Leichhardt, R Aust	107C2
Leiden Neth	56A2
Leie, R Belg	46B1

Leigh Creek

Leigh Creek *Aust*	106C4
Leighton Buzzard *Eng*	43D4
Leine, R *W Germ*	56B2
Leinster, Region *Irish Rep*	45C2
Leipzig *E Germ*	57C2
Leiria *Port*	50A2
Leirvik *Nor*	39F7
Leitrim, County *Irish Rep*	45B1
Leiyang *China*	73C4
Leizhou Bandao, Pen *China*	73B5
Leizhou Wan, B *China*	73C5
Lek, R *Neth*	56A2
Lekemti *Eth*	99D2
Leland *USA*	19B3
Lelija, Mt *Yugos*	54A2
Le Locle *France*	47B1
Le Mans *France*	48C2
Lemicux Is *Can*	6D3
Lemmon *USA*	8C2
Lemoore *USA*	21B2
Lempdes *France*	49C2
Lemro, R *Burma*	86C2
Le Murge, Region *Italy*	52C2
Lena, R *USSR*	63C2
Lendery *USSR*	38L6
Lengshujiang *China*	73C4
Leninabad *USSR*	82A1
Leninakan *USSR*	65F5
Leningrad *USSR*	60D2
Leningradskaya, Base *Ant*	112B7
Leninogorsk, Tatar ASSR *USSR*	61H3
Leninogorsk *USSR*	68A1
Leninsk-Kuznetskiy *USSR*	65K4
Leninskoye *USSR*	69F2
Lenkoran' *USSR*	65F6
Lenne, R *W Germ*	46E1
Lenox *USA*	16C1
Lens *France*	46B1
Lensk *USSR*	63D1
Lentini *Italy*	53B3
Lenya, R *Burma*	76B3
Leoben *Austria*	52B1
Leominster *Eng*	43C3
Leominster *USA*	16D1
Leon *Mexico*	24B2
León *Nic*	25D3
Leon, Region *Spain*	50A1
León *Spain*	50A1
Leonardville *Namibia*	100A3
Leonora *Aust*	106B3
Leopoldina *Brazil*	35C2
Lepel *USSR*	60C3
Leper *Belg*	46B1
Leping *China*	73D4
Le Puy *France*	49C2
Léré *Chad*	98B2
Leribe *Lesotho*	101G1
Lerici *Italy*	47C2
Lérida *Spain*	51C1
Lerma, R *Mexico*	23A1
Lermoos *Austria*	47D1
Léros, I *Greece*	55C3
Lerwick *Scot*	40C1
Les Andelys *France*	46A2
Les Cayes *Haiti*	26C3
Les Ecrins, Mt *France*	47B2
Leshan *China*	73A4
Leskovac *Yugos*	54B2
Les Landes, Region *France*	48B3
Leslie *S Africa*	101G1
Lesnoy *USSR*	61H2
Lesosibirsk *USSR*	63B2
Lesotho, Kingdom *S Africa*	101G1
Lesozavodsk *USSR*	69F2
Les Sables-d'Olonne *France*	48B2
Lesser Antarctica, Region *Ant*	80E
Lesser Antilles, Is *Caribbean*	27D4
Lesser Slave L *Can*	13E1
Lésvos, I *Greece*	55C3
Leszno *Pol*	58B2
Letha Range, Mts *Burma*	86C2
Lethbridge *Can*	5G5
Lethem *Guyana*	33F3
Letichev *USSR*	59D3
Let Oktyobr'ya *USSR*	63D2
Letong *Indon*	78B2
Le Touquet-Paris-Plage *France*	46A1
Letpadan *Burma*	76B2
Le Tréport *France*	48C1
Leuk *Switz*	47B1
Leuven *Belg*	57A2
Levádhia *Greece*	55B3
Levanger *Nor*	38G6
Levanna, Mt *Italy*	47B2
Lévêque,C *Aust*	71D5
Leverkusen *W Germ*	46D1
Levice *Czech*	59B3
Levico *Italy*	47D1
Levin *NZ*	110C2
Lévis *Can*	7C5
Levittown *USA*	15D2
Lévka Óri, Mt *Greece*	55B3
Levkás *Greece*	55B3
Levkás, I *Greece*	55B3
Lévque,C *Aust*	106B2
Levski *Bulg*	54C2
Lewes *Eng*	43E4
Lewis, I *Scot*	40B2
Lewisburg *USA*	16A2
Lewis P *NZ*	111B2
Lewis Range, Mts *USA*	8B2
Lewiston, Idaho *USA*	8B2
Lewiston, Maine *USA*	10C2
Lewistown, Montana *USA*	8C2
Lewistown, Pennsylvania *USA*	15C2
Lewisville *USA*	19B3
Lexington, Kentucky *USA*	11B3
Lexington, Missouri *USA*	18B2
Lexington Park *USA*	15C3
Leyte G *Phil*	79C3
Lezhe *Alb*	54A2
Lhasa *China*	82D3
Lhazê *China*	86B1
Lhokseumawe *Indon*	70A3
Lhozhag *China*	86C1
Lhunze *China*	68B4
Lianga *Phil*	79C4
Liangdang *China*	72B3
Lianjiang *China*	73C5
Lianping *China*	73C5
Lian Xian *China*	73C5
Lianyungang *China*	72D3
Liaoding Bandao, Pen *China*	72E1
Liaodong Wan, B *China*	72E1
Liao He, R *China*	72E1
Liaoning, Province *China*	72E1
Liaoyang *China*	72E1
Liaoyuan *China*	72E1
Liaoyuang *China*	74B2
Liard, R *Can*	4F3
Liard River *Can*	4F4
Liart *France*	46C2
Libenge *Zaïre*	98B2
Liberal *USA*	9C3
Liberec *Czech*	57C2
Liberia, Republic *Africa*	97A4
Liberty, Missouri *USA*	18B2
Liberty, New York *USA*	15D2
Liberty, Texas *USA*	19B3
Libourne *France*	48B3
libres *Mexico*	23B2
Libreville *Gabon*	98A2
Libya, Republic *Africa*	95A2
Libyan Desert *Libya*	95B2
Libyan Plat *Egypt*	95B1
Licata *Italy*	53B3
Lichfield *Eng*	43D3
Lichinga *Mozam*	101C2
Lichtenburg *S Africa*	101G1
Licking, R *USA*	14B3
Lick Observatory *USA*	22B2
Lida *USSR*	60C3
Lidköping *Sweden*	39G7
Lido di Ostia *Italy*	53B2
Liechtenstein, Principality *Europe*	52A1
Liège *Belg*	57B2
Lielupe, R *USSR*	58C1
Lienart *Zaïre*	98C2
Lienz *Austria*	57C3
Liepäja *USSR*	60B2
Lier *Belg*	46C1
Liestal *Switz*	47B1
Liévre, R *Can*	15C1
Liezen *Austria*	57C3
Liffey, R *Irish Rep*	45C2
Lifford *Irish Rep*	45C1
Lifu, I *Nouvelle Calédonie*	107F3
Lightning Ridge *Aust*	109C1
Ligny-en-Barrois *France*	46C2
Ligonha, R *Mozam*	101C2
Liguria, Region *Italy*	47C2
Ligurian, S *Italy*	52A2
Lihue *Hawaiian Is*	21C4
Likasi *Zaïre*	100B2
Lille *France*	49C1
Lillehammer *Nor*	39G6
Lillers *France*	46B1
Lillestøm *Nor*	39G7
Lillooet *Can*	13C2
Lillooet, R *Can*	13C2
Lilongwe *Malawi*	101C2
Liloy *Phil*	79B4
Lim, R *Yugos*	54A2
Lima *Peru*	32B6
Lima *Spain*	50A1
Lima *USA*	10B2
Limassol *Cyprus*	92B3
Limavady *N Ire*	45C1
Limay, R *Arg*	34B3
Limay Mahuida *Arg*	34B3
Limbe *Malawi*	101C2
Limburg *W Gem*	57B2
Limeira *Brazil*	31B6
Limerick, County *Irish Rep*	45B2
Limerick *Irish Rep*	41B3
Limfjorden, L *Den*	56B1
Limmen Bight, B *Aust*	106C2
Límnos, I *Greece*	55C3
Limoeiro *Brazil*	31D3
Limoges *France*	48C2
Limón *Costa Rica*	25D4
Limon *USA*	8C3
Limousin, Region *France*	48C2
Linapacan Str *Phil*	79A3
Linares *Chile*	29B3
Linares *Mexico*	9D4
Linares *Spain*	50B2
Lincang *China*	68B4
Lincoln *Arg*	29D2
Lincoln, California *USA*	18A1
Lincoln, County *Eng*	42D3
Lincoln *Eng*	42D3
Lincoln, Illinois *USA*	18C1
Lincoln, Nebraska *USA*	8D2
Lincoln, New Hampshire *USA*	15D2
Lincoln *NZ*	111B2
Lincoln, S *Greenland*	80A
Lincoln City *USA*	20B2
Lincoln Park *USA*	14B2
L'Incudina, Mt *Corse*	52A2
Lindau *W Germ*	57B3
Linden *Guyana*	33F2
Lindesnes, C *Nor*	39F7
Lindi *Tanz*	99D3
Lindi, R *Zaïre*	98C2
Lindley *S Africa*	101G1
Lindos *Greece*	55C3
Lindsay *Can*	15C2
Line Is *Pacific O*	105J3
Linfen *China*	72C2
Lingao *China*	76D2
Lingayen *Phil*	79B2
Lingen *W Germ*	56B2
Lingling *China*	73C4
Lingshan *China*	73B5
Lingshi *China*	72C2
Linguère *Sen*	97A3
Linhai, Rhejiang *China*	73E4
Linhares *Brazil*	31D5
Linhe *China*	72B1
Linjiang *China*	74B2
Linköping *Sweden*	39H7
Linqing *China*	72D2
Lins *Brazil*	35B2
Lintao *China*	72A2
Linthal *Switz*	47C1
Linxi *China*	68D2
Linxia *China*	72A2
Linz *Austria*	57C3
Lipa *Phil*	79B3
Lipari, I *Italy*	53B3
Lipetsk *USSR*	61E3
Lipova *Rom*	54B1
Lippe, R *W Germ*	56B2
Lippstadt *W Germ*	46E1
Lira *Uganda*	99D2
Liranga *Congo*	98B3
Lisala *Zaïre*	98C2
Lisboa *Port*	50A2
Lisburn *N Ire*	45C1
Liscannor B *Irish Rep*	45B2
Lishui *China*	73D4
Li Shui, R *China*	73C4
Lisichansk *USSR*	60E4
Lisieux *France*	48C2
L'Isle-Adam *France*	46B2
L'Isle-sur-le-Doubs *France*	47B1
Lismore *Aust*	107E3
Listowel *Irish Rep*	45B2
Litang *China*	73B5
Litani, R *Leb*	94B2
Litani, R *Suriname*	33G3
Litchfield *USA*	18C2
Lithgow *Aust*	107E4
Lititz *USA*	16A2
Litovko *USSR*	69F2
Litovskaya SSR, Republic *USSR*	60B2
Little, R *USA*	19A3
Little Abaco, I *Bahamas*	11C4
Little Barrier I *NZ*	110C1
Little Bow, R *Can*	13E2
Little Cayman, I *Caribbean*	25D3
Little Egg Harbor, B *USA*	16B3
Little Inagua, I *Caribbean*	26C2
Little Nicobar, I *Nicobar Is*	77A4
Little Rock *USA*	11A3
Littlerock *USA*	22D3
Little Smoky *Can*	13D2
Little Smoky, R *Can*	13D2
Littlestown *USA*	16A3
Littleton, New Hampshire *USA*	15D2
Liuhe *China*	74B2
Liuzhou *China*	73B5
Livanátais *Greece*	55B3
Livāni *USSR*	58D1
Livengood *USA*	12E1
Live Oak *USA*	17B1
Livermore *USA*	21A2
Liverpool *USA*	7D5
Liverpool *Eng*	42C3
Liverpool B *Can*	4E2

Lubefu

Lubefu *Zaïre*	98C3
Lubefu, R *Zaïre*	98C3
Lubero *Zaïre*	99C3
Lubilash, R *Zaïre*	98C3
Lublin *Pol*	59C2
Lubny *USSR*	60D3
Lubok Antu *Malay*	78C2
Lubudi *Zaïre*	98C3
Lubudi, R *Zaïre*	98C3
Lubukinggau *Indon*	78A3
Lubumbashi *Zaïre*	100B2
Lubutu *Zaïre*	98C3
Lucban *Phil*	79B3
Lucca *Italy*	52B2
Luce, B *Scot*	42B2
Lucedale *USA*	19C3
Lucena *Phil*	79B3
Lucenec *Czech*	59B3
Luchuan *China*	73C5
Luckenwalde *E Germ*	56C2
Luckhoff *S Africa*	101F1
Lucknow *India*	86A1
Lucusse *Angola*	100B2
Lüda *China*	72E2
Lüdenscheid *W Germ*	46D1
Lüderitz *Namibia*	100A3
Ludhiana *India*	84D2
Ludington *USA*	14A2
Ludlow *Eng*	43C3
Ludogorie, Upland *Bulg*	54C2
Ludowici *USA*	17B1
Luduş *Rom*	54B1
Ludvika *Sweden*	39H6
Ludwigsburg *W Germ*	57B3
Ludwigshafen *W Germ*	57B3
Ludwigslust *E Germ*	56C2
Luebo *Zaïre*	98C3
Luema, R *Zaïre*	98C3
Luembe, R *Angola*	98C3
Luena *Angola*	100A2
Luene, R *Angola*	100B2
Lüeyang *China*	72B3
Lufeng *China*	73D5
Lufkin *USA*	11A3
Luga *USSR*	60C2
Luga, R *USSR*	60C2
Lugano *Switz*	52A1
Lugela *Mozam*	101C2
Lugenda, R *Mozam*	101C2
Lugo *Spain*	50A1
Lugoj *Rom*	54B1
Luhuo *China*	72A3
Lui, R *Angola*	98B3
Luiana *Angola*	100B2
Luiana, R *Angola*	100B2
Luino *Italy*	47C2
Luionga, R *Zaïre*	98B2
Luipan Shan, Upland *China*	72B2
Luishia *China*	100B2
Luixi *China*	68B4
Luiza *Zaïre*	98C3
Luján *Arg*	34B2
Luján *Arg*	34D2
Lujiang *China*	73D3
Lukenie, R *Zaïre*	98B3
Luki *USSR*	64E4
Lukolela *Zaïre*	98B3
Luków *Pol*	58C2
Lukuga, R *Zaïre*	98C3
Lukulu *Zambia*	100B2
Lule, R *Sweden*	38J5
Luleå *Sweden*	38J5
Lüleburgaz *Turk*	54C2
Lüliang Shan, Mts *China*	72C2
Luling *USA*	19A4
Lulonga, R *Zaïre*	98C2
Lumbala *Angola*	100B2
Lumberton *USA*	11C3
Lumbis *Indon*	78D1
Lumding *India*	86C1
Lumeje *Angola*	100B2
Lumsden *NZ*	111A3
Lund *Sweden*	39G7
Lundazi *Zambia*	101C2
Lundi, R *Zim*	100C3
Lundy, I *Eng*	43B4
Lüneburg *W Germ*	56C2
Lunéville *France*	46D2
Lunga, R *Zambia*	100B2
Lunglei *India*	86C2
Lungue Bungo, R *Angola*	100A2
Luninec *USSR*	58D2
Luobomo *Congo*	98B3
Luocheng *China*	73B5
Luoding *China*	73C5
Luohe *China*	72C3
Luo He, R, Henan *China*	72C3
Luo He, R, Shaanxi *China*	72B2
Luoxiao Shan, Hills *China*	73C4
Luoyang *China*	72C3
Luozi *Zaïre*	98B3
Lupane *Zim*	100B2
Lupilichi *Mozam*	101C2
Luque *Par*	30E4
Lurgan *N Ire*	45C1
Lurio, R *Mozam*	101C2
Lusaka *Zambia*	100B2
Lusambo *Zaïre*	98C3
Lushnjë *Alb*	55A2
Lushoto *Tanz*	99D3
Lushui *China*	68B4
Lushun *China*	72E2
Luton *Eng*	43D4
Lutsk *USSR*	60C3
Luuq *Somalia*	99E2
Luvua, R *Zaïre*	99C3
Luwegu, R *Tanz*	99D3
Luwingu *Zambia*	100C2
Luwuk *Indon*	71D4
Luxembourg, Grand Duchy *N W Europe*	46D2
Luxembourg *Lux*	49D2
Luxi *China*	73A5
Luxor *Egypt*	95C2
Luza *USSR*	61G1
Luza, R *USSR*	61G1
Luzern *Switz*	52A1
Luzhai *China*	73B5
Luzhi *China*	73B4
Luzhou *China*	73B4
Luziânia *Brazil*	35B1
Luzon, I *Phil*	79B2
Luzon Str *Phil*	79B1
L'vov *USSR*	59C3
Lybster *Scot*	44C2
Lycksele *Sweden*	38H6
Lydenburg *S Africa*	100B3
Lyell,Mt *USA*	8B3
Lykens *USA*	16A2
Lyme B *Eng*	43C4
Lyme Regis *Eng*	43C4
Lynchburg *USA*	11C3
Lyndhurst *Aust*	108A2
Lynn *USA*	15D2
Lynn Canal, Sd *USA*	12G3
Lynn Haven *USA*	17A1
Lynn Lake *Can*	5H4
Lynx L *Can*	5H3
Lyon *France*	49C2
Lyon Canal, Sd *USA*	12G3
Lyons, Georgia *USA*	17B1
Lyons, R *Aust*	106A3
Lys, R *Italy*	47B2
Lys'va *USSR*	61J2
Lyttelton *NZ*	111B2
Lytton *Can*	13C2
Lytton *USA*	22A1
Lyubeshov *USSR*	58D2
Lyublino *USSR*	60E2

M

Ma, R *Viet*	76C1
Ma'agan *Jordan*	94B2
Ma'alot Tarshīha *Israel*	94B2
Ma'an *Jordan*	92C3
Ma'anshan *China*	73D3
Ma'arrat an Nu'mān *Syria*	92C2
Maas, R *Neth*	46C1
Maaseik *Belg*	46C1
Maasin *Phil*	79B3
Maastricht *Belg*	57B2
Mabalane *Mozam*	101C3
Mabaruma *Guyana*	33F2
Mablethorpe *Eng*	42E3
Mabote *Mozam*	101C3
Mabrita *USSR*	58C2
M'adel *USSR*	58D2
Macaé *Brazil*	35C2
McAlester *USA*	9D3
McAllen *USA*	9D4
Macaloge *Mozam*	101C2
Macapá *Brazil*	33G3
Macarani *Brazil*	35C1
Macas *Ecuador*	32B4
Macaú *Brazil*	31D3
Macau, Dependency *China*	73C5
M'Bari, R *CAR*	98C2
McBride *Can*	13C2
McCarthy *USA*	12F2
McCauley I *Can*	13A2
Macclesfield *Eng*	42C3
McClintock B *Can*	6B1
McClintock Chan *Can*	4H2
McClure *USA*	16A2
McClure,L *USA*	22B2
McClure Str *Can*	4G2
McComb *USA*	19B3
McCook *USA*	8C2
Macculloch,C *Can*	6C2
McCusker,Mt *Can*	13C1
McDame *Can*	4F4
McDermitt *USA*	20C2
Macdonald, R *Can*	13E2
Macdonnell Ranges, Mts *Aust*	106C3
Macedo de Cavaleiros *Port*	50A1
Maceió *Brazil*	31D3
Macenta *Guinea*	97B4
Macerata *Italy*	52B2
Macfarlane,L *Aust*	108A2
McGehee *USA*	19B3
MacGillycuddys Reeks Mts *Irish Rep*	45B3
McGrath *USA*	4C3
Machado *Brazil*	35B2
Machaíla *Mozam*	101C3
Machakos *Kenya*	99D3
Machala *Ecuador*	32B4
Machaze *Mozam*	101C3
Mācherla *India*	87B1
Machgharab *Leb*	94B2
Machilīpatnam *India*	87C1
Machiques *Ven*	32C1
Machu-Picchu, Hist Site *Peru*	32C6
Macia *Mozam*	101C3
MacIntyre, R *Aust*	109C1
Mackay *USA*	107D3
Mackay *Aust*	107D3
Mackay,L *Aust*	106B3
McKeesport *USA*	14C2
Mackenzie *Can*	13C1
Mackenzie, R *Can*	4F3
Mackenzie, Region *Can*	4F3
Mackenzie B *Can*	4E3
Mackenzie King I *Can*	4G2
Mackenzie Mts *Can*	4E3
Mackinac,Str of *USA*	14B1
Mackinaw City *USA*	14B1
McKinley,Mt *USA*	12D2
McKinney *USA*	19A3
Mackinson Inlet, B *Can*	6C2
Macksville *Aust*	109D2
Mclaoughlin,Mt *USA*	20B2
Maclean *Aust*	109D1
Maclear *S Africa*	100B4
McLennan *Can*	5G4
McLeod, R *Can*	13D2
McLeod B *Can*	4G3
McLeod,L *Aust*	106A3
McLeod Lake *Can*	13C1
Macmillan, R *Can*	4E3
Macmillan P *Can*	12H2
McMinnville, Oregon *USA*	20B1
McMurdo, Base *Ant*	112B7
McNaughton L *Can*	13D2
Macomb *USA*	18B1
Macomer *Sardegna*	53A2
Macomia *Mozam*	101C2
Mâcon *France*	49C2
Macon, Georgia *USA*	11B3
Macon, Missouri *USA*	18B2
Macondo *Angola*	100B2
McPherson *USA*	18A2
Macquarie, Is *Aust*	104F6
Macquarie, R *Aust*	109C2
Macquarie Harbour, B *Aust*	109C4
Macquarie,L *Aust*	109D2
McRae *USA*	17B1
MacRobertsn Land, Region *Ant*	112B11
Macroom *Irish Rep*	45B3
M'Sila *Alg*	96C1
McTavish Arm, B *Can*	4G3
Macumba, R *Aust*	108A1
Macunaga *Italy*	47C2
McVicar Arm, B *Can*	4F3
M'yaróvár *Hung*	59B3
Mādabā *Jordan*	94B3
Madadi, Well *Chad*	95A3
Madagascar, I *Indian O*	89J10
Madama *Niger*	95A2
Madang *PNG*	71F4
Madaoua *Niger*	97C3
Madaripur *Bang*	86C2
Madau *USSR*	90B2
Madawaska, R *Can*	15C1
Madeira, I *Atlantic O*	96A1
Madeira, R *Brazil*	33E5
Madera *Mexico*	24B2
Madera *USA*	21A2
Madgaon *India*	87A1
Madhubani *India*	86B1
Madhya Pradesh, State *India*	86A2
Madikeri *India*	87B2
Madimba *Zaïre*	98B3
Madingo Kayes *Congo*	98B3
Madingou *Congo*	98B3
Madison, Indiana *USA*	10B3
Madison, Wisconsin *USA*	10B2
Madisonville, Kentucky *USA*	18C2
Madisonville, Texas *USA*	19A3
Madiun *Indon*	78C4
Mado Gashi *Kenya*	99D2
Madonna Di Campiglio *Italy*	47D1
Madras *India*	87C2
Madras *USA*	20B2
Madre de Dios, I *Chile*	29A6
Madre de Dios, R *Bol*	32D6
Madrid *Spain*	50B1
Madridejos *Spain*	50B2
Madura, I *Indon*	78C4
Madurai *India*	87B3
Maebashi *Japan*	75B1
Mae Khlong, R *Thai*	76B3
Mae Nam Lunang, R *Thai*	77B4
Mae Nam Mun, R *Thai*	76C2
Mae Nam Ping, R *Thai*	76C2
Maevatanana *Madag*	101D2
Mafeteng *Lesotho*	101G1
Maffra *Aust*	109C3
Mafia, I *Tanz*	99D3
Mafikeng *S Africa*	101G1
Mafra *Brazil*	30G4
Mafraq *Jordan*	92C3
Magangué *Colombia*	32C2
Magdalena *Arg*	34D3
Magdalena *Mexico*	9B3

Manzanares

Mayaguana, I Bahamas	11C4
Mayagüez Puerto Rico	27D3
Mayahi Niger	97C3
Mayama Congo	98B3
Mayamey Iran	90C2
Maybole Scot	42B2
May,C USA	10C3
Maydena Aust	109C4
Mayen W Germ	46D1
Mayenne France	48B2
Mayerthorpe Can	13D2
Mayfield USA	18C2
Maykop USSR	61E5
Maymaneh Afghan	65H6
Maymyo Burma	76B1
Mayo Can	4E3
Mayo, County Irish Rep	45B2
Mayo USA	16A3
Mayo,Mts of Irish Rep	45B1
Mayon, Mt Phil	79B3
Mayor, Mt Spain	51C2
Mayor Buratovich Arg	34C3
Mayor I NZ	110C1
Mayor P Lagerenza Par	30D2
Mayotte, I Indian O	101D2
May Pen Jamaica	27H2
May Point,C USA	16B3
Mayrhofen Austria	47D1
Mays Landing USA	16B3
Maysville USA	14B3
Mayumba Gabon	98B3
Mazabuka Zambia	100B2
Mazaffarnagar India	84D3
Mazar China	84D1
Mazär Jordan	94B3
Mazara del Vallo Italy	53B3
Mazar-i-Sharif Afghan	84B1
Mazatlán Mexico	24B2
Mazeikiai USSR	60B2
Mazra Jordan	94B3
Mbabane Swaziland	101C3
Mbaïki CAR	98B2
Mbala Zambia	99D3
Mbalabala Zim	100B3
Mbale Uganda	99D2
Mbalmayo Cam	98B2
Mbam, R Cam	98B2
Mbamba Bay Tanz	101C2
Mbandaka Zaïre	98B2
Mbanza Congo Angola	98B3
Mbanza-Ngungu Zaïre	98B3
Mbarara Uganda	99D3
Mbènza Congo	98B2
Mbére, R Cam	98B2
Mbeya Tanz	99D3
Mbinda Congo	98B3
Mbout Maur	97A3
Mbuji-Mayi Zaïre	98C3
Mbulu Tanz	99D3
Mcherrah, Region Alg	96B2
Mchinji Malawi	101C2
Mdrak Viet	76D3
Mead,L USA	9B3
Meadow Lake Can	5H4
Meadville USA	14B2
Mealy Mts Can	7E4
Meandarra Aust	109C1
Meander River Can	5G4
Meath, County Irish Rep	45C2
Meaux France	49C2
Mechanicville USA	16C1
Mechelen Belg	56A2
Mecheria Alg	96B1
Mecklenburger Bucht, B E Germ	56C2
Meconta Mozam	101C2
Mecuburi Mozam	101C2
Mecufi Mozam	101D2
Mecula Mozam	101C2
Medan Indon	70A3
Medanos Arg	34C3
Médanos Arg	34D2
Medecine Hat Can	13E2
Medellin Colombia	32B2
Medenine Tunisia	96D1
Medford USA	8A2
Medgidia Rom	54C2
Media Agua Arg	34B2
Mediaş Rom	54B1
Medical Lake USA	20C1
Medicine Hat Can	5G5
Medina Brazil	35C1
Medina S Arabia	80B3
Medinaceli Spain	50B1
Medina del Campo Spain	50B1
Medina de Rio Seco Spain	50A1
Medinipur India	86B2
Mediterranean S Europe	88E4
Medley Can	13F2
Mednogorsk USSR	61J3
Mêdog China	86D1
Medouneu Gabon	98B2
Medvedista, R USSR	61F3
Medvezh'yegorsk USSR	64E3
Meekatharra Aust	106A3
Meerut India	84D3
Mega Eth	99D2
Megalópolis Greece	55B3
Mégara Greece	55B3
Meghālaya, State India	86C1
Meghna, R Bang	86C2
Megido, Hist Site Israel	94B2
Mohran, R Iran	91D4
Mehriz Iran	90B3
Meia Ponte, R Brazil	35B1
Meiganga Cam	98B2
Meiktila Burma	76B1
Meiringen Switz	47C1
Meishan China	73A4
Meissen E Germ	57C2
Mei Xian China	73D5
Meizhou China	73D5
Mejillones Chile	30B3
Mekambo Gabon	98B2
Meknès Mor	96B1
Mekong, R Camb	76D3
Mekrou, R Benin	97C3
Melaka Malay	77C5
Melanesia, Region Pacific O	104F4
Melawi, R Indon	78C3
Melbourne Aust	107D4
Melbourne USA	11B4
Melchor Muzquiz Mexico	9C4
Melfi Chad	98B1
Melfort Can	5H4
Melilla N W Africa	96B1
Melimoyu, Mt Chile	29B4
Melincué Arg	34C2
Melipilla Chile	34A2
Melitopol' USSR	60E4
Meliville Bugt, B Greenland	6D2
Melmoth S Africa	101H1
Melo Arg	34C2
Melo Urug	29F2
Melones Res USA	22B2
Melozitna, R USA	12D1
Mels Switz	47C1
Melton Mowbray Eng	43D3
Melun France	49C2
Melville Can	5H4
Melville,C Dominica	27Q2
Melville Hills, Mts Can	4F3
Melville I Aust	106C2
Melville I Can	4G2
Melville,L Can	7E4
Melville Pen Can	6B3
Melvin,L Irish Rep	45B1
Memba Mozam	101D2
Memboro Indon	106A1
Memmingen W Germ	57C3
Mempawan Indon	78B2
Memphis, Tennessee USA	11B3
Mena USA	19B3
Menai Str Wales	43B3
Ménaka Mali	97C3
Menasha USA	14A2
Mende France	49C3
Mendebo, Mts Eth	99D2
Mendip Hills, Upland Eng	43C4
Mendocino,C USA	20B2
Mendocino Seascarp Pacific O	105J2
Mendota, California USA	22B2
Mendoza Arg	29C2
Mendoza, State Arg	29C3
Menemen Turk	55C3
Menen Belg	46B1
Mengcheng China	72D3
Menggala Indon	78B3
Menghai China	76B1
Mengla China	73A5
Menglian China	76B1
Mengzi China	73A5
Menindee Aust	107D4
Menindee L Aust	108B2
Meningie Aust	108A3
Menominee USA	14A1
Menomonee Falls USA	14A2
Menongue Angola	100A2
Menorca, I Spain	51C1
Mentasta Mts USA	12F2
Mentok Indon	78B3
Mentor USA	14B2
Ménu France	46B2
Menyuan China	72A2
Menzelinsk USSR	61H2
Meppen W Germ	56B2
Merah Indon	78D2
Meramec, R USA	18B2
Merano Italy	52B1
Merauke Indon	71F4
Merced USA	8A3
Merced, R USA	22B2
Mercedario, Mt Chile	29B2
Mercedes Arg	29C2
Mercedes, Buenos Aires Arg	29E2
Mercedes, Corrientes Arg	30E4
Mercedes Urug	29E2
Mercury B NZ	110C1
Mercury Is NZ	110C1
Mercy B Can	4F2
Mercy,C Can	6D3
Meregh Somalia	99E2
Mergui Burma	76B3
Mergui Arch Burma	76B3
Mérida Mexico	25D2
Mérida Spain	50A2
Mérida Ven	32C2
Meridian USA	11B3
Merimbula Aust	109C3
Meringur Aust	108B2
Merowe Sudan	95C3
Merredin Aust	106A4
Merrick, Mt Scot	42B2
Merrillville USA	14A2
Merritt Can	13C2
Merritt Island USA	17B2
Merriwa Aust	109D2
Mersa Fatma Eth	99E1
Mers el Kebir Alg	51B2
Mersey, R Eng	42C3
Merseyside, Metropolitan County Eng	42C3
Mersin Turk	92B2
Mersing Malay	77C5
Merta India	85C3
Merthyr Tydfil Wales	43C4
Mertola Port	50A2
Meru Mt Tanz	99D3
Merzifon Turk	60E5
Merzig W Germ	46D2
Mesa USA	9B3
Meschede W Germ	46E1
Mescit Dağ, Mt Turk	93D1
Meshik USA	12C3
Meshra Er Req Sudan	99C2
Mesocco Switz	47C1
Mesolóngion Greece	55B3
Mesquite, Texas USA	19A3
Messalo, R Mozam	101C2
Messina Italy	53C3
Messina S Africa	100B3
Messíni Greece	55B3
Messiniakós Kólpos, G Greece	55B3
Mesta, R Bulg	54B2
Mestre Italy	52B1
Meta, R Colombia	32C3
Meta, R USSR	60D2
Meta, R Ven	32D2
Meta Incognito Pen Can	6C3
Metairie USA	19B4
Metaline Falls USA	20C1
Metán Arg	30D4
Metangula Mozam	101C2
Metaponto Italy	53C2
Methil Scot	44C3
Methuen USA	16D1
Methven NZ	111B2
Metlakatla USA	12H3
Metropolis USA	18C2
Mettūr India	87B2
Metz France	49D2
Meulaboh Indon	70A3
Meulan France	46A2
Meuse, Department France	46C2
Meuse, R France	49D2
Mexia USA	19A3
Mexicali Mexico	24A1
Mexico, Federal Republic Central America	24B2
México Mexico	24C3
México, State Mexico	23A2
Mexico USA	18B2
Mexico,G of C America	24C2
Mezada, Hist Site Israel	94B3
Mezcala Mexico	23B2
Mezen' USSR	64F3
Mezhdusharskiy, I USSR	64G3
Mhow India	85D4
Miahuatlán Mexico	23B2
Miami, Florida USA	11B4
Miami, Oklahoma USA	18B2
Miami Beach USA	11B4
Miandowāb Iran	90A2
Miandrivazo Madag	101D2
Miāneh Iran	90A2
Mianwali Pak	84C2
Mianyang China	73A3
Mianyang China	73C3
Mianzhu China	73A3
Miaodao Qundao, Arch China	72E2
Miao Ling, Upland China	73B4
Miass USSR	61K3
Michalovce Czech	59C3
Miches Dom Rep	27D3
Michigan, State USA	10B2
Michigan City USA	14A2
Michigan,L USA	10B2
Michipicoten I Can	7B5
Michoacan, State Mexico	23A2
Michunnsk USSR	65F4
Michurin Bulg	54C2
Michurinsk USSR	61F3
Micronesia, Region Pacific O	104F3
Midai, I Indon	78B2
Mid Atlantic Ridge Atlantic O	102F4
Middelburg Neth	46B1

Middle Alkali L

Middle Alkali L *USA*	20B2
Middleboro *USA*	16D2
Middleburg, Cape Province *S Africa*	100B4
Middleburg, Pennsylvania *USA*	16A2
Middleburg, Transvaal *S Africa*	101G1
Middleburgh *USA*	16B1
Middlebury *USA*	15D2
Middlesboro *USA*	11B3
Middlesbrough *Eng*	42D2
Middletown, Connecticut *USA*	16C2
Middletown, Delaware *USA*	16B3
Middletown, New York *USA*	15D2
Middletown, Ohio *USA*	14B3
Middletown, Pennsylvania *USA*	16A2
Midelt *Mor*	96B1
Mid Glamorgan, County *Wales*	43C4
Mid Indian Basin *Indian O*	104B4
Mid Indian Ridge *Indian O*	104B4
Midland *Can*	7C5
Midland, Michigan *USA*	14B2
Midland, Texas *USA*	9C3
Midongy Atsimo *Madag*	101D3
Mid Pacific Mts *Pacific O*	105G2
Midvale *USA*	20C2
Midway Is *Pacific O*	105H2
Midwest City *USA*	18A2
Midyat *Turk*	93D2
Midžor, Mt *Yugos*	54B2
Mielec *Pol*	59B2
Miercurea-Ciuc *Rom*	54C1
Mieres *Spain*	50A1
Mifflintown *USA*	16A2
Mihara *Japan*	75A2
Mijun Shuiku, Res *China*	72D1
Mikhayiovka *USSR*	65F4
Mikhaylovgrad *Bulg*	54B2
Mikhaylovka *USSR*	61F3
Mikhaylovskiy *USSR*	65J4
Mikkeli *Fin*	38K6
Míkonos, I *Greece*	55C3
Mikulov *Czech*	59B3
Mikumi *Tanz*	99D3
Mikuni-sammyaku, Mts *Japan*	74D3
Mikura-jima, I *Japan*	75B2
Milagro *Ecuador*	32B4
Milana *Alg*	51C2
Milange *Mozam*	101C2
Milano *Italy*	52A1
Milas *Turk*	92A2
Mildura *Aust*	107D4
Mile *China*	73A5
Mileh Tharthār, L *Iraq*	93D3
Miles *Aust*	107E3
Miles City *USA*	8C2
Milford, Connecticut *USA*	16C2
Milford, Delaware *USA*	15C3
Milford, Massachusetts *USA*	15D2
Milford, Nebraska *USA*	18A1
Milford, Pennsylvania *USA*	16B2
Milford Haven *Wales*	43B4
Milford Haven, Sd *Wales*	43B4
Milford L *USA*	18A2
Milford Sd *NZ*	111A2
Milk River *Can*	13E2
Millau *France*	49C3
Millbrook *USA*	16C2
Milledgeville *USA*	17B1
Miller,Mt *USA*	12F2
Millerovo *USSR*	61F4
Millersburg *USA*	16A2
Millers Creek *Aust*	108A1
Millers Falls *USA*	16C1
Millerton *USA*	16C2
Millerton L *USA*	22C2
Millicent *Aust*	108B3
Millmerran *Aust*	109D1
Milltown Malbay *Irish Rep*	45B2
Mill Valley *USA*	22A2
Millville *USA*	15D3
Milne Land, I *Greenland*	6H2
Milolii *Hawaiian Is*	21C4
Mílos, I *Greece*	55B3
Milparinka *Aust*	107D3
Milroy *USA*	16A2
Milton *NZ*	111A3
Milton, Pennsylvania *USA*	16A2
Milwaukee *USA*	10B2
Mina, R *Alg*	51C2
Mīnā' al Ahmadī *Kuwait*	93E4
Mīnāb *Iran*	91C4
Minamata *Japan*	74C4
Minas *Indon*	78A2
Minas *Urug*	29E2
Minas Gerais, State *Brazil*	31B5
Minas Novas *Brazil*	35C1
Minatitlan *Mexico*	25C3
Minbu *Burma*	76A1
Minbya *Burma*	76A1
Mincha *Chile*	34A2
Minch,Little, Sd *Scot*	44A3
Minch,North, Sd *Scot*	44A2
Minch,The, Sd *Scot*	40B2
Minchumina,L *USA*	12D2
Mincio, R *Italy*	47D2
Mindanao, I *Phil*	79B4
Minden, Louisiana *USA*	19B3
Minden *W Germ*	56B2
Mindona L *Aust*	108B2
Mindoro, I *Phil*	79B3
Mindoro Str *Phil*	79B3
Mine Hd, C *Irish Rep*	45C3
Minehead *Eng*	43C4
Mineiros *Brazil*	30F2
Mineola *USA*	19A3
Mineral de Monte *Mexico*	23B1
Minersville *USA*	16A2
Mingary *Aust*	108B2
Minhe *China*	72A2
Minicoy, I *India*	87A3
Min Jiang, R, Fujian *China*	73D4
Min Jiang, R, Sichuan *China*	73A4
Minkler *USA*	22C2
Minlaton *Aust*	108A2
Minle *China*	72A2
Minna *Nig*	97C4
Minneapolis *USA*	10A2
Minnedosa *Can*	5J4
Minnesota, State *USA*	10A2
Miño, R *Spain*	50A1
Minot *USA*	8C2
Minqin *China*	72A2
Min Shan, Upland *China*	72A3
Minsk *USSR*	60C3
Minsk Mazowiecki *Pol*	58C2
Minto *USSR*	12E2
Minto Inlet, B *Can*	4G2
Minto,L *Can*	7C4
Minusinsk *USSR*	63B2
Min Xian *China*	72A3
Miquelon *Can*	7E5
Mirage L *USA*	22D3
Miraj *India*	87A1
Miramar *Arg*	29E3
Miram Shah *Pak*	84B2
Miranda de Ebro *Spain*	50B1
Mirandola *Italy*	47D2
Mir Bachchen Kūt *Afghan*	84B2
Miri *Malay*	78D1
Mirik,C *Maur*	96A3
Mirnoye *USSR*	63A1
Mirnyy *USSR*	63D1
Mirnyy, Base *Ant*	112C9
Mirpur *Pak*	84C2
Mirpur Khas *Pak*	85B3
Mírtoan S *Greece*	55B3
Miryang *S Korea*	74B3
Mīrzāpur *India*	86A1
Misantla *Mexico*	23B2
Misgar *Pak*	84C1
Mishawaka *USA*	14A2
Misheguk Mt *USA*	12B1
Mi-shima, I *Japan*	75A2
Misima, I *Solomon Is*	107E2
Misiones, State *Arg*	30F4
Miskolc *Hung*	59C3
Mismīyah *Syria*	94C2
Misoöl, I *Indon*	71E4
Misrātah *Libya*	95A1
Missinaibi, R *Can*	7B5
Mission City *Can*	20B1
Mississauga *Can*	15C2
Mississippi, State *USA*	11A3
Mississippi, R *USA*	11A3
Mississippi Delta *USA*	19C3
Missoula *USA*	8B2
Missour *Mor*	96B1
Missouri, State *USA*	11A3
Missouri, R *USA*	10A2
Mistassini,L *Can*	10C1
Misti, Mt *Peru*	30B2
Mitchell *Aust*	109C1
Mitchell *USA*	8D2
Mitchell, R *Aust*	107D2
Mitchell,Mt *USA*	11B3
Mitchelstown *Irish Rep*	45B2
Mithankot *Pak*	84C3
Mitilíni *Greece*	55C3
Mitla *Mexico*	23B2
Mitu *Colombia*	32C3
Mitumbar, Mts *Zaïre*	99C3
Mitwaba *Zaïre*	98C3
Mitzic *Gabon*	98B2
Miura *Japan*	75B1
Mi Xian *China*	72C3
Miyake, I *Japan*	69F3
Miyake-jima, I *Japan*	75B2
Miyako, I *Japan*	69E4
Miyakonojō *Japan*	74C4
Miyazaki *Japan*	74C4
Miyazu *Japan*	75B1
Miyoshi *Japan*	74C4
Miyun *China*	72D1
Mizan Teferi *Eth*	99D2
Mizdah *Libya*	95A1
Mizen Hd, C *Irish Rep*	45B3
Mizil *Rom*	54C1
Mizo Hills *India*	86C2
Mizoram, Union Territory *India*	86C2
Mizpe Ramon *Israel*	94B3
Mizuho, Base *Ant*	112B11
Mizusawa *Japan*	74E3
Mjolby *Sweden*	39H7
Mkushi *Zambia*	100B2
Mkuzi *S Africa*	101H1
Mladá Boleslav *Czech*	57C2
Mława *Pol*	58C2
Mljet, I *Yugos*	52C2
Mmabatho *S Africa*	100B3
Mnadi *India*	84D2
Moa, R *Sierra Leone*	97A4
Moab, Region *Jordan*	94B3
Moab *USA*	9C3
Moanda *Congo*	98B3
Moanda *Gabon*	98B3
Moba *Zaïre*	99C3
Mobara *Japan*	75C1
Mobaye *CAR*	98C2
Mobayi *Zaire*	98C2
Moberly *USA*	10A3
Mobile *USA*	11B3
Mobile B *USA*	11B3
Mobridge *USA*	8C2
Moçambique *Mozam*	101D2
Moc Chau *Viet*	76C1
Mochudi *Botswana*	100B3
Mocimboa da Praia *Mozam*	101D2
Mocoa *Colombia*	32B3
Mococa *Brazil*	35B2
Mocoreta, R *Arg*	34D2
Moctezuma, R *Mexico*	23B1
Mocuba *Mozam*	101C2
Modane *France*	47B2
Modder, R *S Africa*	101G1
Modena *Italy*	52B2
Moder, R *France*	46D2
Modesto *USA*	8A3
Modesto Res *USA*	22B2
Modica *Italy*	53B3
Mödling *Austria*	59B3
Moe *Aust*	107D4
Moesa, R *Switz*	47C1
Moffat *Scot*	42C2
Moga *India*	84D2
Mogi das Cruzes *Brazil*	35B2
Mogilev *USSR*	60C3
Mogilev Podolskiy *USSR*	60C4
Mogi-Mirim *Brazil*	35B2
Mogincual *Mozam*	101D2
Mogliano *Italy*	47E2
Mogna *Arg*	34B2
Mogocha *USSR*	68D1
Mogochin *USSR*	65K4
Moguer *Spain*	50A2
Mohaka, R *NZ*	110C1
Mohanganj *Bang*	86C2
Mohawk, R *USA*	15D2
Mohoro *Tanz*	99D3
Mointy *USSR*	65J5
Mo i Rana *Nor*	38G5
Moissac *France*	48C3
Mojave *USA*	21B2
Mojave, R *USA*	22D3
Mojave Desert *USA*	9B3
Mojokerto *Indon*	78C4
Mokama *India*	86B1
Mokau, R *NZ*	110B1
Mokelumne Aqueduct *USA*	22B1
Mokelumne Hill *USA*	22B1
Mokelumne North Fork, R *USA*	22B1
Mokhotlong *Lesotho*	101G1
Moknine *Tunisia*	96D1
Mokokchūng *India*	86C1
Mokolo *Cam*	98B1
Mokp'o *S Korea*	74B4
Moksha, R *USSR*	61F3
Molango *Mexico*	23B1
Moláoi *Greece*	55B3
Moldavskaya SSR, Republic *USSR*	60C4
Molde *Nor*	38F6
Moldoveanu, Mt *Rom*	54B1
Molepolole *Botswana*	100B3
Molfetta *Italy*	53C2
Molina *Chile*	34A3
Mollendo *Peru*	30B2
Molodechno *USSR*	60C3
Molodezhnaya, Base *Ant*	112C11
Molokai, I *Hawaiian Is*	21C4
Moloma, R *USSR*	61G2
Molong *Aust*	109C2
Molopo, R *Botswana*	100B3
Molounddu *Cam*	98B2
Molson L *Can*	8D1
Molucca, S *Indon*	71D4
Moluccas, Is *Indon*	71D4
Moma *Mozam*	101C2
Mombaca *Brazil*	31C3
Mombasa *Kenya*	99D3
Mompono *Zaïre*	98C2
Mon, I *Den*	56C2

Moudon

Moudon *Switz*	47B1
Mouila *Gabon*	98B3
Moulamein *Aust*	108B2
Mould Bay *Can*	4G2
Moulins *France*	49C2
Moulmein *Burma*	76B2
Moulouya, R *Mor*	96B1
Moultrie *USA*	17B1
Moultrie,L *USA*	17C1
Mound City, Illinois *USA*	18C2
Mound City, Missouri *USA*	18A1
Moundou *Chad*	98B2
Moundsville *USA*	14B3
Mountain, R *Can*	12J1
Mountain Brook *USA*	17A1
Mountain Grove *USA*	18B2
Mountain Home, Arkansas *USA*	18B2
Mountain View *USA*	22A2
Mountain Village *USA*	12B2
Mount Airy, Maryland *USA*	16A3
Mount Carmel *USA*	16A2
Mount Dutton *Aust*	108A1
Mount Eba *Aust*	108A2
Mount Gambier *Aust*	108B3
Mount Holly *USA*	16B3
Mount Holly Springs *USA*	16A2
Mount Hope *Aust*	108A2
Mount Isa *Aust*	106C3
Mount Lofty Range, Mts *Aust*	108A2
Mount McKinley Nat Pk *USA*	12D2
Mount Magnet *Aust*	106A3
Mount Manara *Aust*	108B2
Mount Morgan *Aust*	107E3
Mount Pleasant, Texas *USA*	19B3
Mount Rainier Nat Pk *USA*	20B1
Mounts B *Eng*	43B4
Mount Shasta *USA*	20B2
Mount Vernon, Illinois *USA*	11B3
Mount Vernon, Kentucky *USA*	19A3
Mount Vernon, Washington *USA*	20B1
Mourne Mts *N Ire*	45C1
Moussoro *Chad*	98B1
Mouth of the Indus *Pak*	85B4
Mouths of the Ganga *India/Bang*	86B2
Mouths of the Mekong *Viet*	77D4
Mouths of the Niger *Nigeria*	97C4
Moutier *Switz*	47B1
Moûtiers *France*	47B2
Mouydir, Mts *Alg*	96C2
Mouyondzi *Congo*	98B3
Mouzon *France*	46C2
Moyahua *Mexico*	23A1
Moyale *Kenya*	99D2
Moyamba *Sierra Leone*	97A4
Moyen Atlas, Mts *Mor*	96B1
Moyeni *Lesotho*	100B4
Moyo *Uganda*	99D2
Moyobamba *Peru*	32B5
Moyu *China*	84D1
Mozambique, Republic *Africa*	101C3
Mozambique Chan *Mozam/Madag*	101C3
Mozhga *USSR*	61H2
Mozyr *USSR*	60C3
Mpanda *Tanz*	99D3
Mpika *Zambia*	101C2
Mporokosa *Zambia*	99D3
Mposhi *Zambia*	100B2
Mpulungu *Zambia*	99D3
Mpwapwa *Tanz*	99D3
Mtsensk *USSR*	60E3
Mtubatuba *S Africa*	101H1
Mtwara *Tanz*	101D2
Muang Chainat *Thai*	76C2
Muang Chiang Rai *Thai*	76C2
Muang Kalasin *Thai*	76C2
Muang Khon Kaen *Thai*	76C2
Muang Lampang *Thai*	76B2
Muang Lamphun *Thai*	76B2
Muang Loei *Thai*	76C2
Muang Lom Sak *Thai*	76C2
Muang Nakhon Phanom *Thai*	76C2
Muang Nakhon Sawan *Thai*	76B2
Muang Nan *Thai*	76C2
Muang Phayao *Thai*	76C2
Muang Phetchabun *Thai*	76C2
Muang Phichit *Thai*	76C2
Muang Phitsanulok *Thai*	76C2
Muang Phrae *Thai*	76C2
Muang Roi Et *Thai*	76C2
Muang Sakon Nakhon *Thai*	76C2
Muang Samut Prakan *Thai*	76C3
Muang Uthai Thani *Thai*	76C2
Muang Yasothon *Thai*	76C2
Muar *Malay*	77C5
Muara *Brunei*	78C2
Muara *Indon*	70B4
Muaralakitan *Indon*	78A3
Muaratebo *Indon*	78A3
Muaratewah *Indon*	78C3
Muarenim *Indon*	78A3
Muaungmaya *Burma*	76A2
Mubende *Uganda*	99D2
Muchinga, Mts *Zambia*	100C2
Muck, I *Scot*	44A3
Muckadilla *Aust*	109C1
Mucuri *Brazil*	35D1
Mucuri, R *Brazil*	35C1
Mucusso *Angola*	100B2
Mudanjiang *China*	69E2
Mudgee *Aust*	109C2
Mudon *Burma*	76B2
Mueda *Mozam*	101C2
Mueo *Nouvelle Calédonie*	107F3
Mufulira *Zambia*	100B2
Mufu Shan, Hills *China*	73C4
Mugadzhary, Mts *USSR*	61J4
Mughayra *S Arabia*	93C4
Mugla *Turk*	92A2
Mugodzhary, Mts *USSR*	65G5
Muguaping *China*	73A3
Muhaywir *Iraq*	93D3
Mühldorf *W Germ*	57C3
Muhlhausen *E Germ*	57C2
Muhos *Fin*	38K6
Mui Bai Bung, C *Camb*	77C4
Muine Bheag *Irish Rep*	45C2
Mujimbeji *Zambia*	100B2
Mukacheva *USSR*	59C3
Mukah *Malay*	78C2
Muko-jima, I *Japan*	69G4
Muktinath *Nepal*	86A1
Mukur *Afghan*	84B2
Mulberry *USA*	18B2
Mulchatna, R *USA*	12C2
Mulchén *Chile*	34A3
Mulde, R *E Germ*	56C2
Mulgrave I *Aust*	71F5
Mulhacén, Mt *Spain*	50B2
Mülheim *W Germ*	46D1
Mulhouse *France*	49D2
Muli *China*	73A4
Mull, I *Scot*	44B3
Mullaitvu *Sri Lanka*	87C3
Mullaley *Aust*	109C2
Mullewa *Aust*	106A3
Mullica, R *USA*	16B3
Mullingar *Irish Rep*	45C2
Mull of Kintyre, Pt *Scot*	42B2
Mull of Oa, C *Scot*	45C1
Mullumbimby *Aust*	109D1
Mulobezi *Zambia*	100B2
Multan *Pak*	84C2
Mumbwa *Zambia*	100B2
Mumra *USSR*	61G4
Muna, I *Indon*	71D4
München *W Germ*	57C3
Muncie *USA*	14A2
Muncy *USA*	15C2
Münden *W Germ*	56B2
Mundubbera *Aust*	109D1
Mungallala *Aust*	109C1
Mungallala, R *Aust*	109C1
Mungbere *Zaïre*	99C2
Mungeli *India*	86A2
Munger *India*	86B1
Mungindi *Aust*	109C1
Munising *USA*	14A1
Muñoz Gomero,Pen *Chile*	29B6
Munster, Region *Irish Rep*	45B2
Münster *Switz*	47C1
Münster *W Germ*	56B2
Muntii Apuseni, Mts *Rom*	54B1
Muntii Călimanilor, Mts *Rom*	54B1
Muntii Carpaţii Meridionali, Mts *Rom*	54B1
Muntii Rodnei, Mts *Rom*	54B1
Muntii Zarandului, Mts *Rom*	54B1
Munzur Silsilesi, Mts *Turk*	93C2
Muomio *Fin*	64D3
Muong Khoua *Laos*	76C1
Muong Man *Viet*	76D3
Muong Nong *Laos*	76D2
Muong Ou Neua *Laos*	76C1
Muong Sai *Laos*	76C1
Muong Sen *Viet*	76C2
Muong Sing *Laos*	76C1
Muong Son *Laos*	76C1
Muonio *Fin*	38J5
Muonio, R *Sweden/Fin*	38J5
Muqdisho *Somalia*	99E2
Mur, R *Austria*	52B1
Murakami *Japan*	74D3
Murallón, Mt *Chile/Arg*	29B5
Murashi *USSR*	61G2
Murat, R *Turk*	93D2
Muravera *Sardegna*	53A3
Murayama *Japan*	75C1
Murcheh Khvort *Iran*	90B3
Murchison *NZ*	111B2
Murchison, R *Aust*	106A3
Murcia, Region *Spain*	51B2
Murcia *Spain*	51B2
Mureş, R *Rom*	54B1
Muresui, R *Rom*	54B1
Murg, R *W Germ*	46E2
Murgab, R *USSR*	65H6
Murgha Kibzai *Pak*	84B2
Murgon *Aust*	109D1
Muri *India*	86B2
Muriaé *Brazil*	35C2
Muriege *Angola*	98C3
Murmansk *USSR*	64E3
Murom *USSR*	61F2
Muroran *Japan*	74E2
Muros *Spain*	50A1
Muroto *Japan*	74C4
Muroto-zaki, C *Japan*	75A2
Murphy, Idaho *USA*	20C2
Murphys *USA*	22B1
Murray, Kentucky *USA*	18C2
Murray, R *Aust*	108B2
Murray, R *Can*	13C2
Murray Bridge *Aust*	108A3
Murray,L *PNG*	71F4
Murray,L *USA*	17B1
Murray Seacarp *Pacific O*	105J2
Murrumbidgee, R *Aust*	108B2
Murrumburrah *Aust*	109C2
Murrurundi *Aust*	109D2
Murten *Switz*	47B1
Murtoa *Aust*	108B3
Murupara *NZ*	110C1
Murwāra *India*	86A2
Murwillimbah *Aust*	109D1
Muş *Turk*	93D2
Musala, Mt *Bulg*	54B2
Musan *N Korea*	74B2
Musandam, Pen *Oman*	91C4
Muscat, Region *Oman*	91C5
Musgrave Range, Mts *Aust*	106C3
Mushie *Zaïre*	98B3
Muskegon *USA*	14A2
Muskegon, R *USA*	14A2
Muskogee *USA*	18A2
Muskoka,L *Can*	15C2
Musmar *Sudan*	95C3
Musoma *Tanz*	99D3
Musselshell, R *USA*	8C2
Mussende *Angola*	100A2
Mussidan *France*	48C2
Mustafa-Kemalpasa *Turk*	55C2
Mustang *Nepal*	86A1
Muswelibrook *Aust*	109D2
Mut *Egypt*	95B2
Mutarara *Mozam*	101C2
Mutari *Zim*	101C2
Mutoko *Zim*	101C2
Mutsamudu *Comoros*	101D2
Mutshatsha *Zaïre*	100B2
Mutsu *Japan*	74E2
Mutsu-wan, B *Japan*	74E2
Mutton, I *Irish Rep*	45B2
Mu Us Shamo, Desert *China*	72B2
Muxima *Angola*	98B3
Muya *USSR*	63D2
Muyezerskiy *USSR*	38L6
Muyinga *Burundi*	99D3
Muyumba *Zaïre*	98C3
Muyun Kum, Desert *USSR*	82A1
Muzaffarābad *Pak*	84C2
Muzaffargarh *Pak*	84C2
Muzaffarpur *India*	86B1
Muzhi *USSR*	64H3
Muztag, Mt *China*	82C2
Muztagata, Mt *China*	82B2
Mvuma *Zim*	100C2
Mwanza *Tanz*	99D3
Mwanza *Zaïre*	98C3
Mweka *Zaïre*	98C3
Mwene Ditu *Zaïre*	98C3
Mwenezi *Zim*	100C3
Mwenga *Zaïre*	99C3
Mweru, L *Zambia*	99C3
Mwinilunga *Zambia*	100B2
Myanaung *Burma*	83D4
Myingyan *Burma*	86D2
Myingyao *Burma*	76B1
Myinmoletkat, Mt *Burma*	76B3
Myitkyina *Burma*	82D3
Myitta *Burma*	76B3
Mymensingh *Bang*	86C2
Myojin, I *Japan*	69F3
Myrdal *Nor*	39F6
Myrdalsjökur, Mts *Iceland*	38B2
Myrtle Beach *USA*	17C1
Myrtle Creek *USA*	20B2
Mysen *Nor*	39G7
Mysiloborz *Pol*	56C2

Mys Kanin Nos, C USSR 64F3
Myślenice Pol 59B3
Mys Lopatka, C USSR 69H1
Mysore India 87B2
Mys Sarych, C USSR 60D5
Mystic USA 16D2
Mys Tyub-Karagan, Pt USSR 61H5
Mys Yelizavety, C USSR 63G2
Mys Zhelaniya, C USSR 64H2
My Tho Viet 77D3
Mytle Point USA 20B2
Mzimba Malawi 101C2
Mzuzú Malawi 101C2

N

Naalehu Hawaiian Is 21C4
Naantali Fin 39J6
Naas Irish Rep 45C2
Nabari Japan 75B2
Nabosna, R USA 12F2
Nabeul Tunisia 96D1
Nablus Israel 94B2
Nacala Mozam 101D2
Naches USA 20B1
Nachingwea Tanz 101C2
Nacogdoches USA 19B3
Nacondam, I Indian O 76A3
Nacozari Mexico 24B1
Nadiäd India 85C4
Nador Mor 50B2
Nadushan Iran 90B3
Nadvornaya USSR 59C3
Naestved Den 56C1
Nafoora Libya 95B2
Nagahama Japan 75A2
Naga Hills Burma 82D3
Nagai Japan 75B1
Nägäland, State India 86C1
Nagano Japan 74D3
Nagaoka Japan 74D3
Nägappattinam India 87B2
Nagar Parkar Pak 85C4
Nagasaki Japan 74B4
Nagashima Japan 75B2
Nagato Japan 75A2
Nägaur India 85C3
Nägercoil India 87B3
Nagha Kalat Pak 85B3
Nagina India 84D3
Nagoya Japan 74D3
Nägpur India 85D4
Nagqu China 82D2
Nagykanizsa Hung 59B3
Nagykörös Hung 59B3
Naha Japan 69E4
Nahaimo Can 8A2
Nähan India 84D2
Nahanni Butte Can 4F3
Nahariya Israel 94B2
Nahävand Iran 90A3
Nahe, R W Germ 46D2
Nahpu China 72D2
Naimen Qi China 72E1
Nain Can 7D4
Nä'in Iran 90B3
Naini Tai India 84D3
Nairn Scot 44C3
Nairobi Kenya 99D3
Najafäbäd Iran 90B3
Najin N Korea 74C2
Nakama Japan 75A2
Nakaminato Japan 74E3
Nakamura Japan 75A2
Nakano Japan 75B1
Nakano-shima, I Japan 75A1
Nakatsu Japan 74C4
Nakatsu-gawa Japan 75B1
Nakfa Eth 95C3
Nakhichevan USSR 93E2
Nakhl Egypt 92B4
Nakhodka USSR 74C2
Nakhon Pathom Thai 76C3

Nakhon Ratchasima Thai 76C3
Nakhon Si Thammarat Thai 77C4
Nakina Can 12H3
Nakina, Ontario Can 7B4
Naknek USA 12C3
Naknek L USA 12C3
Nakrek USA 4C4
Nakskov Den 39G8
Nakuru Kenya 99D3
Nakusp Can 13D2
Nal'chik USSR 61F5
Nalgonda India 87B1
Nallamala Range, Mts India 87B1
Nälüt Libya 95A1
Namaacha Mozam 101H1
Namak, L Iran 65G6
Namakzar-e Shadad, Salt Flat Iran 90C3
Namangan USSR 65J5
Namapa Mozam 101C2
Namaqualand, Region S Africa 100A4
Nambour Aust 109D1
Nambucca Heads Aust 109D2
Nam Can Viet 77D4
Namcha Barwa, Mt China 82D3
Nam Co, L China 82D2
Nam Dinh Viet 76D1
Nametil Mozam 101C2
Namhae-do, I S Korea 74B4
Namib Desert Namibia 100A2
Namibe Angola 100A2
Namibia, Dependency Africa 100A3
Namlea Indon 71D4
Namoi, R Aust 109C2
Nampa Can 13D1
Nampa USA 20C2
Nampala Mali 97B3
Nam Phong Thai 76C2
Namp'o N Korea 74B3
Nampula Mozam 101C2
Namsos Nor 38G6
Namton Burma 76B1
Namtu Burma 86D2
Namu Can 13B2
Namuno Mozam 101C2
Namur Belg 46C1
Namutoni Namibia 100A2
Namwŏn S Korea 74B3
Nanaimo Can 13C3
Nanam N Korea 74B2
Nanango Aust 109D1
Nanao Japan 74D3
Nanatsu-jima, I Japan 75B1
Nanbu China 73B3
Nanchang China 73D4
Nanchong China 73B3
Nancy France 49D2
Nänded India 87B1
Nandewar Range, Mts Aust 109D2
Nandurbar India 85C4
Nandyäl India 87B1
Nanga Eboko Cam 98B2
Nanga Parbat, Mt Pak 84C1
Nangapinoh Indon 78C3
Nangatayap Indon 78C3
Nangnim Sanmaek, Mts N Korea 74B2
Nang Xian China 86C1
Nangzhou China 67F3
Nanjangüd India 87B2
Nanjing China 72D3
Nankou Japan 75A2
Nan Ling, Region China 73C4
Nanliu, R China 76D1
Nanning China 73B5
Nanortalik Greenland 6F3
Nanpan Jiang, R China 73A5
Nänpära India 86A1

Nanping China 73D4
Nansen Sd Can 6A1
Nansio Tanz 99D3
Nantes France 48B2
Nanton Can 13E2
Nantong China 72E3
Nantucket, I USA 10C2
Nanuque Brazil 35C1
Nanyang China 72C3
Nanyang Hu, L China 72D2
Nanyuki Kenya 99D2
Naoetsu Japan 74D3
Naokot Pak 85B4
Napa USA 22A1
Napaiskak USA 12B2
Napanee Can 15C2
Napas USSR 65K4
Napassoq Greenland 6E3
Nape Laos 76D2
Napier NZ 110C1
Naples, Florida USA 17B2
Naples, Texas USA 19B3
Napo China 73B5
Napo, R Peru/Ecuador 32C4
Napoli Italy 53B2
Naqadeh Iran 90A2
Naqb Ishtar Jordan 92C4
Nara Japan 75B2
Nara Mali 97B3
Naracoorte Aust 107D4
Naranjos Mexico 23B1
Narasaräopet India 87C1
Narathiwat Thai 77C4
Narayanganj Bang 86C2
Näräyenpet India 87B1
Norbonne France 49C3
Narendranagar India 84D2
Nares Str Can 6C2
Narew, R Pol 58C2
Narita Japan 75C1
Narmada, R India 85C4
Närnaul India 84D3
Naro Fominsk USSR 60E2
Narok Kenya 99D3
Narowal Pak 84C2
Narrabri Aust 107D4
Narran, L Aust 109C1
Narran, R Aust 109C1
Narrandera Aust 109C2
Narrogin Aust 106A4
Narromine Aust 109C2
Narsimhapur India 85D4
Narsipatnam India 87C1
Narssalik Greenland 6F3
Narssaq Greenland 6F3
Narssarssuaq Greenland 6F3
Narugo Japan 75C1
Naruto Japan 75A2
Narva USSR 60C2
Narvik Nor 38H5
Narwäna India 84D3
Nar'yan Mar USSR 64G3
Narylico Aust 108B1
Naryn USSR 65J5
Nasarawa Nig 97C4
Nasca Ridge Pacific O 103D5
Nashua USA 16D1
Nashville, Arkansas USA 19B3
Nashville, Tennessee USA 11B3
Našice Yugos 54A1
Näsik India 85B4
Nasir Sudan 99D2
Nass, R Can 13B1
Nassau Bahamas 26B1
Nassau USA 16C1
Nasser,L Egypt 95C2
Nässjö Sweden 39G7
Nastapoka Is Can 7C4
Nata Botswana 100B3
Natal Brazil 31D3
Natal Indon 70A3
Natal, Province S Africa 101H1
Natanz Iran 90B3
Natashquan Can 7D4

Natashquan, R Can 7D4
Natchez USA 19B3
Natchitoches USA 19B3
Nathalia Aust 108C3
Nathorsts Land, Region Greenland 6H2
Nation, R Can 13C1
National City USA 21B3
Natori Japan 75C1
Natovl'a USSR 58D2
Natron, L Tanz 99D3
Naturaliste,C Aust 106A4
Nauders Austria 47D1
Nauen E Germ 56C2
Naugatuck USA 16C2
Naumburg E Germ 57C2
Naur Jordan 94B3
Nauru, I Pacific O 105G4
Naushki USSR 63C2
Nautla Mexico 23B1
Navajo Res USA 9C3
Navalmoral de la Mata Spain 50A2
Navarino, I Chile 29C7
Navarra, Province Spain 51B1
Navarro Arg 34D3
Navasota USA 19A3
Navasota, R USA 19A3
Navia, R Spain 50A1
Navidad Chile 34A2
Navlakhi India 85C4
Navlya USSR 60D3
Navojoa Mexico 24B2
Návpaktos Greece 55B3
Návplion Greece 55B3
Navsäri India 85C4
Nawá Syria 94C2
Nawäda India 86B2
Nawah Afghan 84B2
Nawrabshah Pak 85B3
Naxi China 73B4
Náxos, I Greece 55C3
Nayar Mexico 23A1
Nay Band Iran 90C3
Nay Band Iran 91B4
Nayoro Japan 74E2
Nazareth Israel 94B2
Nazay France 48B2
Nazca Peru 32C6
Nazilli Turk 92A2
Nazimovo USSR 63B2
Nazko, R Can 13C2
Nazwa Oman 91C5
Nazyvayevsk USSR 65J4
Ndalatando Angola 98B3
Ndélé CAR 98C2
Ndendé Gabon 98B3
N'Djamena Chad 98B1
Ndjolé Gabon 98B3
Ndola Zambia 100B2
Neabul Aust 109C1
Neales, R Aust 108A1
Neápolis Greece 55B3
Neath Wales 43C4
Nebine, R Aust 109C1
Nebit Dag USSR 65G6
Nebraska, State USA 8C2
Nebraska City USA 18A1
Nechako, R Can 13C2
Neches, R USA 19A3
Necochea Arg 34D3
Nêdong China 86C1
Needles USA 9B3
Neenah USA 14A2
Neepawa Can 5J4
Neerpelt Belg 46C1
Neftelensk USSR 63C2
Negelli Eth 99D2
Negev, Desert Israel 94B3
Negolu, Mt Rom 60B4
Negombo Sri Lanka 87B3
Negrais,C Burma 76A2
Negritos Peru 32A4
Negro, R, Amazonas Brazil 33E4
Negro, R Arg 29C4
Negro, R Urug 34D2

Negros

Nuristan

Oologah L USA	18A2
Oostende Belg	46B1
Oosterschelde, Estuary Neth	46B1
Ootacamund India	87B2
Ootsa L Can	13B2
Opala USSR	69H1
Opala Zaïre	98C3
Opanake Sri Lanka	87C3
Oparino USSR	61G2
Opava Czech	59B3
Opelika USA	17A1
Opelousas USA	19B3
Ophir USA	12C2
Opochka USSR	58D1
Opole Pol	59B2
Opotiki NZ	110C1
Opp USA	17A1
Oppdal Nor	38F6
Opunake NZ	110B1
Oradea Rom	54B1
Oraefajökull, Mts Iceland	38B2
Orai India	85D3
Oran Alg	96B1
Orán Arg	30D3
Orange Aust	109C2
Orange, California USA	22D4
Orange France	49C3
Orange, Texas USA	19B3
Orange, R S Africa	100A3
Orangeburg USA	17B1
Orange Free State, Province S Africa	101G1
Orange Park USA	17B1
Orangeville Can	14B2
Oranienburg E Germ	56C2
Oras Phil	79C3
Orăstie Rom	54B1
Oravita Rom	54B1
Orbetello Italy	52B2
Orbost Aust	109C3
Orchies France	46B1
Orco, R Italy	47B2
Ord, R Aust	106B2
Ord,Mt Aust	106B2
Ordu Turk	93C1
Ordzhonikidze USSR	61F5
Örebro Sweden	39H7
Oregon, State USA	8A2
Oregon USA	14B2
Oregon City USA	20B1
Oregrund Sweden	39H6
Orekhovo Zuyevo USSR	60E2
Orel USSR	60E3
Orenburg USSR	61H3
Orense Arg	34D3
Orense Spain	50A1
Oresund, Str Den/Sweden	56C1
Oreti, R NZ	111A3
Orhaneli, R Turk	55C3
Orhon Gol, R Mongolia	68C2
Oriental Mexico	23B2
Orientos Aust	108B1
Orihuela Spain	51B2
Orillia Can	15C2
Orinoco, R Ven	33E2
Orissa, State India	86A2
Oristano Sardegna	53A3
Orivesi, L Fin	38K6
Oriximina Brazil	33F4
Orizaba Mexico	23B2
Orizona Brazil	35B1
Orkney, I Scot	44C2
Orlândia Brazil	35B2
Orlando USA	17B2
Orléanais, Region France	48C2
Orléans France	48C2
Orlik USSR	63B2
Ormara Pak	82A3
Ormoc Phil	79B3
Ormond Beach USA	17B2
Ornain, R France	46C2
Ornans France	47B1
Orne, R France	48B2
Örnsköldsvik Sweden	38H6
Orocué Colombia	32C3
Oron Israel	94B3
Oroquieta Phil	79B4
Orosháza Hung	59C3
Oroville, California USA	21A2
Oroville, Washington USA	20C1
Orsières Switz	47B1
Orsk USSR	65G4
Ørsta Nor	38F6
Orthez France	48B3
Ortigueira Spain	50A1
Ortles, Mts Italy	47D1
Ortoire, R Trinidad	27L1
Oruro Bol	30C2
Osa USSR	61J2
Osage, R USA	18B2
Osaka Japan	75B1
Osa,Pen de Costa Rica	25D4
Osceola, Arkansas USA	18C2
Osceola, Iowa USA	18B1
Osgood Mts USA	20C2
Oshawa Can	15C2
O-shima, I Japan	75B2
Oshkosh USA	10B2
Oshogbo Nig	97C4
Oshosh USA	7B5
Oshwe Zaïre	98B3
Osijek Yugos	54A1
Osinniki USSR	65K5
Osipovichi USSR	58D2
Oskaloosa USA	18B1
Oskarshamn Sweden	60A2
Oslo Nor	39G7
Osmaniye Turk	92C2
Osnabrück W Germ	56B2
Osório Brazil	30F4
Osorno Chile	29B4
Osorno Spain	50B1
Osoyoos Can	20C1
Ospika, R Can	13C1
Ossa,Mt Aust	107D5
Ossining USA	16C2
Ostashkov USSR	60D2
Østerdalen, V Nor	38G6
Östersund Sweden	38G6
Ostfriesische Inseln, Is W Germ	56B2
Östhammär Sweden	39H6
Ostia Italy	53B2
Ostiglia Italy	47D2
Ostrava Czech	59B3
Ostróda Pol	58B2
Ostroleka Pol	58B2
Ostrov USSR	60C2
Ostrov Belyy, I USSR	64J2
Ostrov Green Bell, I Barents S	64H1
Ostrov Kolguyev, I USSR	64F3
Ostrov Kunashir, I USSR	74F2
Ostrov Mechdusharskiy, I Barents S	64F2
Ostrov Ogurchinskiy, I USSR	90B2
Ostrov Rudol'fa, I Barents S	64G1
Ostrov Vaygach, I USSR	64G2
Ostrov Vrangelya, I USSR	1B7
Ostrów Pol	58B2
Ostrowiec Pol	59C2
Ostrów Mazowiecka Pol	58C2
Osuna Spain	50A2
Osweg USA	15C2
Oswego USA	15C2
Oswestry Eng	43C3
Oświęcim Pol	59B2
Ota Japan	75B1
Otago Pen NZ	111B3
Otaki NZ	110C2
Otaru Japan	74E2
Otavalo Ecuador	32B3
Otavi Namibia	100A2
Otawara Japan	75C1
Othello USA	20C1
Óthris, Mt Greece	55B3
Otis, Massachusetts USA	16C1
Otish Mts Can	10C1
Otisville USA	16B2
Otjiwarongo Namibia	100A3
Otog Qi China	72B2
Otorohanga NZ	110C1
Otranto Italy	55A2
Otranto,Str of, Chan Italy/Alb	55A2
Otsego USA	14A2
Otsu Japan	75B1
Otta Nor	39F6
Otta, R Nor	39F7
Ottawa Can	15C1
Ottawa, Kansas USA	18A2
Ottawa, R Can	15C1
Ottawa Is Can	7B4
Otter Rapids Can	7B4
Otto Fjord Can	6B1
Ottosdal S Africa	101G1
Ottumwa USA	18B1
Ottweiler W Germ	46D2
Oturkpo Nig	97C4
Otusco Peru	32B5
Otway,C Aust	108B3
Otwock Pol	58C2
Ötz Austria	47D1
Otzal, Mts Austria	47D1
Ou, R Laos	76C1
Ouachita, R USA	19B3
Ouachita,L USA	19B3
Ouachita Mts USA	19B3
Ouadane Maur	96A2
Ouadda CAR	98C2
Ouaddai, Desert Region Chad	98C1
Ouagadougou U Volta	97B3
Ouahigouya U Volta	97B3
Ouaka CAR	98C2
Oualam Niger	97C3
Ouanda Djallé CAR	98C2
Ouarane, Region Maur	96A2
Ouargla Alg	96C1
Ouarra, R CAR	98C2
Ouarzazate Mor	96B1
Ouassel, R Alg	51C2
Oubangui, R Congo	98B2
Oudenaarde Belg	46B1
Oudtshoorn S Africa	100B4
Oued Tlélat Alg	51B2
Oued Zem Mor	96B1
Ouesso Congo	98B2
Ouezzane Mor	96B1
Ouham, R Chad	98B2
Ouidah Benin	97C4
Oujda Mor	96B1
Oulainen Fin	38J6
Oulu Fin	38K5
Oulu, R Fin	38K6
Oulujärvi, L Fin	38K6
Oum Chalouba Chad	95B3
Oum Hadjer Chad	98B1
Oum Haouach, Watercourse Chad	95B3
Ounas, R Fin	38K5
Ounianga Kébir Chad	95B3
Our, R W Germ	46D1
Ourcq, R France	46B2
Ouricuri Brazil	31C3
Ourinhos Brazil	35B2
Ouro Prêto Brazil	35C2
Ourthe, R Belg	46C1
Ouse, R Eng	42D2
Ouse, R Eng	43E3
Outer Hebrides, Is Is	40B2
Outer Santa Barbara, Chan USA	22C4
Outjo Namibia	100A3
Outokumpu Fin	38K6
Ouyen Aust	108B3
Ovada Italy	47C2
Ovalle Chile	34A2
Ovamboland, Region Namibia	100A2
Ova Tyuleni, Is USSR	61H5
Övertorneå Sweden	38J5
Oviedo Spain	50A1
Ovruch USSR	60C3
Ovsyanka USSR	63E2
Owaka NZ	111A3
Owase Japan	75B2
Owensboro USA	11B3
Owens L USA	21B2
Owen Sound Can	14B2
Owen Stanley Range, Mts PNG	107D1
Owerri Nig	97C4
Owo Nig	97C4
Owosso USA	14B2
Owyhee, R USA	20C2
Owyhee Mts USA	20C2
Oxapampa Peru	32B6
Oxelösund Sweden	39H7
Oxford, County Eng	43D4
Oxford Eng	43D4
Oxford, Massachusetts USA	16D1
Oxford, Mississippi USA	19C3
Ox Mts Irish Rep	45B1
Oxnard USA	22C3
Oyama Japan	74D3
Oyen Can	13E2
Oyen Gabon	98B2
Oykel, R Scot	44B3
Øyre Nor	39F6
Oyster B Aust	109C4
Ozamiz Phil	79B4
Ozark USA	17A1
Ozark Plat USA	18B2
Ozarks,L of the USA	18B2
Ózd Hung	59C3
Ozero Alakol, L USSR	65K5
Ozero Balkhash, L USSR	65J5
Ozero Baykal, L USSR	63C2
Ozero Chany, L USSR	65J4
Ozero Chudskoye, L USSR	60C2
Ozero Il'men, L USSR	60D2
Ozero Imandra, L USSR	38L5
Ozero Issyk Kul', L USSR	82B1
Ozero Khanka, L USSR/China	69F2
Ozero Kovdozero, L USSR	38L5
Ozero Kuyto, L USSR	38L5
Ozero Pyaozero, L USSR	38L5
Ozero Tengiz, L USSR	65H4
Ozero Topozero, L USSR	38L5
Ozero Zaysan USSR	65K5
Ozuluama Mexico	23B1

P

Paarl S Africa	100A4
Pabbay, I Scot	44A3
Pabianice Pol	58B2
Pabna Bang	86B2
Pabrade USSR	58D2
Pacasmayo Peru	32B5
Pachuca Mexico	23B1
Pacific-Antarctic Ridge Pacific O	105K6
Pacific Grove USA	22B2
Pacitan Indon	78C4
Pacuí, R Brazil	35C1
Padang Indon	70B4
Paderborn W Germ	56B2
Padlei Can	5J3
Padma, R Bang	86C2

Padova

Piedade

56

Popondetta PNG	71F4	Port Macquarie Aust	109D2
Popovo Bulg	54C2	Port Moller USA	12B3
Porbandar India	85B4	Port Moresby PNG	107D1
Porcher I Can	13A2	Port Nolloth S Africa	100A3
Porcupine, R USA/		Port Norris USA	16B3
Can	12F1	Port Novo Benin	89E7
Poreč Yugos	52B1	Porto Port	50A1
Porecatu Brazil	35A2	Pôrto Alegre Brazil	30F5
Pori Fin	39J6	Pôrto Artur Brazil	33F6
Porirua NZ	111B2	Pôrto 15 de	
Porjus Sweden	38H5	Novembro Brazil	35A2
Poronaysk USSR	69G2	Pôrto E Cunha Brazil	30F3
Porrentruy Switz	47B1	Portoferraio Italy	52B2
Porsangen, Inlet Nor	38K4	Port of Spain Trinidad	27E4
Porsgrunn Nor	39F7	Portomaggiore Italy	47D2
Portadown N Ire	45C1	Porto Novo Benin	97C4
Portage la Prairie Can	8D2	Port Orchard USA	20B1
Port Alberni Can	13C3	Port Orford USA	20B2
Portalegre Port	50A2	Porto Santo, I	
Portales USA	9C3	Medeira	96A1
Port Alfred Can	7C5	Pôrto Seguro Brazil	31D5
Port Alfred S Africa	100B4	Porto Torres Sardegna	53A2
Port Alice Can	13B2	Porto Vecchio Corse	53A2
Port Allen USA	19B3	Pôrto Velho Brazil	33E5
Port Angeles USA	20B1	Port Pegasus, B NZ	111A3
Port Antonio Jamaica	26B3	Port Phillip B Aust	108B3
Portarlington Irish Rep	45C2	Port Pirie Aust	108A2
Port Arthur USA	19B4	Portree Scot	44A3
Port Augusta Aust	108A2	Port Renfrew Can	20B1
Port-au-Prince Haiti	26C3	Port Royal Jamaica	27J2
Port Austin USA	14B2	Port Royal Sd USA	17B1
Port Campbell Aust	108B3	Portrush N Ire	45C1
Port Canning India	86B2	Port Said Egypt	92B3
Port Cartier Can	7D5	Port St Joe USA	17A2
Port Chalmers NZ	111B3	Port St Johns S Africa	100B4
Port Charlotte USA	17B2	Port Saunders Can	7E4
Port Chester USA	16C2	Port Shepstone S	
Port Colborne Can	15C2	Africa	100C4
Port Credit Can	15C2	Port Simpson Can	13A2
Port Davey Aust	109C4	Portsmouth Dominica	27Q2
Port-de-Paix Haiti	26C3	Portsmouth Eng	43D4
Port Dickson Malay	77C5	Portsmouth, Ohio	
Port Edward S Africa	100C4	USA	14B3
Porteirinha Brazil	35C1	Portsmouth, Virginia	
Port Elgin Can	14B2	USA	11C3
Port Elizabeth S Africa	100B4	Port Stephens, B Aust	109D2
Porter Pt St Vincent	27N2	Port Sudan Sudan	95C3
Porterville USA	21B2	Port Sulphur USA	19C3
Port Fairy Aust	107D4	Porttipahdan Tekojärvi	
Port Gentil Gabon	98A3	Res Fin	38K5
Port Gibson USA	19B3	Portugal, Republic	
Port Graham USA	12D3	Europe	50A2
Port Hammond Can	20B1	Port Washington USA	14A2
Port Harcourt Nigeria	89E7	Port Weld Malay	77C5
Port Hardy Can	13B2	Porvenir Bol	32D6
Port Hawkesbury Can	7D5	Posadas Arg	30E4
Port Hedland Aust	106A3	Posadas Spain	50A2
Porthmadog Wales	43B3	Poschiavo Switz	47D1
Port Hope Simpson		Posheim Pen Can	6B2
Can	7E4	Posht-e Badam Iran	90C3
Port Hueneme USA	22C3	Poso Indon	71D4
Port Huron USA	14B2	Postavy USSR	58D1
Portimão Port	50A2	Post Clinton USA	14B2
Port Jackson, B Aust	109D2	Poste-de-la-Baleine	
Port Jefferson USA	16C2	Can	7C4
Port Jervis USA	16B2	Postmasburg S Africa	100B3
Port Kembla Aust	109D2	Postojna Yugos	52B1
Portland, Indiana USA	14B2	Pos'yet USSR	74C2
Portland, Maine USA	10C2	Potchetstroom S	
Portland, New South		Africa	101G1
Wales Aust	109C2	Poteau USA	19B2
Portland, Oregon USA	20B1	Potenza Italy	53C2
Portland, Victoria Aust	108B3	Potgietersrus S Africa	100B3
Portland Bight, B		Potiskum Nig	97D3
Jamaica	27H2	Potlatch USA	20C1
Portland Bill, Pt Eng	43C4	Potomac, R USA	15C3
Portland,C Aust	109C4	Potosi Bol	30C2
Portland Canal USA/		Potrerillos Chile	30C4
Can	13A1	Potsdam E Germ	56C2
Portland I NZ	110C1	Pottstown USA	16B2
Portland Pt Jamaica	27H2	Pottsville USA	16A2
Port Laoise Irish Rep	45C2	Poughkeepsie USA	16C2
Port Lincoln Aust	108A2	Pouso Alegre Brazil	35B2
Port Loko Sierra		Poverty B NZ	110C1
Leone	97A4	Povorino USSR	61F3
Port Louis Mauritius	101E3	Povungnituk Can	7C4
Port MacDonnell Aust	108B3	Powder, R USA	8C2
Port McNeill Can	13B2	Powell Creek Aust	106C2

Powell,L USA	9B3	Primorsko-Akhtarsk	
Powell River Can	13C3	USSR	60E4
Power, R USA	8C2	Primrose L Can	13F2
Powys, County Wales	43C3	Prince Albert Can	5H4
Poyang Hu, L China	73D4	Prince Albert,C Can	4F2
Pozantı Turk	92B2	Prince Albert Pen Can	4G2
Poza Rica Mexico	23B1	Prince Albert Sd Can	4G2
Poznań Pol	58B2	Prince Charles I Can	6C3
Pozo Colorado Par	30E3	Prince Charles Mts	
Pozzuoli Italy	53B2	Ant	112B10
Pra, R Ghana	97B4	Prince Edward I Can	7D5
Prachin Buri Thai	76C3	Prince George Can	13C2
Prachuap Khiri Khan		Prince Gustaf Adolp,	
Thai	76B3	S Can	4H2
Praděd, Mt Czech	59B2	Prince of Wales, I	
Pradelles France	49C3	USA	5E4
Prado Brazil	35D1	Prince of Wales I Aust	71F5
Praha Czech	57C2	Prince of Wales I Can	4H2
Praia Cape Verde	97A4	Prince of Wales Str	
Prainha Brazil	33E5	Can	4G2
Prairie Village USA	18B2	Prince Patrick I Can	4F2
Prakhon Chai Thai	76C3	Prince Regent Inlet,	
Prata Brazil	35B1	Str Can	6A2
Prata, R Brazil	35B1	Prince Rupert Can	13A2
Prato Italy	49E3	Princess Charlotte B	
Prattsville USA	16B1	Aust	107D2
Prattville USA	17A1	Princess Royal I Can	13B2
Prawle Pt Eng	48B1	Princes Town Trinidad	27L1
Praya Indon	78D4	Princeton Can	13C3
Predazzo Italy	47D1	Princeton, Kentucky	
Predivinsk USSR	63B2	USA	18C2
Prek Kak Camb	76D3	Princeton, Missouri	
Prenzlau E Germ	56C2	USA	18B1
Preparis, I Burma	76A3	Princeton, New Jersey	
Preparis North Chan		USA	16B2
Burma	76A2	Prince William USA	4D3
Přerov Czech	59B3	Prince William Sd	
Presa del Infiernillo		USA	12E2
Mexico	23A2	Principe, I W Africa	97C4
Prescott, Arizona USA	9B3	Prinoville USA	20B2
Prescott, Arkansas		Pringle,Mt USA	12E1
USA	19B3	Prins Christian Sund,	
Prescott Can	15C2	Sd Greenland	6F3
Presidencia Roque		Prinsesse Astrid Kyst,	
Sáenz Peña Arg	30D4	Region Ant	112B12
Presidente Epitácio		Prinsesse Ragnhild	
Brazil	35A2	Kyst, Region Ant	112B12
Presidente Frei, Base		Prins Karls Forland, I	
Ant	112C2	Barents S	64B2
Presidente Migúel		Prinzapolca Nic	25D3
Aleman, L Mexico	23B2	Pripyat', R USSR	58D2
Presidente Prudente		Priština Yugos	54B2
Brazil	35A2	Pritzwalk E Germ	56C2
Presidenté Vargas		Privolzhskaya	
Brazil	30F3	Vozvyshennost',	
Presidente Venceslau		Upland USSR	61F3
Brazil	35A2	Prizren Yugos	54B2
Prešov Czech	59C3	Probolinggo Indon	78C4
Prespansko Jezero, L		Procatello USA	5G5
Yugos	55B2	Proddatür India	87B2
Presque Isle USA	10D2	Progreso Mexico	25D2
Preston Eng	42C3	Project City USA	20B2
Preston, Idaho USA	8B2	Prokhladnyy USSR	61F5
Preston, Missouri USA	18B2	Prokop'yevsk USSR	65K4
Prestwick Scot	42B2	Proletarskaya USSR	61F4
Prêto Brazil	31B6	Proliv Karskiye Vorota,	
Prêto, R Brazil	35B1	Str USSR	64G2
Pretoria S Africa	101G1	Prome Burma	83D4
Préveza Greece	55B3	Propriá Brazil	31D4
Prey Veng Camb	76D3	Prospect, Oregon	
Price USA	8B3	USA	20B2
Price I Can	13B2	Prosperine Aust	107D3
Prichernomorskaya		Prostějov Czech	59B3
Nizmennost',		Prøven Greenland	6E2
Lowland USSR	60D4	Provence, Region	
Prickly Pt Grenada	27M2	France	49D3
Priekule USSR	58C1	Providence USA	16D2
Prieska S Africa	100B3	Provincetown USA	15D2
Priest L USA	20C1	Provins France	49C2
Priest River USA	20C1	Provo USA	8B2
Prikaspiyskaya		Provost Can	13E2
Nizmennost', Region		Prudhoe Bay USA	4D2
USSR	61G4	Prudhoe Land	
Prilep Yugos	55B2	Greenland	6D2
Priluki USSR	60D3	Pruszkow Pol	58C2
Primero, R Arg	34C2	Prutul, R USSR	60C4
Primorsk USSR	39K6	Pruzhany USSR	58C2
		Pryor USA	18A2

Przemys'l

58

Queziot *Israel*	94B3
Quezon City *Phil*	79B3
Quibala *Angola*	100A2
Quibaxe *Angola*	98B3
Quibdó *Colombia*	32B2
Quiberon *France*	48B2
Quicama Nat Pk *Angola*	98B3
Quijing *China*	73A4
Quilima *Chile*	34A2
Quilino *Arg*	34C2
Quillabamba *Peru*	32C6
Quillacollo *Bol*	30C2
Quillan *France*	48C3
Quill L *Can*	5H4
Quill Lakes *Can*	5H4
Quillota *Chile*	34A2
Quilon *India*	87B3
Quilpie *Aust*	108B1
Quilpué *Chile*	34A2
Quimbele *Angola*	98B3
Quimper *France*	48B2
Quimperlé *France*	48B2
Quincy, California *USA*	21A2
Quincy, Illinois *USA*	10A3
Quincy, Massachusetts *USA*	16D1
Quines *Arg*	34B2
Quinhagak *USA*	12B3
Qui Nhon *Viet*	76D3
Quintanar de la Orden *Spain*	50B2
Quintero *Chile*	34A2
Quinto, R *Arg*	34C2
Quirihue *Chile*	34A3
Quirima *Angola*	100A2
Quirindi *Aust*	109D2
Quissanga *Mozam*	101D2
Quissico *Mozam*	101C3
Quito *Ecuador*	32B4
Quixadá *Brazil*	31D2
Quorn *Aust*	108A2
Quseir *Egypt*	95C2
Outdligssat *Greenland*	6E3
Qu Xian, Sichuan *China*	73B3
Qu Xian, Zhejiang *China*	73D4
Quynh Luu *Viet*	76D2
Quzhou *China*	72C2
Qüzü *China*	86C1

R

Raahe *Fin*	38J6
Raasay, I *Scot*	44A3
Raasay,Sound of, Chan *Scot*	44A3
Rab, I *Yugos*	52B2
Raba *Indon*	78D4
Rába, R *Hung*	59B3
Rabat *Mor*	96B1
Rabba *Jordan*	94B3
Rabigh *S Arabia*	80B3
Racconigi *Italy*	47B2
Race,C *Can*	7E5
Rachaya *Leb*	94B2
Rachel, Mt *W Germ*	57C3
Rach Gia *Viet*	76D3
Racine *USA*	14A2
Rădăuţi *Rom*	59D3
Radhanpur *India*	85C4
Radix,Pt *Trinidad*	27L1
Radom *Pol*	58C2
Radomsko *Pol*	59B2
Radviliškis *USSR*	58C1
Rae *Can*	4G3
Rāe Bareli *India*	86A1
Rae Isthmus *Can*	6B3
Rae L *Can*	4G3
Raetihi *NZ*	110C1
Rafaela *Arg*	34C2
Rafah *Egypt*	94B3
Rafai *CAR*	98C2
Rafhā Al Jumaymah *S Arabia*	93D3
Rafsanjān *Iran*	91C3

Raga *Sudan*	98C2
Ragged Pt *Barbados*	27R3
Raguba *Libya*	95A2
Ragusa *Italy*	53B3
Rahad, R *Sudan*	99D1
Rahimyar Khan *Pak*	84C3
Rähjerd *Iran*	90B3
Raíces *Arg*	34D2
Räichur *India*	87B1
Raigarh *India*	86A2
Rainbow *Aust*	108B3
Rainbow City *USA*	17A1
Rainier *USA*	20B1
Rainier,Mt *USA*	20B1
Rainy L *Can*	10A2
Rainy P *USA*	12D2
Rainy River *Can*	10A2
Raipur *India*	86A2
Räjahmundry *India*	87C1
Rajang, R *Malay*	78C2
Rajanpur *Pak*	84C3
Räjapälaiyam *India*	87B3
Räjasthan, State *India*	85C3
Räjgarh *India*	84D3
Räjgarh, State *India*	85D4
Räjkot *India*	85C4
Räjmahäl Hills *India*	86B2
Raj Nändgaon *India*	86A2
Räjpïpla *India*	85C4
Rajshahi *Bang*	86B2
Rajur *India*	85D4
Rakaia, R *NZ*	111B2
Rakata, I *Indon*	78B4
Raka Zangbo, R *China*	82C3
Rakhov *USSR*	59C3
Rakops *Botswana*	100B3
Rakov *USSR*	58D2
Raleigh *USA*	11C3
Ralny L *Can*	7A5
Rama *Israel*	94B2
Ramallah *Israel*	94B3
Rämanäthapuram *India*	87B3
Ramapo Deep *Pacific Oc*	69G3
Ramat Gan *Israel*	94B2
Rambouillet *France*	46A2
Rämgarh, Bihar *India*	86B2
Rämgarh, Rajasthan *India*	85C3
Rämhormoz *Iran*	90A3
Ramla *Israel*	94B3
Ramlat Al Wahibah, Region *Oman*	91C5
Ramona *USA*	21B3
Rämpur *India*	84D3
Rämpura *India*	85D4
Rämsar *Iran*	90B2
Ramsey *Eng*	42B2
Ramsey, I *Eng*	16B2
Ramsey I *Wales*	43B4
Ramsgate *Eng*	43E4
Ramtha *Jordan*	94C2
Ramu, R *PNG*	71F4
Rancagua *Chile*	34A2
Ränchi *India*	86B2
Ränchi Plat *India*	86A2
Randers *Den*	39G7
Randfontein *S Africa*	101G1
Randolph, Vermont *USA*	15D2
Ranfurly *NZ*	111B3
Rangamati *Bang*	86C2
Rangiora *NZ*	111B2
Rangitaiki, R *NZ*	110C1
Rangitate, R *NZ*	111B2
Rangitikei, R *NZ*	110C1
Rangoon *Burma*	76B2
Rangpur *India*	86B1
Ränibennur *India*	87B2
Ranier,Mt, Mt *USA*	8A2
Räniganj *India*	86B2
Rankins Springs *Aust*	109C2
Ranklin Inlet *Can*	6A3
Rann of Kachchh, Flood Area *India*	85B4
Ranong *Thai*	77B4
Rantauparapat *Indon*	70A3

Rantoul *USA*	18C1
Rapallo *Italy*	49D3
Rapel, R *Chile*	34A2
Raper,C *Can*	6D3
Rapid City *USA*	8C2
Rapid River *USA*	14A1
Rappahannock, R *USA*	15C3
Rapperswil *Switz*	47C1
Raritan B *USA*	16B2
Ras Abu Shagara, C *Sudan*	95C2
Ra's al 'Ayn *Syria*	93D2
Ra's al Hadd, C *Oman*	91C5
Ras al Kaimah *UAE*	91C4
Ras-al-Kuh, C *Iran*	91C4
Ra's al Madrakah, C *Oman*	81D4
Ra's az Zawr, C *S Arabia*	91A4
Räs Bânas, C *Egypt*	95C2
Ras Burûn, C *Egypt*	94A3
Ras Dashan, Mt *Eth*	99D1
Ra's-e-Barkan, Pt *Iran*	90A3
Rås el Kenâyis, Pt *Egypt*	92A3
Ra's Fartak, C *S Yemen*	81D4
Rås Ghârib *Egypt*	95C2
Rashad *Sudan*	99D1
Rashädïya *Jordan*	94B3
Rashïd *Egypt*	92B3
Rasht *Iran*	90A2
Ra's Jibish, C *Oman*	91C5
Ras Khanzira, C *Somalia*	99E1
Ras Koh, Mt *Pak*	84B3
Rås Muhammad, C *Egypt*	95C2
Ras Nouadhibou, C *Maur*	96A2
Rasshua, I *USSR*	69H2
Rasskazovo *USSR*	61F3
Ra's Tanäqib, C *S Arabia*	91A4
Ra's Tannürah *S Arabia*	91B4
Rastatt *W Germ*	57B3
Ras Xaafuun, C *Somalia*	99F1
Ratangarh *India*	84C3
Rat Buri *Thai*	76B3
Rath *India*	85D3
Ratherow *E Germ*	56C2
Rathkeale *Irish Rep*	45B2
Rathlin, I *N Ire*	45C1
Ráth Luirc *Irish Rep*	45B2
Ratläm *India*	85D4
Ratnägiri *India*	87A1
Ratnapura *Sri Lanka*	87C3
Ratno *USSR*	58C2
Rattenberg *Austria*	47D1
Rättvik *Sweden*	39H6
Ratz,Mt *Can*	12H3
Rauch *Arg*	34D3
Raukumara Range, Mts *NZ*	110C1
Raul Soares *Brazil*	35C2
Rauma *Fin*	39J6
Raurkela *India*	86A2
Ravänsar *Iran*	90A3
Råvar *Iran*	90C3
Rava Russkaya *USSR*	59C2
Ravena *USA*	16C1
Ravenna *Italy*	52B2
Ravensburg *W Germ*	57B3
Ravenshoe *Aust*	107D2
Ravi, R *Pak*	84C2
Rawalpindi *Pak*	84C2
Rawicz *Pol*	58B2
Rawlinna *Aust*	106B4
Rawlins *USA*	8C2
Rawndïz *Iraq*	93D2
Rawson *Arg*	29C4
Raya, Mt *Indon*	78C3
Räyadurg *India*	87B2
Rayak *Leb*	94C2
Ray,C *Can*	7E5
Räyen *Iran*	91C4

Raymond, California *USA*	22C2
Raymond, Washington *USA*	20B1
Raymond Terrace *Aust*	109D2
Ray Mts *USA*	12D1
Rayon *Mexico*	23B1
Razan *Iran*	90A2
Razgrad *Bulg*	54C2
Razim, L *Rom*	54C2
Reading *Eng*	43D4
Reading *USA*	16B2
Read Island *Can*	4G3
Readsboro *USA*	16C1
Real de Padre *Arg*	34B2
Realicó *Arg*	34C3
Rebiana, Well *Libya*	95B2
Rebiana Sand Sea *Libya*	95B2
Reboly *USSR*	38L6
Recherche,Arch of the Is *Aust*	106B4
Recife *Brazil*	31E3
Hécifs D'Entrecasteaux *Nouvelle Calédonie*	107F2
Recklinghausen *W Germ*	46D1
Reconquista *Arg*	30E4
Red, R *USA*	19B3
Redang, I *Malay*	77C4
Red Bank, New Jersey *USA*	16B2
Red Bluff *USA*	21A1
Redcar *Eng*	42D2
Redcliff *Can*	13E2
Redcliffe *Aust*	109D1
Red Cliffs *Aust*	108B2
Red Deer *Can*	13E2
Red Deer, R *Can*	13E2
Redding *USA*	20B2
Red L *USA*	10A2
Red Lake *Can*	7A4
Redlands *USA*	22D3
Red Lion *USA*	16A3
Redmond *USA*	20B2
Red Oak *USA*	18A1
Redon *France*	48B2
Redondo Beach *USA*	22C4
Redoubt V *USA*	12D2
Red River Delta *Vietnam*	73B5
Red Sea *Africa/ Arabian Pen*	80B3
Redwater *Can*	13E2
Redwood City *USA*	22A2
Reed City *USA*	14A2
Reedley *USA*	22C2
Reedsport *USA*	20B2
Reefton *NZ*	111B2
Refahiye *Turk*	93C2
Regência *Brazil*	35D1
Regensburg *W Germ*	57C3
Reggane *Alg*	96C2
Reggio di Calabria *Italy*	53C3
Reggio Nell'Emilia *Italy*	47D2
Reghin *Rom*	54B1
Regina *Can*	5H4
Rehoboth *Namibia*	100A3
Rehoboth Beach *USA*	15C3
Rehovot *Israel*	94B3
Reicito *Ven*	32D1
Reigate *Eng*	43D4
Reims *France*	46C2
Reindeer, R *Can*	5H4
Reinosa *Spain*	50B1
Reisterstown *USA*	16A3
Reitz *S Africa*	101G1
Reliance *Can*	4H3
Remarkable,Mt *Aust*	108A2
Rembang *Indon*	78C4
Remeshk *Iran*	91C4
Remscheid *W Germ*	46D1
Rend,L *USA*	18C2
Rendsburg *W Germ*	56B2

Renfrew

Renfrew Can	15C1
Rengat Indon	78A3
Rengo Chile	34A2
Reni USSR	59D3
Renk Sudan	99D1
Renland, Pen Greenland	6H2
Renmark Aust	108B2
Rennell, I Solomon Is	107F2
Rennes France	48B2
Reno USA	21B2
Reno, R Italy	47D2
Renovo USA	15C2
Rensselaer USA	16C1
Renton USA	20B1
Reo Indon	70D4
Reprêsa de Furnas, Dam Brazil	35B2
Reprêsa Três Marias, Dam Brazil	35B1
Republic USA	20C1
Republic of Ireland NW Europe	41B3
Repulse Bay Can	6B3
Réservoir Baskatong, Res Can	15C1
Réservoire Cabonga, Res Can	7C5
Réservoire Gouin, Res Can	7C5
Réservoire Manicouagan, Res Can	10D1
Reshteh-ye Alborz, Mts Iran	90B2
Reshui China	72A2
Resistencia Arg	30E4
Resita Rom	54B1
Resolute Can	6A2
Resolution I NZ	111A3
Resolution Island Can	6D3
Ressano Garcia Mozam	101H1
Retamito Arg	34B2
Rethel France	46C2
Réthimnon Greece	55B3
Reunion, I Indian O	89K10
Reus Spain	51C1
Reuss, R Switz	47C1
Reutte Austria	47D1
Revda USSR	61K3
Revelstoke Can	13D2
Revillagigedo, Is Mexico	24A3
Revillagigedo I USA	12H3
Revin France	46C2
Revivim Israel	94B3
Rewa India	86A2
Rewari India	84D3
Rexburg USA	8B2
Reykjavik Iceland	38A2
Reynosa Mexico	24C2
Rezé France	48B2
Rezekne USSR	58D1
Rezh USSR	61K2
Rhätikon, Mts Austria/Switz	47C1
Rhazir, Republic Leb	94B1
Rhein, R W Europe	56B2
Rheine W Germ	56B2
Rheinfielden Switz	47B1
Rheinland Pfalz, Region W Germ	49D2
Rheinwaldhorn, Mt Switz	47C1
Rhinebeck USA	16C2
Rhinelander USA	10B2
Rho Italy	47C2
Rhode Island, State USA	15D2
Rhode Island Sd USA	16D2
Rhône, R France	49C3
Rhyl Wales	43C3
Riachão do Jacuipe Brazil	31D4
Ria de Arosa, B Spain	50A1
Ria de Betanzos, B Spain	50A1
Ria de Corcubion, B Spain	50A1
Ria de Lage, B Spain	50A1
Ria de Sta Marta, B Spain	50A1
Ria de Vigo, B Spain	50A1
Riäsi Pak	84C2
Ribadeo Spain	50A1
Ribas do Rio Pardo Brazil	35A2
Ribauè Mozam	101C2
Ribble, R Eng	42C3
Ribeira Brazil	35B2
Ribeirão Prêto Brazil	35B2
Riberalta Bol	32D6
Rice L Can	15C2
Rice Lake USA	10A2
Richard's Bay S Africa	101H1
Richardson USA	19A3
Richardson Mts Can	12G1
Richfield USA	8B3
Richland USA	20C1
Richmond, California USA	22A2
Richmond, Natal S Africa	101H1
Richmond, New South Wales Aust	109D2
Richmond NZ	111B2
Richmond, Queensland Aust	107D3
Richmond, Virginia USA	10C3
Richmond Range, Mts NZ	111B2
Rideau,L Can	15C2
Ridgeland USA	17B1
Ridgway USA	15C2
Riecito Ven	27D4
Rienza, R Italy	47D1
Riesa E Germ	57C2
Riesco, I Chile	29B6
Riet, R S Africa	101F1
Rieti Italy	52B2
Rif, Mts Mor	50B2
Riga USSR	58C1
Riga,G of USSR	60B2
Rigän Iran	91C4
Riggins USA	20C1
Rigolet Can	7E4
Riihimaki Fin	39J6
Rijeka Yugos	52B1
Rimbey Can	13E2
Rimbo Sweden	39H7
Rimini Italy	52B2
Rîmnicu Sârat Rom	54C1
Rîmnicu Vîlcea Rom	54B1
Rimouski Can	10D2
Rincón de Romos Mexico	23A1
Ringkøbing Den	39F7
Rio Benito Eq Guinea	98A2
Rio Branco Brazil	32D5
Rio Bravo del Norte, R USA/Mexico	24B1
Riochacha Colombia	32C1
Rio Claro Brazil	35B2
Rio Claro Trinidad	27L1
Rio Colorado Arg	34C3
Rio Cuarto Arg	34C2
Rio de Jacuipe Brazil	31D4
Rio de Janeiro Brazil	35C2
Rio de Janeiro, State Brazil	35C2
Rio de la Plata, Est Arg/Urug	29E3
Rio Gallegos Arg	29C6
Rio Grande Arg	29C6
Rio Grande Brazil	30F5
Rio Grande Nic	26A4
Rio Grande, R Nicaragua	25D3
Rio Grande, R USA/Mexico	24B2
Rio Grande de Santiago Mexico	23A1
Rio Grande do Norte, State Brazil	31D3
Rio Grande do Sul, State Brazil	30F4
Rio Grande Rise Atlantic O	103G6
Riohacha Colombia	26C4
Riom France	49C2
Riombamba Ecuador	32B4
Rio Mulatos Bol	30C2
Río Negro, State Arg	29C3
Rio Pardo Brazil	30F4
Rio Tercero Arg	34C2
Rio Theodore Roosevelt, R Brazil	33E6
Rio Turbio Arg	29B6
Rio Verde Brazil	35A1
Rio Verde Mexico	23A1
Ripley, Ohio USA	14B3
Ripley, West Virginia USA	14B3
Ripon Eng	42D2
Ripon USA	22B2
Rishon le Zion Israel	94B3
Rising Sun USA	16A3
Risør Nor	39F7
Ritenberk Greenland	6E2
Ritter,Mt USA	22C2
Ritzville USA	20C1
Rivadavia Arg	34B2
Rivadavia Chile	34A1
Rivadavia Gonzalez Moreno Arg	34C3
Riva de Garda Italy	47D2
Rivera Arg	34C3
Rivera Urug	29E2
Riverbank USA	22B2
River Cess Lib	97B4
Riverhead USA	16C2
Riverina Aust	108B3
Riversdale NZ	111A3
Riverside USA	22D4
Rivers Inlet Can	13B2
Riverton NZ	111A3
Riverton USA	8C2
Riviera Beach USA	17B2
Rivière aux Feuilles, R Can	7C4
Rivière de la Baleine, R Can	7D4
Rivière du Petit Mècatina, R Can	7D4
Rivigny-sur-Ornain France	46C2
Riyadh S Arabia	91A5
Rize Turk	93D1
Rizhao China	72D2
Rjukan Nor	39F7
Roanes Pen Can	6B2
Roanne France	49C2
Roanoke, Alabama USA	17A1
Roanoke, Virginia USA	11C3
Roanoke, R USA	11C3
Roaringwater B Irish Rep	45B3
Robertsforz Sweden	38J6
Robert S Kerr Res USA	19B2
Robertsport Lib	97A4
Roberval Can	7C5
Robinson Crusoe, I Chile	30H6
Robinvale Aust	108B2
Robson,Mt Can	13D2
Roca Partida, I Mexico	24A3
Rocas, I Atlantic O	103G5
Rocas, I Brazil	31E2
Rocha Urug	29F2
Rochdale Eng	42C3
Rochefort France	48B2
Rocher River Can	5G3
Rochester Aust	108B3
Rochester Can	7C5
Rochester Eng	43E4
Rochester, Minnesota USA	10A2
Rochester, New Hampshire USA	15D2
Rochester, New York USA	10C2
Rockford USA	10B2
Rock Hill USA	11B3
Rock Island USA	10A2
Rocklands Res Aust	108B3
Rockledge USA	17B2
Rock Springs, Wyoming USA	8C2
Rocks Pt NZ	110B2
Rock,The Aust	109C3
Rockville, Connecticut USA	16C2
Rockville, Indiana USA	14A3
Rockville, Maryland USA	16A3
Rocky Island L Can	14B1
Rocky Mountain House Can	13E2
Rocky Mts Can/USA	8B1
Rocky Pt USA	12B2
Rødbyhavn Den	56C2
Rodeo Arg	34B2
Rodez France	49C3
Ródhos Greece	55C3
Ródhos, I Greece	55C3
Rodi Garganico Italy	52C2
Rodopi Planina, Mts Bulg	54B2
Roebourne Aust	106A3
Roer, R Neth	46D1
Roermond Neth	46C1
Roeselare Belg	46B1
Roes Welcome Sd Can	6B3
Rogers USA	18B2
Rogers City USA	14B1
Rogue, R USA	20B2
Rohn Pak	85B3
Rohtak India	84D3
Roja USSR	58C1
Rolândia Brazil	35A2
Rolla USA	18B2
Roma Aust	109C1
Roma Italy	52B2
Romagnano Italy	47C2
Romain,C USA	17C1
Roman Rom	54C1
Romanche Gap Atlantic O	103H5
Romang, I Indon	71D4
Romania, Republic E Europe	60B4
Romano,C USA	17B2
Romans sur Isère France	49D2
Romblon Phil	79B3
Rome, Georgia USA	17A1
Rome, New York USA	15C2
Romilly-sur-Seine France	49C2
Romney USA	15C3
Romny USSR	60D3
Rømø, I Den	56B1
Romont Switz	47B1
Romoratin France	48C2
Ronda Spain	50A2
Rondônia Brazil	33E6
Rondônia, State Brazil	24F6
Rondonópolis Brazil	30F2
Rong'an China	73B4
Rongchang China	73B4
Rongcheng China	72E2
Rongjiang China	73B4
Rong Jiang, R China	73B4
Rongklang Range, Mts Burma	76A1
Rønne Denmark	39G7
Ronneby Sweden	39H7
Ronne Ice Shelf Ant	112B2
Ronse Belg	46B1
Ronthieu, Region France	46A1
Roof Butte, Mt USA	9C3
Roorkee India	84D3
Roosendaal Neth	46C1

St Étienne

San Bartolo Mexico	23A1
San Benedicto, I Mexico	24A3
San Benito, R USA	22B2
San Benito Mt USA	22B2
San Bernardino USA	22D3
San Bernardo Chile	34A2
San Blas,C USA	17A2
San Carlos Chile	34A3
San Carlos Nic	32A1
San Carlos Phil	79B2
San Carlos de Bariloche Arg	29B4
San-chung Taiwan	69E4
Sanchursk USSR	61G2
San Clemente Chile	34A3
San Clemente USA	22D4
San Clemente I USA	21B3
San Cristóbal Arg	34C2
San Cristóbal Mexico	25C3
San Cristóbal Ven	32C2
San Cristóbal, I Ecuador	32J7
San Cristobal, I Solomon Is	107F2
Sancti Spíritus Cuba	25E2
Sandai Indon	78C3
Sandakan Malay	70C3
Sanday, I Scot	44C2
Sanderson USA	9C3
Sandfly L Can	13F1
San Diego USA	21B3
Sandikli Turk	92B2
Sandïla India	86A1
Sandnes Nor	39F7
Sandnessjøen Nor	38G5
Sandø Faroes	38D3
Sandoa Zaïre	98C3
Sandomierz Pol	59C2
Sandpoint USA	20C1
Sandrio Italy	49D2
Sand Springs USA	18A2
Sandstone Aust	106A3
Sandu China	73C4
Sandusky USA	14B2
Sandviken Sweden	39H6
Sandy L Can	7A4
San Elcano Arg	34C2
San Felipe, Baja Cal Mexico	9B3
San Felipe Chile	34A2
San Felipe, Guanajuato Mexico	23A1
San Felipe Ven	27D4
San Feliu de Guixols Spain	51C1
San Felix, I Pacific O	28A5
San Fernando Chile	34A2
San Fernando Phil	79B2
San Fernando Phil	79B2
San Fernando Spain	50A2
San Fernando Trinidad	27E4
San Fernando USA	22C3
San Fernando Ven	32D2
Sanford, Florida USA	17B2
Sanford,Mt USA	12F2
San Francisco Arg	34C2
San Francisco Dom Rep	27C3
San Francisco USA	22A2
San Francisco B USA	22A2
San Francisco del Oro Mexico	24B2
San Francisco del Rincon Mexico	23A1
San Gabriel Mts USA	22D3
Sangamner India	85C5
Sangamon, R USA	18C2
Sangan, I Pacific O	71F2
Sangāreddi India	87B1
Sangeang, I Indon	78D4
Sanger USA	22C2
Sanggan He, R China	72C2
Sanggau Indon	78C2
Sangha, R Congo	98B2
Sanghar Pak	85B3
Sangkhla Buri Thai	76B3
Sangkulirang Indon	78D2
Sāngli India	87A1
Sangmélima Cam	98B2
San Gorgonio Mt USA	9B3
Sangre de Cristo, Mts USA	9C3
San Gregorio Arg	34C2
San Gregorio USA	22A2
Sangrūr India	84D2
San Ignacio Arg	30E4
San Isidro Phil	79B3
San Jacinto Colombia	32B2
San Jacinto Peak, Mt USA	21B3
San Javier Chile	34A3
San Javier, Sante Fe Arg	34D2
Sanjō, I Japan	74D3
San João del Rei Brazil	31C6
San Joaquin, R USA	22B2
San Joaquin Valley USA	22B2
San José Costa Rica	32A1
San José Guatemala	25C3
San Jose, Luzon Phil	79B2
San Jose, Mindoro Phil	79B3
San Jose USA	22B2
San José, I Mexico	9B4
San José de Chiquitos Bol	30D2
San José de Feliciano Arg	34D2
San José de Jachal Arg	34B2
San José de la Dormida Arg	34C2
San José do Rio Prêto Brazil	31B6
San José del Cabo Mexico	24B2
San Juan Arg	34B2
San Juan Puerto Rico	27D3
San Juan, State Arg	34B2
San Juan Trinidad	27L1
San Juan Ven	32D2
San Juan, Mt Cuba	26B2
San Juan, Mts USA	8C3
San Juan, R Arg	34B2
San Juan, R Mexico	23B2
San Juan, R Nicaragua/Costa Rica	25D3
San Juan Bautista Mexico	23B2
San Juan Bautista Par	30E4
San Juan Bautista USA	22B2
San Juan del Norte Nic	25D3
San Juan de los Cayos Ven	27D4
San Juan de loz Lagoz Mexico	23A1
San Juan del Rio Mexico	23A1
San Juan del Sur Nicaragua	25D3
San Juan Is USA	20B1
San Juan Tepozcolula Mexico	23B2
San Julián Arg	29C5
San Justo Arg	34C2
Sankuru, R Zaïre	98C3
San Leandro USA	22A2
San Lorenzo Ecuador	32B3
San Lorenzo Arg	34C2
San Lucas USA	22B2
San Luis Arg	34B2
San Luis, State Arg	34B2
San Luis de la Paz Mexico	23A1
San Luis Obispo USA	21A2
San Luis Potosi Mexico	23A1
San Luis Res USA	22B2
Sanluri Sardegna	53A3
San Maigualida, Mts Ven	33D2
San Manuel Arg	34D3
San Marcos Chile	34A2
San Marcos Mexico	23B2
San Marino, Republic Europe	52B2
San Martin, Mendoza Arg	34B2
San Martin, Base Ant	112C3
San Martino di Castroza Italy	47D1
San Martin Tuxmelucan Mexico	23B2
San Mateo USA	22A2
San Matias Bol	30E2
Sanmenxia China	72C3
San Miguel El Salvador	25D3
San Miguel, I USA	22B3
San Miguel del Allende Mexico	23A1
San Miguel del Monte Arg	34D3
San Miguel de Tucumán Arg	30C4
Sanming China	73D4
San Nicolas, I USA	9B3
San Nicolás de los Arroyos Arg	34C2
Sannieshof S Africa	101G1
Sanniquellie Lib	97B4
Sanok Pol	59C3
San Onofore Colombia	26B5
San Onofre USA	22D4
San Pablo Phil	79B3
San Pablo B USA	22A1
San Pedro, Buenos Aires Arg	34D2
San Pédro Ivory Coast	97B4
San Pedro, Jujuy Arg	30D3
San Pedro Par	30E3
San Pedro Chan USA	22C4
San Pedro de los Colonias Mexico	9C4
San Pedro Sula Honduras	25D3
San Pietro, I Medit S	53A3
San Quintin Mexico	24A1
San Rafael Arg	34B2
San Rafael USA	22A2
San Rafael Mts USA	22C3
San Remo Italy	49D3
San Salvador Arg	34D2
San Salvador, I Caribbean	26C2
San Salvador, I Ecuador	32J7
San Salvador de Jujuy Arg	30C3
San Sebastian Spain	51B1
San Severo Italy	53C2
Santa Ana Bol	30C2
Santa Ana Guatemala	25C3
Santa Ana USA	22D4
Santa Ana Mts USA	22D4
Santa Bárbara Chile	34A3
Santa Barbara Mexico	24B2
Santa Barbara USA	22D4
Santa Barbara, I USA	22C4
Santa Barbara Chan USA	22B3
Santa Barbara Res USA	22C3
Santa Catalina, I USA	22C4
Santa Catalina,G of USA	22C4
Santa Catarina, State Brazil	30F4
Santa Clara Cuba	26B2
Santa Clara USA	22B2
Santa Clara, R USA	22C3
Santa Cruz Arg	29C6
Santa Cruz Bol	30D2
Santa Cruz Phil	79B3
Santa Cruz, State Arg	29B5
Santa Cruz USA	22A2
Santa Cruz, I USA	22C4
Santa Cruz Cabrália Brazil	35D1
Santa Cruz Chan USA	22C3
Santa Cruz de la Palma Canary Is	96A2
Santa Cruz del Sur Cuba	26B2
Santa Cruz de Tenerife Canary Is	96A2
Santa Cruz do Cuando Angola	100B2
Santa Cruz do Rio Pardo Brazil	35B2
Santa Cruz Mts USA	22A2
Santa Elena Arg	34D2
Santa Elena Ven	33E3
Santa Fe Arg	34C2
Santa Fe, State Arg	34C2
Santa Fe USA	9C3
Santa Helena de Goiás Brazil	35A1
Santai China	73B3
Santa Inés, I Chile	29B6
Santa Isabel, La Pampa Arg	34B3
Santa Isabel, Sante Fe Arg	34C2
Santa Isabel, I Solomon Is	107E1
Santa Lucia, Ra USA	21A2
Santa Lucia Range, Mts USA	21A2
Santa Luzia, I Cape Verde	97A4
Santa Margarita, I Mexico	9B4
Santa Margarita, R USA	22D4
Santa Maria Brazil	30F4
Santa Maria Colombia	26C4
Santa Maria USA	21A3
Santa Maria, I Açores	96A1
Santa Maria, R, Queretaro Mexico	23B1
Santa Maria del Rio Mexico	23A1
Santa Marta Colombia	32C1
Santa Monica USA	22C3
Santa Monica B USA	22C4
Santana do Livramento Brazil	29E2
Santander Colombia	32B3
Santander Spain	50B1
Santañy Spain	51C2
Santa Paula USA	22C3
Santa Quitéria Brazil	31C2
Santarem Brazil	33G4
Santarém Port	50A2
Santa Rosa, California USA	22A1
Santa Rosa Honduras	25D3
Santa Rosa, La Pampa Arg	34C3
Santa Rosa, Mendoza Arg	34B2
Santa Rosa, San Luis Arg	34B2
Santa Rosa, I USA	22B3
Santa Rosalía Mexico	24A2
Santa Rosa Range, Mts USA	20C2
Santa Talhada Brazil	31D3
Santa Teresa Brazil	35C1
Santa Teresa de Gallura Sardegna	53A2
Santa Ynez, R USA	22B3
Santa Ynez Mts USA	22B3
Santee, R USA	17C1
Santhia Italy	47C2
Santiago Chile	34A2
Santiago Dom Rep	27C3
Santiago Panama	32A2
Santiago Phil	79B2
Santiago, R Peru	32B4
Santiago de Compostela Spain	50A1

Santiago de Cuba

Santiago de Cuba Cuba	26B2
Santiago del Estero Arg	30D4
Santiago del Estero, State Arg	30D4
Santiago Peak, Mt USA	22D4
Santo, State Brazil	31C5
Santo Anastatácio Brazil	35A2
Santo Angelo Brazil	30F4
Santo Antão, I Cape Verde	97A4
Santo Antonio da Platina Brazil	35A2
Santo Domingo Dom Rep	27D3
Santos Brazil	35B2
Santos Dumont Brazil	35C2
Santo Tomé Arg	30E4
San Valentin, Mt Chile	29B5
San Vicente Chile	34A2
Sanza Pomba Angola	98B3
São Borja Brazil	30E4
São Carlos Brazil	35B2
São Félix, Mato Grosso Brazil	33G5
São Fidélis Brazil	35C2
São Francisco Brazil	35C1
São Francisco, R Brazil	31D3
São Francisco do Sul Brazil	30G4
São Gotardo Brazil	35B1
Sao Hill Tanz	99D3
São João da Barra Brazil	35C2
São João da Boa Vista Brazil	35B2
São João da Ponte Brazil	35C1
São João del Rei Brazil	35C2
São Joaquim da Barra Brazil	35B2
São Jorge, I Açores	96A1
São José do Rio Prêto Brazil	35B2
São José dos Campos Brazil	35B2
São Luis Brazil	31C2
São Marcos, R Brazil	35B1
São Maria do Suaçui Brazil	35C1
São Mateus Brazil	35D1
São Mateus, R Brazil	35C1
São Miguel, I Açores	96A1
Saône, R France	49C2
São Nicolau, I Cape Verde	97A4
São Paulo Brazil	35B2
São Paulo, State Brazil	35A2
São Raimundo Nonato Brazil	31C3
São Romão Brazil	35B1
São Sebastia do Paraiso Brazil	35B2
São Simão, Goias Brazil	35A1
São Simão, Sao Paulo Brazil	35B2
São Tiago, I Cape Verde	97A4
São Tomé, I W Africa	97C4
São Tomé and Principe, Republic W Africa	97C4
Saoura, Watercourse Alg	96B2
São Vicente Brazil	35B2
São Vincente, I Cape Verde	97A4
Sápai Greece	55C2
Sape Indon	78D4
Sapele Nig	97C4
Sapporo Japan	74E2
Sapri Italy	53C2
Sapulpa USA	18A2
Saqqez Iran	90A2
Saquenay, R Can	10C2
Sarāb Iran	90A2
Sarafa USSR	54C1
Sarajevo Yugos	54A2
Sarakhs Iran	90D2
Saraktash USSR	61J3
Sarala USSR	63A2
Saranac L USA	15D2
Saranac Lake USA	15D2
Sarandë Alb	55B3
Sarangani Is Phil	79C4
Saransk USSR	61G3
Sarapul USSR	61H2
Sarasota USA	17B2
Saratoga Springs USA	15D2
Saratok Malay	78C2
Saratov USSR	61G3
Saratovskoye Vodokhranilishche, Res USSR	61G3
Sarawak, State Malay	67F4
Saraykoy Turk	92A2
Sarbīsheh Iran	90C3
Sarca, R Italy	47D1
Sardalais Libya	95A2
Sar Dasht Iran	90A2
Sardegna, I Medit S	52A2
Sarektjåkkå, Mt Sweden	38H5
Sargodha Pak	84C2
Sarh Chad	98B2
Sārī Iran	90B2
Sarida, R Isreal	94B2
Sarikamiş Turk	93D1
Sarina Aust	107D3
Sarine, R Switz	47B1
Sar-i-Pul Afghan	84B1
Sarir Libya	95B2
Sarir Tibesti, Desert Libya	95A2
Sariwŏn N Korea	74B3
Sark, I UK	48B2
Šarkišla Turk	92C2
Sarmi Indon	71E4
Sarmiento Arg	29C5
Särna Sweden	39G6
Sarnen Switz	47C1
Sarnia Can	14B2
Sarny USSR	58D2
Saroaq Greenland	6E2
Sarobi Afghan	84B2
Sarolangun Indon	78A3
Saronikós Kólpos, G Greece	55B3
Saronno Italy	47C2
Saros Körfezi, B Turk	55C2
Sarpsborg Nor	39G7
Sarralbe France	46D2
Sarrebourg France	46D2
Sarreguemines France	46D2
Sarre-Union France	46D2
Sarrion Spain	51B1
Sartanahu Pak	85B3
Sartène Corse	53A2
Sarthe, R France	48B2
Sarykamys USSR	61H4
Sarysu, R USSR	65H5
Sasarām India	86A2
Sasebo Japan	74B4
Saskatchewan, Province Can	5H4
Saskatchewan, R Can	5H4
Saskatoon Can	13F2
Sasolburg S Africa	101G1
Sasovo USSR	61F3
Sassandra Ivory Coast	97B4
Sassandra, R Ivory Coast	97B4
Sassari Sardegna	53A2
Sassnitz E Germ	56C2
Sassuolo Italy	47D2
Sastre Arg	34C2
Sātāra India	87A1
Satellite B Can	4G2
Satengar, Is Indon	78D4
Säter Sweden	39H6
Satilla, R USA	17B1
Satka USSR	61J2
Satluj, R India	84D2
Satna India	86A2
Sātpura Range, Mts India	85C4
Satu Mare Rom	54B1
Sauce Arg	34D2
Sauda Nor	39F7
Saudi Arabia, Kingdom Arabian Pen	80C3
Sauer, R W Germ/Lux	46D2
Sauerland, Region W Germ	46D1
Sauðárkrókur Iceland	38B1
Saugatuck USA	14A2
Saugerties USA	16C1
Saugstad,Mt Can	13B2
Sault Sainte Marie Can	7B5
Sault Ste Marie Can	14B1
Sault Ste Marie USA	14B1
Saumlaki Indon	71E4
Saumur France	48B2
Saurimo Angola	98C3
Sauteurs Grenada	27M2
Sava, R Yugos	54A2
Savalou Benin	97C4
Savannah, Georgia USA	17B1
Savannah, R USA	17B1
Savannakhet Laos	76C2
Savanna la Mar Jamaica	26B3
Savant Lake Can	7A4
Savarane Laos	76D2
Savé Benin	97C4
Save, R Mozam	101C3
Sāveh Iran	90B3
Saverne France	46D2
Savigliano Italy	47B2
Savigny France	46B2
Savoie, Region France	49D2
Savona Italy	49D3
Savonlinna Fin	38K6
Savoonga USA	4A3
Savukoski Fin	38K5
Savu S Indon	71D4
Saw Burma	76A1
Sawai Mādhopur India	85D3
Sawang Indon	78A2
Sawankhalok Thai	76B2
Sawara Japan	75C1
Sawk700 Mt USA	12E1
Sawu, I Indon	106B2
Say Niger	97C3
Sayghan Afghan	84B1
Sayhandulaan Mongolia	72B1
Sayhūt S Yemen	91B5
Saykhin USSR	61G4
Saynshand Mongolia	68D2
Say-Utes USSR	61H5
Sayville USA	16C2
Sayward Can	13B2
Sázava, R Czech	57C3
Sbisseb, R Alg	51C2
Scafell Pike, Mt Eng	42C2
Scalloway Scot	44D1
Scapa Flow, Sd Scot	44C2
Scarborough Can	15C2
Scarborough Eng	42D2
Scarborough Tobago	27E4
Scarp, I Scot	44A2
Scarriff Irish Rep	45B2
Schaffhausen Switz	52A1
Scharding Austria	57C3
Scharteberg, Mt W Germ	46D1
Schefferville Can	7D4
Schelde, R Belg	46B1
Schenectady USA	10C2
Schio Italy	47D2
Schleiden W Germ	46D1
Schleswig W Germ	56B2
Schleswig Holstein, State W Germ	56B2
Schoharie USA	16B1
Schouten, Is PNG	71F4
Schreiber Can	7B5
Schurz USA	21B2
Schuykill Haven USA	16A2
Schuylkill, R USA	16B2
Schwabische Alb, Upland W Germ	57B3
Schwarzwald, Mts W Germ	49D2
Schwarzwald, Upland W Germ	57B3
Schwatka Mts USA	12C1
Schwaz Austria	47D1
Schweinfurt W Germ	57C2
Schweizer Reneke S Africa	101G1
Schwerin E Germ	56C2
Schwyz Switz	47C1
Sciacca Italy	53B3
Scioto, R USA	14B3
Scone Aust	109D2
Scoresby Sd Greenland	6H2
Scotia Ridge Atlantic O	103F7
Scotia S Atlantic O	103F7
Scotland, Country U K	44B3
Scott, Base Ant	112B7
Scott,C Can	13B2
Scott City USA	9C2
Scott I Ant	112C6
Scott Inlet, B Can	6C2
Scott,Mt USA	20B2
Scott Reef Timor S	106B2
Scottsbluff USA	8C2
Scottsboro USA	17A1
Scottsdale Aust	109C4
Scranton USA	10C2
Scuol Switz	47D1
Seal, R Can	5J4
Sea Lake Aust	108B3
Searcy USA	18B2
Seaside, California USA	22B2
Seaside, Oregon USA	20B1
Seaside Park USA	16B3
Seattle USA	20B1
Sebastopol USA	22A1
Sebez USSR	58D1
Sebring USA	17B2
Secretary I NZ	111A2
Sedalia USA	18B2
Sedan France	46C2
Seddonville NZ	111B2
Sede Boqer Israel	94B3
Sederot Israel	94B3
Séдhiou Sen	97A3
Sedom Israel	94B3
Seeheim Namibia	100A3
Sefton,Mt NZ	111B2
Segamat Malay	77C5
Segorbe Spain	51B2
Ségou Mali	97B3
Segovia Spain	50B1
Segre, R Spain	51C1
Séguéla Ivory Coast	97B4
Seguia el Hamra, Watercourse Mor	96A2
Segundo, R Arg	34C2
Seguntur Indon	78D2
Segura, R Spain	50B2
Sehwan Pak	85B3
Seille, R France	46D2
Seinäjoki Fin	38J6
Seine, R France	48C2
Seine-et-Marne, Department France	46B2
Sekenke Tanz	99D3
Selah USA	20B1
Selaru, I Indon	71E4
Selat Alas, Str Indon	78D4
Selat Bangka, Str Indon	78B3
Selat Berhala, B Indon	78A3

Selat Dampier, Str *Indon*	71E4
Selat Gaspar, Str *Indon*	78B3
Selat Lombok, Str *Indon*	78D4
Selat Sape, Str *Indon*	78D4
Selat Sunda, Str *Indon*	78B4
Selat Wetar, Chan *Indon*	71D4
Selawik *USA*	12B1
Selawik, R *USA*	12C1
Selawik L *USA*	12B1
Selby *Eng*	42D3
Selçuk *Turk*	55C3
Seldovia *USA*	12D3
Selebi Pikwe *Botswana*	100B3
Selfoss *Iceland*	6H3
Selima Oasis *Sudan*	95B2
Selkirk *Can*	5J4
Selkirk *Scot*	42C2
Selkirk Mts *Can*	13D2
Selma, California *USA*	22C2
Selouane *Mor*	50B2
Selous,Mt *USA*	12H2
Selta Karimata, Str *Indon*	78B3
Selvas, Region *Brazil*	32C5
Selwyn *Aust*	107D3
Selwyn Mts *Can*	4E3
Semarang *Indon*	78C4
Semenov *USSR*	61E2
Semidi Is *USA*	12C3
Semiluki *USSR*	60E3
Seminole, Oklahoma *USA*	19A2
Seminole,L *USA*	17B1
Semipalatinsk *USSR*	65K4
Semirara Is *Phil*	79B3
Semirom *Iran*	90B3
Semitau *Indon*	78C2
Semnān *Iran*	90B2
Semois, R *Belg*	46C2
Sempoala, Hist Site *Mexico*	23B2
Sena Madureira *Brazil*	32D5
Senanga *Zambia*	100B2
Senatobia *USA*	19C3
Sendai, Honshū *Japan*	74E3
Sendai, Kyūshū *Japan*	74C4
Sendwha *India*	85D4
Seneca Falls *USA*	15C2
Senegal, Republic *Africa*	97A3
Sénégal, R *Maur Sen*	97A3
Senekal *S Africa*	101G1
Senhor do Bonfim *Brazil*	31D4
Senigallia *Italy*	52B2
Senj *Yugos*	52C2
Senkaku Gunto, Is *Japan*	69E4
Senlis *France*	46B2
Sennar *Sudan*	99D1
Senneterre *Can*	7C5
Sens *France*	49C2
Senta *Yugos*	54A1
Sentery *Zaïre*	98C3
Sentinel Peak, Mt *Can*	13C2
Seoni *India*	85D4
Separation Pt *NZ*	110B2
Sepone *Laos*	76D2
Sept-Iles *Can*	7D4
Séquédine *Niger*	95A2
Sequoia, Nat Pk *USA*	21B2
Seram, I *Indon*	71D4
Serang *Indon*	78B4
Serasan, I *Indon*	78B2
Serbia, Region *Yugos*	54A2
Serdobsk *USSR*	61F3
Seremban *Malay*	77C5
Serengeti Nat Pk *Tanz*	99D3
Serenje *Zambia*	100C2
Seret, R *USSR*	59D3
Sergach *USSR*	61G2
Sergino *USSR*	65H3
Sergipe, State *Brazil*	31D4
Seria *Brunei*	78C2
Serian *Malay*	78C2
Sérifos, I *Greece*	55B3
Serio, R *Italy*	47C2
Serir Calanscio, Desert *Libya*	95B2
Sermaize-les-Bains *France*	46C2
Sermata, I *Indon*	71D4
Sernovodsk *USSR*	61H3
Serov *USSR*	65H4
Serowe *Botswana*	100B3
Serpa *Port*	50A2
Serpukhov *USSR*	60E3
Serra da Canastra, Mts *Brazil*	35B2
Serra da Estrela, Mts *Port*	50A1
Serra da Mantiqueira, Mts *Brazil*	35B2
Serra da Mombuca *Brazil*	35A1
Serra do Cabral, Mt *Brazil*	35C1
Serra do Cachimbo, Mts *Brazil*	33F5
Serra do Caiapó, Mts *Brazil*	35A1
Serra do Cantu, Mts *Brazil*	35A2
Serra do Caparaó, Mts *Brazil*	35C2
Serra do Chifre *Brazil*	31C5
Serra do Espinhaço, Mts *Brazil*	35C1
Serra do Mar, Mts *Brazil*	35B2
Serra do Mirante, Mts *Brazil*	35A2
Serra do Navio *Brazil*	33G3
Serra do Paranapiacaba, Mts *Brazil*	35B2
Serra dos Caiabis, Mts *Brazil*	33F6
Serra dos Dourados, Mts *Brazil*	35A2
Serra dos Parecis, Mts *Brazil*	33E6
Serra dos Pilões, Mts *Brazil*	35B1
Serra Dourada, Mts *Brazil*	35A1
Serra Formosa, Mts *Brazil*	33F6
Sérrai *Greece*	55B2
Serrana Bank, Is *Caribbean*	25D3
Serrana de Cuenca, Mts *Spain*	51B1
Serranópolis *Brazil*	35A1
Serra Pacaraima, Mts *Brazil/Ven*	33E3
Serra Parima, Mts *Brazil*	33E3
Serra Tumucumaque *Brazil*	33G3
Serre, R *France*	46B2
Serrezuela *Arg*	34B2
Serrinha *Brazil*	31D4
Serrmilik *Greenland*	6G3
Serro *Brazil*	35C1
Sertanópolis *Brazil*	35A2
Sêrtar *China*	72A3
Seruyan, R *Indon*	78C3
Sesfontein *Namibia*	100A2
Sesheke *Zambia*	100B2
Sestriere *Italy*	47B2
Setana *Japan*	74D2
Sète *France*	49C3
Sete Lagoas *Brazil*	35C1
Sétif *Alg*	96C1
Seto *Japan*	75B1
Seto Naikai, S *Japan*	75A2
Settat *Mor*	96B1
Settle *Eng*	42C2
Settler *Can*	5G4
Sêtúbal *Port*	50A2
Sevan,Oz, L *USSR*	93E1
Sevastopol' *USSR*	60D5
Severn, R *Can*	7B4
Severn, R *Eng*	43C3
Severnaya Zemlya, I *USSR*	1B9
Severo-Baykalskoye Nagorye, Mts *USSR*	63C2
Severo Donets *USSR*	60E4
Severodvinsk *USSR*	64E3
Severo Sos'va, R *USSR*	64H3
Sevier, R *USA*	8B3
Sevier L *USA*	8B3
Sevilla *Spain*	50A2
Sevlievo *Bulg*	54C2
Sewa, R *Sierra Leone*	97A4
Seward, Alaska *USA*	12E2
Seward, Nebraska *USA*	18A1
Seward Pen *USA*	12A1
Sexsmith *Can*	13D1
Seychelles, Is *Indian O*	89K8
Seyðisfjörður *Iceland*	38C1
Seyhan *Turk*	92C2
Seym, R *USSR*	60E3
Seymour *Aust*	108C3
Seymour, Connecticut *USA*	16C2
Seymour, Indiana *USA*	14A3
Sézanne *France*	46B2
Sfax *Tunisia*	96D1
Sfîntu Gheorghe *Rom*	54C1
's-Gravenhage *Neth*	56A2
Shaanxi, Province *China*	72B7
Shabunda *Zaïre*	98C3
Shache *China*	82B2
Shackleton Ice Shelf *Ant*	112C9
Shadadkot *Pak*	85B3
Shādhām, R *Iran*	91B3
Shaftesbury *Eng*	43C4
Shag Rocks, Is *South Georgia*	29G8
Shāhābād *Iran*	90A3
Shahbā *Syria*	94C2
Shahdap *Iran*	91C3
Shahdol *India*	86A2
Shāhīn Dezh *Iran*	90A2
Shāh Kūh *Iran*	90C3
Shahr-e Bābak *Iran*	91C3
Shahr Kord *Iran*	90B3
Shājābād *India*	87B1
Shājahānpur *India*	84D3
Shājāpur *India*	85D4
Shakhty *USSR*	61F4
Shakhun'ya *USSR*	61G2
Shaki *Nig*	97C4
Shaktoolik *USA*	12B2
Shamary *USSR*	61J2
Shambe *Sudan*	99D2
Shamokin *USA*	16A2
Shandaken *USA*	16B1
Shandong, Province *China*	72D2
Shangchuan Dao, I *China*	73C5
Shangdu *China*	72C1
Shanghai *China*	73E3
Shangnan *China*	72C3
Shangombo *Zambia*	100B2
Shangra *China*	73D4
Shangsi *China*	73B5
Shang Xian *China*	72C3
Shannon, R *Irish Rep*	41B3
Shanqiu *China*	72D3
Shansonggang *China*	74B2
Shantarskiye Ostrova, I *USSR*	63F2
Shantou *China*	73D5
Shanxi, Province *China*	72C2
Shan Xian *China*	72D3
Shaoguan *China*	73C5
Shaoxing *China*	73E4
Shaoyang *China*	73C4
Shapinsay, I *Scot*	44C2
Shaqqā *Syria*	94C2
Sharīfābād *Iran*	90C2
Sharjah *UAE*	91C4
Shark B *Aust*	106A3
Sharlauk *USSR*	90C2
Sharon,Plain of *Israel*	94B2
Sharya *USSR*	61G2
Shashamanna *Eth*	99D2
Shashi *China*	73C3
Shasta L *USA*	20B2
Shasta,Mt *USA*	20B2
Shatt al Gharrat, R *Iraq*	93E3
Shaubak *Jordan*	94B3
Shaunavon *Can*	13F3
Shaver L *USA*	22C2
Shawangunk Mt *USA*	16B2
Shawinigan *Can*	15D1
Shawnee, Oklahoma *USA*	19A2
Sha Xian *China*	73D4
Shay Gap *Aust*	106B3
Shaykh Miskīn *Syria*	94C2
Shaykh 'Uthmān *S Yemen*	99E1
Shchigry *USSR*	60E3
Shchors *USSR*	60D3
Shchuchinsk *USSR*	65J4
Sheboygan *USA*	14A2
Shebshi, Mts *Nig*	98B2
Sheenjek, R *USA*	12F1
Sheep Haven, Estuary *Irish Rep*	45C1
Sheerness *Eng*	43E4
Shefar'am *Israel*	94B2
Sheffield *Eng*	42D3
Shekhupura *Pak*	84C2
Shelagyote Peak, Mt *Can*	13B1
Shelburne Falls *USA*	16C1
Shelby, Michigan *USA*	14A2
Shelby, Montana *USA*	8B2
Shelbyville, Indiana *USA*	14A3
Sheldon,Mt *Can*	12H2
Shelikof Str *USA*	12D3
Shellharbour *Aust*	109D2
Shelter Pt *NZ*	111A3
Shelton *USA*	20B1
Shemakha *USSR*	93E1
Shenandoah *USA*	18A1
Shenandoah, R *USA*	15C3
Shenandoah Nat Pk *USA*	15C3
Shendam *Nig*	97C4
Shendi *Sudan*	95C2
Shenmu *China*	72C2
Shenyang *China*	72E1
Shenzhen *China*	73C5
Sheopur *India*	85D3
Shepetovka *USSR*	59D2
Shepparton *Aust*	108C3
Sherard,C *Can*	6B2
Sherborne *Eng*	43C4
Sherbro I *Sierra Leone*	97A4
Sherbrooke *Can*	15D1
Shergarh *India*	85C3
Sheridan, Arkansas *USA*	19B3
Sheridan, Wyoming *USA*	8C2
Sherman *USA*	19A3
s-Hertogenbosch *Neth*	56B2
Sheslay *Can*	12H3
Shetland, Is *Scot*	40C1
Shevchenko *USSR*	61H5
Sheykh Sho'eyb, I *Iran*	91B4
Shiashkotan, I *USSR*	69H2
Shibarghan *Afghan*	84B1
Shibata *Japan*	74D3
Shibeli, R *Eth*	99E2
Shibin el Kom *Egypt*	95C1
Shibukawa *Japan*	75B1
Shijiazhuang *China*	72C2
Shikarpur *Pak*	84B3
Shikoku, I *Japan*	67G3
Shikoku-sanchi, Mts *Japan*	75A2

Shiliguri

Shiliguri *India*	86B1	Sibiu *Rom*	54B1	Sierra de Zongolica	
Shilka *USSR*	68D1	Sibolga *Indon*	70A3	*Mexico*	23B2
Shilka, R *USSR*	68D1	Sibsägär *India*	86C1	Sierra Grande, Mts	
Shillington *USA*	16B2	Sibu *Malay*	78C2	*Arg*	34C2
Shillong *India*	86C1	Sibuguay B *Phil*	79B4	Sierra Leone, Republic	
Shilovo *USSR*	61F3	Sibut *CAR*	98B2	*Africa*	97A4
Shimabara *Japan*	75A2	Sibuyan, I *Phil*	79B3	Sierra Leone,C *Sierra*	
Shimada *Japan*	75B2	Sibuyan S *Phil*	79B3	*Leone*	97A4
Shimanovsk *USSR*	69E1	Sichuan, Province		Sierra Madre, Mts *Phil*	79B2
Shimizu *Japan*	74D3	*China*	73A3	Sierra Madre del Sur,	
Shimoda *Japan*	75B2	Sicilia, I *Medit S*	53B3	Mts *Mexico*	23A2
Shimoga *India*	87B2	Sicilian, Chan *Italy/*		Sierra Madre	
Shimonoseki *Japan*	74C4	*Tunisia*	53B3	Occidental, Mts	
Shinano, R *Japan*	75B1	Sicuani *Peru*	32C6	*Mexico*	24B2
Shinâş *Oman*	91C5	Siddhapur *India*	85C4	Sierra Malanzan, Mts	
Shingü *Japan*	74D4	Siddipet *India*	87B1	*Arg*	34B2
Shinjö *Japan*	75C1	Sidhi *India*	86A2	Sierra Mojada *Mexico*	9C4
Shinminato *Japan*	74D3	Sidi Barrani *Egypt*	95B1	Sierra Morena, Mts	
Shinshär *Syria*	94C1	Sidi bel Abbès *Alg*	96B1	*Spain*	50A2
Shinyanga *Tanz*	99D3	Sidlaw Hills *Scot*	44C3	Sierra Nevada, Mts	
Shiogama *Japan*	74E3	Sidley,Mt *Ant*	112B5	*Spain*	50B2
Shiono-misaki, C		Sidney *Can*	20B1	Sierra Nevada, Mts	
Japan	75B2	Sidney, Nebraska *USA*	8C2	*USA*	21A2
Shiping *China*	73A5	Sidney, New York		Sierra Nevada de	
Shippensburg *USA*	16A2	*USA*	15C2	santa Marta, Mts	
Shiquan *China*	72B3	Sidney, Ohio *USA*	14B2	*Colombia*	32C1
Shirakawa *Japan*	75C1	Sidney Lanier,L *USA*	17B1	Sierra Pié de Palo,	
Shirane-san, Mt *Japan*	75B1	Siedlce *Pol*	58C2	Mts *Arg*	34B2
Shirani-san, Mt *Japan*	75B1	Sieg, R *W Germ*	46D1	Sierre *Switz*	47B1
Shīrāz *Iran*	91B4	Siegburg *W Germ*	46D1	Sífnos, I *Greece*	55B3
Shīr Küh *Iran*	90B3	Siegen *W Germ*	46D1	Sighet *Rom*	59C3
Shirotori *Japan*	75B1	Siem Reap *Camb*	76C3	Sighisoara *Rom*	54B1
Shirvān *Iran*	90C2	Siena *Italy*	52B2	Siglufjörður *Iceland*	38B1
Shishmaref *USA*	12A1	Sierpc *Pol*	58B2	Sigüenza *Spain*	50B1
Shishmaref Inlet *USA*	12A1	Sierra Andrés Tuxtla		Siguiri *Guinea*	97B3
Shishmaref *USA*	4B3	*Mexico*	23B2	Sihora *India*	85E4
Shitanjing *China*	72B2	Sierra Auca Mahuida,		Siirt *Turk*	93D2
Shively *USA*	14A3	Mts *Arg*	34B3	Sikai Hu, L *China*	68B3
Shivpuri *India*	85D3	Sierra Blanca *USA*	9C3	Sikar *India*	85D3
Shivta, Hist Site *Israel*	94B3	Sierra de Albarracin,		Sikaram, Mt *Afghan*	84B2
Shiwa Ngandu *Zambia*	101C2	Mts *Spain*	51B1	Sikasso *Mali*	97B3
Shiyan *China*	72C3	Sierra de Alcaraz, Mts		Sikeston *USA*	18C2
Shizuishan *China*	72B2	*Spain*	50B2	Síkinos, I *Greece*	55C3
Shizuoka *Japan*	75B1	Sierra de Cordoba,		Sikioniá *Greece*	55B3
Shkodër *Alb*	54A2	Mts *Arg*	34B2	Sikkim, State *India*	86B1
Shoalhaven, R *Aust*	109D2	Sierra de Gredos, Mts		Sil, R *Spain*	50A1
Shobara *Japan*	75A2	*Spain*	50A1	Silandro *Italy*	47D1
Shoranür *India*	87B2	Sierra de Guadalupe,		Silao *Mexico*	23A1
Shorāpur *India*	87B1	Mts *Spain*	50A2	Silay *Phil*	79B3
Shoshone Mts *USA*	21B2	Sierra de Guadarrama,		Silchar *India*	86C2
Shostka *USSR*	60D3	Mts *Spain*	50B1	Silet *Alg*	96C2
Shreveport *USA*	19B3	Sierra de Guara, Mts		Silgarhi *Nepal*	86A1
Shrewsbury *Eng*	43C3	*Spain*	51B1	Silifke *Turk*	92B2
Shropshire, County		Sierra de Gudar, Mts		Siling Co, L *China*	82C2
Eng	43C3	*Spain*	51B1	Silistra *Bulg*	54C2
Shuanglia *China*	72E1	Sierra de Juárez		Silkeborg *Den*	39F7
Shuangyanan *China*	69F2	*Mexico*	23B2	Sillian *Austria*	47E1
Shubar kuduk *USSR*	61J4	Sierra de la Ventana,		Siloam Springs *USA*	18B2
Shu He, R *China*	72D2	Mts *Arg*	34C3	Silsbee *USA*	19B3
Shuicheng *China*	73A4	Sierra del Codi, Mts		Siltou, Well *Chad*	95A3
Shujaabad *Pak*	84C3	*Spain*	51C1	Silvan *Turk*	93D2
Shujälpur *India*	85D4	Sierra del Morro, Mt		Silvania *Brazil*	35B1
Shule He *China*	68B2	*Arg*	34B2	Silvassa *India*	85C4
Shumen *Bulg*	54C2	Sierra del Nevado,		Silver City, Nevada	
Shumerlya *USSR*	61G2	Mts *Arg*	34B3	*USA*	21B2
Shuncheng *China*	73D4	Sierra de los Alamitos,		Silver City, New	
Shungnak *USA*	12C1	Mts *Mexico*	24B2	Mexico *USA*	9C3
Shuo Xian *China*	72C2	Sierra de los Filabres		Silver Lake *USA*	20B2
Shūr Gaz *Iran*	91C4	*Spain*	50B2	Silver Spring *USA*	16A3
Shurugwi *Zim*	100B2	Sierra de los		Silverthrone Mt *Can*	13B2
Shuswap L *Can*	13D2	Huicholes *Mexico*	23A1	Silverton *Aust*	108B2
Shuya *USSR*	61F2	Sierra de Miahuatlán		Silvretta, Mts *Austria/*	
Shuyak I *USA*	12D3	*Mexico*	23B2	*Switz*	47C1
Shwebo *Burma*	82D3	Sierra de Morones,		Simanggang *Malay*	78C2
Shwegyin *Burma*	76B2	Mts *Mexico*	23A1	Simao *China*	76C1
Siah Koh, Mts *Afghan*	84A2	Sierra de Ronda, Mts		Simareh, R *Iran*	90A3
Sialkot *Pak*	84C2	*Spain*	50A2	Simav *Turk*	55C3
Siarao, I *Phil*	79C4	Sierra de San Luis,		Simav, R *Turk*	55C3
Siaton *Phil*	79B4	Mts *Arg*	34B2	Simcoe,L *Can*	15C2
Šiauliai *USSR*	58C1	Sierra de Segura, Mts		Simeulue, I *Indon*	70A3
Sibay *USSR*	65G4	*Spain*	50B2	Simferopol' *USSR*	60D5
Sibayi L *S Africa*	101H1	Sierra de Urbion, Mts		Sími, I *Greece*	55C3
Šibenik *Yugos*	52C2	*Spain*	50B1	Simla *India*	84D2
Siberut, I *Indon*	70A4	Sierra de Uspallata,		Simmern *W Germ*	46D1
Sibi *Pak*	84B3	Mts *Arg*	34B2	Simoon Sound *Can*	13B2
Sibirskoye *USSR*	68C1	Sierra de Valle Fértil,		Simplon, Mt *Switz*	49D2
Sibiti *Congo*	98B3	Mts *Arg*	34B2	Simplon, P *Switz*	47C1
Sibiti, R *Tanz*	99D3				

Simpson,C *USA*	4C2
Simpson Desert *Aust*	106C3
Simpson Pen *Can*	6B3
Simrishamn *Sweden*	39G7
Simushir, I *USSR*	69H2
Sinadogo *Somalia*	99E2
Sinai, Pen *Egypt*	92B4
Sincelejo *Colombia*	32B2
Sinclair,L *USA*	17B1
Sind *Pak*	85B3
Sind, R *India*	85D3
Sindirği *Turk*	55C3
Sindri *India*	86B2
Sines *Port*	50A2
Singa *Sudan*	99D1
Singapore, Republic *S*	
E Asia	77C5
Singapore,Str of *S E*	
Asia	77C5
Singaraja *Indon*	78D4
Singida *Tanz*	99D3
Singkawang *Indon*	78B2
Singleton *Aust*	109D2
Singtep, I *Indon*	78A3
Singu *Burma*	76B1
Siniscola *Sardgena*	53A2
Sinjär *Iraq*	93D2
Sinkai Hills, Mts	
Afghan	84B2
Sinkat *Sudan*	95C3
Sinkiang, Autonomous	
Region	82C2
Sinnamary *French*	
Guiana	33G2
Sinop *Turk*	92C1
Sintana *Rom*	54B1
Sintang *Indon*	78C2
Sintra *Port*	50A2
Sinú, R *Colombia*	32B2
Sinŭiju *N Korea*	74A2
Siofok *Hung*	59B3
Sion *Switz*	47B1
Sioux City *USA*	8D2
Sioux Falls *USA*	8D2
Sioux Lookout *Can*	10A2
Sipalay *Phil*	79B4
Siparia *Trinidad*	27L1
Siping *China*	69E2
Siple, Base *Ant*	112B3
Siple I *Ant*	112B5
Sipocot *Phil*	79B3
Sipora *Indon*	70A4
Siquijor, I *Phil*	79B4
Sira *India*	87B2
Siracusa *Italy*	53C3
Sirajganj *Bang*	86B2
Sir Alexander,Mt *Can*	13C2
Sīr Banī Yās, I *UAE*	91B5
Sir Edward Pellew	
Group, Is *Aust*	106C2
Siret, R *Rom*	54C1
Sir James McBrien,Mt	
Can	12J2
Sir Kälahasti *India*	87B2
Sir Laurier,Mt *Can*	13D2
Şirnak *Turk*	93D2
Širohi *India*	85C4
Sironcha *India*	87B1
Sironj *India*	85D4
Síros, I *Greece*	55B3
Sirri, I *Iran*	91B4
Sirsa *India*	84D3
Sir Sandford,Mt *Can*	13D2
Sirsi *India*	87A2
Sirt *Libya*	95A1
Sirte Desert *Libya*	95A1
Sirte,G of *Libya*	95A1
Sisak *Yugos*	52C1
Sisaket *Thai*	76C2
Sisophon *Camb*	76C3
Sissonne *France*	46B2
Sistan, Region *Iran/*	
Afghan	90D3
Sisteron *France*	49D3
Sistig Khem *USSR*	63B2
Sitäpur *India*	86A1
Sitía *Greece*	55C3
Sitka *USA*	4E4

Sitkalidak I USA	12D3	
Sitkinak, I USA	12D3	
Sittang, R Burma	76B2	
Sittard Neth	46C1	
Sittwe Burma	86C2	
Situbondo Indon	78C4	
Sivas Turk	92C2	
Siverek Turk	93C2	
Sivrihisar Turk	92B2	
Siwa Egypt	95B2	
Siwalik Range, Mts India	84D2	
Siwalik Range, Mts Nepal	86A1	
Siyang China	72D3	
Sjaelland, I Den	56C1	
Skagen Den	39G7	
Skagerrak, Str Nor/ Den	39F7	
Skagit, R USA	20B1	
Skagit Mt USA	20B1	
Skagway USA	4E4	
Skara Sweden	39G7	
Skarzysko-Kamlenna Pol	59C2	
Skeena, R Can	5F4	
Skeena Mts Can	13B1	
Skeenjek, R USA	4D3	
Skegness Eng	42E3	
Skellefte, R Sweden	38H5	
Skellefteå Sweden	38J6	
Skíathos, I Greece	55B3	
Skibbereen Irish Rep	45B3	
Skidegate Can	5E4	
Skiemiewice Pol	58C2	
Skien Nor	39F7	
Skikda Alg	96C1	
Skikoku, I Japan	74C4	
Skipton Eng	42D3	
Skíros, I Greece	55B3	
Skive Den	39F7	
Skjern Den	56B1	
Skjoldungen Greenland	6F3	
Skokie USA	14A2	
Skópelos, I Greece	55B3	
Skopje Yugos	54B2	
Skövde Sweden	39G7	
Skovorodino USSR	63E2	
Skwentna USA	4C3	
Skwierzyna Pol	58B2	
Skye, I Scot	40B2	
Slagelse Den	39G7	
Slaney, R Irish Rep	45C2	
Slatina Rom	54B2	
Slaung Indon	78C4	
Slav Brod Yugos	54A1	
Slave, R Can	5G3	
Slave Lake Can	13E1	
Slavgorod, Rossiyskaya USSR	65J4	
Slavuta USSR	59D2	
Slavyansk USSR	60E4	
Sleat,Sound of, Chan Scot	44B3	
Sleetmute USA	12C2	
Sleeve Bloom, Mts Irish Rep	45C2	
Slidell USA	19C3	
Slide Mt USA	16B2	
Sligo, County Irish Rep	45B1	
Sligo Irish Rep	41B3	
Sligo, B Irish Rep	41B3	
Sliven Bulg	54C2	
Slobozia Rom	54C2	
Slocan Can	13D3	
Slonim USSR	58D2	
Slough Eng	43D4	
Slough, R USA	22B2	
Slovensko, Region Czech	59B3	
Slubice Pol	56C2	
Sluch', R USSR	59D2	
Sludyanka USSR	68C1	
Słupsk Pol	58B2	
Slutsk USSR	58D2	
Slutsk, R USSR	58D2	
Slyne Head, Pt Irish Rep	41A3	
Slyudyanka USSR	63C2	
Smallwood Res Can	7D4	
Smara Mor	96A2	
Smederevo Yugos	54B2	
Smederevska Palanka Yugos	54B2	
Smela USSR	60D4	
Smethport USA	15C2	
Smith Can	13E1	
Smith Arm, B Can	4F3	
Smithers Can	13B2	
Smith I Can	7C3	
Smith Sd Can	13B2	
Smiths Falls Can	15C2	
Smithton Aust	109C4	
Smoky, R Can	13D1	
Smoky C Aust	109D2	
Smoky Lake Can	13E2	
Smøla, I Nor	38F6	
Smolensk USSR	60D3	
Smólikas, Mt Greece	55B2	
Smolyan Bulg	54B2	
Smorgon' USSR	58D2	
Smyrna, Delaware USA	16B3	
Smyrna, Georgia USA	17B1	
Snaefell, Mt Eng	42B2	
Snafell, Mt Iceland	38B2	
Snake, R USA	8B2	
Snake River Canyon USA	8B2	
Sneek Neth	56B2	
Sneem Irish Rep	45B3	
Snelling USA	22B2	
Snežka, Mt Pol/Czech	59B2	
Snøhetta, Mt Nor	38F6	
Snohomish USA	20B1	
Snoqualmie P USA	20B1	
Snoul Camb	76D3	
Snowdon, Mt Wales	43B3	
Snowdonia Nat Pk Wales	43B3	
Snowdrift Can	4G3	
Snow Lake Can	5H4	
Snowtown Aust	108A2	
Snowy Mts Aust	109C3	
Snyder USA	9C3	
Soan-kundo, I S Korea	74B4	
Sobat, R Sudan	99D2	
Sobral Brazil	31C2	
Sochaczew Pol	58C2	
Sochi USSR	61E5	
Socorro USA	9C3	
Socorro, I Mexico	24A3	
Socos Chile	34A2	
Socotra, I S Yemen	81D4	
Sodankylä Fin	38K5	
Soddo Eth	99D2	
Soderhamn Sweden	39H6	
Södertälje Sweden	39H7	
Sodiri Sudan	99C1	
Soest W Germ	46E1	
Sofala Mozam	101C2	
Sofiya Bulg	54B2	
Sofu Gan, I Japan	69G4	
Sogamoso Colombia	32C2	
Sognefjorden, Inlet Nor	39F6	
Sog Xian China	82D2	
Sohâg Egypt	95C2	
Sohipat India	84D3	
Soignies Belg	46B1	
Soissons France	46B2	
Sojat India	85C3	
Sŏjosŏn-man, B N Korea	74A3	
Söke Turk	92A2	
Sokodé Togo	97C4	
Sokol USSR	61E2	
Sokołka Pol	58C2	
Sokolo Mali	97B3	
Sokota Eth	99D1	
Sokoto Nig	97C3	
Sokoto, R Nig	97C3	
Solander I NZ	111A3	
Solano Phil	79B2	
Solapur India	87B1	
Solbad Hall Austria	47D1	
Sölden Austria	47D1	
Soldotna USA	12D2	
Soledad Colombia	26C4	
Solent, Sd Eng	43D4	
Solesmes France	46B1	
Soligorsk USSR	58D2	
Solikamsk USSR	61J2	
Solimões Peru	32C4	
Solingen W Germ	46D1	
Sol'Itesk USSR	65G4	
Solleftebå Sweden	38H6	
Sol'lletsk USSR	61H3	
Solok Indon	70B4	
Solomon, Is Pacific O	105G4	
Solothurn Switz	47B1	
Soltau W Germ	39F8	
Solvang USA	22B3	
Solway Firth, Estuary Scot/Eng	42C2	
Solwezi Zambia	100B2	
Sōma Japan	75C1	
Soma Turk	55C3	
Somalia, Republic E Africa	81C5	
Sombor Yugos	54A1	
Somerset Aust	107D2	
Somerset, County Eng	43C4	
Somerset, Massachusetts USA	16D2	
Somerset, Pennsylvania USA	15C2	
Somerset East S Africa	100B4	
Somerset I Can	6A2	
Somers Point USA	16B3	
Somerville USA	16B2	
Somerville Res USA	19A3	
Somes, R Rom	54B1	
Somme, Department France	46B2	
Somme, R France	46B2	
Sommesous France	46C2	
Son, R India	86A2	
Sŏnch'ŏn N Korea	74A3	
Sønderborg Den	39F8	
Søndre Strømfjord Greenland	6E3	
Sondrio Italy	47C1	
Song Ba, R Viet	76D3	
Song Cau Viet	76D3	
Songea Tanz	101C2	
Songjiang China	73E3	
Songkhla Thai	77C4	
Songnim N Korea	74B3	
Sŏng Pahang, R Malay	77C5	
Songpan China	72A3	
Sonid Youqi China	72C1	
Son La Viet	76C1	
Sonmiani Pak	85B3	
Sonmiani Bay Pak	85B3	
Sonoma USA	22A1	
Sonora, California USA	22B2	
Sonora, R Mexico	24A2	
Sonoran Desert USA	9B3	
Sonora P USA	22C1	
Sonsonate El Salvador	25D3	
Sonsorol, I Pacific O	71E3	
Soo Canals USA/Can	10B2	
Sooke Can	13C3	
Sopot Pol	58B2	
Sopron Hung	59B3	
Soquel USA	22B2	
Sora Italy	53B2	
Sored, R Israel	94B3	
Sorel Can	15D1	
Sorell Aust	109C4	
Sorgun Turk	92C2	
Soria Spain	50B1	
Sørkjosen Nor	38J5	
Sørksop, I Barents S	64C2	
Sor Mertvyy Kultuk, Plain USSR	61H4	
Sorocaba Brazil	35B2	
Sorochinsk USSR	61H3	
Soroi, I Pacific O	71F3	
Sorok USSR	60C4	
Sorong Indon	71E4	
Sorong, Province Indon	71E4	
Soroti Uganda	99D2	
Sørøya, I Nor	38J4	
Sorrento Italy	53B2	
Sorsatunturi, Mt Fin	38K5	
Sorsele Sweden	38H5	
Sorsogon Phil	79B3	
Sortavala USSR	38L6	
Sōsan S Korea	74B3	
Sosnowiec Pol	59B2	
Sos'va USSR	65H4	
Souanké Congo	98B2	
Soubré Ivory Coast	97B4	
Souderton USA	16B2	
Soufrière St Lucia	27P2	
Soufrière, V St Vincent	27N2	
Souillac France	48C3	
Souk Ahras Alg	96C1	
Souk S Korea	74B3	
Soummam, R Alg	51C2	
Sources,Mt aux Lesotho	101G1	
Sousa Brazil	31D3	
Sousse Tunisia	96D1	
South Africa, Republic Africa	100B4	
South Amboy USA	16B2	
Southampton Can	14B2	
Southampton Eng	43D4	
Southampton USA	16C2	
Southampton I Can	6B3	
South Atlantic O	28F6	
South Aulatsivik I Can	7D4	
South Australia, State Aust	106C3	
South Australian Basin Indian O	104E5	
Southaven USA	19C3	
South Bay USA	17B2	
South Baymouth Can	14B1	
South Bend, Indiana USA	14A2	
South Bend, Washington USA	20B1	
Southbridge USA	16D1	
South Carolina, State USA	11B3	
South China S S E Asia	70C2	
South Dakota, State USA	8C2	
South Deerfield USA	16C1	
South Downs Eng	43D4	
South East C Aust	109C4	
Southen Alps, Mts NZ	111A2	
Southend Can	5H4	
Southend-on-Sea Eng	43E4	
Southern Alps, Mts NZ	111A2	
Southern Cross Aust	106A4	
Southern Indian L Can	5J4	
Southfield Jamaica	27H2	
South Fiji Basin Pacific O	105G5	
South Fork, R, Alaska USA	12D2	
South Fork, R, California USA	22B1	
South Georgia, I S Atlantic O	28F8	
South Glamorgan, County Wales	43C4	
South Haven USA	14A2	
South Henik L Can	5J3	
South Honshu Ridge Pacific O	104F3	
South I NZ	111A2	
Southington USA	16C2	
South Korea, Republic S E Asia	74B3	
South Lake Tahoe USA	21A2	

South Magnetic Pole

Sukkur *Pak*	85B3	
Sukma *India*	87C1	
Sukses *Namibia*	100A3	
Sukumo *Japan*	75A2	
Sukunka, R *Can*	13C1	
Sula, R *USSR*	60E3	
Sulaiman Range, Mts *Pak*	84B3	
Sulawesi, I *Indon*	70C4	
Sulaymānīyah *Iraq*	93E3	
Sulina *Rom*	54C1	
Sulitjelma *Nor*	38H5	
Sullana *Peru*	32A4	
Sullivan *USA*	18B2	
Sullivan Bay *Can*	13B2	
Sullivan L *Can*	13E2	
Sulmona *Italy*	52B2	
Sulphur, Louisiana *USA*	19B3	
Sulphur, Oklahoma *USA*	19A3	
Sulphur Springs *USA*	19A3	
Sultânpur *India*	86A1	
Sulu Arch *Phil*	79B4	
Sulu S *Philip*	70C3	
Sumampa *Arg*	30D4	
Sumba, I *Indon*	70C4	
Sumbawa, I *Indon*	78D4	
Sumbawa Besar *Indon*	78D4	
Sumbawanga *Tanz*	99D3	
Sumbe *Angola*	100A2	
Sumburgh Head, Pt *Scot*	44D2	
Sumenep *Indon*	78C4	
Sumisu, I *Japan*	69G3	
Summerland *Can*	13D3	
Summit Lake *Can*	5F4	
Summit Mt *USA*	21B2	
Sumner,L *NZ*	111B2	
Sumoto *Japan*	75A2	
Sumter *USA*	17B1	
Sumy *USSR*	60D3	
Sunbury *USA*	16A2	
Sunchales *Arg*	34C2	
Sunch'ŏn *N Korea*	74B3	
Sunch'ŏn *S Korea*	74B4	
Sundargarh *India*	86A2	
Sunderbans, Swamp *India*	86B2	
Sunderland *Eng*	42D2	
Sundre *Can*	13E2	
Sundridge *Can*	15C1	
Sundsvall *Sweden*	38H6	
Sungaianyar *Indon*	78D3	
Sungaisalak *Indon*	78A3	
Sunnyside *USA*	20C1	
Sunnyvale *USA*	21A2	
Suntar *USSR*	63D1	
Sunyani *Ghana*	97B4	
Suō-nada, B *Japan*	75A2	
Suonejoki *Fin*	38K6	
Supaul *India*	86B1	
Superior, Nebraska *USA*	18A1	
Superior, Wisconsin *USA*	10A2	
Superior,L *USA/Can*	10B2	
Suphan Buri *Thai*	76C3	
Süphan Dağ *Turk*	93D2	
Supiori, I *Indon*	71E4	
Suq ash Suyukh *Iraq*	93E3	
Suqian *China*	72D3	
Sür *Oman*	91C5	
Surabaya *Indon*	78C4	
Suraga-wan, B *Japan*	75B2	
Surakarta *Indon*	78C4	
Surar, R *USSR*	61G3	
Surat *Aust*	109C1	
Sürat *India*	85C4	
Süratgarh *India*	84C3	
Surat Thani *Thai*	77B4	
Surendranagar *India*	85C4	
Surf City *USA*	16B3	
Surgut *USSR*	64J3	
Suriāpet *India*	87B1	
Sürich *Switz*	49D2	
Surlgao *Phil*	79C4	
Surin *Thai*	76C3	

Surinam, Republic	33F3	
Surrey, County *Eng*	43D4	
Sursee *Switz*	47C1	
Surtsey, I *Iceland*	38A2	
Surulangan *Indon*	78A3	
Susa *Italy*	47B2	
Susa *Japan*	75A2	
Susaki *Japan*	75A2	
Susanville *USA*	21A1	
Süsch *Switz*	47D1	
Susitna, R *USA*	12E2	
Susquehanna, R *USA*	16A3	
Sussex *USA*	16B2	
Sussex West *Eng*	43D4	
Sustut Peak, Mt *Can*	13B1	
Sutherland *S Africa*	100B4	
Sutlej, R *Pak*	84C2	
Sutter Creek *USA*	21A2	
Sutton *USA*	14B3	
Sutwik I *USA*	12C3	
Suwa *Japan*	74D3	
Suwałki *Pol*	58C2	
Suwannee, R *USA*	17B2	
Suweilih *Jordan*	94B2	
Suwŏn *S Korea*	74B3	
Su Xian *China*	72D3	
Suzaka *Japan*	75B1	
Suzhou *China*	73E3	
Suzu *Japan*	74D3	
Suzuka *Japan*	75B2	
Suzu-misaki, C *Japan*	75B1	
Svalbard, Is *Barents S*	64C2	
Svalyava *USSR*	59C3	
Svartisen, Mt *Nor*	38G5	
Svay Rieng *Camb*	76D3	
Sveg *Sweden*	38G6	
Svendborg *Den*	39G7	
Sverdlovsk *USSR*	65H4	
Sverdrup Chan *Can*	6A1	
Svetlaya *USSR*	69F2	
Svetlogorsk *USSR*	58C2	
Svetogorsk *USSR*	39K6	
Svetozarevo *Yugos*	54B2	
Svilengrad *Bulg*	54C2	
Svir' *USSR*	58D2	
Švitavy *Czech*	59B3	
Svobodnyy *USSR*	69E1	
Svolvaer *Nor*	38G5	
Swain Reefs *Aust*	107E3	
Swainsboro *USA*	17B1	
Swakopmund *Namibia*	100A3	
Swale, R *Eng*	42D2	
Swallow Reef, I *S E Asia*	70C3	
Swämihalli *India*	87B2	
Swan, I *Honduras*	25D3	
Swanage *Eng*	43D4	
Swan Hill *Aust*	108B3	
Swan Hills *Can*	13D2	
Swan Hills, Mts *Can*	13D2	
Swan I *Caribbean*	26A3	
Swan River *Can*	5H4	
Swansea *Wales*	43C4	
Swansea B *Wales*	43C4	
Swartruggens *S Africa*	101G1	
Swaziland, Kingdom *S Africa*	101H1	
Sweden, Kingdom *N Europe*	39G7	
Sweet Home *USA*	20B2	
Sweetwater *USA*	9C3	
Swellendam *S Africa*	100B4	
Świdnica *Pol*	59B2	
Swidwin *Pol*	58B2	
Swiebodzin *Pol*	58B2	
Swiecie *Pol*	58B2	
Swift Current *Can*	5H4	
Swindon *Eng*	43D4	
Swinford *Irish Rep*	45B2	
Świnoujście *Pol*	56C2	
Switzerland, Federal Republic *Europe*	49D2	
Swords *Irish Rep*	45C2	
Syderø *Faeroes*	38D3	
Sydney *Aust*	109D2	
Sydney *Can*	7D5	
Syktyvkar *USSR*	64G3	
Sylacauga *USA*	17A1	

Sylarna, Mt *Sweden*	38G6	
Sylhet *Bang*	86C2	
Sylt, I *W Germ*	56B1	
Sylvania *USA*	14B2	
Syowa, Base *Ant*	112C11	
Syracuse, New York *USA*	10C3	
Syracuse *USA*	15C2	
Syrdal'ya, R *USSR*	65H5	
Syria, Republic *S W Asia*	93C2	
Sysert' *USSR*	61J2	
Syzran' *USSR*	61G3	
Szczecin *Pol*	56C2	
Szczecinek *Pol*	58B2	
Szczytno *Pol*	58C2	
Szeged *Hung*	59C3	
Székesfehérvar *Hung*	59B3	
Szekszard *Hung*	59B3	
Szolnok *Hung*	59B3	
Szombathely *Hung*	59B3	
Szprotawa *Pol*	58B2	

T

Tabas *Iran*	90C3	
Tabasco *Mexico*	23A1	
Tabatinga *Brazil*	32D4	
Tabelbala *Alg*	96B2	
Tabeng *Camb*	76C3	
Taber *Can*	13E2	
Tablas, I *Phil*	79B3	
Table Mt *S Africa*	100A4	
Table Mt *USA*	12F1	
Table Rock Res *USA*	18B2	
Taboali *Indon*	78B3	
Tábor *Czech*	57C3	
Tabora *Tanz*	99D3	
Tabou *Ivory Coast*	97B4	
Tabrīz *Iran*	90A2	
Tabūk *S Arabia*	92C4	
Tacámbaro *Mexico*	23A2	
Tacheng *China*	82C1	
Tacloban *Phil*	79C3	
Tacna *Peru*	30B2	
Tacoma *USA*	8A2	
Tadjoura *Djibouti*	99E1	
Tādpatri *India*	87B2	
Tadzhen *USSR*	65H6	
Tadzhikskaya SSR, Republic *USSR*	82A2	
Taebaek Sanmaek, Mts *S Korea*	74B3	
Taegu *S Korea*	74B3	
Taehŭksan, I *S Korea*	74B4	
Taejŏn *S Korea*	74B3	
Tafalla *Spain*	51B1	
Tafasaset, Watercourse *Alg*	96C2	
Taff, R *Wales*	43C4	
Tafila *Jordan*	94B3	
Tagant, Region *Maur*	97A3	
Tagbilaran *Phil*	79B4	
Taguenout Hagguerete, Well *Maur*	96B2	
Tagula, I *Solomon Is*	107E2	
Tagum *Phil*	79C4	
Tahat, Mt *Alg*	96C2	
Tahiti, I *Pacific O*	105J4	
Tahlequah *USA*	18A2	
Tahoe City *USA*	21A2	
Tahoe,L *USA*	21A2	
Tahoua *Niger*	97C3	
Tahuna *Indon*	71D3	
Tai'an *China*	72D2	
Taibai Shan, Mt *China*	72B3	
Taibus Qi *China*	72D1	
T'ai-chung *Taiwan*	73E5	
Taieri, R *NZ*	111B3	
Taihang Shan *China*	72C2	
Taihape *NZ*	110C1	
Tai Hu, L *China*	72E3	
Tailem Bend *Aust*	108A3	
Tain *Scot*	44B3	
T'ai-nan *Taiwan*	73E5	
Taiobeiras *Brazil*	35C1	
T'ai pei *Taiwan*	73E5	

Taiping *Malay*	77C5	
Taira *Japan*	75C1	
Tais *Indon*	78A3	
Taisha *Japan*	75A1	
Taitao,Pen de *Chile*	29B5	
T'ai-tung *Taiwan*	73E5	
Taivelkoski *Fin*	38K5	
Taiwan, Republic *China*	69E4	
Taiyuan *China*	72C2	
Taizhou *China*	72D3	
Ta 'izz *Yemen*	81C4	
Tajo, R *Spain*	50B1	
Tak *Thai*	76B2	
Takada *Japan*	74D3	
Takahashi *Japan*	75A2	
Takaka *NZ*	110B2	
Takamatsu *Japan*	74C4	
Takaoka *Japan*	74D3	
Takapuna *NZ*	110B1	
Takasaki *Japan*	74D3	
Takayama *Japan*	75B1	
Takefu *Japan*	74D3	
Takeo *Camb*	76C3	
Takeo *Japan*	75A2	
Takestān *Iran*	90A2	
Taketa *Japan*	75A2	
Takingeun *Indon*	70A3	
Takjvak L *Can*	4G3	
Takkaze, R *Eth*	99D1	
Takla L *Can*	13B1	
Takla Landing *Can*	13B1	
Takslesluk L *USA*	12B2	
Taku Arm, R *Can*	12H2	
Tala *Mexico*	23A1	
Talabanya *Hung*	59B3	
Talagang *Pak*	84C2	
Talagante *Chile*	34A2	
Talaimannar *Sri Lanka*	87B3	
Talak, Desert, Region *Niger*	97C3	
Talangbetutu *Indon*	78A3	
Talara *Peru*	32A4	
Talavera de la Reina *Spain*	50B2	
Talca *Chile*	34A3	
Talcahuano *Chile*	34A3	
Tālcher *India*	86B2	
Taldy Kurgan *USSR*	82B1	
Taliabu *Indon*	71D4	
Tali Post *Sudan*	99D2	
Taliwang *Indon*	78D4	
Talkeetna *USA*	12D2	
Talkeetna Mts *USA*	12E2	
Talladega *USA*	17A1	
Tall 'Afar *Iraq*	93D2	
Tallahassee *USA*	17B1	
Tall Bîsah *Syria*	94C1	
Tallinn *USSR*	60B2	
Tall Kalakh *Syria*	92C3	
Tallulah *USA*	19B3	
Tal'noye *USSR*	60D4	
Talpaki *USSR*	58C2	
Taltal *Chile*	30B4	
Talwood *Aust*	109C1	
Tamabo Range, Mts *Malay*	78D1	
Tamale *Ghana*	97B4	
Tamanrasset *Alg*	96C2	
Tamanrasset, Watercourse *Alg*	96C2	
Tamaqua *USA*	16B2	
Tamazula, Jalisco *Mexico*	23A2	
Tamazulapán *Mexico*	23B2	
Tamazunchale *Mexico*	23B1	
Tambacounda *Sen*	97A3	
Tambov *USSR*	61F3	
Tambre, R *Spain*	50A1	
Tambura *Sudan*	98C2	
Tamchaket *Maur*	97A3	
Tamega, R *Port*	50A1	
Tamiahua *Mexico*	23B1	
Tamil Nādu, State *India*	87B2	
Tamie, R *Rom*	54B1	
Tam Ky *Viet*	76D2	

Tampa

Tampa USA	17B2
Tampa B USA	17B2
Tampere Fin	39J6
Tampico Mexico	23B1
Tamsagbulag Mongolia	68D2
Tamu Burma	86C2
Tamuis Mexico	23B1
Tamworth Aust	109D2
Tamworth Eng	43D3
Tana Nor	38K4
Tana, L Eth	99D1
Tana, R Kenya	99E3
Tana, R Nor/Fin	38K5
Tanabe Japan	75B2
Tanafjord, Inlet Nor	38K4
Tanahgrogot Indon	78D3
Tanahmerah Indon	71E4
Tanana USA	12D1
Tanana, R USA	12E2
Tanaro, R Italy	47C2
Tanch'ŏn N Korea	74B2
Tandaho Eth	99E1
Tandil Arg	34D3
Tandjong Datu, Pt Indon	78B2
Tandjung d'Urville, C Indon	71E4
Tandjung Layar, C Indon	78D3
Tandjung Lumut, C Indon	78B3
Tandjung Mangkalihet C Indon	78D2
Tandjung Sambar, C Indon	78C3
Tandjung Sirik, C Malay	78C2
Tandjung Vals, C Indon	71E4
Tando Adam Pak	85B3
Tando Muhammad Khan Pak	85B3
Tandou L Aust	108B2
Tāndūr India	87B1
Taneatua NZ	110C1
Tanen Range, Mts Burma/Thai	76B2
Tanezrouft, Desert Region Alg	96B2
Tang Iran	91C4
Tanga Tanz	99D3
Tanganrog USSR	60E4
Tanganyika,L Tanz/Zaïre	99C3
Tanger Mor	96B1
Tanggula Shan, Mts China	82C2
Tangjungpinang Indon	78A2
Tangra Yumco, L China	82C2
Tangshan China	72D2
Tangub Phil	79B4
Tanguy USSR	63C2
Tanjay Phil	79B4
Tanjong Bugel, C Indon	78C4
Tanjong Cangkuang, C Indon	78B4
Tanjong Puting, C Indon	78C3
Tanjong Selatan, C Indon	78C3
Tanjung Indon	78D3
Tanjungbalai Indon	70A3
Tanjung Jabung, Pt Indon	78A3
Tanjungpandan Indon	78B3
Tanjung Priok Indon	78B4
Tanjungredeb Indon	78D2
Tanjungselor Indon	78D2
Tank Pak	84C2
Tannu Ola, Mts USSR	68B1
Tano, R Ghana	97B4
Tanout Niger	97C3
Tanquián Mexico	23B1
Tan-shui Taiwan	73E4
Tansing Nepal	86A1
Tanta Egypt	95C1
Tan-Tan Mor	96A2
Tanunak USA	4B3
Tanzania, Republic Africa	99D3
Tao He, R China	72A3
Taolañaro Madag	101D3
Taole China	72B2
Taourirt Mor	96B1
Tapa USSR	60C2
Tapachula Mexico	25C3
Tapajós, R Brazil	33F4
Tapalquén Arg	34C3
Tapan Indon	70B4
Tapanui NZ	111A3
Tapauá, R Brazil	32D5
Tapi, R India	85D4
Taplejung Nepal	86B1
Tapuaeniku, Mt NZ	111B2
Tapuaritinga Brazil	35B2
Tapul Group, Is Phil	79B4
Tapurucuara Brazil	33E4
Tara Aust	109D1
Tara USSR	65J4
Tara, R USSR	65J4
Tara, R Yugos	54A2
Taraba, R Nig	97D4
Tarabuco Bol	30D2
Taracón Spain	50B1
Taradale NZ	110C1
Tarakan Indon	78D2
Taransay, I Scot	44A3
Taranto Italy	53C2
Tarapoto Peru	32B5
Tarare France	49C2
Tararua Range, Mts NZ	110C2
Tarat Alg	96C2
Tarawera NZ	110C1
Tarazona Spain	51B1
Tarbat Ness, Pen Scot	44C3
Tarbela Res Pak	84C2
Tarbert, Strathclyde Scot	42B2
Tarbert, Western Isles Scot	44A3
Tarbes France	48C3
Tarcoola Aust	106C4
Tarcoon Aust	109C2
Taree Aust	109D2
Tarfaya Mor	96A2
Tarhūnah Libya	95A1
Tarif UAE	91B5
Tarija Bol	30D3
Tarikere India	87B2
Tarim S Yemen	81C4
Tarime Tanz	99D3
Tarim He, R China	82C1
Tarim Pendi, Basin China	82C2
Tarin Kut Afghan	84B2
Tarkio USA	18A1
Tarlac Phil	79B2
Tarma Peru	32B6
Tarn, R France	49C3
Tarnobrzeg Pol	59C2
Tarnów Pol	59C3
Taroom Aust	107D3
Tarragona Spain	51C1
Tarraleah Aust	109C4
Tarrasa Spain	51C1
Tarrytown USA	16C2
Tarsus Turk	92B2
Tartan, Oilfield N Sea	44D2
Tartaro, R Italy	47D2
Tartu USSR	60C2
Tartūs Syria	92C3
Tarumirim Brazil	35C1
Tarutung Indon	70A3
Tarvisio Italy	52B1
Tashauz USSR	80D1
Tashigang Bhutan	86C1
Tashkent USSR	82A1
Tashtagol USSR	65K4
Tashtyp USSR	63A2
Tasikmalaya Indon	78B4
Tasil Syria	94B2
Tasiussaq Greenland	6E2
Tasker, Well Niger	95A3
Tasman B NZ	110B2
Tasmania, I Aust	107D5
Tasman Mts NZ	111B2
Tasman Pen Aust	109C4
Tasman S NZ Aust	107E4
Taşova Turk	92C1
Tassili du Hoggar, Desert, Region Alg	96C2
Tassili N'jjer, Desert, Region Alg	96C2
Tata Mor	96B2
Tataouine Tunisia	96D1
Tatarsk USSR	65J4
Tatarskaya ASSR, Republic USSR	61G2
Tatarskiy Proliv, Str USSR	69G2
Tateyama Japan	75B1
Tathlina L Can	5G3
Tatitlek USA	12E2
Tatla Lake Can	13C2
Tatry, Mts Pol/Czech	59B3
Tatsuno Japan	75A2
Tatta Pak	85B4
Tatuí Brazil	35B2
Tatvan Turk	93D2
Tauá Brazil	31C3
Taubaté Brazil	35B2
Taumarunui NZ	110C1
Taung S Africa	101F1
Taungdwingyi Burma	76B2
Taung-gyi Burma	76B1
Taungup Burma	76A2
Taunsa Pak	84C2
Taunton Eng	43C4
Taunton USA	16D2
Taunus, Region W Germ	46E1
Taupo NZ	110C1
Taupo,L NZ	110C1
Taurage USSR	58C1
Tauranga NZ	110C1
Tauranga Harbour, B NZ	110C1
Tauroa Pt NZ	110B1
Tavani Can	7A3
Tavira Port	50A2
Tavistock Eng	43B4
Tavoy Burma	76B3
Tavoy Pt Burma	76B3
Tavsanli Turk	92A2
Tawa NZ	111B2
Tawakoni,L USA	19A3
Tawas City USA	14B2
Tawau Malay	70C3
Taweisha Sudan	98C1
Tawitawi, I Phil	79B4
Tawitawi Group, Is Phil	79B4
Taxco Mexico	23B2
Taxcoco Mexico	23B2
Tay, R Scot	44C3
Tayan Indon	78C3
Taylor, Alaska USA	12B1
Taylor Can	13C1
Taylor, Michigan USA	14B2
Taylor, Texas USA	19A3
Taylorville USA	18C2
Taymá' S Arabia	80B3
Taymura, R USSR	63B1
Tay Ninh Viet	76D3
Tayshet USSR	63B2
Tayshir Mongolia	68B2
Tayside, Region Scot	44C3
Taytay Phil	79A3
Tayyebāt Iran	90D3
Taza Mor	96B1
Tazerbo, Region Libya	95B2
Tazlina L USA	12E2
Tazovskiy USSR	64J3
Tbilisi USSR	65F5
Tchibanga Gabon	98B3
Tchigai,Plat du Niger	95A2
Tchin Tabaradene Niger	97C3
Tcholliré Cam	98B2
Tczew Pol	58B2
Te Anau NZ	111A3
Te Anau,L NZ	111A3
Te Aroha NZ	110C1
Te Awamutu NZ	110C1
Tébessa Alg	96C1
Teboman Mexico	23A2
Tecailtlän Mexico	23A2
Tecate Mexico	21B3
Techa, R USSR	61K2
Tecolotlán Mexico	23A1
Tećpan Mexico	23A2
Tecuci Rom	54C1
Tecumseh USA	18A1
Tedzhen USSR	80E2
Tedzhen, R USSR	65H6
Tees, R Eng	42D2
Tefé Brazil	33E4
Tegal Indon	78B4
Tegineneng Indon	78B4
Tegucigalpa Honduras	25D3
Tehachapi Mts USA	21B3
Tehachapi P USA	21B2
Tehek L Can	4J3
Tehrān Iran	90B2
Tehuacán Mexico	23B2
Tehuantepec Mexico	23B2
Tehuitzingo Mexico	23B2
Teifi, R Wales	43B3
Tejo, R Port	50A2
Tejupilco Mexico	23A2
Tekapo,L NZ	111B2
Tekeli USSR	82B1
Tekirdağ Turk	92A1
Tekir Dağlari, Mts Turk	55C2
Teknaf Bang	86C2
Te Kuiti NZ	110C1
Tela Honduras	25D3
Tel Aviv Yafo Israel	94B2
Telén Arg	34B3
Telescope Peak, Mt USA	21B2
Teles Pires, R Brazil	33F5
Telfs Austria	47D1
Teli USSR	63A2
Tell el Meise, Mt Jordan	94B3
Teller USA	12A1
Tellicherry India	87B2
Telok Anson Malay	77C5
Tělok Darvel Malay	78D2
Tělok Flamingo, B Indon	71E4
Tělok Kumai, B Indon	78C3
T14elok Pelabuanratu, B Indon	78B4
Tělok Saleh, B Indon	78B4
Tělok Sampit, B Indon	78C3
Tělok Sukadona, B Indon	78B3
Teloloapán Mexico	23B2
Telšiai USSR	58C1
Telukbatang Indon	78C3
Teluk Berau, B Indon	71E4
Telukbetung Indon	78B4
Teluk Bone, B Indon	70D4
Teluk Cendrawasih, B Indon	71E4
Teluk Mandar, B Indon	78D3
Teluk Tolo, B Indon	71D4
Teluk Tomini, B Indon	70D3
Těluk Weda, B Indon	71D3
Temanggui,L Can	14B1
Temascal Mexico	23B2
Tembesi, R Indon	78A3
Tembilahan Indon	78A3
Temblador Ven	27E5
Temerloh Malay	77C5
Temir USSR	65G5
Temirtau USSR	65J4
Temiscaming Can	15C1
Temora Aust	109C2
Tempe Aust	9B3
Temple USA	19A3
Templemore Irish Rep	45C2
Tempoal Mexico	23B1
Temuco Chile	34A3

Temuka *NZ*	111B2	Tewantin *Aust*	109D1	Three Pagodas P *Thai*	76B2	Timétrine Monts, Mts *Mali*	97B3
Tena *Ecuador*	32B4	Têwo *China*	72A3	Three Rivers, Michigan *USA*	14A2	Timia *Niger*	97C3
Tenâli *India*	87C1	Texarkana *USA*	19B3	Three Sisters, Mt *USA*	20B2	Timimoun *Alg*	96C2
Tenancingo *Mexico*	23B2	Texarkana,L *USA*	19B3	Thule *Greenland*	6D2	Timişoara *Rom*	54B1
Tenasserim *Burma*	76B3	Texas *Aust*	109D1	Thun *Switz*	47B1	Timmins *Can*	10B2
Tenby *Wales*	43B4	Texas, State *USA*	9C3	Thundar Bay *Can*	10B2	Timor, I *Indon*	106B1
Ten Degree Chan Indian O	83D5	Texas City *USA*	19B4	Thuner See, L *Switz*	47B1	Timor S *Aust/Indon*	106B2
Ténéré, Desert Region *Niger*	98B1	Texel, I *Neth*	56A2	Thung Song *Thai*	77B4	Timote *Arg*	34C3
Tenerife, I *Canary Is*	96A2	Texoma,L *USA*	19A3	Thur, R *Switz*	47C1	Tinaca Pt *Phil*	79C4
Teng, R *Burma*	76B1	Teyateyaneng *Lesotho*	101G1	Thüringen Wald, Upland *E Germ*	57C2	Tinaco *Ven*	27D5
Tenggarong *Indon*	78D3	Teziutlán *Mexico*	23B2	Thurles *Irish Rep*	45C2	Tindivanam *India*	87B2
Tengger Shamo, Desert *China*	72A2	Tezpur *India*	86C1	Thursday I *Aust*	71F5	Tindouf *Alg*	96B2
Tenkãsi *India*	87B3	Tha *Laos*	76C1	Thurso *Scot*	44C2	Tinfouchy *Alg*	96B2
Tenke *Zaïre*	100B2	Thabana Ntlenyana, Mt *Lesotho*	101G1	Thurston I *Ant*	112B4	Tin Fouye *Alg*	96C2
Tenkodogo *U Volta*	97B3	Thaba Putsoa, Mt *Lesotho*	101G1	Thusis *Switz*	47C1	Tingmiarmiut *Greenland*	6F3
Tennant Creek *Aust*	106C2	Thagyettaw *Burma*	76B3	Thylungra *Aust*	108B1	Tingo Maria *Peru*	32B5
Tennessee, State *USA*	11B3	Thai Binh *Viet*	76D1	Tiandong *China*	73B5	Tingrela *Ivory Coast*	97B3
Tennessee, R *USA*	18C2	Thailand, Kingdom *S E Asia*	76C2	Tian'e *China*	73B5	Tingri *China*	86B1
Teno *Chile*	34A2	Thailand,G of *Thai*	76C3	Tianjin *China*	72D2	Tinian *Pacific O*	71F2
Tenom *Malay*	78D1	Thai Nguyen *Viet*	76D1	Tianlin *China*	73B5	Tinogasta *Arg*	30C4
Tenosique *Mexico*	25C3	Thakhek *Laos*	76C2	Tiân Shan, Mts *C Asia*	82C1	Tínos, I *Greece*	55C3
Tenterfield *Aust*	109D1	Thal *Pak*	84C2	Tianshui *China*	72B3	Tintagel Head, Pt *Eng*	43B4
Ten Thousand Is *USA*	17B2	Thale Luang, L *Thai*	77C4	Tianzhu *China*	72A2	Tin Tarabine, Watercourse *Alg*	96C2
Teocaltiche *Mexico*	23A1	Thallon *Aust*	109C1	Tiaret *Alg*	96C1	Tintinara *Aust*	108B2
Teófilo Otôni *Brazil*	35C1	Thames *NZ*	110C1	Tibagi, R *Brazil*	35A2	Tin Zaouaten *Alg*	96C2
Teotihiucan, Hist Site *Mexico*	23B2	Thames, R *Eng*	43E4	Tiberias *Israel*	94B2	Tioga P *USA*	22C2
Teotitlan *Mexico*	23B2	Thanh Hoah *Viet*	76D2	Tiberias,L *Israel*	94B2	Tioman, I *Malay*	77C5
Tepatitlan *Mexico*	23A1	Thanjavur *India*	87B2	Tibesti, Mountain Region *Chad*	95A2	Tione *Italy*	47D1
Tepehuanes *Mexico*	24B2	Thar Desert *India*	85C3	Tibet, Autonomous Region *China*	82C2	Tipperary, County *Irish Rep*	45C2
Tepeji *Mexico*	23B2	Thargomindah *Aust*	108B1	Tibooburra *Aust*	108B1	Tipperary *Irish Rep*	41B3
Tepic *Mexico*	23A1	Thásos, I *Greece*	55B2	Tibrikot *Nepal*	86A1	Tipton, Missouri *USA*	18B2
Teplice *Czech*	57C2	Thaton *Burma*	76B2	Tiburón, I *Mexico*	24A2	Tiptūr *India*	87B2
Te Puke *NZ*	110C1	Thayetmyo *Burma*	76B2	Tichitt *Maur*	97B3	Tiquicheo *Mexico*	23A2
Tequila *Mexico*	23A1	The Dalles *USA*	5F5	Tichla *Mor*	96A2	Tiranë *Alb*	55A2
Tequistepec *Mexico*	23B2	The Gulf *S W Asia*	91B4	Ticino, R *Italy/Switz*	47C2	Tirano *Italy*	47D1
Ter, R *Spain*	51C1	Thelon, R *Can*	4H3	Ticonderoga *USA*	15D2	Tiraspol *USSR*	60C4
Téra *Niger*	97C3	Theodore *Aust*	107E3	Ticul *Mexico*	25D2	Tirchchiräppalli *India*	87B2
Teradomari *Japan*	75B1	Theodore Roosevelt L *USA*	9B3	Tidjikja *Maur*	97A3	Tire *Turk*	55C3
Teramo *Italy*	52B2	Thermaïkós Kólpos, G *Greece*	55B2	Tiefencastel *Switz*	47C1	Tirebolu *Turk*	93C1
Terceira, I *Açores*	96A1	Thermopolis *USA*	8C2	Tieling *China*	74A2	Tiree, I *Scot*	44A3
Tereboviya *USSR*	59D3	Thesiger B *Can*	4F2	Tielt *Belg*	46B1	Tîrgovişte *Rom*	54C2
Teresina *Brazil*	31C3	Thessalon *Can*	14B1	Tienen *Belg*	46C1	Tîrgu Jiu *Rom*	54B1
Teresópolis *Brazil*	35C2	Thessaloníki *Greece*	55B2	Tien Shan, Mts *USSR/China*	65J5	Tîrgu Mureş *Rom*	54B1
Terme *Turk*	92C1	Thetford *Eng*	43E3	Tientsin *China*	72D2	Tirich Mir, Mt *Pak*	84C1
Termez *USSR*	80E2	Thetford Mines *Can*	15D1	Tierp *Sweden*	39H6	Tiris, Region *Mor*	96A2
Termoli *Italy*	52B2	Theunissen *S Africa*	101G1	Tiorra Blanca *Mexico*	23B2	Tirlyanskiy *USSR*	61J3
Ternate *Indon*	71D3	Thibodaux *USA*	19B4	Tierra Colorada *Mexico*	23B2	Tîrnăveni *Rom*	54B1
Terni *Italy*	52B2	Thicket Portage *Can*	5J4	Tierra del Fuego, Territory *Arg*	29C6	Tírnavos *Greece*	55B3
Ternopol *USSR*	59D3	Thief River Falls *USA*	8D2	Tierra del Fuego, I *Chile/Arg*	28C8	Tirodi *India*	85D4
Terrace *Can*	13B2	Thielsen,Mt *USA*	20B2	Tietê *Brazil*	35B2	Tirol, Province *Austria*	47D1
Terracina *Italy*	53B2	Thiers *France*	49C2	Tiete, R *Brazil*	35A2	Tirso, R *Sardegna*	53A2
Terrafirma *S Africa*	100B3	Thiès *Sen*	97A3	Tiffin *USA*	14B2	Tiruchchendür *India*	87B3
Terre Adélie, Region *Ant*	112C8	Thika *Kenya*	99D3	Tifton *USA*	17B1	Tirunelveli *India*	87B3
Terre Bonne B *USA*	19B4	Thimphu *Bhutan*	86B1	Tigre, R *Peru*	32B4	Tirupati *India*	87B2
Terre Haute *USA*	14A3	Thionville *France*	49D2	Tigre, R *Ven*	33E2	Tiruppattür *India*	87B2
Terrell *USA*	19A3	Thíra, I *Greece*	55C3	Tigris, R *Iraq*	93E3	Tiruppur *India*	87B2
Terschelling, I *Neth*	56B2	Thirsk *Eng*	42D2	Tihuatlán *Mexico*	23B1	Tiruvannamalai *India*	87B2
Teruel *Spain*	51B1	Thisted *Den*	39F7	Tijuana *Mexico*	21B3	Tishomingo *USA*	19A3
Teshekpuk *USA*	4C2	Thívai *Greece*	55B3	Tikamgarh *India*	85D4	Tisïyah *Syria*	94C2
Teshekpuk L *USA*	4C2	Thiviers *France*	48C2	Tikhin *USSR*	60D2	Tisza, R *Hung*	59C3
Teshio, R *Japan*	74E2	Thomaston, Georgia *USA*	17B1	Tikhoretsk *USSR*	61F4	Titlagarh *India*	86A2
Tesiyn Gol, Mts *Mongolia*	68B2	Thomastown *Irish Rep*	45C2	Tikrit *Iraq*	93D3	Titograd *Yugos*	54A2
Teslin *Can*	12H2	Thomasville, Georgia *USA*	17B1	Tiksi *USSR*	1B8	Titovo Užice *Yugos*	54A2
Teslin, R *Can*	12H3	Thom Bay *Can*	6A2	Tilburg *Neth*	46C1	Titov Veles *Yugos*	54B2
Teslin L *Can*	12H2	Thompson *Can*	5J4	Tilbury *Eng*	43E4	Titule *Zaïre*	98C2
Teslyn Gol, R *Mongolia*	63B3	Thompson, R *USA*	18B1	Tilcara *Arg*	30C3	Titusville *USA*	17B2
Tessalit *Mali*	96C2	Thompson Landing *Can*	4G3	Tilcha *Aust*	108B1	Tiverton *Eng*	43C4
Tessaoua *Niger*	97C3	Thompson R *Can*	13C2	Tilin *Burma*	76A1	Tivoli *Italy*	52B2
Tete *Mozam*	101C2	Thompsonville *USA*	16C2	Tillabéri *Niger*	97C3	Tixtla *Mexico*	23B2
Tetela *Mexico*	23A2	Thomson *USA*	17B1	Tillamook *USA*	20B1	Tiyeglow *Somalia*	99E2
Tetouan *Mor*	96B1	Thomson, R *Aust*	107D3	Tillia *Niger*	97C3	Tizayuca *Mexico*	23B2
Tetyushi *USSR*	61G2	Thon Buri *Thai*	76C3	Tílos, I *Greece*	55C3	Tizimin *Mexico*	25D2
Teuco, R *Arg*	30D3	Thongwa *Burma*	76B2	Tilpa *Aust*	108B2	Tizi Ouzou *Alg*	96C1
Teúl de Gonzalez Ortega *Mexico*	23A1	Thonon-les-Bains *France*	47B1	Tiluá *Colombia*	32B3	Tiznit *Mor*	96B2
Teun, I *Indon*	71D4	Thornhill *Scot*	42C2	Timaru *NZ*	111B2	Tizpan el Alto *Mexico*	23A1
Tevere, R *Italy*	52B2	Thouars *France*	48B2	Timashevsk *USSR*	60E4	Tlacolula *Mexico*	23B2
Teviot, R *Scot*	42C2	Thousand Is *Can/USA*	15C2	Timbákion *Greece*	55B3	Tlacotalpan *Mexico*	23B2
Tevriz *USSR*	65J4	Three Hills *Can*	13E2	Timbalier B *USA*	19B4	Tlalchana *Mexico*	23A2
Te Waewae B *NZ*	111A3	Three Kings Is *NZ*	7G4	Timbédra *Maur*	97B3	Tlalnepantla *Mexico*	23B2
Tewah *Indon*	78C3					Tlalpan *Mexico*	23B2
						Tlaltenango *Mexico*	23A1
						Tlancualpicán *Mexico*	23B2
						Tlapa *Mexico*	23B2
						Tlapacoyan *Mexico*	23B2

Tlaquepaque Mexico	23A1
Tlaxcala Mexico	23B2
Tlaxcala, State Mexico	23B2
Tlaxiaco Mexico	23B2
Tlemcem Alg	96B1
Toamasina Madag	101D2
Toay Arg	34C3
Toba Japan	75B2
Toba and Kakar Ranges, Mts Pak	84B2
Tobago, I Caribbean	27E4
Toba Inlet, Sd Can	13C2
Tobelo Indon	71D3
Tobermory Can	14B1
Tobermory Scot	44A3
Tobi, I Pacific O	71E3
Tobin,Mt USA	21B1
Tobol, R USSR	65H4
Tobol'sk USSR	65H4
Tocantins, R Brazil	31B2
Toccoa USA	17B1
Toce, R Italy	47C1
Tocopilla Chile	30B3
Tocorpuri, Mt Chile	30C3
Tocuyo, R Ven	32D1
Toda India	85D3
Tödi, Mt Switz	47C1
Todong S Korea	75A1
Todos Santos Mexico	9B4
Tofield Can	13E2
Tofino Can	13B3
Togiak USA	12B3
Togiak B USA	12B3
Togo, Republic Africa	97C4
Togtoh China	72C1
Tok USA	12F2
Tokachi, R Japan	74E2
Tokamachi Japan	75B1
Tokar Sudan	95C3
Tokara Retto, Arch Japan	69E4
Tokat Turk	92C1
Tökchök-kundo, Arch S Korea	74B3
Tok-do, I S Korea	75A1
Tokmak USSR	82B1
Tokomaru Bay NZ	110C1
Toku, R Can/USA	12H3
Tokung Indon	78C3
Tokuno, I Japan	69E4
Tokushima Japan	74C4
Tokuyama Japan	75A2
Tökyö Japan	74D3
Tolaga Bay NZ	110C1
Toledo Brazil	30F3
Toledo Spain	50B2
Toledo USA	14B2
Toledo Bend Res USA	19B3
Toliara Madag	101D3
Toliman Mexico	23B1
Tolina, Mt Colombia	32B3
Tolosa Spain	51B1
Toltén Chile	29B3
Toluca Mexico	23B2
Tol'yati USSR	61G3
Tomakomai Japan	74E2
Tomani Malay	78D1
Tomaszów Mazowiecka Pol	58C2
Tombigbee, R USA	11B3
Tomboco Angola	98B3
Tombos Brazil	35C2
Tombouctou Mali	97B3
Tombua Angola	100A2
Tomé Chile	34A3
Tomelloso Spain	50B2
Tomer Port	50A2
Tomkinson Range, Mts Aust	106B3
Tommot USSR	63E2
Tomorrit, Mt Alb	55B2
Tomsk USSR	65K4
Toms River USA	16B3
Tonalá Mexico	25C3
Tonasket USA	20C1
Tonawanda USA	15C2
Tonga, Is Pacific O	105H4
Tongaat S Africa	101H1
Tongcheng China	73D3
Tongchuan China	72B2
Tongde China	72A2
Tongeren Belg	46C1
Tonggu Jiao, I China	76E2
Tonghai China	73A5
Tonghua China	74B2
Tongjosön-man N Korea	74B3
Tongkin,G of Viet/China	76D1
Tonglia China	72E1
Tongling China	73D3
Tongo Aust	108B2
Tongoy Chile	34A2
Tongren, Guizhou China	73B4
Tongren, Qinghai China	72A2
Tongsa Bhutan	86C1
Tongta Burma	76B1
Tongtian He, R China	68B3
Tongue Scot	44B2
Tong Xian China	72D2
Tongxin China	72B2
Tongzi China	73B4
Tonhil Mongolia	63B3
Tonich Mexico	9C4
Tonj Sudan	99C2
Tonk India	85D3
Tonkawa USA	18A2
Tonle Sap, L Camb	76C3
Tonopah USA	21B2
Tonsina USA	12E2
Tooele USA	8B2
Toogoolawah Aust	109D1
Toompine Aust	108B1
Toowoomba Aust	109D1
Topaz L USA	22C1
Topeka USA	18A2
Topolobampo Mexico	9C4
Toppenish USA	20B1
Torbali Turk	55C3
Torbat-e-Heydarīyeh Iran	90C2
Torbat-e Jām Iran	90D2
Torbay Eng	43C4
Torbert,Mt USA	12D2
Tordesillas Spain	50A1
Torgau E Germ	56C2
Torhout Belg	46B1
Tori Eth	99D2
Tori, I Japan	69G3
Torino Italy	47B2
Torit Sudan	99D2
Torixoreu Brazil	35A1
Tormes, R Spain	50A1
Tornado Mt Can	13E2
Torne, L Sweden	38J5
Torneträsk Sweden	38H5
Torngat, Mts Can	7D4
Tornio Fin	38J5
Tornquist Arg	34C3
Toronto Can	15C2
Toropets USSR	60D2
Tororo Uganda	99D2
Toros Dağlari, Mts Turk	92B2
Torrance USA	22C4
Torrão Port	50A2
Torreblanca Spain	51C1
Torre del Greco Italy	53B2
Torrelavega Spain	50B1
Torremolinos Spain	50B2
Torrens,L Aust	108A2
Torreón Mexico	24B2
Torre Pellice Italy	47B2
Torres Str Aust	107D2
Torres Vedras Port	50A2
Torrington, Connecticut USA	16C2
Torrington, Wyoming USA	8C2
Torrón Mexico	9C4
Torshavn Faeroes	38D3
Tortona Italy	47C2
Tortosa Spain	51C1
Torūd Iran	90C2
Toruń Pol	58B2
Tory, I Irish Rep	40B2
Torzhok USSR	60D2
Tosa Japan	75A2
Tosa-shimizu Japan	74C4
Tosa-wan, B Japan	74C4
To-shima, I Japan	75B2
Tosno USSR	39L7
Tosno USSR	60D2
Tosu Japan	75A2
Tosya Turk	92B1
Tot'ma USSR	61F1
Totnes Eng	43C4
Totness Surinam	33F2
Totolapan Mexico	23B2
Totona Spain	51B2
Tottenham Aust	109C2
Tottori Japan	74C3
Touba Ivory Coast	97B4
Touba Sen	97A3
Toubkal, Mt Mor	96B1
Tougan U Volta	97B3
Touggourt Alg	96C1
Tougué Guinea	97A3
Toul France	46C2
Toulon France	49D3
Toulouse France	48C3
Toumodi Ivory Coast	97B4
Toungoo Burma	76B2
Tourcoing France	46B1
Tourine Maur	96A2
Tournai Belg	46B1
Tours France	48C2
Towada Japan	74E2
Towada-ko, L Japan	74E2
Towanda USA	15C2
Townsville Aust	107D2
Towson USA	16A3
Towy, R Wales	43C4
Toyama Japan	74D3
Toyama-wan, B Japan	75B1
Toyohashi Japan	75B2
Toyonaka Japan	75B2
Toyooka Japan	75A1
Toyota Japan	74D3
Tozeur Tunisia	96C1
Traben-Trarbach W Germ	46D2
Trabzon Turk	93C1
Tracy, California USA	22B2
Traiguén Chile	34A3
Trail Can	13D3
Tralee Irish Rep	41B3
Tralee B Irish Rep	45B2
Tramore Irish Rep	45C2
Tranås Sweden	39G7
Trang Thai	77B4
Trangan, I Indon	71E4
Trangie Aust	109C2
Transalaskan Pipeline USA	12E2
Transvaal, Province S Africa	100B3
Trapani Italy	53B3
Traralgon Aust	109C3
Trarza, Region Maur	97A3
Trat Thai	76C3
Traveller's, L Aust	108B2
Travemünde W Germ	56C2
Traverse City USA	14A2
Traverse Peak, Mt USA	12C1
Travers,Mt NZ	111B2
Trebbia, R Italy	47C2
Trebič Czech	59B3
Trebinje Yugos	54A2
Trebon Czech	57C3
Treinta y Tres Urug	29F2
Trelew Arg	29C4
Trelleborg Sweden	39G7
Tremadog B Wales	43B3
Tremblant,Mt Can	15D1
Trembleur L Can	13C2
Tremont USA	16A2
Trenčín Czech	59B3
Trenque Lauquén Arg	34C3
Trent, R Eng	43D3
Trentino, Region Italy	47D1
Trento Italy	47D1
Trenton Can	15C2
Trenton, Missouri USA	18B1
Trenton, New Jersey USA	16B2
Trepassey Can	7E5
Tres Arroyos Arg	34C3
Tres Corações Brazil	35B2
Três Lagoas Brazil	30F3
Tres Lomas Arg	34C3
Tres Pinos USA	22B2
Três Rios Brazil	35C2
Treviglio Italy	47C2
Treviso Italy	47E2
Trezzo Italy	47C2
Trichūr India	87B2
Trida Aust	108C2
Trier W Germ	46D2
Trieste Italy	52B1
Trim Irish Rep	45C2
Trincomalee Sri Lanka	87C3
Trinidad Bol	33E6
Trinidad Urug	29E2
Trinidad USA	9C3
Trinidad, I Arg	34C3
Trinidad, I Caribbean	27E4
Trindade, I Atlantic O	103G6
Trinidad & Tobago, Is Republic Caribbean	27E4
Trinity USA	19A3
Trinity, R USA	9D3
Trinity B Can	7E5
Trinity Is USA	12D3
Trion USA	17A1
Tripoli Leb	94B1
Tripoli Libya	95A1
Tripolis Greece	55B3
Tripura, State India	86C2
Tristan da Cunha, Is Atlantic O	103H6
Trivandrum India	87B3
Trnava Czech	59B3
Trobriand Is PNG	107E1
Trois-Riviéres Can	15D1
Troitsk USSR	65H4
Trollhättan Sweden	39G7
Trollheimen, Mt Nor	38F6
Tromelin, I Indian O	89K9
Tromsø Nor	38H5
Trondheim Nor	38G6
Trondheimfjord, Inlet Nor	38G6
Troon Scot	42B2
Tropic of Cancer	102J3
Tropic of Capricorn	103J6
Troudenni Mali	96B2
Trout L, Ontario Can	7A4
Troy, Alabama USA	17A1
Troy, New York USA	16C1
Troy, Ohio USA	14B2
Troyan Bulg	54B2
Troyes France	49C2
Trucial Coast, Region UAE	91B5
Truckee, R USA	21A2
Trujillo Honduras	25D3
Trujillo Peru	32B5
Trujillo Spain	50A2
Trujillo Ven	32C2
Trundle Aust	109C2
Truro Can	7D5
Truro Eng	43B4
Trust Territories of the Pacific Is Pacific O	71E3
Tsagaan Nuur, L Mongolia	68B2
Tsagan-Tologoy USSR	68B1
Tsaratanana Madag	101D2
Tsau Botswana	100B3
Tsavo Kenya	99D3
Tsavo Nat Pk Kenya	99D3
Tselinograd USSR	65J4
Tses Namibia	100A3
Tsetserleg Mongolia	68B2
Tsetserleg Mongolia	68C2
Tsévié Togo	97C4

Union City

Vergara Arg	34D3
Verin Spain	50A1
Verissimo Sarmento Angola	98C3
Verkh Angara, R USSR	63D2
Verkhneural'sk USSR	61J3
Verkhnevilyuysk USSR	63E1
Verkhoyansk USSR	1C8
Vermelho, R Brazil	35A1
Vermilion Can	13E2
Vermont, State USA	10C2
Vernalis USA	22B2
Vernon Can	13D2
Vernon France	46A2
Vernon USA	9D3
Vero Beach USA	17B2
Veroia Greece	54B2
Verolanuova Italy	47D2
Verona Italy	47D2
Versailles France	46B2
Verulam S Africa	101H1
Verviers Belg	46C1
Vervins France	46B2
Vesle, R France	46C2
Vesoul France	49D2
Vesterålen, Is Nor	38G5
Vestfjorden, Inlet Nor	38G5
Vestmannaeyjar Iceland	38A2
Vesuvio, Mt Italy	53B2
Veszprém Hung	59B3
Vetlanda Sweden	39H7
Vetluga, R USSR	61F2
Veurne Belg	46B1
Vevey Switz	47B1
Vexin, Region France	46A2
Veynes France	47A2
Viana do Castelo Port	50A1
Viareggio Italy	49E3
Viborg Den	39F7
Vibo Valentia Italy	53C3
Vice-commodoro Marambio, Base Ant	112C2
Vicenza Italy	52B1
Vich Spain	51C1
Vichada, R Colombia	32D3
Vichuga USSR	61F2
Vichy France	49C2
Vicksburg USA	19B3
Vicosa Brazil	35C2
Victor Harbour Aust	106C4
Victoria Arg	34C2
Victoria Can	13C3
Victoria Chile	34A3
Victoria Hong Kong	73C5
Victoria Malay	78D1
Victoria, State Aust	108B3
Victoria USA	9D4
Victoria, R Aust	106C2
Victoria, State Aust	107D4
Victoria de las Tunas Cuba	26B2
Victoria Falls Zambia/Zim	100B2
Victoria I Can	4G2
Victoria,L Aust	108B2
Victoria,L C Africa	99D3
Victoria Land, Region Ant	112B2
Victoria,Mt Burma	86C2
Victoria Nile, R Uganda	99D2
Victoria Range, Mts NZ	111B2
Victoria River Downs Aust	106C2
Victoria Str Can	4H3
Victoriaville Can	15D1
Victoria West S Africa	100B4
Victorica Arg	34B3
Victorville USA	21B3
Vicuña Chile	34A2
Vicuña Mackenna Arg	34C2
Vidalia USA	17B1
Videle Rom	54C2
Vidin Bulg	54B2
Vidisha India	85D4
Vidzy USSR	58D1
Viedma Arg	29D4
Viéjo Costa Rica	26A4
Viella Spain	51C1
Vienna, Illinois USA	18C2
Vienna, W Virginia USA	14B3
Vienne France	49C2
Vienne, R France	48C2
Vientiane Laos	76C2
Vierwaldstätter See, L Switz	47C1
Vierzon France	48C2
Vieste Italy	53C2
Vietnam, Republic S E Asia	70B2
Vietri Viet	76D1
Vieux Fort St Lucia	27P2
Vigan Phil	79B2
Vigevano Italy	47C2
Vignemale, Mt France	48B3
Vigo Spain	50A1
Vijayawāda India	87C1
Vijosë, R Alb	55A2
Vik Iceland	38B2
Vikhren, Mt Bulg	54B2
Viking Can	13E2
Vikna, I Nor	38G6
Vila da Maganja Mozam	101C2
Vila Machado Mozam	101C2
Vilanculos Mozam	101C3
Vila Real Port	50A1
Vila Vasco da Gama Mozam	101C2
Vila Velha Brazil	35C2
Vileyka USSR	58D2
Vilhelmina Sweden	38H6
Vilhena Brazil	33E6
Viljandi USSR	60C2
Viljoenskroon S Africa	101G1
Vilkovo USSR	59D3
Villa Ahumada Mexico	9C3
Villa Atuel Arg	34B2
Villaba Spain	50A1
Villa Carranza Mexico	23A2
Villach Austria	52B1
Villa Colon Arg	34B2
Villa Constitución Arg	34C2
Villa de Maria Arg	34C1
Villa de Reyes Mexico	23A1
Villa Dolores Arg	34B2
Villafranca di Verona Italy	47D2
Villa General Mitre Arg	34C2
Villa General Roca Arg	34B2
Villaguay Arg	34D2
Villahermosa Mexico	25C3
Villa Hidalgo Mexico	23A1
Villa Huidobro Arg	34C2
Villa Iris Arg	34C3
Villa Maria Arg	34C2
Villa Montes Bol	30D3
Villanueva Mexico	23A1
Villa Nova de Gaia Port	50A1
Villanueva de la Serena Spain	50A2
Villanueva-y-Geltrú Spain	51C1
Villa Regina Arg	34B3
Villarreal Spain	51B2
Villarrica Chile	29B3
Villarrica Par	30E4
Villarrobledo Spain	50B2
Villa San José Arg	34D2
Villa Valeria Arg	34C2
Villavicencio Colombia	32C3
Villefranche France	49C2
Ville-Marie Can	7C5
Villena Spain	51B2
Villeneuve-St-Georges France	46B2
Villeneuve-sur-Lot France	48C3
Ville Platte USA	19B3
Villers-Cotterêts France	46B2
Villeurbanne France	49C2
Villiers S Africa	101G1
Villupuram India	87B2
Vilnius USSR	58D2
Vilyuy USSR	63D1
Vilyuysk USSR	63E1
Viña del Mar Chile	34A2
Vinaroz Spain	51C1
Vincennes USA	14A3
Vindel, R Sweden	38H5
Vindhya Range, Mts India	85D4
Vineland USA	16B3
Vineyard Haven USA	16D2
Vinh Viet	76D2
Vinh Cam Ranh, B Viet	76D3
Vinh Loi Viet	77D4
Vinh Long Viet	77D3
Vinita USA	18A2
Vinkovci Yugos	54A1
Vinnitsa USSR	60C4
Vinson Massif, Upland Ant	112B3
Vioolsdrift S Africa	100A3
Vipiteno Italy	47D1
Virac Phil	79B3
Virddhāchalam India	87B2
Virei Angola	100A2
Virgem da Lapa Brazil	35C1
Virginia S Africa	101G1
Virginia, State USA	10C3
Virginia USA	10A2
Virginia City USA	21B2
Virgin Is Caribbean	27E3
Virovitica Yugos	52C1
Virton Belg	46C2
Virudunagar India	87B3
Vis, I Yugos	52C2
Visalia USA	21B2
Visayan S Phil	79B3
Visby Sweden	39H7
Viscount Melville Sd Can	4H2
Višegrad Yugos	54A2
Viseu Port	50A1
Vishākhapatnam India	83C4
Visp Switz	47B1
Vissingen Neth	49C1
Vista USA	21B3
Vitavia, R Czech	57C3
Vite India	87A1
Vitebsk USSR	60D2
Viterbo Italy	52B2
Vitigudino Spain	50A1
Vitim, R USSR	63D2
Vitora Spain	50B1
Vitoria Brazil	31C6
Vitória da Conquista Brazil	31C4
Vitré France	48B2
Vitry-le-Francois France	46C2
Vittangi Sweden	38J5
Vittoria Italy	53B3
Vittorio Veneto Italy	47E2
Vityaz Depth Pacific O	69H2
Vivero Spain	50A1
Vivi, R USSR	63B1
Vivorata Arg	34D3
Vizhne-Angarsk USSR	63C2
Vizianagaram India	83C4
Vladeasa, Mt Rom	54B1
Vladimir USSR	65F4
Vladimir Volynskiy USSR	59C2
Vladivostok USSR	74C2
Vlieland, I Neth	56A2
Vlissingen Neth	46B1
Vlorë Alb	55A2
Vöcklabruck Austria	57C3
Voeune Sai Camb	76D3
Voghera Italy	47C2
Vohibinany Madag	101D2
Vohimarina Madag	101E2
Voi Kenya	99D3
Voinjama Lib	97B4
Voiron France	49D2
Volcán Baru, Mt Panama	26A5
Volcán Citlaltepetl, Mt Mexico	23B2
Volcán Lullaillaco, Mt Chile	30C3
Volcáno Copahue, Mt Chile	34A3
Volcáno Domuyo, Mt Arg	34A3
Volcáno Lanin, Mt Arg	29B3
Volcán Ollagüe, Mt Chile	30C3
Volcáno Llaima, Mt Chile	34A3
Volcáno Maipo, Mt Arg	34B2
Volcáno Peteroa, Mt Chile	34A3
Volcáno Tromen, V Arg	34B3
Volcán Paracutin, Mt Mexico	23A2
Volcán Puraće, Mt Colombia	32B3
Volcán Tinguiririca, Mt Chile/Arg	34A2
Volchansk USSR	61J2
Volga, R USSR	61G4
Volgodonsk USSR	61F4
Volgograd USSR	61F4
Volgogradskoye Vodokhranilishche, Res USSR	61G3
Volkhov USSR	60D2
Volkhov, R USSR	60D2
Volkovysk USSR	58C2
Volksrust S Africa	101G1
Vologda USSR	61F2
Volognes France	48B2
Vólos Greece	55B3
Vol'sk USSR	61G3
Volta USA	22B2
Volta Blanche, R U Volta	97B3
Volta,L Ghana	97B4
Volta Noire, R U Volta	97B3
Volta Redonda Brazil	35C2
Volta Rouge, R U Volta	97B3
Volynskiy USSR	60C3
Volzhskiy USSR	61F4
Von Frank Mt USA	12D2
Vopnafjörður Iceland	6J3
Voralberg, Province Austria	47C1
Vorder Rhein, R Switz	47C1
Vordingborg Den	56C1
Vorkuta USSR	64H3
Vorma, R Nor	39G6
Voronezh USSR	60E3
Voron'ya, R USSR	38M5
Voroshilovgrad USSR	60E4
Võru USSR	39K7
Vosges, Mt France	49D2
Voshnyy Saytocan, Mts USSR	68B1
Voss Nor	39F6
Vostochnyy Sayan, Mts USSR	63B2
Vostok, Base Ant	112B9
Votkinsk USSR	61H2
Vouziers France	46C2
Voznesensk USSR	60D4
Vranje Yugos	54B2
Vratsa Bulg	54B2
Vrbas Yugos	54A1
Vrbas, R Yugos	52C2
Vrbovsko Yugos	52B1
Vrede S Africa	101G1
Vreed en Hoop Guyana	33F2
Vršac Yugos	54B1
Vrtoče Yugos	52C2
Vryburg S Africa	100B3
Vryheid S Africa	101H1

Vukovar

Weishan Hu, L *China*	72D3
Weissenfels *E Germ*	57C2
Weiss L *USA*	17A1
Welkom *S Africa*	101G1
Welland *Can*	15C2
Welland, R *Eng*	43D3
Wellesley Is *Aust*	106C2
Wellesley L *Can*	12G2
Wellingborough *Eng*	43D3
Wellington *Aust*	109C2
Wellington, Kansas *USA*	18A2
Wellington *NZ*	111B2
Wellington Chan *Can*	6A2
Wells *Can*	13C2
Wells *Eng*	43C4
Wellsford *NZ*	110B1
Wells,L *Aust*	106B3
Wels *Austria*	57C3
Welshpool *Wales*	43C3
Wembley *Can*	13D1
Wenatchee *USA*	20B1
Wenatchee, R *USA*	20C1
Wenchi *Ghana*	97B4
Wondon *China*	72E2
Wenling *China*	73E4
Wenman, I *Ecuador*	32J7
Wenshan *China*	73A5
Wenthaggi *Aust*	107D4
Wentworth *Aust*	108B2
Wen Xian *China*	72A3
Wenzhou *China*	73E4
Wenzhu *China*	73C4
Wepener *S Africa*	101G1
Wernecke Mts *Can*	12G1
Werra, R *E Germ*	57C2
Werris Creek *Aust*	109D2
Wesel *W Germ*	56B2
Weser, R *W Germ*	56B2
Wessel Is *Aust*	106C2
West Allis *USA*	14A2
West Australian Basin *Indian O*	104C4
West Australian Ridge *Indian O*	104C5
West B *USA*	19C3
West Bengal, State *India*	86B2
West Bromwich *Eng*	43D3
West Chester *USA*	16B3
Westerburg *W Germ*	46D1
Westerland *W Germ*	56B2
Westerly *USA*	16D2
Western Australia, State *Aust*	106A3
Western Ghats, Mts *India*	87A1
Western Isles *Scot*	44A3
Western Sahara, Region *Mor*	96A2
Western Samoa, Is *Pacific O*	105H4
Westerschelde, Estuary *Neth*	46B1
Westerwald, Region *W Germ*	46D1
Westfalen, Region *W Germ*	49D1
West Falkland, I *Falkland Is*	29D6
Westfield, Massachusetts *USA*	16C1
Westfield, New York *USA*	15C2
West Frankfort *USA*	18C2
Westgate *Aust*	109C1
West Germany, Federal Republic *Europe*	57B2
West Glamorgan, County *Wales*	43C4
West Indies, Is *Caribbean S*	102E3
Westlock *Can*	13E2
West Lorne *Can*	14B2
Westmeath, County *Irish Rep*	45C2
West Memphis *USA*	18B2
West Midlands, County *Eng*	43D3
Westminster *Eng*	43D4
Westminster, Maryland *USA*	16A3
Westminster, S Carolina *USA*	17B1
West Nicholson *Zim*	100B3
Weston *Malay*	78D1
Weston *USA*	14B3
Weston-super-Mare *Eng*	43C4
West Palm Beach *USA*	17B2
West Plains *USA*	18B2
West Point, California *USA*	22B1
West Point, Mississippi *USA*	19C3
West Point, New York *USA*	16C2
West Point, Mt *USA*	12F2
Westport *Irish Rep*	45B2
Westport *NZ*	111B2
Westray, I *Scot*	40C2
West Road, R *Can*	13C2
West Side, Oilfield *N Sea*	42E3
West Virginia, State *USA*	11B3
West Walker, R *USA*	22C1
West Wyalong *Aust*	109C2
West Yorkshire, County *Eng*	42D3
Wetar, I *Indon*	71D4
Wetaskiwin *Can*	13E2
Wete *Tanz*	99D3
Wetzlar *W Germ*	46E1
Wewak *PNG*	71F4
Wewoka *USA*	19A2
Wexford, County *Irish Rep*	45C2
Wexford *Irish Rep*	45C2
Weyburn *Can*	5H5
Weymouth *Eng*	43C4
Weymouth *USA*	16D1
Whakatane *NZ*	110C1
Whakatane, R *NZ*	110C1
Whalsay, I *Scot*	44D1
Whangarei *NZ*	110B1
Wharfe, R *Eng*	42D3
Wharton *USA*	19A4
Whataroa *NZ*	111B2
Wheaton, Maryland *USA*	16A3
Wheeler Peak, Mt, Nevada *USA*	8B3
Wheeler Peak, Mt, New Mexico *USA*	9C3
Wheeling *USA*	14B2
Whistler *Can*	13C3
Whitby *Can*	15C2
Whitby *Eng*	42D2
White, R, Arkansas *USA*	18B2
White, R *Can*	12F2
White, R, Indiana *USA*	14A3
White, R, S Dakota *USA*	8C2
White B *Can*	7E4
White Cliffs *Aust*	108B2
White Coomb, Mt *Scot*	40C2
Whitecourt *Can*	13D2
Whitefish Pt *USA*	14A1
Whitegull L *Can*	7D4
Whitehall, New York *USA*	15D2
Whitehall, Pennsylvania *USA*	16B2
Whitehaven *Eng*	42C2
Whitehorse *Can*	12G2
White I *NZ*	110C1
White L *USA*	19B4
Whitemark *Aust*	109C4
White Mountain Peak, Mt *USA*	21B2
White Mts, Alaska *USA*	12E1
White Mts, New Hampshire *USA*	15D2
White Plains *USA*	16C2
White River *Can*	7B5
White River Junction *USA*	15D2
Whitesail L *Can*	13B2
White Salmon *USA*	20B1
Whiteville *USA*	17C1
White Volta, R *Ghana*	97B4
Whithorn *Scot*	42B2
Whitmire *USA*	17B1
Whitney,Mt *USA*	21B2
Whittier, Alaska *USA*	12E2
Whittier, California *USA*	22C4
Wholdia L *Can*	5H3
Whyalla *Aust*	108A2
Wiarton *Can*	14B2
Wichita *USA*	18A2
Wichita Falls *USA*	9D3
Wick *Scot*	44C2
Wicklow, County *Irish Rep*	45C2
Wicklow *Irish Rep*	45C2
Wicklow, Mts *Irish Rep*	45C2
Widgeegoara, R *Aust*	109C1
Wied, R *W Germ*	46D1
Wielun *Pol*	59B2
Wien *Austria*	59B3
Wiener Neustadt *Austria*	59B3
Wieprz, R *Pol*	58C2
Wiesbaden *W Germ*	46E1
Wigan *Eng*	42C3
Wiggins *USA*	19C3
Wigtown *Scot*	42B2
Wigtown B *Scot*	42B2
Wil *Switz*	47C1
Wilbur *USA*	20C1
Wilcannia *Aust*	108B2
Wildcat Peak, Mt *USA*	21B2
Wildhorn, Mt *Switz*	47B1
Wild Horse *Can*	13E2
Wildspitze, Mt *Austria*	47D1
Wildwood, Florida *USA*	17B2
Wildwood, New Jersey *USA*	16B3
Wilge, R *S Africa*	101G1
Wilhelmshaven *W Germ*	56B2
Wilkes-Barre *USA*	15C2
Wilkes Land *Ant*	112B8
Wilkie *Can*	13F2
Willamette, R *USA*	20B2
Willandra, R *Aust*	108B2
Willapa B *USA*	20B1
Willcox *USA*	9C3
Willemstad *Curaçao*	27D4
William Creek *Aust*	108A1
William,Mt *Aust*	108B3
Williams, California *USA*	21A2
Williams Lake *Can*	13C2
Williamsport *USA*	15C2
Williamstown, Massachusetts *USA*	16C1
Williamstown, W Virginia *USA*	14B3
Willimantic *USA*	16C2
Willingboro *USA*	16B2
Willingdon,Mt *Can*	13D2
Willis Group, Is *Aust*	107E2
Williston, Florida *USA*	17B2
Williston *S Africa*	100B4
Williston L *Can*	13C1
Willmar *USA*	8D2
Willoughby,C *Aust*	108A3
Willow, R *Can*	13C2
Willow Ranch *USA*	20B2
Willows *USA*	21A2
Willow Springs *USA*	18B2
Wilmington *Aust*	108A2
Wilmington, Delaware *USA*	16B3
Wilmington, N Carolina *USA*	17C1
Wilnona *USA*	7A5
Wilson *USA*	11C3
Wilson, R *Aust*	108B1
Wilson,C *Can*	6B3
Wilson,Mt, California *USA*	22C3
Wilson,Mt, Oregon *USA*	20B1
Wilsons Promontory, Pen *Aust*	109C3
Wiltshire, County *Eng*	43D4
Wiltz *Lux*	46C2
Wiluna *Aust*	106B3
Winamac *USA*	14A2
Winburg *S Africa*	101G1
Winchendon *USA*	16C1
Winchester *USA*	15C1
Winchester *Eng*	43D4
Winchester, New Hampshire *USA*	16C1
Winchester, Virginia *USA*	15C3
Windermere *Eng*	42C2
Windhoek *Namibia*	100A3
Windorah *Aust*	107D3
Wind River Range, Mts *USA*	8C2
Windsor *Aust*	109D2
Windsor, Connecticut *USA*	16C2
Windsor *Eng*	43D4
Windsor, Nova Scotia *Can*	7D5
Windsor, Ontario *Can*	14B2
Windsor, Quebec *Can*	15D1
Windsor Forest *USA*	17B1
Windsor Locks *USA*	16C2
Windward Is *Caribbean*	27E4
Windward Pass *Caribbean*	26C3
Winefred L *Can*	13E1
Winfield, Kansas *USA*	18A2
Wingham *Aust*	109D2
Winifreda *Arg*	34C3
Winisk, R *Can*	7B4
Winisk L *Can*	7B4
Winkana *Burma*	76B2
Winlock *USA*	20B1
Winneba *Ghana*	97B4
Winnebago,L *USA*	14A2
Winnemucca *USA*	20C2
Winnfield *USA*	19B3
Winnipeg *Can*	5J4
Winnipeg,L *Can*	5J4
Winnipegosis *Can*	5J4
Winnipesaukee,L *USA*	15D2
Winona, Minnesota *USA*	10A2
Winona, Mississippi *USA*	19C3
Winooski *USA*	15D2
Winslow *USA*	9B3
Winsted *USA*	16C2
Winston-Salem *USA*	11B3
Winterberg *W Germ*	46E1
Winter Garden *USA*	17B2
Winter Park *USA*	17B2
Winters *USA*	22B1
Winterthur *Switz*	47C1
Winton *Aust*	107D3
Winton *NZ*	111A3
Wisbech *Eng*	43E3
Wisconsin, State *USA*	10B2
Wisconsin Rapids *USA*	7B5
Wiseman *USA*	12D1
Wisla, R *Pol*	58B2
Wismar *E Germ*	56C2
Witagron *Surinam*	33F2
Witbank *S Africa*	101G1
Witchita Falls *USA*	9D3
Witham, R *Eng*	43D3
Withernsea *Eng*	42E3

Witney

Witney *Eng*	43D4	Wuhua *China*	73D5
Witten *W Germ*	46D1	Wüjang *China*	84D2
Wittenberg *E Germ*	56C2	Wujia He, R *China*	72B1
Wittenoom *Aust*	106A3	Wu Jiang, R *China*	73B4
Wittlich *W Germ*	46D1	Wukari *Nig*	97C4
Wladyslawowo *Pol*	58B2	Wuling Shan, Mts *China*	73B4
Włocławek *Pol*	58B2	Wum *Cam*	97D4
Włodawa *Pol*	58C2	Wumeng Shan, Upland *China*	73A4
Wodonga *Aust*	109C3	Wuppertal *W Germ*	46D1
Wohlen *Switz*	47C1	Wuqi *China*	72B2
Wokam *Indon*	71E4	Wuqing *China*	72D2
Woking *Eng*	43D4	Würzburg *W Germ*	57B3
Woleai, I *Pacific O*	71F3	Wurzen *E Germ*	57C2
Wolf Creek *USA*	20B2	Wutai Shan, Mt *China*	72C2
Wolf Point *USA*	8C2	Wuvulu, I *Pacific O*	71F4
Wolfsberg *Austria*	57C3	Wuwei *China*	72A2
Wolfsburg *W Germ*	56C2	Wuxi *China*	73E3
Wollaston L *Can*	5H4	Wuxing *China*	73E3
Wollaston Lake *Can*	5H4	Wuyang *China*	72C2
Wollaston Pen *Can*	4G3	Wuyi Shan, Mts *China*	73D4
Wollongong *Aust*	109D2	Wuzhi Shan, Mts *China*	76D2
Wolmaransstad *S Africa*	101G1	Wuzhong *China*	72B2
Wolow *Pol*	59B2	Wuzhou *China*	73C5
Wolseley *Aust*	108B3	Wyandotte *USA*	14B2
Wolverhampton *Eng*	43C3	Wyandra *Aust*	109C1
Womelsdorf *USA*	16A2	Wye, R *Eng*	43C4
Wondai *Aust*	109D1	Wylye, R *Eng*	43C4
Wŏnju *S Korea*	74B3	Wymondham *Eng*	43E3
Wonominta, R *Aust*	108B2	Wyndham *Aust*	106B2
Wonowon *Can*	13C1	Wynne *USA*	18B2
Wŏnsan *N Korea*	74B3	Wynniatt B *Can*	4G2
Wonthaggi *Aust*	108C3	Wynyard *Aust*	109C4
Woocalla *Aust*	108A2	Wyoming, State *USA*	8C2
Woodbine *USA*	16B3	Wyoming *USA*	14A2
Woodbridge *USA*	15C3	Wyong *Aust*	109D2
Wood Buffalo Nat Pk *Can*	5G4		

X

Xaidulla *China*	84D1
Xai Moron He, R *China*	72D1
Xai Xai *Mozam*	101C3
Xaltinguis *Mexico*	23B2
Xangongo *Angola*	100A2
Xanten *W Germ*	46D1
Xánthi *Greece*	55B2
Xau,L *Botswana*	100B3
Xenia *USA*	14B3
Xiaguan *China*	68B4
Xiahe *China*	72A2
Xiamen *China*	73D5
Xi'an *China*	72B3
Xianfeng *China*	73B4
Xiangfan *China*	73C3
Xiang Jiang, R *China*	73C4
Xiangtan, Province *China*	73C4
Xianning *China*	73C4
Xianyang *China*	72B3
Xiao Shui, R *China*	73C4
Xiapu *China*	73D4
Xichang *China*	73A4
Xicotepec *Mexico*	23B1
Xieng Khouang *Laos*	76C2
Xifeng *China*	73B4
Xi He, R *China*	72A1
Xiji *China*	72B2
Xi Jiang, R *China*	73C5
Xiliao He, R *China*	72E1
Xilin *China*	73B5
Xilitla *Mexico*	23B1
Xinfeng *China*	73D4
Xinghe *China*	72C1
Xingning *China*	73D5
Xingren *China*	73B4
Xingtai *China*	72C2
Xingu, R *Brazil*	33G4
Xingxingxia *China*	68B2
Xingyi *China*	73A4
Xining *China*	72A2
Xinjin, Liaoning *China*	72E2
Xinjin, Sichuan *China*	73A3
Xinwen *China*	72D2

Continued:

Xin Xian *China*	72C2
Xinxiang *China*	72C2
Xinyang *China*	73C3
Xinyi, Guangdong *China*	73C5
Xinyi, Jiangsu *China*	72D3
Xi Ujimqin Qi *China*	72D1
Xiuyan *China*	74A2
Xochimilco *Mexico*	23B2
Xuancheng *China*	73D3
Xuanhan *China*	73B3
Xuanhua *China*	72D1
Xuanwei *China*	73A4
Xuchang *China*	72C3
Xuddur *Somalia*	99E2
Xunhua *China*	72A2
Xun Jiang, R *China*	73C5
Xunke *China*	69E2
Xunwu *China*	73D5
Xupu *China*	73C4
Xuwen *China*	76D2
Xuwen *China*	76E1
Xuyong *China*	73B4
Xuzhou *China*	72D3

Y

Ya'an *China*	73A4	Yangshan *China*	73C5
Yaapeet *Aust*	108B3	Yangtze Gorges *China*	73C3
Yabassi *Cam*	98B2	Yangtze,Mouths of the *China*	72E3
Yablonovyy Khrebet, Mts *USSR*	68C1	Yangzhou *China*	72D3
Yabrūd *Syria*	94C2	Yanhe *China*	73B4
Yachats *USA*	20B2	Yanji *China*	74B2
Yacuiba *Bol*	30D3	Yanko, R *Aust*	108C3
Yādgīr *India*	87B1	Yankton *USA*	8D2
Yafran *Libya*	95A1	Yanqi *China*	68A2
Yahualica *Mexico*	23A1	Yan Shan, Hills *China*	72D1
Yahuma *Zaïre*	98C2	Yantabulla *Aust*	108B1
Yaita *Japan*	75B1	Yantai *China*	72E2
Yaizu *Japan*	75B2	Yanzhou *China*	72D2
Yajiang *China*	73A4	Yaoundé *Cam*	98B2
Yakima *USA*	20B1	Yapen, I *Indon*	71E4
Yakima, R *USA*	20B1	Yap Is *Pacific O*	71E3
Yako *U Volta*	97B3	Yaqui, R *Mexico*	24B2
Yakoma *Zaïre*	98C2	Yaransk *USSR*	61G2
Yakumo *Japan*	74E2	Yargon, R *Israel*	94B2
Yakutat *USA*	12G3	Yari, R *Colombia*	32C3
Yakutat B *USA*	12G3	Yariga-dake, Mt *Japan*	74D3
Yakutsk *USSR*	63E1	Yarkant He, R *China*	82B2
Yala *Thai*	77C4	Yarlung Zangbo Jiang, R *China*	86C1
Yalalag *Mexico*	23B2	Yarmouth *Can*	7D5
Yalinga *CAR*	98C2	Yarmük, R *Syria/Jordan*	94B2
Yallourn *Aust*	109C3	Yaroslavl' *USSR*	61E2
Yalong, R *China*	68B3	Yarram *Aust*	109C3
Yalong Jiang, R *China*	73A4	Yarraman *Aust*	109D1
Yalova *Turk*	54C2	Yarrawonga *Aust*	109C3
Yalta *USSR*	60D5	Yartsevo *USSR*	60D2
Yalu Jiang, R *China*	74B2	Yartsevo *USSR*	63B1
Yamagata *Japan*	74D3	Yarumal *Colombia*	32B2
Yamaguchi *Japan*	74C4	Yashi *Nig*	97C3
Yamarovka *USSR*	68D1	Yashikera *Nig*	97C4
Yamba, New S Wales *Aust*	109D1	Yashkul' *USSR*	61F4
Yamba, S Australia *Aust*	108B2	Yasin *Pak*	84C1
Yambio *Sudan*	99C2	Yasinya *USSR*	59C3
Yambol *Bulg*	54C2	Yass *Aust*	109C2
Yamdena, I *Indon*	71E4	Yass, R *Aust*	109C2
Yamma Yamma,L *Aust*	108B1	Yasugi *Japan*	75A1
Yamuna, R *India*	85D3	Yates Center *USA*	18A2
Yamzho Yumco, L *China*	86C1	Yatolema *Zaïre*	98C2
Yana, R *USSR*	63F1	Yatsushiro *Japan*	74C4
Yanac *Aust*	108B3	Yatta *Israel*	94B3
Yanagawa *Japan*	75A2	Yavari *Peru*	32C4
Yanam *India*	87C1	Yavatmāl *India*	85D4
Yan'an *China*	72B2	Yawatahama *Japan*	74C4
Yanbu'al Bahr *S Arabia*	80B3	Ya Xian *China*	76D2
Yancannia *Aust*	108B2	Yazd *Iran*	90B3
Yancheng *China*	72E3	Yazd-e Khvāst *Iran*	90B3
Yanchi *China*	72B2	Yazoo, R *USA*	19B3
Yandama, R *Aust*	108B1	Yazoo City *USA*	19B3
Yangambi *Zaïre*	98C2	Ye *Burma*	76B2
Yang He, R *China*	72C1	Yedintsy *USSR*	59D3
Yangjiang *China*	73C5	Yeelanna *Aust*	108A2
Yangquan *China*	72C2	Yefremov *USSR*	60E3
		Yegorlyk, R *USSR*	61F4
		Yei *Sudan*	99D2
		Yelets *USSR*	60E3
		Yell, I *Scot*	40C1
		Yellandu *India*	87C1
		Yellowhead P *Can*	8B1
		Yellowknife *Can*	4G3
		Yellowmead P *Can*	5G4
		Yellow Mt *Aust*	109C2
		Yellow Sea *China/Korea*	69E3
		Yellowstone, R *USA*	8C2
		Yellowstone L *USA*	8B2
		Yelverton B *Can*	6B1
		Yelwa *Nig*	97C3
		Yemen, Republic *Arabian Pen*	81C4
		Yen Bai *Viet*	76C1
		Yendi *Ghana*	97B4
		Yengan *Burma*	76B1
		Yeniseysk *USSR*	63B2
		Yeniseyskiy Kryazh, Ridge *USSR*	63B1
		Yeniseyskiy Zai, B *USSR*	64J2
		Yentna, R *USA*	12D2
		Yeo, R *Eng*	43C4
		Yeoval *Aust*	109C2
		Yeovil *Eng*	43C4

Ziller

Ziller, R *Austria*	**47D1**	Ziya He, R *China*	**72D2**	Zrenjanin *Yugos*	**54B1**	Zuyevka *USSR*	**61H2**

Ziller, R *Austria* **47D1**
Zillertaler Alpen, Mts
  Austria **47D1**
Zilupe *USSR* **58D1**
Zima *USSR* **63C2**
Zimapan *Mexico* **23B1**
Zimatlan *Mexico* **23B2**
Zin, R *Israel* **94B3**
Zinacatepec *Mexico* **23B2**
Zinapécuaro *Mexico* **23A2**
Zinder *Niger* **97C3**
Zi Shui *China* **73C4**
Zitácuaro *Mexico* **23A2**
Zittau *E Germ* **57C2**

Ziya He, R *China* **72D2**
Ziyang *China* **72A3**
Zlatoust *USSR* **61J2**
Zmeinogorsk *USSR* **65K4**
Znin *Pol* **58B2**
Znoimo *Czech* **59B3**
Zofinger *Switz* **47B1**
Zoigê *China* **72A3**
Zolochev *USSR* **59D3**
Zomba *Malawi* **101C2**
Zongo *Zaïre* **98B2**
Zonguldak *Turk* **92B1**
Zorzor *Lib* **97B4**
Zouerate *Maur* **96A2**

Zrenjanin *Yugos* **54B1**
Zug *Switz* **47C1**
Zugspitze, Mt *W*
  Germ **47D1**
Zújar, R *Spain* **50A2**
Zumbo *Mozam* **100C2**
Zumpango *Mexico* **23B2**
Zungeru *Nig* **97C4**
Zunyi *China* **73B4**
Zuo, R *China* **76D1**
Zuo Jiang, R *China* **73B5**
Zürich *Switz* **47C1**
Zürichsee, L *Switz* **47C1**
Zuwārah *Libya* **95A1**

Zuyevka *USSR* **61H2**
Zvishavane *Zim* **100B4**
Zvolen *Czech* **59B3**
Zvornik *Yugos* **54A2**
Zweibrücken *W Germ* **46D2**
Zweisimmen *Switz* **47B1**
Zwickau *E Germ* **57C2**
Zwolle *Neth* **56B2**
Zyrardów *Pol* **58C2**
Zyryanovsk *USSR* **65K5**
Żywiec *Pol* **59B3**
Zyyi *Cyprus* **94A1**